T0345018

RELIGION AND CULTURE IN THE MIDDLE AGES

Reading Medieval Anchoritism

RELIGION AND CULTURE IN THE MIDDLE AGES

Reading Medieval Anchoritism

IDEOLOGY AND SPIRITUAL PRACTICES

MARI HUGHES-EDWARDS

UNIVERSITY OF WALES PRESS
CARDIFF
2012

www.uwp.co.uk

British Library CIP Data
A catalogue record for this book is available from the British Library.

ISBN   978-0-7083-2504-9 (hardback)
          978-0-7083-2505-6 (paperback)
e-ISBN 978-0-7083-2506-3

Printed by CPI Antony Rowe, Chippenham, Wiltshire

Contents

Series Editors' Preface ix
Acknowledgements xi
Abbreviations xiii
Introduction 1

I ANCHORITIC SPIRITUALITY IN ISOLATION: THE ENGLISH ANCHORITIC GUIDES

1 Introducing the Guides 15

2 Anchoritic Enclosure 32

3 Anchoritic Solitude and Sociability 41

II ANCHORITIC SPIRITUALITY IN CONTEXT: ENGLISH ANCHORITISM AND THE WIDER MEDIEVAL WORLD

4 Anchoritism and Asceticism 59

5 Anchoritism and Contemplative Experience 81

Conclusion 108

Notes 111
Appendix: Guidance Text Overview 159
Select Bibliography 169
Index 185

Et ad astra doloribus itur
(Prudentius, *Cathemerinon*, 10: 92)

This book is dedicated to my parents
William George and Marian Joyce Hughes-Edwards

SERIES EDITORS' PREFACE

Religion and Culture in the Middle Ages aims to explore the interface between medieval religion and culture, with as broad an understanding of those terms as possible. It puts to the forefront studies which engage with works that significantly contributed to the shaping of medieval culture. However, it also gives attention to studies dealing with works that reflect and highlight aspects of medieval culture that have been neglected in the past by scholars of the medieval disciplines. For example, devotional works and the practice they infer illuminate our understanding of the medieval subject and its culture in remarkable ways, while studies of the material space designed and inhabited by medieval subjects yield new evidence on the period and the people who shaped it and lived in it. In the larger field of religion and culture, we also want to explore further the roles played by women as authors, readers and owners of books, thereby defining them more precisely as actors in the cultural field. The series as a whole investigates the European Middle Ages, from c.500 to c.1500. Our aim is to explore medieval religion and culture with the tools belonging to such disciplines as, among others, art history, philosophy, theology, history, musicology, the history of medicine, and literature. In particular, we would like to promote interdisciplinary studies, as we believe strongly that our modern understanding of the term applies fascinatingly well to a cultural period marked by a less tight confinement and categorization of its disciplines than the modern period. However, our only criterion is academic excellence, with the belief that the use of a large diversity of critical tools and theoretical approaches enables a deeper understanding of medieval culture. We want the series to reflect this diversity, as we believe that, as a collection of outstanding contributions, it offers a more subtle representation of a period that is marked by paradoxes and contradictions and which necessarily reflects diversity and difference, however difficult it may sometimes have proved for medieval culture to accept these notions.

ACKNOWLEDGEMENTS

Loving thanks must first go to my parents, William and Joyce Hughes-Edwards, for all their support during the fourteen years I spent writing this book. My father was a deep spiritual thinker, and the first person who inspired me to seek knowledge for its own sake. My mother's strength anchored him, as it does me. Without my mother this book could not have been finished; without my father it could not have been started.

I would also like to thank my doctoral supervisors, Felicity Riddy and Jeremy Goldberg, who guided me during the research that formed the basis of some earlier sections of this book. They encouraged me, listened to me, challenged me intellectually and supported me to an extent far beyond that which could ever have been expected of them.

I am also grateful to my doctoral external examiner, Bella Millett, who has been characteristically kind and supportive of my work from my student days, and whose scholarship of medieval spirituality continues to inspire me with awe.

Robert Hasenfratz made helpful suggestions for improvements to the manuscript in its final stages, and I am grateful to him for his clear-sighted advice and for his belief in the book.

Thanks are also due to Katy Cubitt, Joseph Gribbin (now Brother Anselm), Liz Herbert McAvoy and her family, Cate Gunn, Catherine Innes-Parker, Alexandra Barratt and Eddie Jones. I am also grateful to the late Philip Stell, whose scholarship funded the original doctoral research at the Centre for Medieval Studies, University of York, on which some of this book is based, and to Edge Hill University for awarding me a research grant to support the writing's final stages.

I would also like to thank Elizabeth McConnell, Effie Knights, Rachel Nott, Kathy Powell, Hilary Arnold, Roz Ferguson, Gill Parrott and Elke Weißmann.

Last, but not least, my loving thanks go to James Binns for his unfailing encouragement, guidance and care, for giving me a quiet place to write in, and for telling me when it was time to stop: 'Is est amicus qui in re dubia re iuvat, ubi re est opus'.

ABBREVIATIONS

This page gives the full details of the abbreviations used to denote the anchoritic guidance texts which are cited parenthetically in this monograph.

Anselm   Francis S. Schmitt (ed.), *Sancti Anselmi Cantuariensis Archiepiscopi, Opera Omnia*, 6 vols (Edinburgh: T. Nelson, 1946–63). This abbreviation refers to specific Latin letters of Anselm's, each of which is explicitly identified in a suffix to this abbreviation in each case: 'Letter 112' in vol. 3, pp. 244–6; 'Letter 230' in vol. 4, pp. 134–5 and 'Letter 414' in vol. 5, pp. 359–62.

AW, Corpus   Bella Millett (ed.), with Eric J. Dobson and Richard Dance, *Ancrene Wisse. A Corrected Edition of the Text in Cambridge, Corpus Christi College, MS 402, With Variants from Other Manuscripts*, vol. 1, Early English Text Society, original series, 325 (2005).

DII   Aelred of Rievaulx, *De institutione inclusarum*, in *Aelredi Rievallensis Opera Omnia: I Opera Ascetica*, in *Corpus Christianorum Continuatio Mediaeualis I*, ed. Anselm Hoste and Charles Hugh Talbot (Turnhout: Brepols, 1971), pp. 635–82.

DII, MS Bodley 423 This refers to the late-medieval redaction of Aelred of Rievaulx's anchoritic guide, *De institutione inclusarum*, in John Ayto and Alexandra Barratt (eds), *Aelred of Rievaulx's 'De institutione inclusarum': Two English Versions*, Early English Text Society, original series, 287 (1984), pp. 1–25.

Form   This refers to the edition of Richard Rolle's anchoritic guide, *The Form of Living* in Sarah J. Ogilvie-Thompson (ed.), *Richard Rolle: Prose and Verse from MS Longleat 29 and Related Manuscripts*, Early English Text Society, original series, 293 (1988), pp. 3–25.

Fröhlich   Walter Fröhlich (ed. and trans.), *The Letters of Saint Anselm of Canterbury*, 3 vols (Kalamazoo: Cistercian Publications, 1990–4). This abbreviation refers to specific English translations of certain Latin letters of Anselm's, each of which is explicitly identified in a suffix to this abbreviation in each case:

'Letter 112' is in vol. 1, pp. 268–71; 'Letter 230' is in vol. 2, pp. 199–200 and 'Letter 414' is in vol. 3, pp. 184–7.

Liber   Goscelin of St Bertin, 'The *Liber confortatorius* of Goscelin of Saint Bertin', *Analecta monastica*, ed. Charles Hugh Talbot, series 3, *Studia Anselmiana*, fasc. 37 (Rome: Pontifical Institute of St Anselm, 1955), pp. 1–117.

MacPherson   Aelred of Rievaulx, 'A rule of life for a recluse', in *Aelred of Rievaulx: Treatises and Pastoral Prayer*, trans. Mary Paul MacPherson (Kalamazoo: Cistercian Studies Series, 1971), pp. 40–102.

Millett   Bella Millett, *Ancrene Wisse: Guide for Anchoresses. A Translation* (Exeter: Exeter University Press, 2009).

Myrour   Marta Powell Harley (ed.), *The Myrour of Recluses* (Madison and Teaneck: Fairleigh Dickinson University Press, 1995).

Otter   Goscelin of St Bertin, *The Book of Encouragement and Consolation (Liber confortatorius). The Letter of Goscelin to the Recluse Eva*, trans. Monika Otter (Cambridge: D. S. Brewer, 2004).

Scale I   This refers to the first book of Walter Hilton's anchoritic guide, *The Scale of Perfection*, in *Walter Hilton: The Scale of Perfection*, ed. Thomas H. Bestul (Kalamazoo: Medieval Institute Publications, 2000), pp. 31–133.

Speculum   P. Livario Oliger (ed.), '*Speculum inclusorum*', *Lateranum*, n.s., 4 (1938), 1–148.

Introduction

This book is the first study of normative English anchoritic ideology from *c*.1080 to *c*.1450. A survey of the diachronic development of anchoritic ideological thought, it focuses on eight anchoritic guidance texts, including every extant guide originally intended for female English recluses, some of which have received comparatively little critical attention. It reveals an important, self-referential tradition of guidance writing in England, in operation throughout the entirety of the Middle Ages. This tradition quotes, revises and re-translates itself frequently, inspired by the desire to interrogate and solve what it sees as the vocation's persistent problems and by the need to charter new ideological territory. The book's fundamental argument is that the guidance tradition is founded on the inculcation of four common anchoritic ideals – enclosure, solitude, chastity and orthodoxy – and in the context of two crucial spiritual practices: asceticism and contemplative experience. The extent to which each of the guides focuses on the four ideals will be shown to be different, but every guidance writer, nonetheless, focuses on them and adapts and develops them for his own purposes. This book's detailed analysis of each ideal in turn renders the changes and continuities in anchoritic ideology visible here for the first time. It clarifies important differences between earlier and later medieval anchoritic guides and also vital similarities, which have not hitherto been fully understood.[1] While its analysis of the guides sometimes focuses on them as two groups, early and late, this does not mean that their ideologies are wholly distinct. Grouping them thus best renders visible the extent to which later medieval anchoritic ideology grows out of earlier normative thought, even, as this book will show, when their perspectives appear to be very different.

Scrutinizing the anchoritic ideals of enclosure, solitude, chastity and orthodoxy enables the rejection, as myth, of the medieval anchorhold as simply a solitary death cell and the recluse as simply a living corpse, locked up in death-like darkness. The book shows this to be just one of a host of reclusive images used as part of the ideological construction of the vocation, amongst which is also the less critically prominent, but equally valid, depiction of a busy woman who willingly interrupts her devotions to be of spiritual service to a steady stream of visitors to the reclusorium. The anchorhold is thereby concurrently revealed, in ideological terms, as the potential site of intellectual exchange, spiritual progression and growth. This is further reinforced by the book's contextualization of the two spiritual practices constructed by the guides as most vital to the vocation: asceticism and contemplative experience. Placing these within the wider theologies of medieval Europe enables the book to demonstrate many intersections between insular anchoritic spirituality and wider medieval spirituality. Ultimately then, the book reveals the extent to which anchoritic spirituality is in sync with the spirituality of the wider medieval world.

The book is split into two sections: part I focuses on the English anchoritic guidance tradition in isolation, in order to establish the ideological foundations of the vocation clearly, so that part II can contextualize insular anchoritic theology within the theology of wider medieval Europe. Part II can read the vocation in its wider contexts only when the guides have been analysed in full in their own right. The book reads the largest number of guides ever analysed together as ideological texts, in order to map their constructions of the vocation onto the wider medieval world. It moves outwards in scope, taking the anchorite's cell as its starting point. Part I explores the textual confines of the reclusorium in isolation; part II opens that reclusorium up to the world.

Part I contains three chapters. Chapter 1 introduces the guides, their manuscript traditions, their writers and reclusive audience(s). Much is known about the provenance and textual transmission of some guides but little about others. Chapter 1 cannot therefore be uniform in its coverage, but it introduces each guide as fully as possible, outlines their basic contents and gives information on the controversies that surrounded their writers. Chapter 2 focuses on the ideal of enclosure and chapter 3 on solitude (and inevitably therefore anchoritic sociability, for each is defined in terms of the other). The guides themselves indicate that enclosure and solitude are the common foundation stones upon which their ideological constructions of the vocation are built. Therefore the book's focus is first and foremost on them. The third and fourth ideals of chastity and orthodoxy remain important throughout the Middle Ages, yet the guides as a collective group do not focus on them to the same shared extent.[2] The ideal of chastity is therefore explored in chapter 2, as part of its elaboration of the threats to solitude posed by social interaction (chief amongst which, for earlier guidance writers especially, is the potential loss of chastity that may ensue). Yet, in addition to exploring sociability-as-threat, chapter 3 re-evaluates the extent to which the English recluse is encouraged by the guidance tradition to engage in acceptable social interaction, problematizing scholarship which reads anchoritic sociability as only, or chiefly, transgressive. The fourth anchoritic ideal, of orthodoxy, is explored in chapter 5's treatment of contemplative experience, since the two are inextricably linked by the guides themselves.

Part II of this book is split into two chapters, both of which seek to break new ground as they track the variety of cultural and intellectual changes evident in the guides, across the whole of wider medieval Europe.[3] Chapter 4 historicizes asceticism and seeks to demonstrate the extent to which the anchoritic guidance writing tradition's increasing tendency to replace physical mortification with mental asceticism harmonizes with wider medieval spiritual thought. Chapter 5 historicizes contemplative experience. It proposes that three contemplative states are common to the guides: meditation, vision and a rarer experience, which this book terms contemplative fusion, whereby God and the contemplative are fused together; the two rendered one. These three states are extrapolated from a reading of the contemplative trajectory of the guidance tradition as a whole. Each writer operates with an awareness of the differences between them, placing different emphases upon each for a variety of reasons to be explicated in part II in greater detail. The guides themselves do not, of course, use this modern-day threefold vocabulary and chapter 5 initially focuses on the language that they do use to describe these contemplative states before suggesting its own, new terminology. Chapter 5 ends with the negotiation of two powerful medieval spiritual controversies. The first centres on contemplative experience, anchoritism and heresy in the book's negotiation of the anchoritic ideal of spiritual orthodoxy (the final ideal of the four ideals upon which it argues anchoritic ideology is founded). The second controversy centres upon the role of anchoritic ideology in wider medieval debates about the value of the active and the contemplative life.

Ultimately, part II's historicization of the spirituality of the English anchorhold enables the book to draw wider conclusions about the transitional nature of medieval religion and culture and its shifting preoccupations, prejudices, demands and developments. It thereby completes the book's revelation of a textually constructed anchorhold that, despite its idealized, relative isolation and potential liminality, is far from cut-off from the outside world.

The origins of anchoritism

Religious men and women have sought lives of solitude since ancient times, finding spiritual fulfilment through the rejection of society's expectations and burdens. The desert fathers and mothers were the earliest-known Christian solitaries: holy men and women who lived in the deserts of Egypt, Syria, Palestine and Arabia during the fourth and fifth centuries. They withdrew from society so that they might better come to know themselves and through that self-knowledge forge a more intimate connection with God. They abandoned the world, considering themselves the richer for it; their minds attuned to the eternal, not the temporal, scheme.[4] In England, during the Middle Ages, the same urge to experience religious solitude was expressed in a number of ways, mediated through the practice of physical enclosure. Coenobitic withdrawal from the world involved comparative solitude, but was nonetheless a life lived in community. Eremites – hermits and anchorites – sought to withdraw in isolation and thereby experienced the harshest and most extreme form of solitude open to the medieval Christian.

The term anchorite descends from the Greek ἀναχωρητής (anachoretes) itself derived from the ancient Greek verb ἀναχωρειν (anachorein, 'to withdraw').[5] Anchorites commonly withdrew, in the tradition of the desert solitaries, to a small arena; an anchorhold was often a single cell adjoining a church or religious building. Yet, the distinction between anchoritic and hermitic eremitism was not reinforced by the pre-medieval church. St Benedict (c.480–c.550) potentially conflates them in his influential Rule:

> Deinde secundum genus est anachoritarum, id est heremitarum, horum qui non conversationis fervore novicio, sed monasterii probatione diuturna, qui didicerunt contra diabolum multorum solacio iam docti pugnare, et bene exstructi fraterna ex acie ad singularem pugnam heremi, securi iam sine consolatione alterius, sola manu vel brachio contra vitia carnis vel cogitationum, Deo auxiliante, pugnare sufficiunt.[6]

Ann K. Warren, in her influential monograph on anchoritic patronage, argues that in the fourth century, 'hermit and anchorite were one in meaning … The recluse was *anachoreta* or *eremita* interchangeably'.[7] Edward A. Jones argues for the gradual development of the terminology of solitude: a shift from St Benedict's synonymous usage, 'general in the West until around the end of the first millennium', to two distinct forms: '"Anchorite" … begins to refer … specifically to one who is strictly enclosed (effectively incarcerated)'.[8] Although, in the earlier Middle Ages, some anchorites may have shared their solitude with others and, as Henrietta Leyser has shown, some hermits lived in quasi-anchoritic seclusion, by the later medieval period, the vocations had become increasingly separate.[9] Tom Licence concludes: 'In eleventh-century England, the term *ancer* covered a spectrum of practices, but the twelfth century's interest in precision began to reduce its elasticity'.[10] Rotha Mary Clay, in her seminal study of English eremitism, *The Hermits and Anchorites of England*, notes the development of 'two distinct classes of solitaries: the *anchorite*, enclosed within four walls, and the *hermit* who … mingled with his fellow-men'.[11] Warren argues:

> to be an *anchorite* meant to take on a narrowly defined vocation … *inclusus/inclusa* or *reclusus/reclusa*. Enclosed and stable … [the anchorite] inhabited only a limited space within what was broadly considered to be an eremitic life; the hermit remained free to encounter his destiny in the remainder of that space.[12]

She emphasizes a further difference: 'Once they [anchorites] entered the cell they could not retreat. Solitary by choice, they became solitary by law and in this way distinct from hermits'.[13] Unable and, ideally, unwilling, to leave the spiritual arena, caught firmly between two worlds, the medieval anchorite had no choice but to stand her ground and fight.[14]

Introduction to medieval anchoritism

The extant written evidence for the English anchoritic vocation, more extensive for the later medieval period, includes ceremonies of enclosure, wills, court documents, bishop's registers, ecclesiastical documents, personal correspondence and anchoritic guides. The earliest ceremony of enclosure, detailing the final liturgical moments of an anchorite's life in the world, is found in a twelfth-century pontifical and the latest in a printed sixteenth-century manual.[15] Such ceremonies are textually constructed rites of passage. In theory they were undertaken after episcopal permission for enclosure was granted, satisfactory financial arrangements made and an anchorhold built or selected.[16] Not every recluse would have participated in one; the basic requirements for enclosure were only investigation into the candidate's spiritual integrity, financial security, intended abode and the granting of a licence for enclosure. Nonetheless, some elaborate ceremonies exist. At the climax of a twelfth-century rite, psalms are chanted from the Office of the Dead, the postulant is given extreme unction and, once she has entered the anchorhold, the command 'Obstruant hostium domus' is given by the officiant, the door is blocked up and the recluse left alone within her enclosure.[17] Jones identifies the death rhetoric of the rite as 'dispensable' in the eyes of some (busy) bishops from a note at the end of the Lacy Pontifical's version which states: 'Many prelates omit Extreme Unction and Commendations and go straight from [the] *Exaudi* [*Domine* prayer] to the blocking of the door'.[18] Whether the rhetoric of death was vital to some bishops or not, the ceremonials all share the same need to signal an end to the postulant's earthly life, to demonstrate permanent separation from the world and to vivify the recluse's new fixity of abode. They also reveal significant clerical participation in the vocation. Enclosure ceremonies also offer, in Jones's words: 'rhetorically powerful … liturgical perform-ance' which constructs enclosure as the point of entry into a new life; a focus then, on rebirth as much as on death.[19] Through their spectacle, the anchorhold and its occupant are potentially elevated and set apart from the community; the visible and invisible boundaries of anchoritic experience liturgically established and rendered potentially sacrosanct.

The extant wills which mention anchorites usually document small individual bequests and, sometimes, gifts made to the recluses of one geographical area. Infrequently, they detail lifetime endowments for a favoured recluse. The percentage of wills that mentions anchorites is relatively small. Warren notes only 10 per cent calen-dared at the London Court of Husting between 1351 and 1360.[20] Nonetheless, they demonstrate the visible support which the, often lay, community gave to the vocation and the esteem in which it was held. Other indicators of esteem include the visits of those of high status to the reclusorium for advice. Westminster recluses were consulted by Richard II and Henry V, while a female anchorite from Winchester was brought to see Richard Beauchamp in London because he was too busy to travel to her.[21] Emma Rawghton, of All Saint's Church, North Street, York, esteemed for her visions of Mary, was also linked to Beauchamp and made predictions, to be explored in chapter 5 below, about his future.[22] Clay cites these as examples of the influence exercised by contempla-tive anchorites in public affairs.[23] Jones acknowledges renowned later medieval recluses like Julian of Norwich (c.1342–c.1416), Rawghton and the Winchester anchorite as 'rare … But … not unique' examples of 'a female anchorite occupying a position of spiritual authority', but notes also the ambiguity of Beauchamp's reclusive associations: 'Such deference to female visionaries carries some irony in a man who played a promin-ent role in the … condemnation of Joan of Arc'.[24] He reminds us that 'Beauchamp goes to his anchoresses for guidance *from God*, not from the women themselves per se.[25] Nonetheless, the medieval recluse is evidently considered and consulted as an agent of the Lord and these visits suggest the potential respect with which medieval society treated some of its solitaries.

Ecclesiastical documentation, including episcopal registers and court documents, details the vocation's clerical support and frequently addresses its operational problems. The episcopal registers of John Stratford, Bishop of Winchester from 1323–33, note, for instance, the case of Christine, anchorite of St James's Church in Shere in Surrey, who sought enclosure in 1329 but fled her cell by 1332.[26] Other sensational accounts of anchoritism record alleged sexual scandal, notably at Whalley in Lancashire. An account of the supposed sexual misconduct of the servants of the anchorite Isolda de Heton (enclosed in 1436) potentially implies that the anchorite absconded: 'dyvers that had been anchores and recluses in the seyd plase aforetyme, contrary to thyre own oth … have broken owte of the seyd plase'.[27] Like Christine, Isolda seems to have left her reclusorium. A widow with a young child, she may have gone into hiding with her son. The Cistercians of Whalley Abbey seized upon her flight, petitioning Henry VI to allow them to convert the anchorhold to other uses. Anna Palmer, anchorite of St Peter's Church, Leicester, was accused of incontinence by Bishop Buckingham in 1393, although she denied the charges.[28] Usually, however, the operational documents that surround the vocation are less dramatic. They detail pre-enclosure background investigations and post-enclosure arrangements for practical and spiritual support. Licences and mandates are also extant which detail the building of anchorholds, the substitution of suitable for unsuitable cells and even the legislation of diet.[29] On rare occasions they document permission given to recluses to leave their cells temporarily, as in the case of Emma Scherman, who seems to have been permitted the right to make annual pilgrimage.[30]

The documentation that surrounds anchoritism also implies community involvement in the vocation. Henry Mayr-Harting, in a case study of the socially active recluse Wulfric of Haselbury, concludes: 'Anyone living in twelfth-century England would very probably ... have had contact with a recluse'.[31] Robert Hasenfratz's argument that 'many anchorites withdrew from the world only to find themselves squarely in the center of village life' is echoed by Licence's conclusion: 'Set at the heart of the community ... it was an unwise recluse that entered her cell to achieve peace and quiet'.[32] Licence argues that, even in the earlier medieval period, recluses potentially 'provide a ministry different from the priest's', involving three key elements: inspiring repentance, interceding (constituting interaction with a 'circle of clients ... the anchorite's confraternity') and, lastly, mediating God's power.[33]

Many of the sources that surround anchoritism imply then that anchorites were not cut off from society, but rather attempted, as much as was possible, to withdraw from it. Ironically, they could not do this without the approval of the very society that they strove to reject. Christopher Daniell argues that from the time of the Norman Conquest, England's spirituality was so strongly fostered by the relationship between church and lay patron that the entire church was 'dependent upon the wealth and patronage of the laity'.[34] It is in this context, notwithstanding the reforms of the twelfth century (which were, as Daniell has shown, partly intended to wrest 'churches out of the hands of the laity'), that anchoritism is best understood.[35] For, as Warren concludes:

> The medieval Englishman who passed by the cell of the anchorite was more than a passive observer. He was part of a network of support that enabled the anchorite to exist and persist ... [the recluse's] choice implied a culture in consonance with his views, one that ... encouraged it by responding to its demands.[36]

Anchoritism thus read is not just a private statement, but a public proclamation, with ramifications for the recluse, the church and the world. Denis Renevey argues for a darker aspect to community support in his work on medieval death. The dying man knew that 'once dead, he depended on the goodwill of the living for their prayers'; therefore, the 'community of the living ... had the upper hand in ... the economy of salvation'.[37] Anchoritism, the 'living death', would seem, on one level, to subvert this. The community's dependence upon the intercessionary support of the recluse is codified in its extension to her of practical aid and professional respect. Liz Herbert McAvoy identifies the 'communal investments in the anchoritic body', which offer the 'ordinary parishioner a stake in the salvific process'.[38] Yet, concurrently, that same recluse depends upon the community for her survival. In spiritual terms the recluse might appear to have the upper hand; in practical terms she might not.

Archaeological evidence of the vocation also exists, although it is scarcer for the earlier medieval period. It suggests the prevalence of small, one-roomed cells, not multi-roomed establishments.[39] Licence argues for the makeshift nature of the earlier medieval anchorhold: 'the vast majority were lean-to, timber structures rather than the solid domiciles of stones which first came into view in the fourteenth century'.[40] Many cells were attached or close to churches, although some were part of convents, monasteries and even castles.[41] Roberta Gilchrist concludes that the majority were built on the inhospitable northern side of the chancel, although the placement of some female-inhabited cells may have been to the west.[42] The smallest known cells are those of Leatherhead and Compton in Surrey. Leatherhead's cell was eight feet square, with a window of twenty-one inches square, while Compton's was six foot eight inches by four foot four inches, with a loft where the recluse may have slept.[43] Warren's plan of Compton in the twelfth century illustrates its tiny dimensions, yet this cell knew anchoritic occupation from 1185 to the early fourteenth century.[44] Gilchrist describes both sites, noting the existence of two cells at Compton, one to the south of the chancel and an upper chapel at its east end which may have served as 'the oratory for an anchorite-priest'.[45] Later medieval anchoritic architectural remains imply that the cell continued to be a small one- or two-roomed structure, although notable exceptions include the four-roomed anchorhouse at Chester-le-Street and the twenty-nine foot by twenty-four foot cell of one fifteenth-century anchorite priest.[46] Some later cells may even have had gardens, although again this appears to be exceptional. Of the fifteenth-century reclusorium at the Charterhouse of Sheen, Warren states: 'The anchorite paid an annual rent of eight pence for a garden "newly walled"'.[47] Emma Scherman of Pontefract was given permission to be rehoused because her present garden was too noisy.[48]

If a recluse entered the anchorhold while still relatively young, then her enclosure could last many years. Norman Tanner argues that the Norwich recluse Elizabeth Scott was enclosed for thirty years at St Julian's, Conisford, while at nearby Carrow Priory, Julian Lampett may have passed fifty years in solitude.[49] Warren, on the basis of the evidence available to her in the mid-1980s, based on Clay's invaluable tabulated lists of cells published in 1914, proposes the recorded existence of at least 780 English recluses on 601 sites.[50] She suggests that more English women than men were enclosed at every stage of the medieval period. She locates anchorholds in all but four counties of medieval England (Buckinghamshire, Rutland, Cumberland and Westmorland).[51] Some counties evidence strong anchoritic identities, including Oxfordshire, Sussex, Worcestershire and Hampshire, during the twelfth and thirteenth centuries and Lincolnshire, Middlesex (including London) and Norfolk, throughout the Middle Ages. Some demonstrate strong anchoritic links only at times, connections which are later lost, for instance in Yorkshire, where anchoritism appears to have declined by the end of the fifteenth century.[52]

Anchoritism began as a largely rural phenomenon, but the number of English urban anchorholds steadily increased until the sixteenth century when they dominated their rural counterparts and, Gilchrist argues, the anchorhold became 'an integral element of the ecclesiastical topography of medieval towns'.[53] This shift is implied by the arguments of the English canonist, William Lyndwood, in 1433 that 'a recluse might be more readily supplied in his needs in a town where there are plenty of people than in the country where there are few and those often too poor to help anyone'.[54] The height of anchoritism's popularity in England seems to have been the fourteenth century, when Warren identifies London, York and Norwich as having twelve, eight and six anchoritic sites respectively.[55] Yet, at every stage of the medieval period, the rural anchorhold retained its importance and its dominance (with the exception of the sixteenth century).[56]

English anchoritism's reclusive data, gendered differentials, geographical locations and chronological development are, however, still emergent. Warren's and Clay's statistical picture will alter as new sites and solitaries are discovered. Jones is currently revising Clay's 1914 study of eremitism. In updating Clay's lists of solitaries, he draws on revisionary principles laid down by Clay herself and continued by Basil Cottle between Clay's death in 1961 and his own in 1994.[57] Jones's investigations have thus far resulted in the publication of updated lists for medieval Bedfordshire, Hertfordshire and Huntingdonshire which, when combined, feature fifty solitaries compared with Clay's twenty-four.[58] The alterations which new data will make to our understanding of anchoritism are, as yet, unknown. Yet they need not imply radical change in anchoritism's gendered, geographical or chronological make-up. Warren's original depiction of the vocation as 'a wide-ranging and far-reaching religious phenomenon: many anchorites all over the country ... Not one in every parish, but in many', may yet remain true.[59] Nonetheless, the vocation was evidently more widespread than either Clay or Warren could have anticipated.

Introduction to the anchoritic guidance writing genre

To be physically enclosed within the same four walls for life required a strength of character and of purpose far beyond most medieval Christians. English anchoritic guides were therefore written, revised and translated, chiefly from Latin into English and vice versa, throughout the Middle Ages to enable the recluse to come to terms with the enormity of her choice. They perceive the anchoritic life to be one of privation and paradoxical joy, because of the God-given grace required to make it bearable. Frequently written in the form of a letter from one writer to one recluse, these guides differ in size from short epistles to intricately subdivided works. Warren argues that thirteen English guides are extant but it is difficult to be precise about numbers.[60] Textual revision is so common to the tradition and some guides are so altered, for different, even non-anchoritic, audiences, that to identify all the revisions or translations of one guide as the same guide is problematic. As chapter 1 will show, in the case of some guides, like *Ancrene Wisse*, there can be as many as seventeen texts. More scholarly debate on this issue is needed and the question of what constitutes an anchoritic guide needs to be more widely addressed.[61]

It is tempting to read anchoritic guides as evidence of widespread reclusive practice, especially given the dramatic, visual nature of earlier medieval guidance, coupled with the relative lack of documentary evidence for that early period. Yet, the guides do not show us how recluses actually lived. They show us what a handful of men hoped a number of recluses could achieve at their best, or fail to achieve at their worst; often they are the conclusions of just one man for just one woman. The guides are rich in the rhetorical theory of anchoritism. Complex normative works of instruction, they are shaped by the ideological agendas of their age. We can know, as Patricia Ranft states: 'from accounts like [Aelred's] ... what the ideal anchorite life was', but we cannot know, as she also argues, that: 'often the ideal was not attained'.[62] Aelred's demonizations (and idealizations) of the recluse are comparative rhetoric; part of a broader strategy, intended to shape his readers' behaviour through the inculcation of fear. They are demonstrative of far wider early medieval anxieties (in this case, chiefly about sexuality). Anchoritic guides like Aelred's are grounded, as chapters 2 and 3 will show in more detail, in common cultural fears that they can never wholly quieten.[63]

It is not known how many recluses actually used an anchoritic guide. Some may have used several, while others used none. Bella Millett makes a useful distinction between 'actual and potential anchoritic readers'.[64] My own work argues elsewhere for their separation into 'generative or incidental' readerships.[65] Many guides are presented as the result of persistent requests, implying a network of personal relationships which pre-exist enclosure and persist beyond it. Ironically, the bond between some guidance writers and recluses gives birth to a genre devoted to the severance of such ties. These texts, in the earlier medieval period especially, are meant to facilitate the destruction of the very relationships that have generated their production.

To analyse every extant anchoritic guide is, sadly, beyond the scope of this current monograph. To do all the guides and their many revisions justice, interrogating them in any useful depth, would require a volume of at least twice its length.[66] This book focuses instead on eight guides, but this does not mean that it analyses just eight texts. Some guides, as chapter 1 will show, are extant in numerous revisions, many of which this book also explores.[67] Each guide has been chosen carefully on four key grounds: first, if in its original conception, or revised usage, it was intended for a reclusive audience. Those guides, or their revised and translated texts, widened to include other audiences are largely excluded, as are those where reclusive readership is uncertain, as in the case of the Vernon manuscript.[68] Secondly, texts have been selected from a full chronological range (from 1080 to 1450), giving a solid basis for measuring ideological developments across the majority of the Middle Ages. This sample has been balanced, so that the book's conclusions are based on a relatively equal number of earlier and later guides (four base guides, and their revisions, have been selected, from each sub-period). Longer guides and guides that circulated in manuscript form in significant numbers have been chosen over fragmentary letters, although some short guides and guides extant in single manuscripts are included as comparatives. Finally, every guide intended originally for women has been selected, so that the book can make conclusive arguments about the basis of the ideological constructions of the vocation for at least one gender. Women were chosen because female recluses commonly outnumbered their male counterparts.[69] To offer some comparatives, however, the book does also analyse some guidance intended for men, such as the later medieval *Speculum inclusorum* and possibly the vernacular redaction of *De institutione* extant in Oxford, Bodleian Library, MS Bodley 423 (since it may be of Carthusian provenance).[70]

Specifically, this book focuses upon the following guides and their revisions:[71] (from the early medieval period) Goscelin of St Bertin's Latin *Liber confortatorius* (*c*.1080); two letters by St Anselm for lay female recluses and one for a male solitary (*c*.1078–*c*.1105); Aelred of Rievaulx's *De institutione inclusarum* (*c*.1160–2); the thirteenth-century, oft-revised guide, *Ancrene Wisse* – specifically those texts extant in London, British Library, MS Cotton Nero A. xiv (*c*.1240s), in Cambridge, Corpus Christi College, MS 402 (*c*.1230s–1280s, but after 1224), in London, British Library, MS Cotton Cleopatra C. vi (1230s), in London, British Library, MS Cotton Titus D. xviii (1240s) and in Cambridge, Gonville and Caius College, MS 234/120 (third quarter of the thirteenth century). From the later medieval period: Richard Rolle's *The Form of*

Living (*c.*1348); the anonymously authored *Speculum inclusorum* (*c.*1349–*c.*1382/92); Walter Hilton's *Scale of Perfection*, Book I only (*c.*1384–6); the vernacular Bodley redaction of *De institutione* (*c.*1430–40) and the anonymous *Myrour of Recluses* (*c.*1450), a vernacular translation of *Speculum*.

Traditionally, the guides' generic classification has been problematic. Licence calls them manuals or handbooks.[72] Warren terms them treatises or rules.[73] Others, such as Charlotte D'Evelyn, classify some, such as *Speculum*, as 'borderline' rules.[74] Yet, they are not rules in a monastic sense. Only on rare occasions are they prescriptive, for enclosure has taken the recluse beyond mere human command. As Linda Georgianna argues in a study of *Ancrene Wisse* contextualized within the different traditions of the Benedictine and Augustinian rules, anchoritic guidance writers move:

> beyond the prescriptiveness of religious rules … toward a more self-conscious awareness of their interior lives … in opposition to those who would demand a fixed and particular set of external precepts as the only legitimate definition of an individual's spiritual goals.[75]

Anchoritic guides are composite texts, collections of writings that trouble and resist generic boundaries. They combine vocational guidance with lyrical passages of biblical exegesis. They intersect liberal quotations from and glosses of the work of a wide range of ancient and newer authors, with material on contemporary economics, politics and theology. Each writer gathers together in one compendium all the texts and all the genres that he feels he needs to support his constructions of anchoritic ideology. Anchoritic guidance, then, is an inclusive generic form, one dictated by necessity. As Monika Otter remarks, the guide 'has to fulfil … many functions' and that very functionality invokes 'fullness … it is all you have, but also all you need'.[76]

Anchoritic scholarship has tended until now to centre on a small number of guides or ideals.[77] Earlier medieval guidance has dominated the critical field and much of this work has focused on a single guide, *Ancrene Wisse*, to the comparative exclusion of later medieval guidance. This has created an imbalance in critical perceptions of anchoritism. Yet, understanding *Speculum*, *Myrour* and the Bodley redaction of Aelred's guide is just as vital to the comprehension of the ideology of the vocation as a whole. Whilst alongside *Ancrene Wisse, The Form of Living* and the *Scale of Perfection* have formed the focus of influential theories on the continuity of English prose, comparatively little analysis of some of the later guides as anchoritic texts exists.[78] Rollian and Hiltonian criticism tends to focus on the relevance of their writing for the laity, or on them as contemplative not anchoritic writers, as if the two are mutually exclusive.[79] While *Form* and *Scale* have become justifiably known for their lay relevance, their anchoritic origins should not be passed over critically. In returning them to their reclusive roots, this book seeks to facilitate new understandings of these popular spiritual treatises in their original anchoritic contexts.

Warren argues that the earlier and later guides are different in tone and purpose and this theory has been influential where the guides have, on rare occasions, been considered as a larger group.[80] She identifies a fourteenth-century mystical volte-face, 'a flowering of mysticism', responsible for their marked disparities.[81] The later guides are, as this book will show, in places quite different from their earlier counterparts. Yet Warren's conclusion precludes the notion of gradual developments in anchoritic ideology and theology and discounts the possibility of subtle relationships between the earlier and later guides. Some guidance writers, including the original author of *Ancrene Wisse*, the *Speculum* author, Walter Hilton and Aelred's Bodley redactor, signal their awareness of the work of their guidance predecessors, consciously placing themselves in an ongoing continuum of anchoritic guidance writing which draws the earlier and later texts together. In choosing to redact an earlier medieval guide, Aelred's Bodley redactor implies his support for earlier constructions of anchoritism. He also deliberately includes an explicit reference to Aelred at the close of his redaction, aligning himself with that earlier guide and with Aelred's considerable spiritual authority in claims that his text is in fact 'the Reule of a Recluse that Seynt Alrede wrote to his suster' (*DII*, MS Bodley 423, p. 25).[82] The two texts are sometimes so different that it may be more useful to regard them as different guides, but this later medieval redactor nonetheless still wishes to align himself with the ideological spirituality of earlier guidance, even as he departs from it. The *Speculum* author signals similar approval of earlier guidance writing, in a passage that has been largely overlooked in critical terms.[83] From a section of part IV, missing in *Myrour*, he implores his recluses to live: 'iuxta vestre professionis sacras observancias et beati Alredi doctrinam de institutione reclusi atque aliorum devotorum egregia documenta' (*Speculum*, p. 140).[84] A later medieval guidance writer again suggests the continued relevance of earlier medieval ideological constructions of the vocation to his own later constructions of it. He implies that a reading of earlier guidance will corroborate, not contradict, a reading of his own late medieval perspectives. Part I of this book seeks to follow the Bodley redactor and the *Speculum* author's lead, in a new interrogation of the relationships between earlier and later guidance. It seeks also to redress the critical imbalance caused by so much focus on earlier guidance in its comparative exploration of the equally important later guides, which it analyses, crucially, as anchoritic texts.

I

Anchoritic Spirituality in Isolation:
The English Anchoritic Guides

1

Introducing the Guides[1]

The earlier medieval guides

The earliest extant English anchoritic guide, Goscelin of St Bertin's *Liber conforta-torius*, was written *c.*1080 for the recluse Eve. It is extant in a single manuscript, London, British Library, MS Sloane 3103, of the abbey of Saint-Sauveur-le-Vicomte in Normandy; the mid-twelfth-century work of more than one scribe.[2] Like Aelred's twelfth-century guide, the *Liber* is a letter and, like the thirteenth-century *Ancrene Wisse*, it is of such a length that it is subdivided – in its case into four books and a prologue. Book I focuses on complaint and comfort. Therein, Goscelin alleges many grievances against Eve for her 'desertion' of him and of England. These were prompted by her, apparently secret, move to an anchorhold at the church of Saint-Laurent du Tertre in Angers.[3] Book II confronts human sinfulness, the battle against which is cast as the route to spiritual success in the tradition of the ultimate struggle: Christ's Passion. In its context, the *Liber* argues, every Christian, but especially the recluse, must fight. Book III seeks to inflame Eve's spiritual desires and offers strategies whereby she can conquer the dejection and doubt constructed as inherent to the solitary vocation. Book IV focuses on the importance of humility as a foundation stone for all virtue. Remarkable for its final section, in which a new Revelation-style heaven and earth are imagined at length, eternal perfection (the reward for a spiritual life well lived) is contrasted with the sinfulness of Goscelin's contemporary world and Eve is exhorted thusly, at the guide's conclusion: 'Sic habeas anime cuncta cupita tue' (*Liber*, p. 117).[4]

In comparison to other earlier medieval guides such as *Ancrene Wisse*, the *Liber* has been less explored by scholars. Yet, in terms of the guidance tradition, it is extraordinary, a text written as much for the sake of its author as its recluse, it makes bold claims and 'petit astra quadrigis' (*Liber*, p. 19).[5] Yet, we do not know whether Eve ever received it, much less that she actually used it as a guide. Otter hypothesizes: 'there seems to have been no reply',[6] but Stephanie Hollis argues that we cannot know whether it was even sent, for although the existence of a continental copy renders it potentially possible: 'There is no evidence that it was known to Goscelin's contemporaries or to later generations'.[7]

Biographical information about Eve is scarce. Hollis suggests she was 'of noble family, the English-born daughter of a Danish father and a Lotharingian mother', possibly the niece of Herman, bishop of Ramsbury and Sherborne.[8] She may have been born in 1058, was perhaps seven when she was dedicated as a child oblate to the Wilton community in 1065, perhaps twenty-two when she became a recluse if 1058 really is the year of her birth, and she died in 1120.[9] It is not certain that she was a nun prior to reclusive enclosure.[10] We do not know what motivated that enclosure, although Hollis argues that Eve 'did not find Wilton conducive to a life of contemplation', citing Hilary of Orléans's commemorative poem, which hints at Eve's spiritual discomfort there.[11] Otter argues that Eve had 'a predecessor at Angers who recruited her and introduced her to the anchoritic life' (Otter, p. 113, n. 10). Hollis remarks: 'At Angers Eve joined a small community of recluses attached to the church ... Some ... twenty years later – she moved to the church of Saint-Eutrope, where she was joined by her niece Ravenissa'.[12] At Saint-Eutrope she seems to have shared her solitude with the male recluse, Hervé of Vendôme, one of the supporters of Robert of Arbrissel, who himself, as Dyan Elliott notes, was 'repeatedly accused of sleeping alongside his female followers'.[13] It seems that Eve repeatedly shared her solitude, with both men and women. Her relationship with Hervé evokes obvious comparisons with the intimacy that Goscelin claims he himself shared with Eve, although it is too extreme to conclude, as Elliott does, that 'Eve, despite her spirited show of independence in unilaterally leaving England ... could be perceived as merely exchanging Goscelin for Hervé'.[14] If nothing else, this overlooks the twenty years of solitude Eve negotiates in-between the move to, and her departure from, Angers. The relative scarcity of biographical information increases the unwise temptation to read Goscelin's guide as biography, as in Daphne Stroud's conclusion: 'For Eve's early life at Wilton the only reliable source is the *Liber*' and her certainty that where Hilary of Orléans's evidence conflicts with Goscelin's 'it must be rejected'.[15] This is exactly the kind of submission to Goscelin's textual authority that he hoped his guide would persuade Eve herself to make. Yet Hollis rightly warns the reader about Goscelin's 'tendency to projection'.[16] This guidance writer has an unusually strong vested interest in constructing his apparent familiarity with his recluse. Part of his attempt to reconcile himself to her loss involves the negotiation of the only connection between them that is now possible. The spectre of their former intimacy enables Goscelin to stake the only claim to Eve he can now make: that of her anchoritic guidance writer.

More is known about Goscelin's own life.[17] Born in northern France, *c.*1040, he was originally a monk of Saint-Bertin, the Benedictine abbey in Saint-Omer. Flemish by birth, he relocated to England prior to 1065, possibly as early as 1058.[18] Part of Bishop Herman's household, he was, Hollis notes: 'foremost among the authors who recreated the Anglo-Saxon past for the Norman regime'.[19] He was an accomplished hagiographer. Joseph P. McGowan notes Goscelin's responsibility for many *vitae*, notably those of Hildelith, Mildred, Æthelburga and the bishops Laurence, Mellitus, Justus and Deusdedit.[20] Speculation exists that Goscelin met Eve as chaplain to the nunnery at Wilton or was even her childhood tutor.[21] Engaged by the Wilton community to write the *Vita* and the *Translatio* of their patron saint Edith (*c.*961–84), he was certainly involved in the business of guiding and celebrating the women of Wilton before he wrote his *Liber*.[22] By the time he did, he had been forced to leave Wiltshire by Herman's successor and by *c.*1090 was permanently resident at St Augustine's, Canterbury, and died *c.*1114.

Goscelin was exiled then, both from Wilton and from Eve, at the time he wrote the *Liber* and finished his Legend of Edith. His guide, therefore, potentially seeks to reunite him with both.[23] In it, he declares that he wishes Eve had never become a recluse; the only guidance writer to claim that he has lost personally because of anchoritism.[24] He alone resents his recluse's choice, preferring for her a vocation that could have safe-guarded their contact: 'sed hoc alibi quam hic et alia cupiebam uia ... cenobialis columba, non turtur solitaria, aut, si malles, turtur fieres in patria ... Vt nos minus deso-lationem plangeremus, te proxima' (*Liber*, p. 36).[25] The closest later guidance writers come to this is, as chapter 5 will show, the later medieval guidance writer's certainty that spiritual salvation is not *only* to be found in the vocation (Rolle and Hilton write extensively of the value of secular life).[26] Even the later guidance writers, however, are certain that anchoritism is the best vocational choice for their specific reclusive charges.

Elizabeth Robertson has argued that Goscelin's contradictory narrative unwittingly fashions Eve as the perfect anchorite.[27] She has severed temporal ties in order to pursue her vocation, despite the consequences for those left behind. It is unfortunate that we know so little of the experiences of the families and friends of anchorites and of the potential effects their vocational choice may have had. Otter suggests that Goscelin's consequent turmoil prompts him 'to write himself free from Eva'.[28] Yet this is not what he does. His narrative attempts rather to drag Eve back to him: 'post querelam disces-sionis commendatum, admissum, susceptum, respice tecum assidentem, ausculta tecum sermocinantem' (*Liber*, p. 34).[29] He seeks their reconnection, not their disconnection. For this reason, judging by the length of his guide, he seems also to have found it hard to stop writing. To do so is to admit defeat; to lose Eve again. He tries, at length, to re-enclose Eve within the walls of his own words, but her migration to France places her permanently beyond his reach – unless she chooses to accept him as guidance writer. He has no interest therefore in the wider, incidental reclusive audience envisaged by many of his guidance-writing successors. Other readers are unwelcome; condemned as 'uenti-lator et cachinnator impurus' (*Liber*, p. 26).[30] Goscelin's chief interest lies in persuading Eve into their new relationship and himself into his new role. Yet this new identity is precarious. Built hopelessly upon the foundations of an older one; when one collapses all collapse:

> dum scribo, grassans dolor non potuit dissimulari; *cecidere manus et usus scriptorii*; rugitus et eiulatus inuasit me; corrui coram altari tui Laurentii ... clamabam frequens in diluuio lacrimarum quasi inter ictus et uerbera Domini ... et cum eiulatu ... intonui ... Similis factus sum pelicano solitudinis ... Magnis clamoribus infremui ... Repetens ergo interruptam inter-rumpente luctu loquelam (*Liber*, p. 27).[31]

The *Liber* often reads more like the (albeit one-sided) narrative of parted lovers than parted spiritual companions. Otter calls it 'an account of a deep, desperate, only half sublimated love'.[32] Its 'erotic valence' may, she argues, be read in the context of the Ovidian paraclausithyron.[33] Yet, Hollis declares it 'innocent of the knowledge of Ovidian *amor*', focusing instead on the doomed context provided by Abelard and Heloise's later love story, itself sublimated into Abelard's guidance of the sisters at the abbey of the Holy Paraclete.[34] Hayward goes further back, to Roman times, arguing for Eve and Goscelin's place in a tradition of writing about friendship stemming from Cicero, Ambrose, Jerome, Augustine, Boniface, Alcuin, and Anselm.[35] More contempor-ary contexts are to be found in the spiritual intimacies of Christina of Markyate and the hermit Roger, of Christina and the Abbot Geoffrey de Gorran, in the bonds between Robert of Arbrissel and his followers and in the correspondence between Peter Damien and Agnes.[36] Elliott argues nonetheless that 'the frantic tenor' of 'Goscelin's relentless focus on Eve is something of an anomaly', even among these examples.[37] Chapters 2 and 3 below will show in more detail that this renders Goscelin's guide one of the very snares from which he argues Eve must free herself.

Eve's silence has inspired some critics to defend her passionately. Stroud declares that Eve 'pursued her vocation in ever-increasing holiness', ascribing any sinfulness in their relationship to 'Goscelin's own barely contained passion'.[38] Others have defended Goscelin instead. H. M. Canatella argues vehemently that the guide reveals 'not a self-sublimated love between a religious man and woman but rather a friendship', non-sexual and purely 'spiritual ... ennobling Goscelin himself and Eve in return'.[39] As yet, since there is little unequivocal evidence for either position, Hayward is right to challenge criticism which seeks only to define the nature of Goscelin's devotion and to ask: 'What element in the text accounts for ... the need to discuss this?'[40] She argues for a return to the text itself as remedy, yet it is the text itself that prompts critical fascination with its forbidden possibilities; and wonderment at Goscelin's veiled self-castigations: 'Et que meis debebantur sceleribus, hec separationis tormenta' (*Liber*, p. 27).[41] Otter rightly reminds us: 'For every passage that seems to hint at a guilty sexual relationship, there are others that speak against it', and Goscelin's penitence makes 'equally good sense if they refer to guilty desires rather than a love affair' (Otter, p. 11). Yet, his tone frequently reads, nonetheless, like that of wronged lover:

> Omnia tempora tempus suum habent ... Habuimus nos quoque nostra tempora. Satis inuicem uidimus, satis collocuti sumus, conuiuati quoque et epulati, sollemnizati et iocundati satis ... si modo quicquam satis esse posset caritati ... Nunc, inquam, tempus eundi in fletus (*Liber*, p. 42).[42]

He is petulant too:

> O quotiens Egidam tuam beatam pensabam, que te ut ar(c)tius diligebat, ita et loci et sexus unitate presentialiter sibi confouebat! Sed ecce sua sollemnia in merorem et solitudinem sunt conuersa, quanquam adhuc eo sit beatior quo abeunti potuit uale dicere (*Liber*, p. 45).[43]

Whatever the real nature of the relationship between Goscelin and Eve may have been, this guide stands as testament to the strength of one man's devotion to one woman and on one point his narrative insists: she left the convent and the country without informing him of her intentions. In part, therefore, the *Liber* seeks not to support anchoritism but to rail against it. This points us to a glorious problematic: this, the first extant example of the English anchoritic guidance genre, forces a widening of that genre. Chapters 2 and 3 will show that this guide functions as the very kind of intrusion of the personal past upon the anchoritic present that the tradition usually encourages its recluses to avoid. This first guide, on one level, functions as a threat to the vocational success of its intended recipient. Its writer is concurrently the reinforcer of Eve's anchoritism and its bitterest critic. Ultimately, Goscelin may seek a measure of acceptance of Eve's 'defection', fashioning his sorrow as the ground of her spiritual growth. Yet, the vehemence of his loss is never fully eradicated and reading his guide as anchoritic guidance remains a difficult, if rewarding, challenge.

Yet, the *Liber* was not only inspired by Goscelin's devotion to Eve. It must also be understood as part of what Michael Frassetto terms the consciousness of a 'millennial generation', stretching across the eleventh century, motivated by the millennium of the Incarnation in the year 1000 and the millennium of the Passion in 1030.[44] It is also, as

Canatella argues, reflective of 'an internal dialogue' sited within the earlier medieval 'discovery of the individual'.[45] Moreover, this guide is motivated by new cultural under-standings of Christ, reflected in reformative drives such as the 1031 peace council of Limoges and the involved programme of religious transformation inspired by apocalyp-ticism in anticipation of the later Gregorian reforms.[46] Goscelin's guide then is not only a personal document. It is, as Hollis argues, also at 'the forefront of cultural change', truly a 'notable harbinger of the "twelfth-century Renaissance"'.[47]

These wider cultural contexts are also relevant to the anchoritic guidance of the Burgundian churchman, St Anselm of Aosta (1033–1109), author of the *Monologion*, the *Proslogion* and *Cur Deus Homo*, amongst other texts. From humble beginnings as a reluctant Benedictine monk (he reputedly found it difficult to choose between coeno-bitism and eremitism), Anselm later became prior and abbot of Bec and, in 1093, succeeded Lanfranc to the archbishopric of Canterbury.[48] By the time he authored the three Latin letters for solitaries to be explored here, Richard Sharpe argues that 'he was an established author, whose books were known in monasteries scattered over much of France'.[49] Anselm wrote many letters and Richard W. Southern identifies London, Lambeth Palace Library, MS 59, as the largest collection of those composed from 1070–1109, arguing for the manuscript's original provenance as Christ Church Canterbury, where it was begun *c*.1125–30, possibly as a posthumous Anselmian memorial.[50] Scholarship is divided over Anselm's potential involvement in shaping the collection of his correspondence prior to his death; debate that goes right to the heart of critical esti-mations of Anselm's episcopal leadership. Colin Gale summarizes the controversy thus:

> Some scholars [e.g. Walter Fröhlich] have argued that Lambeth MS 59 bears witness to Anselm's attempts to … manage his reputation as a scholar-saint and to downplay his involve-ment in the messy, murky world of ecclesiastical politics. Others [e.g. Sally Vaughn] … that behind a carefully nurtured image of simple holiness and profound thinking lay a deceptively astute political player.[51]

Others still, Southern notably among them, conclude that Anselm had no real hand in crafting the collection that lies behind Lambeth MS 59, and 'nursed a deep-seated horror of worldly advancement – a genuinely reluctant Archbishop'.[52]

Whatever may have been Anselm's involvement in shaping his literary legacy, his three letters of eremitic guidance evidently admire vocational enclosure and construct eremitism as a safe haven from the political world in which he is himself immersed. Anselm's letters rarely request others to pray for him, but Licence reveals that he does so twice in his letters to recluses, evidence of his belief in their spiritual prowess.[53] 'Letter 230: Ad Rodbertum, Seit, Edit' (*c*.1102) and 'Letter 414: Ad Robertum eiusque moniales' (*c*.1105), composed while Anselm was archbishop, are addressed to a group of lay female solitaries and to Robert, who was possibly their spiritual advisor. 'Letter 230' is intended for Robert, Seitha and Edith alone, while 'Letter 414' is written also for Thydit, Lwerun, Dirgit and Godit. These women have been described as vowesses, but Licence concludes that the letter implies that 'they were recluses', possibly at Bury St Edmunds.[54] A third, earlier, letter, '112: Ad Hugonem', was written *c*.1086 (although Licence places it no earlier than 1078 and no later than 1093) while Anselm was still at Bec. It is addressed to Hugh, the hermit of Caen.[55] It begins with Anselm's acknow-ledgement of Hugh's request, via two laymen, for a guide, so that he might better advise those who come to his hermitage, inspired by his solitude. 'Letter 414' is similarly described as prompted by requests for guidance from its recipients.

'Letter 112' acknowledges Hugh's superior spiritual abilities as solitary. In it, Anselm synonymizes the Christian and especially the solitary life as one of love, advising Hugh to love his fellow man for God's sake and to submit wholly to God's will. Prayer, spiritual converse and heavenly meditation are recommended; as are poverty, industry and obedience. Anselm ends with a recommendation that Hugh refer to his *Proslogion* for further guidance. 'Letter 230', which is much shorter, recounts a now-burdened and fraught Anselm's joy at a female solitary group's inspirational spirituality: 'me sentiam a spirituali fervore tepere, tamen magna cordi meo generatur laetitia, cum audio alios in amore dei fervere' (Anselm, 'Letter 230', vol. 4, p. 135).[56] In it, Anselm advises diligence in the recognition of even the smallest of flaws and particularly in the regulation of speech. 'Letter 414' again rejoices at this same group's holiness. It begins with a focus on the human will and on the importance of purity of intention as well as action. It outlines the means whereby the women can distinguish good from bad and God's will from their own. It advises the same attention to moral detail in self-assessment as 'Letter 230' and specifically explores the vices of anger, envy and vainglory.

Southern argues that all Anselm's letters, 'even the most intimate, are public statements of a religious ideal'; on the surface addressed to one individual, in reality 'intended to be read by others'.[57] This public and private dichotomy is certainly also exploited by the Latin text *De institutione inclusarum*, composed between 1160 and 1162 by Aelred (c.1110–67), then abbot of the Cistercian foundation at Rievaulx.[58] It too is a letter, addressed on the surface to Aelred's biological sister who had possibly, by the time of writing, been enclosed for some years. Information about her is even scarcer than information about the *Liber*'s Eve. We know neither her name nor the location of her anchorhold. Aelred Squire sites it 'somewhere in the area between Hexham and Durham', but this is speculation.[59] One interpretation of the statement: 'Certe si praeter necessarium uictum et uestitum aliquid habes, monacha non es' (*DII*, p. 639), is that she was a nun before becoming a recluse, but, as with Eve, this is not certain.[60] Her piety, as with Anselm's hermit Hugh, according to *De institutione*, has potentially inspired other would-be solitaries to come to her. For, unlike Goscelin, both Anselm and Aelred deliberately write with wider, incidental audience awareness. Anselm acknowledges Hugh's desire: 'postulastis ut aliquid a me breviter scriptum acciperetis, unde saecularium mentes hominum vos adeuntium ad huius saeculi contemptum et aeterni regni desiderium incitaretis' (Anselm, 'Letter 112', vol. 3, p. 244).[61] Aelred writes: 'sed quia non solum propter te, sed etiam propter adolescentiores quae similem uitam tuo consilio arripere gestiunt' (*DII*, p. 642).[62] There is no proof, however, that Aelred's sister formed the focal point of the kind of community-in-solitude addressed by Anselm in 'Letter 230' and 'Letter 414', or which reputedly surrounded the contemporary solitary, Christina of Markyate.[63] Yet, in writing deliberately for wider audiences, Anselm and Aelred both acknowledge the anchorite's capacity to inspire wider medieval society.

The original copy of *De institutione* is lost and Alexandra Barratt notes that it was subject to 'the usual sort of *mouvance* experienced by such texts'.[64] Incorporated into meditative treatises and ascribed erroneously to the authorship of others, including Anselm himself and also Augustine, it survives in Latin in six complete and four partial manuscript versions. The earliest complete Latin text is found in the thirteenth century

London, British Library, MS Cotton Nero A. III. The guide's Latin composition implies that Aelred's sister was reasonably well educated and its content argues for her spiritual sophistication, especially in ascetical terms (*DII*, p. 648).[65] Aelred suggests that her women may have been less literate (*DII*, p. 645).[66] Anselm too distinguishes between Hugh and one 'qui altiora capere non possit' (Anselm, 'Letter 112', vol. 3, p. 244).[67]

Aelred's guide is divided into thirty-three sections which, in the manuscripts, are not divided into the overarching tripartite structure that Mary Paul MacPherson's translation adopts. Yet she concludes: 'it is clear from the final paragraph' that Aelred saw his guide as 'made up of three sections'.[68] She argues that Part I (sections II to XIII) focuses on outer issues, giving an overview of the history of anchoritism, detailing guidance for the practicalities of the reclusive life and focusing on common problems, the majority of which are occasioned by continued, inevitable worldly contact. Part II (sections XIV to XXVIII) concentrates on inner concerns and the virtues fostered by solitude, chief amongst which, for Aelred, is chastity. It cautions the recluse always to fear the gradual descent into vice, advising a series of protective strategies. Part III (sections XXIX to XXXIII) offers her a threefold meditation. On the past: detailing the life of Christ; on the present: focusing on Aelred and his sister's familial lineage, and on the future: exploring, as did Goscelin, Judgement Day and its retributions and rewards.

De institutione greatly influences another earlier medieval guide: *Ancrene Wisse*, although direct borrowings from it are rare.[69] *Ancrene Wisse*, longer and composed in the vernacular, was originally written for three, well-born, consanguineous sisters known to its original author. The exact identity of both author and original audience remains unknown, although, unlike Eve and Aelred's sister, they may have been only partially literate in Latin, but also partially literate in French.[70] Barratt argues, in an article that questions the perception of earlier medieval female Latinity as elitist, that Aelred's sister 'would not have been exceptional in her ability to read Latin in the mid-twelfth century', and that she and the original audience of *Ancrene Wisse* were 'probably of a similar social status and equivalent educational level'.[71] A reference made uniquely in *Ancrene Wisse*'s Nero text suggests that this original sisterhood entered the anchorhold when young, making no mention of prior coenobitism. Women in the thirteenth century, as Millett notes, increasingly entered the anchorhold 'directly from the world, as an alternative ... to life in a nunnery rather than as a progression from it'.[72] The original three sisters of *Ancrene Wisse* were probably lay women prior to enclosure and their lay status may have some bearing on their primarily vernacular literacy.[73] The later, wider reclusive audiences of the guide's other texts may also have included recluses who entered the anchorhold directly from home.

The original text of *Ancrene Wisse* is lost. Yet, passages found in its Nero and Corpus texts (both relatively close to the lost original in date) reflect the directives of the Fourth Lateran Council of 1215 on confession and penance. It is therefore possible that the lost original was composed between 1215 and 1230, probably later rather than earlier since it would take time for the clergy to incorporate the Council's directives into their writings. Millett proposes a date for the lost original 'between about 1216 and 1230, probably in the later 1220s'.[74] She suggests that the Corpus text be dated between *c*.1230 and the 1280s (the manuscript's *terminus ante quem*), but after 1224. She recently refined the dates of various later texts of the guide using datings by Malcolm Parkes, who assigns the Nero and the Titus texts to the second quarter of the thirteenth century (the 1240s), the Cleopatra text to the early 1230s and the Gonville and Caius text to the third quarter of the thirteenth century.[75]

Seventeen manuscripts of *Ancrene Wisse* are extant which contain material from the lost original, sometimes reworked or with added revisions. Michelle Sauer identifies it as 'The most influential of the Middle English guides'.[76] This is certainly true now: it dominates the critical field, yet it was not necessarily the case in the Middle Ages. The existence of nine vernacular, four Latin and four French manuscripts certainly implies that the guide had a wider circulation than any other earlier medieval anchoritic guide, but in comparison with the larger number of manuscripts of Rolle's and Hilton's guides, its textual transmission seems small. The only overt references made in the later anchoritic guides considered in this book to the influence of earlier guides are, as has already been noted, those of Aelred's Bodley redactor, to his original guide and *Speculum*'s reference to Aelred's guide.[77]

Ancrene Wisse is divided into a preface and eight parts, following a similar schema to Aelred's guide in its separation of inner, spiritual matters from outer, practical considerations. Outer concerns are detailed in the Preface, Part I (in the sense that it outlines the recluse's daily activities, albeit devotional ones) and Part VIII. Parts II to VII seek to foster inner reclusive purity and spiritual growth. The Preface stresses the threefold importance of anchoritic obedience, chastity and fixity of place. It permits variations to the outer rule, but not to the inner. Part I details a full programme of diurnal anchoritic devotions. Part II focuses in turn on the regulation of the five senses, as preparation for contemplative experience. Part III focuses on the inculcation of virtuous inner feelings, using a bestiary motif, notably focusing on birds. Part IV intensifies the guide's inculcation of purity by detailing specific spiritual problems and their remedies. Part V focuses on confession, in reclusive and non-reclusive contexts, arguing that it must be accusatory, bitter, complete, well thought out, willing, wise, frequent and motivated by shame, fear and a sense of hopefulness. Part VI, on penance, characterizes the anchoritic vocation as inherently penitential, but makes a distinction between enjoined penance and ascetic practice, which will be explored in more detail in chapter 4 below. Part VII synonymizes, as did Anselm, the Christian life and the solitary vocation with love, encouraging the recluse to foster and intensify love of God, through her inner purity.

The Nero text of *Ancrene Wisse* is the work of two scribes, the first of whom copied out the text and is responsible, in the words of Mabel Day, for 'many errors left uncorrected'.[78] These errors did not prevent the Nero text being for years the best known among modern scholars, forming the basis of James Morton's influential 1853 edition of the guide, entitled *Ancren Riwle*.[79] It describes the original reclusive readership of three, bound to one geographical area and the patronage of one man: 'euerich of ou haueð of one ureonde al þet hire is neod. ne þerf þet meiden sechen ... bread ... fur þene et his halle' (*AW*, Nero, p. 85).[80] It describes their spiritual renown: 'Muche word is of ou hu gentile wummen 3e beoð. vorgodleic ant for ureoleic i3irned of monie. ant sustren of one ueder ant of one moder. i ne blostme of ower 3uweðe uorheten alle wordes blissen. ant bicomen ancren' (*AW*, Nero, p. 85).[81] This recalls Goscelin's depiction of Eve's youthful enclosure: 'Pupa es, adolescentula es, flos ipse uite repente peristi' (*Liber*, p. 70).[82] Geoffrey Shepherd suggests that Nero is closer in some respects to the original than any other text of *Ancrene Wisse*, citing 'some features of language and the inclusion of certain passages not found in ... Corpus', namely its references to this original sisterhood.[83] The Nero text is certainly early, but unlikely to be the earliest. It has not yet been dated with certainty beyond the 1240s.

Of all *Ancrene Wisse*'s vernacular texts, the Corpus manuscript is now the best known and the only text which refers to itself by this title, meaning 'guide for anchoresses'.[84] It has not been proven conclusively that it is textually or chronologically closest to the lost original, but its revisions are almost certainly authorial, although its scribe was not necessarily its author. Roger Dahood suggests that 'Authorially revised versions, aimed at a wider audience of female recluses, survive in English in MSS Cleopatra ... Corpus ... and Vernon ... and in a French translation in the Vitellius MS'.[85] The Corpus text has inspired much critical work due to the legibility of its script, the relative coherence of its content and its comparative freedom from errors. Millett declares it 'in a class of its own ... an exceptionally good text ... [which goes] back to an annotated form of the author's original draft' and 'our most reliable witness' for the original text.[86] It alone seems to be descended from a lost revision of the original guide, while all the other extant texts seem, in all probability, to have descended from the original guide itself.[87]

The Cleopatra text of *Ancrene Wisse* evidences painstaking revision. Corrections, thought necessary to the work of the original scribe, make it the product of three different scribes: A, B (possibly the original author of *Ancrene Wisse*) and D.[88] Millett documents Dobson's analysis of the 'Scribe B' alterations, concluding that: 'both the "Scribe B" revisions in the Cleopatra manuscript and the more comprehensive revisions behind the Corpus manuscript are probably authorial'.[89] Dobson believes the Cleopatra text predates Corpus,[90] and 'the whole tenor of the additions ... is addressed to the original community', although the passage concerning the three sisters in the main Cleopatra text has been cut so heavily that he considers it now 'pointless'.[91] Millett thinks that the Cleopatra text is 'Probably the earliest surviving copy of *Ancrene Wisse*'.[92] It shares, with Corpus and Nero, a direct address to a female audience and, like Corpus, indicates a division in its audience between a smaller and larger group of anchorites. Scribe B (or C2),[93] whoever he may have been, chiefly focuses on the text as a working tool for recluses and his corrections share the general spirit of earlier forms of the guide without obsessive replication.

In content, the Titus text of *Ancrene Wisse* is strikingly similar to the Nero text, but its audience has been superficially widened to include male recluses, although the mixture of gendered pronouns suggests that this adaptation has been partially reversed.[94] Pronoun inconsistency leads to confusion between masculine and feminine forms.[95] The passage concerning the original sisterhood is reduced to: 'Muche word þat is of ow. hu gentille 3e beon. 3unge of 3eres 3ulden ow. & bi comen ancres. forsoken worldes blisses' (*AW*, Titus, p. 61).[96] Other references to them are suppressed or altered to 'mine leoue frend' and habitually to 'childre' (*AW*, Titus, p. 10).[97]

The Gonville and Caius text is a disordered collection of extracts from the inner rule section of the guide (i.e. from Parts II to VII). It too is adapted to include a male audience and 'mine leoue frend' is often substituted for 'mine leoue sustren' (*AW*, G&C, p. 86).[98] It too is inconsistent in its use of masculine forms. Dobson speculates that it was intended for the use of 'the man who made it ... as an aid to preaching', because of its obvious appeal to the masculine and the inclusion, in the Titus manuscript, immediately after the guide, of Latin excerpts from the *Vitas Patrum*.[99] It is largely preoccupied with confession and this might feasibly interest a priest or, as Millett suggests, a male religious community or mendicant foundation.[100] Yet the list of typically anchoritic sins present in the other aforementioned texts of *Ancrene Wisse* is retained (*AW*, G&C, p. 26) and additional material specific to the vocation remains relevant to a reclusive audience.[101]

The identity of the original author of *Ancrene Wisse* has created sustained controversy. He has been variously identified as the hermit Godwine, Gilbert of Sempringham, Robert Bacon, Herbert Poor, Richard Poor and Simon of Ghent.[102] Dobson's impressive book, *The Origins of Ancrene Wisse*, argues that he belonged to 'an "order" strongly influenced by ... the statutes of Prémontré but not itself Premonstratensian', arguing that he was 'a member of the congregation of St Victor'.[103] He famously identifies him, from an apparent cryptogram found in the Nero, Corpus and Cleopatra texts, as Brian of Lingen, a secular canon of Wigmore Abbey.[104] Dobson provides painstaking analysis of *Ancrene Wisse*'s Augustinian influences and locates the guide's original sisterhood in the Deerfold, west of Wigmore, in the vicinity of a larger religious house identified as Limebrook Priory.[105] Scholars such as Anne Savage and Nicholas Watson have supported many of Dobson's assertions: 'None of all this dazzling argumentation can be proved, but little of it needs to be ... the pieces of the jigsaw fit together'.[106] Subsequent research has contradicted some of his theories, but much of Dobson's exhaustive work remains impressive. Millett reassessed his conclusions, proposing Dominican instead of Victorine or Premonstratensian authorship: 'this would explain a number of its features ... its heavy emphasis on confession, its close relationship to the Dominican constitutions and liturgy and the author's enthusiasm for the friars'.[107] Hasenfratz believes that the struggle to find one single author has itself hampered the guide's investigation, arguing that the text's 'AB' language, identified by J. R. R. Tolkien, 'is a communal language', implying collaborative authorship.[108] Millett thinks it unlikely that the anonymous author(s) and original users of this work will ever be individually identified. She argues of the *Ancrene Wisse* group (the name given to the collection of devotional works which also includes saints' lives, work on virginity and on the custody of the soul and four lyrical meditations on Christ and Mary),[109] that 'we should be thinking in terms of more than one author, or even more than one type of author' and certainly 'more than a single audience'.[110] All the texts in the group may have been composed within the same forty-year period (*c*.1190–*c*.1230) and intended originally for anchoritic audiences. Traditionally, they have been further subdivided into the Wooing and Katherine groups, but Millett argues for them 'at least provisionally as a single group with a common origin', with the proviso that 'there is still no general agreement on whether we are dealing with a single, well-defined *oeuvre* or with a scatter of works by different authors and with ill-defined boundaries'.[111] Hasenfratz concludes that while an Augustinian *Ancrene Wisse* would best be understood as a representative of current monastic, predominately Bernardine, concerns, a Dominican text 'implies a program much more oriented towards lay spirituality'.[112] Cate Gunn suggests that in this, *Ancrene Wisse* anticipates 'the vernacular spirituality that developed in the fourteenth century'.[113] Millett has also shown that the devotions in *Ancrene Wisse* especially anticipate those of later medieval lay books of hours.[114] Gunn correctly identifies an 'incarnational spirituality expressed in *Ancrene Wisse*', arguing for marked intersections between it and the later medieval *Scale of Perfection*, similarities that, as chapters 2 to 5 of this book will reveal, are part of a wider framework of reference between earlier and later medieval anchoritic guidance.[115]

Although the recovery of authorial involvement in the revisionary process of *Ancrene Wisse* is desirable, no anchoritic guide is the exclusive intellectual property of its author, but rather of all those involved with it, especially its audience, to whom, many guides imply, the majority of the task of textual interpretation rightly falls. Its author evidently intended *Ancrene Wisse* to be continually revised and modified, possibly in the light of other works from the *Ancrene Wisse* group. Millett refers to Paul Zumthor's use in his *Essai de poétique médiévale* of the concept of *mouvance*, the 'essential textual instability or fluidity' which can mean that a medieval text is less 'a single, completed entity' than 'something more fluid … constantly adapted through space and time',[116] and to Bernard Cerquiglini's criticism of editions of single manuscript texts as no more than 'snapshots freezing in a single point of textual development rather than representing the process of that development',[117] noting the tendency of this school of textual theory to see the aim of reconstruction of the author's original as 'not only hopeless but misconceived', and grounded in 'a misunderstanding of the nature of the work itself'.[118] *Ancrene Wisse*, then, is not a single guide created by one single author, revelatory of only a single 'snapshot' of anchoritism. It is best read, as Millett argues, as a textual tradition that moves through the hands of different men at different times; the collaborative work of 'a succession of adaptors, translators and what Derek Pearsall has called "participatory scribes"'.[119] This textual tradition persistently modifies and amends the original text at its centre and reshapes itself according to the demands of different audiences and their needs. Thus, the very textual tradition of *Ancrene Wisse* suggests a wider, more generally applicable truth about anchoritic guidance, which will be borne out by close textual analysis of the guides in the remainder of this book: that the ideological constructions of anchoritism and their meanings, as reflected in the English guidance tradition, are not fixed and stable, but mutable and shifting.

The later medieval guides

Every later medieval guide explored in this book was intended, in its original conception at least, for anchorites at a time when anchoritic texts were increasingly being made applicable to wider audiences and anchoritism functioned as an increasingly accessible spiritual model for the laity. *The Form of Living* was composed in the vernacular, *c.*1348, for the anchorite Margaret Kirkby by Richard Rolle, hermit of Hampole (*c.*1290–1349). Rolle was fond of advising women spiritually and, although Watson characterizes his interest in their spiritual needs as unusual in his contemporary context, such concern is a common feature of anchoritic guidance writing.[120] Ralph Hanna argues that this guide is associated with Margaret leaving Hampole (where she was a nun) to be enclosed at East Layton.[121] She is acknowledged in the text's *incipit* and *explicit*, but she is not often addressed directly. Instead, wider references are made to mankind and 'euery synful man' (*Form*, p. 3).

Hope Emily Allen regards *Form* as 'the finest and most mature work' Rolle ever produced.[122] A popular text, extant in over forty vernacular manuscripts, including twenty-seven complete versions dating from the fifteenth to the sixteenth centuries, it was subsequently translated into Latin and also adapted into English verse.[123] It has two main lines of manuscript descent, headed respectively by two unrelated versions of the guide.[124] That found in Longleat, library of the marquess of Bath, MS 29, was copied *c*.1430–50 in an east Midlands dialect. The other manuscript, Cambridge, University Library, MS Dd. v. 64. III, was copied in a northern dialect, *c*.1400. The Longleat manuscript and its group are the closest to the lost original. Sarah Ogilvie-Thompson writes: 'MS. Dd. could be as many as nine removes from the original, whereas, despite its later date of composition, LT. could be as little as two'.[125] The Longleat manuscript contains other spiritual guidance texts by Rolle, including *Ego Dormio, The Commandment, Desire and Delight, Ghostly Gladness, Sweet Jesu* and a prose fragment, all of which are apparently dedicated to Margaret in a manner which suggests their descent from an autograph collection made for her.[126]

This guide is not separated into sections, but begins with an account of the three sins that Rolle believes most afflict humanity: lack of spiritual fervour, enslavement to fleshly desires and delight in temporality. It moves to an admiration of the solitary life as conducive to contemplative spirituality and focuses on the Devil-sent dangers involved. Rolle's desire to help Margaret to overcome these is declared as the motivation for the *Form*'s creation. Through 'þis short fourme of lyvynge' (*Form*, p. 9), Rolle seeks to enable this recluse to emerge triumphant from a lifetime of anchoritic privation. The guide then devotes itself to a series of strategies for reclusive success. Turning entirely to God and placing love at the heart of the Christian life is, as it was in earlier guidance, notably in Anselm's letters and *Ancrene Wisse*, chief amongst these. Four further routes to spiritual purity are explored. In the context of later medieval fears about spiritual orthodoxy, the recluse must understand what defiles and what purifies her. In terms that recall earlier guidance's distinction between inner and outer and its focus on sensory experience, Rolle therefore interrogates the sins of the heart, the mouth, of action and omission. He explores three purificatory activities – heartfelt sorrow, confession and atonement – explains how purity in heart, mouth and deed may be maintained and cites three means whereby the will can be accorded with God's. The rest of the guide is devoted to the inculcation, via contemplative experience, of Rolle's self-acknowledged obsession: love, which, as will be discussed in chapter 3, is split into three degrees, the highest level of which is aligned with the rejection of the world (*Form*, p. 23).[127] The guide ends with an overview of the active and contemplative lives.

Of all the guidance writers whose work forms the subject of this book, Rolle has perhaps been the most censured in scholarly terms. David Knowles famously branded him, because of his emotional fervour, a contemplative beginner, while Warren considers Hilton 'a more experienced (and higher level) mystic'.[128] Yet Renevey's work shows that: 'Rolle is much more than a mystic, a modern label that fails to grasp the extent of his output'.[129] Rolle's theological constructions of love are sophisticated and intertwined with his meditative constructions of Christ, especially of Christ's humanity, itself bound up with his treatment of the Holy Name.[130] The emotional fervour that earned Rolle Knowles's censure is the natural consequence of Rolle's adoption of his own recommended contemplative programme. He is a practitioner, not merely a theorist. His guide seeks not simply to direct the recluse to contemplative experience, but to re-create it for her. Renevey puts it perfectly: 'this epistle [is written] by a solitary for a solitary'.[131] Rolle writes with the authority of first-hand contemplative experience; of real spiritual prowess. This contrasts with Goscelin's distinction between Eve's greater spiritual abilities and his own (although, typically, he does not allow this to limit his own potential importance as Eve's spiritual guide): 'Nam imbellis cantor uel tubicen, quanquam non pugnet, multum tamen pugnantibus confert. Robustos excitat, et uicendi gloria roborat' (*Liber*, p. 36).[132] It also contrasts with Anselm's distinction between himself as a guidance writer, conversant with the theory of solitude, and Hugh as a solitary contemplative practitioner: 'Quod enim ego de sanctae vitae rectitudine utcumque intelligo, vos operibus tractatis; et quod ego utcumque loqui possum, vos faciendo gustatis' (Anselm, 'Letter 112', vol. 3, p. 244).[133] Rolle's affective enthusiasm, if read as evidence of his own sophisticated contemplative prowess, is scarcely grounds for his exclusion from the contemplative canon. It is Rolle, after all, who expends the greatest effort in communicating love's contemplative significance to the recluse and love is acknowledged by every anchoritic guide as the central contemplative motivating force. Rolle's constructions of love as an inebriation, a burning yearning, to be experienced physically, not just understood intellectually, may prompt Watson's judgement that: 'Rolle's experiential spirituality was not … centred around … Christ, but … his own sensations'.[134] Claire McIlroy, however, defends it as a system of spiritual self-reference. It is not self-promotion, but an 'audience-centred … exhortation to the reader to join with him in the perfection of his own contemplation'; a 'relationship of equality'.[135]

The *Scale of Perfection*, a lengthy guide to the contemplative life divided into two books, was begun *c.*1384/6 by Walter Hilton (*c.*1340/5–96). An Augustinian canon at Thurgarton Priory, Nottinghamshire, Hilton began his guide shortly after he entered that community. Book II was completed *c.*1394–6, close to his death. He may have spent some time as a solitary prior to becoming a canon, although he seems also to have had some university training, perhaps at Cambridge.[136] Forty-two extant manuscripts contain one or both books of *Scale*, with a preponderance of manuscripts of Book I. Nineteen vernacular and two Latin manuscripts of either the whole, or part, of *Scale I* on its own are extant, while only four vernacular and one Latin manuscript of *Scale II* on its own survive.[137] Michael Sargent's evaluation of previous attempts to construct *Scale*'s manuscript stemma argues for Carthusian involvement in its production and prioritizes one group of its manuscripts, the London Group.[138] He argues that a single authoritative version of the text never existed, which, when considered in the context of Millett's aforementioned work on Zumthor and Cerquiglini, strengthens this book's suggestion that *Ancrene Wisse* is best read not as a text, but as a textual tradition.[139] Sargent suggests that the scribes of one-fifth of the extant manuscripts would have been aware of more than one form of *Scale*.[140] The decade which elapsed between the creation of *Scale*'s two books has also prompted some to propose that each be regarded as a separate work, although this is challenged by Stanley Hussey, who draws attention to Hilton's own reference to *Scale I* in *Scale II*, which ties the two together: 'as I have seid heer biforn in the firste partie of this writynge' (*Scale II*, p. 172).[141]

Defining the audience of *Scale* has proved contentious. Some critics argue for an anchoritic audience, comprising anything from one to many anchorites, for both books; others discount an anchoritic audience for either.[142] Most later medieval anchoritic guides render themselves concurrently relevant to anchorites and to wider audiences. This is a natural progression from the tendency of some early medieval guides to make themselves relevant to wider reclusive audiences and on rare occasions, for instance in the case of *Ancrene Wisse*, to non-reclusive ones. Material, notably on confession in Part V, is also clearly addressed 'to alle men iliche' (*AW*, Corpus, p. 129), implying clear awareness of a wider-than-anchoritic audience.[143] Yet, as with Goscelin and Rolle's guides, *Scale I* presents itself, in its original conception at least, as intended for one female recluse. It is Hilton's response to a single enclosed anchorite, a 'ghostly sister' in the early stages of her enclosure, known to him personally.[144] *Scale I* makes four direct references to its reader as an 'ankir' or 'ankir incluse' (*Scale I*, p. 79): in chapter 44 (*Scale I*, p. 79), in chapter 61 (*Scale I*, pp. 100–1), which contains two references, and in chapter 83 (*Scale I*, pp. 124–5), the only chapter to signal in its title an exclusively anchoritic focus, which guides the recluse on her attitude to temporal interruptions. The guide also makes frequent wider references to the recluse's state of life or 'callynge' (*Scale I*, p. 31).

Controversy also surrounds *Scale*'s title, which was the subject of some scribal confusion. Different manuscripts refer to it variously as a treatise on 'de uita contempla-tiua', 'þe reformyng of mannys soule' and 'scole of perfeccion'. Vivian Kay Hudson, John P. H. Clark, Joy Russell-Smith and Hussey note that this latter title is derived from '*Scala Perfectionis*, a name attached to some manuscripts produced by the Carmelite Thomas Fishlake before 1400'.[145] Since the ladder metaphor does not dominate the guide, some critics, like Janel Mueller, have taken to referring to *Scale* as *The Reforming of Man's Soul*, although this practice is not widespread.[146]

Book I of *Scale* is divided into ninety-two chapters, each with its own title. Chapter 1 begins by making, in the tradition of earlier guidance, a distinction between inner and outer spirituality and argues, as does Rolle, that without inner holiness, outer sanctity is useless. Chapters 2–9 focus on the three degrees of contemplative experience to which the recluse aspires and chapters 13 and 15 detail contemplative inspirations and occupa-tions. Chapters 10 and 11 encourage the recluse to distinguish between good and bad contemplative experiences, and chapter 12 focuses on strategies (as does *Form*) whereby the recluse may accord her soul with God's will, material reinforced by chap-ters 46–51, which detail how Jesus may be sought, found and valued by the eager contemplative and by the penultimate chapter, 91. Chapters 14 and 16–25 focus on the inculcation of virtue, preparations vital to the understanding of the fire of love, which forms the focus of chapters 26, 30 and 31. Prayer, its uses and potential pitfalls, is the subject of chapters 27–30, 32 and 33. Meditation is interrogated in chapters 34–6. The dangers which beset the contemplative recluse are the subject of chapters 37–40 and also of 42. Sin is a central Hiltonian focus. Chapters 53–60 and chapters 71–4 devote much space, in common with every other guidance writer, to the means whereby the recluse can assess her own corruption, e.g. chapter 52 specifies how the recluse may recognize 'the grounde of synne' in herself (*Scale I*, p. 24) and 78 is devoted to 'the merkenese of the image of synne' (*Scale I*, p. 25), also explored at great length in later chapters, notably 84–8. Hilton constructs sin, in a manner reminiscent of early medieval guidance, strongly in terms of the senses, especially that of sight.

However, it is the recluse's contemplative state that is the chief focus of this guide and the subject with which its final chapter concludes. If the Rollian prioritization of sensation attempts to transcend the intellectualization of contemplation, which Pollard attributes to 'a negative reaction toward the scholasticism' Rolle encountered at

Oxford,[147] Hiltonian constructions of it stress rationality, taking issue with Rollian thought so closely that some critics argue Hilton 'must have known some of Rolle's writing firsthand'.[148] While Rolle constructs himself first and foremost as an eremitic contemplative, communicating his ideas with the energy and enthusiasm of personal experience, Hilton's textual persona is commonly that of teacher; a pose of comparative detachment.

Rolle's and Hilton's positions have traditionally been defined as affectivity in the face of intellectualism. It is certainly true that Hilton distrusts the extremism that Rolle favours, arguing in favour of 'discrecion ... in bodili feelynge bi greet fervour of devocioun ... the mene is the beste' (*Scale I*, p. 56). His qualifications of fire and flame metaphor certainly imply Rollian influence, as do references to prayer as 'the soft swete brennande' (*Scale I*, p. 38) of 'the fier of love' (*Scale I*, pp. 58–9). Yet Hilton refers only once in Book I of *Scale* to that fire (*Scale I*, p. 58), and he does so to correct the mistaken conclusions of others in what could be read as an implied criticism of Rollian spirituality: 'Alle men and women that speken of the fier of love knowe not wel what it is' (*Scale I*, p. 59). Yet, work such as Renevey's study of the little-known fifteenth-century text, *The Doctrine of the Hert*, rightly proposes that affective piety be understood not simply as an emotive response but as an intellectual process.[149] This, as chapters 2 to 5 will show, demands the revaluation of the supposedly sharp differences between these two guidance writers.

The much-condensed, vernacular redaction of Aelred's earlier medieval guide, *De institutione inclusarum*, is extant in Oxford, Bodleian Library, MS Bodley 423, part of a collection of devotional prose and verse. MS Bodley 423 comprises four separate manuscripts bound as one and is possibly of Carthusian provenance (which may suggest a male audience for this redaction, although this is not known for certain). The scribe of sections B and C of Bodley 423 (which contain the translated, redacted, anchoritic guide) was probably Stephen Dodesham.[150] Ayto and Barratt argue that since all earlier vernacular translations of Aelred's guide have been lost, the Bodley text (*c.*1430–40) and the only other extant vernacular translation, in the later medieval Vernon manuscript, cannot bridge the gap in our understanding of the chronological development of the vernacular transmission of Aelred's original work.[151]

In general, the Bodley redaction of *De institutione* is heavily shortened. Aelred's original thirty-three sections are compacted into just sixteen. Ayto and Barratt term it a 'drastic and thorough-going redaction of the Latin' in which 'abbreviation, conflation and omission are extensive'.[152] Aelred's original initial focus on diurnal practicalities and subsequent focus on chastity are retained, but his obsessive focus on chastity is most heavily condensed. His threefold meditation on the past, present and future still form the guide's conclusion, but these final meditative sections of the guide are no longer its dominant focus. The guide is no longer specific to its original audience of Aelred's sister (references to her are removed) and the meditation on the present reflects nothing of her shared lineage with Aelred. The effusive tone is transformed into one of precision and brevity and Aelred's tendency to prolonged explanation has gone and with it many beautiful and lyrical passages (which are retained in the vernacular version found in the Vernon manuscript, although it lacks Aelred's outer rule, i.e. much of his specifically anchoritic content).

Speculum inclusorum is the only guide explored in this book that was written for male recluses. Composed originally in Latin, it is extant in two fourteenth-century manuscripts of English provenance: London, British Library, MS Royal A. V and Oxford, St John's College, MS 177, but the precise dating of the composition of the Latin original is unclear.[153] Oliger proposes a date between 1342 and 1362 because of a potential reference to the 1362 Statute of Pleading.[154] Jones challenges Oliger's dating, citing other internal evidence, notably instances of Eucharistic orthodoxy and proposing a later date, between 1349 and sometime, perhaps as much as ten years, after 1382.[155] The guide is divided into a prologue, four parts (each of which is subdivided into further chapters; there are fourteen in total) and an epilogue. Part I contains five chapters; one as preface and four that outline each of the four motivations for the anchoritic life: 2) to live as one wishes without grave labour; 3) to do penance with great fervour for the things one has done (i.e. for sins); 4) to avoid the opportunities for sin and 5) to be more freely at leisure for the contemplation of God and to praise him. Part II is split into three chapters: 1) on fervent prayer; 2) on devout meditation and 3) on edifying reading. Part III focuses its three chapters again on these three practices in turn, in terms of the advantages to be gained from their proper enactment and the implications of failing to enact them properly. Finally, Part IV focuses on the rewards of the vocation, its three chapters exploring: 1) the hundredfold reward for anchoritism in this life; 2) the heavenly glory of (the anchorite's) body and, finally, 3) the heavenly glory of (the anchorite's) soul.

The editorially titled vernacular translation of *Speculum*, *The Myrour of Recluses*, is preserved in only one, damaged, mid-fifteenth-century manuscript: London, British Library, MS Harley 2372.[156] *Myrour* contains only eight of *Speculum*'s fourteen chapters and lacks the first few lines of the preface as found in *Speculum*, Part I. It also lacks the third chapters from both Parts II and III (on edificatory reading) and the whole of Part IV (on the rewards of the contemplative life). Where it remains intact, however, it is strikingly similar to the Latin guide in form and content. Roger Ellis finds it 'as close to its original as authorised translations of the Bible were expected to be to theirs'.[157] Textual reductions are rare and the translator rarely amends, or alters, the original Latin meaning. *Myrour*'s translator is also careful to gloss the full meaning of the Latin where Latin quotation is included, using, Marta Powell Harley notes: 'more than two hundred doublets to clarify Latin words'.[158]

The *Speculum* author was probably a Carthusian, although his identity and the identity of *Myrour*'s medieval translator remains unknown.[159] Jones concludes that the *Speculum* author 'was less interested than Rolle or Hilton in reaching an audience outside the reclusory' and that *Myrour*'s Middle English translator 'had in mind an equally restricted readership of anchoresses'.[160] The original author's textual persona mixes humility with confidence, persuasion with prescription and adopts a formulaic conclusion, reminiscent of *Ancrene Wisse*.[161] He characterizes himself as the humble vehicle of communication between God and his anchorites: 'O benignissime Ihesu ... revela mihi quod eis proferam' (*Speculum*, p. 66).[162] Part IV of his guide presents him in a far more authoritarian light, however, and there he makes bold claims for the heavenly fate of his anchorites (*Speculum*, p. 125).

By the time of *Speculum*'s later, vernacular translation, *Myrour*, the guide's audience had been widened to include women. *Myrour* therefore retains some of the Latin guide's original male references but also refers to 'ancres & ankeresses' (*Myrour*, p. 13). The audiences of both *Speculum* and *Myrour* remain unidentified, but are clearly addressed as a group of considerable size, reflecting, alongside *Ancrene Wisse*, one of the largest original anchoritic audiences of any extant guide. *Speculum*'s and *Myrour*'s sophisti-cated treatment of contemplative material implies considerable audience spiritual sophistication. Jones seeks to connect the manuscripts to specific anchorites with Carthusian associations: in the case of *Speculum*, a group of anchorite-priests at Henry V's foundation at Sheen, and in the case of *Myrour*, a female anchorite of Stamford (because, by the late fifteenth century, the manuscript had been gifted to William Browne's almshouse by Sir John Trus).[163] As yet, there is not enough evidence to link either *Speculum* or *Myrour* conclusively to these named groups or individuals.[164]

Having introduced each of the eight base guides and some of their many texts in terms of their contents and controversies, their manuscripts and editions, their authors and audiences, chapters 2 and 3 will now analyse the significances of three of the four fundamental anchoritic ideals upon which the English guidance tradition is founded: enclosure, solitude and chastity.

2

Anchoritic Enclosure

Permanent fixity of place

Permanent fixity of place is the ideal which is at the heart of earlier medieval guidance; a conception of enclosure that is terrifying and yet affords the recluse comfort, for the earlier guides suggest that the greatest blessings of anchoritism come in the form of its torments. *Ancrene Wisse* advises its recluses to vow to 'stude-steaðeluestnesse' (*AW*, Corpus, p. 3); to a cell broken open only in the face of extreme violence or on pain of death.[1] Recluses who refuse to leave even then are much admired, as in Goscelin's tale of Brithric, who refuses to leave his cell although remaining there means he will be burnt to death. Brithric's embrace of the permanency of enclosure is constructed as his martyrdom, and Eve is encouraged thereby to welcome similarly permanent enclosure and 'omnem merorem ac laborem, cunctaque mortalitatis dispendia' (*Liber*, p. 36).[2] Permanent spatial fixity must be psychological as well as physical. *Ancrene Wisse* urges: 'Haldeð ow feaste ínne – nawt te bodi ane, for þet is þe unwurðest, ah ower fif wittes, ant te heorte … þer þe sawle lif is' (*AW*, Corpus, p. 90).[3] Aelred writes of those who fruitlessly enclose the body without the mind: 'Sed multi rationem huius ordinis uel ignorantes uel non curantes, membra tantum intra parietes cohibere satis esse putant, cum mens non solum peruagatione dissoluatur, curis et sollicitudinibus dissipetur' (*DII*, p. 638).[4] Wandering outside the cell in the imagination is constructed as a tangible threat, for it breeds dissatisfaction with enclosure (*DII*, p. 644).[5]

The later guides emphasize fixity of place less than earlier guidance, but that does not mean enclosure is less important to the vocation in ideological terms. Permanent geographical fixity is still a defining characteristic of anchoritism, but it is no longer *the* defining characteristic. For the focus of the later guides is not on anchoritic withdrawal per se, but on the contemplative experience it facilitates. Nonetheless, enclosure is not constructed as less severe at this time. Recluses are still expected to dwell apart in relative spatial constriction. Anchoritism is still 'vitam perfectissimam' (*Speculum*, p. 71) because it is experienced 'in silencio, in secretis, et in tenebris' (*Speculum*, p. 83).[6] *Speculum*'s and *Myrour*'s recluses must still vow to a social segregation which 'necessario usque in finem servabitur sub pena dampnacionis eterne' (*Speculum*, p. 73).[7] Indeed, enclosure is now thought severe enough to warrant a year-long period of probation for prospective recluses involving strict supervision (*Speculum*, pp. 73–4).[8] Hilton still depicts the recluse 'as a wrecche, outcaste and refuse of alle men and women … spered in an hous aloone' (*Scale I*, p. 47). The Bodley redaction retains Aelred's original opening explanation of the eremitic impulse and the continued, venerable tradition of enclosure is implied in retained recommendations that the recluse be 'closed in a house out of alle mennes sight' (*DII*, MS Bodley 423, p. 1). The redactor observes that anchorites are still more strictly enclosed than other 'cloistrers', for a recluse must 'vtterly ... forsake al worldly besynesse' (*DII*, MS Bodley 423, p. 17).

Enclosure is, however, accepted as more of a given in the later guides. It is taken more for granted that the recluse will naturally understand its centrality to her vocation. *Speculum* and *Myrour* clearly criticize those who do not take it seriously, desiring instead 'iuxta sue voluntatis arbitrium, fugiunt ab ordine suo, tanquam perdicionis filii, vel aliquam exempcionem non sine consciencie scrupulo procurant, ut puta quod sint capellani pape vel episcopi nullatenses' (*Speculum*, p. 68).[9] Warren details known instances of acceptable and unacceptable reclusive community involvement, noting the comparative freedoms of some male recluses.[10] *Myrour*, in a passage not found in *Speculum*, elaborates upon the necessary severity of anchoritic enclosure for women, arguing, for the sake of its widened audience of female recluses, that lone women require stricter enclosure than the men for which *Speculum* was intended. Female anchorites need to be: 'more streytly closed þan oþir religious men and wommen, enclosed in her houses ... and in alle tymes at her souereyns wyl' (*Myrour*, p. 13). From Goscelin's *Liber* onwards, the guides construct greater anchoritic freedoms for the male recluse. Goscelin's own fantasy anchorhold comes: 'ad sollemnes exitus ... haberet ostiolum' (*Liber*, p. 34), to allow him continued access to the main body of the church during services.[11] For female recluses, whether early or late, the guides construct enclosure as an agreement to permanent geographical fixity of a stricter kind.

The purpose of anchoritic enclosure

The anchorhold exists to facilitate, through comparative isolation, the recluse's closer connection with God. In theory, it is her enclosure that enables her to work unencumbered by worldly constraints. Goscelin declares: 'tu, omnibus exutis, regnantius [*sic*] dilataberis' (*Liber*, p. 78).[12] The guides render the cell the architectural codification of the potential sanctity of its occupant; its archaeology (or material culture, to coin Gilchrist's phrase) is entirely functional, dictated by vocational requirements. *Ancrene Wisse* renders it a public proclamation: 'Euch ancre haueð þis o foreward, ba þurh nome of "ancre" ant þurh þet ha wuneð under þe chirche, [as] to understiprín hire ... ha ne stu[t]eð neauer: ancre wununge ant hire nome ʒeieð eauer þis foreward ʒet hwen ha slepeð' (*AW*, Corpus, p. 56).[13] Wordplay suggests the very etymological importance of geographical fixity: 'For-þi is ancre "ancre" icleopet, ant under chirche iancret as ancre under schipes bord ... Alswa al Hali Chirche (þet is schip icleopet) schal ancrin o þe ancre' (*AW*, Corpus, p. 56).[14]

Earlier guidance ties the need for enclosure into worldly sinfulness. For Goscelin, Judgement Day obviates the necessity of its 'mors ... nox ... tenebre' (*Liber*, p. 112).[15] The cell itself will, along with the nunnery at Wilton, be transformed and the need for enclosure eradicated. In an imperfect world, however, the earlier medieval recluse is encouraged to regard the anchorhold as a refuge which renders her secure while earthly hedonistic excesses pass away. Goscelin states: 'Nauis tibi est ab illius pelagi uastitate, asilum a mundi tempestate, domus refugii a malorum turbine' (*Liber*, p. 78).[16] That worldly 'freedom' leads to damnation is, therefore, the message of an extended juxtaposition of Eve's enclosure with the life of Octavianus Augustus, Caesar's heir. *Ancrene Wisse* argues that the anchorhold's walls and the 'wel-itund windowe' (*AW*, Corpus, p. 159) provide a protective shield.[17] Goscelin romanticizes the cell in his attempts to render it Eve's safe haven: 'Tua quoque portiuncula est hec, tua peregrinalis et pascualis casula, hec domuscula octo pedum' (*Liber*, p. 72).[18] He continues:

> O quotiens suspirabam simile tuo hospitiolum … ubi orare, lectitare scriptitare, dicititare meruissem … turbam euaderem … uentri legem ponerem, ut in loco pascue libris pro epulis incumberem (*Liber*, p. 34).[19]

Here, the vocation is constructed as an escape from life's struggle. Yet earlier guidance constructs it concurrently as a battlefield, since anchoritism forces the recluse to confront all that is worst about her own sinfulness, and the permanency of the cell removes all hope of escape. Goscelin's idealizations are related to his desire to represent himself as the beleaguered victim of Eve's desertion (she lives safely; he suffers). Nonetheless, they construct enclosure's paradoxical freedom: 'Tu in portu es, ego fluctuo. Tu domi resides, ego naufragor. Tu nidificasti in petra, ego arenis illidor' (*Liber*, p. 35).[20] The security of the cell renders enclosure a paradoxical form of spatial liberty. Yet the guides concurrently imply that it affords the earlier medieval recluse the opportunity to escape nothing.

The earlier guides focus on enclosure to such an extent that they give the impression of admiring it as an end in itself. The later guides do not do this. Hilton is particularly insistent that the cell is simply the means to an end; to be valued solely because, in theory, it occasions the solitude that facilitates contemplation. It is by virtue of the contemplation facilitated by enclosure, not by virtue of enclosure per se, that later medieval guidance argues the recluse can transcend her sinfulness. Enclosure, in itself, is not her spiritual purpose. Enclosure is the medium, Hilton argues, whereby the recluse negotiates the greatest of heavenly prizes, potentially gaining the supreme rewards open to all Christians and the accidental rewards, open only to martyrs, preachers, virgins and anchorites (*Scale I*, pp. 79–82). In keeping with the emotive tone of much later guidance, enclosure simply enables the recluse to 'more frely syghe and snobbe after the loue of Iesu with longyng desire' (*DII*, MS Bodley 423, p. 1); an eremitic motivation absent from Aelred's original version of this guide. Enclosure is to be valued for this alone. The later writers are concerned with the spiritual practices and rewards that are facilitated by enclosed space. They are not concerned with enclosed space in itself. They dwell on the enclosure of the mind, for their fascination is with the soul, not the body; the spirit, not the flesh.

By the time of the later guides, the focus on anchoritic temporal practicalities has been discarded. At first glance this seems very different from earlier guidance, yet it is the natural culmination of a process begun in embryo in the earlier texts, for instance in *Ancrene Wisse*'s advice that its recluses should not waste themselves on temporalities to their spiritual detriment (*AW*, Corpus, pp. 3–4).[21] This finds its logical conclusion in statements like those of Rolle, that the anchorite 'loue God stalwarthly' (*Form*, p. 21), not the cell itself. Rolle ties such love naturally into enclosure, advising: 'may no man loue hym bot if he be stalworth' (*Form*, p. 20). The cell gives Hilton's recluse the opportunity to 'hate synne ... withouten cesynge, and ... love vertues and clennesse ... withouten stintynge' (*Scale I*, p. 56). Human nature, not the boundary of the cell itself, is the 'wal' (*Scale I*, p. 83) that now divides, not the recluse from the world, but rather God from the recluse. Christ is still 'the door', but now to contemplation, not the cell. It is the 'gate' (*Scale I*, p. 38), or liminal threshold of contemplation, not of the enclosure itself, that the recluse must cross in the search for contemplative union. It is God, not the anchorite's servant, that is now the recluse's 'porter and withoute his leve and his lyveray mai *there* [i.e. to contemplation] *no man come in*' (*Scale I*, p. 132). Although the recluse is bound to 'stable entencion' (*Scale I*, p. 55) and '*mai wilfulli leve it not*' (*Scale I*, p. 55), Hilton argues, in a logical development from earlier medieval declarations that it is fruitless to enclose the body but not the mind, that it is 'the poynt of thi thought' which must be 'sette upoun noon erthely thynge'; the mind that must be '*enclosid*, rested, softed, anoynted and comfortid thorugh gracious presence of oure Lord Jhesu Crist' (*Scale I*, p. 84).[22]

Anchoritic enclosure and living death

Earlier guides reinforce the severity of enclosure through extended metaphor. They are, as Watson argues, dominated by images of 'wombs, bodies, crucifixions, walls, castles'.[23] Some of these images vivify the outside world, prompting Georgianna's conclusion that *Ancrene Wisse* is 'an uncommonly worldly book'.[24] She reminds us that secular attractions are not entirely evil: 'The anchorite cannot shut out the world altogether without also shutting out ... Christ, who was after all, a man'.[25] Janet Grayson's study of *Ancrene Wisse* proposes a progress in the anchorite's interpretation of worldly images, from an outer, literal meaning to an inner, metaphorical significance, driving the author's deliberate attempts to reprogramme his recluses' natural tendency to remember their former lives.[26] John Burrow reads *The Cloud of Unknowing*, a text with reclusive connections, in this light: 'even if we ... stop thinking *about* created things, we will still go on thinking *with* them'.[27] Worldly imagery, imbued with spiritual significance is used to reinforce, not undermine, enclosure. Cary Howie argues: 'To be inside ... is not to be sealed off: it is to be summoned, paradoxically, into a more concrete, ecstatic relation to what lies not just beyond but within these boundaries'.[28] For the recluse, as heavenly values replace secular ones, so Christ becomes the barn, the store cupboard, the purse of the recluse (*DII*, pp. 676–7).[29] This understanding motivates Watson's argument that anchorites are already 'enclosed within a powerful imaginative structure, and require only a personal and affective realisation of its significance ... [of] a reciprocal relationship, an interpenetration, between these images and the anchoritic image which they "interpret"'.[30] Otter suggests the recluses themselves revelled in this, needing 'to find image after image of what they had become', to 'literalize the metaphor' and 'not only to think it but ... live it'.[31] Christopher Cannon argues that enclosure affords the recluse the tools for securing her 'imaginative boundaries', a 'set of images whereby the anchorite can orient ... [herself] in the context of a larger world'.[32]

We know too little of the actual consumption of anchoritic guides to be certain that such comparative imagery was demanded by the recluses themselves. Clearly, the earlier guidance writers wish to enclose them within an elaborate system of metaphor and simile, intending such descriptions to be affective actualizations and codifications of, crucially, their perceptions of the vocation. Barbara Newman detects in this the male writer's assuagement of his own needs, rather than those of his recluse. She suggests: 'The authors of anchoritic books loved to imagine the solitude of their readers, sometimes with wistful envy', indulging their 'deep satisfaction in the thought of their own textual presence in the lives of their readers'.[33] In this context, the literatures that surround anchoritism (of which guidance texts are, of course, only a part), reflect, not anchoritism per se, but the male writer's fantasy of it; to which he must persuade his recluse to submit. The earlier medieval guidance writer uses metaphor after metaphor to ensure that the recluse understands her place in his system of spiritual signification.

Yet, in metaphorical terms, what dominates earlier guidance is not the imagery of life, but of death. Both the cell and the grave – confined spaces that can never be left – are traditionally situated in the churchyard. The guides expect the recluse to die in her reclusorium, exchanging a metaphorical tomb for a literal one. Yet, for the earlier guidance writers, she is already dead. Goscelin argues: 'Beati enim mortui qui in Domino moriuntur, cui mori uiuere est' (Liber, p. 70).[34] Paradoxically, Eve by 'cotidie moriendo seculo et uiuendo Deo' (Liber, p. 89), stands a far greater chance of life (in the eternal sense).[35] Aelred reminds his sister: 'desiderans non uideri, et quasi mortua saeculo in spelunca Christo consepeliri' (DII, p. 649).[36] Ancrene Wisse asks: 'hwet is ancre-hus bute hire burinesse?' (AW, Corpus, p. 43).[37] The soul 'is her in uncuððe, iput in a prison, bitund in a cwalm-hus' (AW, Corpus, p. 55).[38] Recluses must 'schrapien euche dei þe eorðe up of hare put þet ha schulen rotien in' (AW, Corpus, p. 46).[39] This recommendation has been read, notably by Mary Salu and Georgianna, as literal. Salu translates it as: 'God knows, the sight of her grave near her does many an anchoress much good'.[40] Yet Ancrene Wisse's meaning here is best read as metaphorical. The declaration: 'Godd hit wat, þet put deð muche god moni ancre' (AW, Corpus, p. 46) is best translated, in White's words, as: 'God knows, the grave does a lot of good to many an anchoress'.[41] Passages that precede this section are patently figurative, pitting the whiteness of the anchorite against the blackness of the earth. Grave metaphor suggests that peripherals (here, beauty) have no place in the anchorhold; enclosure liberates the recluse from temporal judgements and pursuits.

Death imagery does not reduce the guides' portrayal of earlier medieval anchoritism to the passive level of permanent suffering. It also implies a creative spiritual regeneration. The anchorhold is a place of life as well as death, or rather, life in death. If Eve is 'ut altile in cauea non carne, sed anima, non epularum illecebra, sed lectione diuina' (Liber, p. 72), she is being fattened for a fight, not cold-blooded slaughter.[42] Such metaphor conveys the positive significance of death. It constructs it as an active regenerative process, as in the natural world, where the cycle of life involves necessary renewal: 'arbor … in multam propaginem reuiuiscit a sepultura' (Liber, p. 79).[43] The crucified recluse awaits rejuvenation or, more properly, resurrection in heaven. For now, she lies hidden within her anchor-grave in jubilant submission to its narrow constraints. Eve can 'in angusto loco amplificare securitate' (Liber, p. 78),[44] for, as Aelred writes joyfully: 'mors beatitudinis principium est, laborum meta, peremptoria uitiorum' (DII, p. 677).[45] This is why Aelred envisages the reclusive body as senseless at the peak of its spiritual fulfilment (DII, p. 672).[46] Thus, anchoritic worldly renunciation is constructed as the beginning, not the end, of the recluse's spiritual journey. Goscelin thereby converts mortality into immortality: 'Non nocet sepultura resurrecturis' (*Liber*, p. 79).[47]

Regeneration is also implied by the earlier guides' juxtaposition of tomb and womb.[48] Eve's enclosure reconfigures her as a spiritual mother: 'Hoc equidem semper optaui, et ad hoc peperi te ac dilexi, ut in Christi transires uiscera, ac tota Christi fieres uictima' (*Liber*, p. 36).[49] Womb/tomb metaphor fosters an analogy between cell and flesh; life and death. Body, cell and soul merge into a threefold enclosure. Goscelin synonymizes these: 'Ibi egreditur de clauso utero, hic de clauso mausoleo' (*Liber*, p. 83).[50] *Ancrene Wisse* uses womb metaphor to construct Jesus as recluse: 'Marie wombe ant þis þruh weren his ancre-huses' (*AW*, Corpus, p. 142).[51] Aelred constructs his and his sister's gestation in the same womb as an enclosure (*DII*, pp. 673–4) and celebrates the fertile constraints of Mary's womb: 'Beati uentres in quibus totius mundi salus exoritur, pulsisque tristitiae tenebris, sempiterna laetitia prophetatur' (*DII*, p. 663).[52] Miri Rubin argues: 'Mary was attractive not only for her purity, but for the intimacy that linked her to the redemption promised by her son ... Being of a single substance, mother and son enjoyed an incomparable closeness'.[53] Like the developing foetus and in the tradition of Christ himself, the enclosed recluse is nurtured as foetus, until, (re)birthed by death, her suffering transports her into paradise and she resigns: 'ba þine ancre-huses ... þet an is þe licome; þet oþer is þe uttre hus' (*AW*, Corpus, p. 142).[54]

Like the womb itself, the anchorhold is cast, in earlier guidance, as a threshold place, a liminal space between two worlds, belonging to neither. Social anthropologist Victor Turner argues: 'Liminal entities are neither here nor there; they are betwixt and between the positions assigned ... by ... convention ... Thus liminality is frequently likened to death, to being in the womb, to invisibility, to darkness'.[55] Goscelin argues: 'Venisti ad ianuam paradisi uere uoluptatis; persiste et pulsa assidua importunitate, donec intres Domino ueniente' (*Liber*, p. 37).[56] The enclosed recluse inhabits the threshold between life and death, heaven and hell, between inner and outside worlds. Aelred writes: 'Sta nunc quasi in medio, nesciens quibus te iudicis sententia deputabit. O dura expectatio! Timor et tremor uenerunt super me, et contexerunt me tenebrae' (*DII*, p. 679).[57] The earlier medieval recluse is textually constructed as bound by a double exile; unwilling to remain in the world and unable to enter heaven.

Enclosed space functions less, in the later guides, as a creative canvas open to metaphorical manipulation. Earlier medieval guidance may cast the cell as anything from a prison to a paradise, from a refuge to a place of exile, but later guides 'read' the cell less; later writers take it for granted that the recluse already understands the importance of enclosure. To focus on earthly temporalities is, the later guides imply, to limit the recluse to them (no matter how cleverly transformed by simile and metaphor). The virtues of chastity, humility, charity and the rejection of worldly materialism are more real to these writers and are meant to be more real to their recluses than the bricks and mortar of the enclosure which facilitates their development. Earlier medieval analogies between the cell and the flesh and connections between anchorhold and womb are largely absent. The later guides deliberately break down attachment to time, place and material possession, for if the recluse associates herself with her physical surroundings, or with her body, even if only to construct their rejection, then she chains herself to them.

Where metaphorical constructions of enclosure do, however, persist in the later texts, those that link anchoritism to death remain most dominant. Aelred's redactor retains his description of an anchorite as 'deed and buryed to the worlde' (*DII*, MS Bodley 423, p. 16) and continues to construct the cell as an oven in which the fire of temptation can either refine or destroy the clay-covered vessel of the recluse's body (*DII*, MS Bodley 423, p. 10). *Speculum* and *Myrour* do not focus on death metaphor directly, although their constructions of the silent recluse locked down, with her senses stopped up, implicitly recall the grave. Rolle argues that the recluse 'hath joy þat men reproue hym and spek il of hym, as a dede man, what so men doth or seith, answareth nat' (*Form*, p. 21), although his recluse is now 'stille in a stid' (*Form*, p. 23), not in the grave specifically. This is celebrated purely because it facilitates God's 'comynge and thy goynge' (*Form*, p. 18). Hilton argues that the recluse is 'as it were a deed man' (*Scale I*, p. 31). He still admires anchoritism, urging his recluse: 'in plenté of gode bodili werkes and goostli vertues entre thi grave, that is the reste in contemplacioun' (*Scale I*, p. 46). Yet, it is anchoritic contemplation (facilitated by enclosure) rather than anchoritic enclosure in itself which renders his recluse dead to the world. The shift is slight, but nonetheless discernible.

For the later guides do not only construct enclosure as deprivation, but as an indulgence. Such comparisons recall Goscelin's complaints about Eve's comparative happiness and are reminiscent too of wider earlier medieval notions of the cell as refuge. Yet, the emphasis of new juxtapositions of the advantages of enclosure with the tribulations of active life is different. Enclosure is now cast almost as a luxury, unaffordable to most. For the later medieval recluse is told to compare her lot with that of actives who 'suffren many tribulacions and greet temptaciones which thu sittynge in thyn hous felist not of' (*Scale I*, p. 49). The *Speculum* author concludes similarly: 'Vos enim estis paradisicole, nos mundi miserabiles incole; vos estis in porta celi, et nos in limo profundi; vos in speculo veritatis, et nos in tenebris falsitatis' (*Speculum*, p. 135).[58] Hilton constructs a contemporary envy of the recluse: 'manye ... hadde wel lyvere serve God, yif thei myghten, as thou doost in bodili reste' (*Scale I*, p. 49). The world is not a hedonistic place of excess that she must escape, but a place of suffering of which she, luckily, knows nothing. These perspectives are motivated, as chapter 5 will show, by a wider contemporary controversy about the value of the active and contemplative lives; a controversy that potentially begs the question of whether anchoritism is needed at all.[59]

The invisible anchorhold

Despite their frequent, metaphorical constructions of the cell, it is all but impossible to visualize the specific anchorhold under discussion in any earlier medieval guide. Even at its most descriptive, *Ancrene Wisse* gives only the vague impression of a multi-roomed structure close enough to the church to glimpse the elevation of the host (*AW*, Corpus, p. 13).[60] Goscelin is unfamiliar with the layout of Eve's cell – after all, he has never seen it and he never will. Yet, at times, he does visualize the cell's spatial multivalency: 'Hic sanctuarium, hic oratorium, hic refectorium, hic dormitorium, aulam, cubiculum, uestibulum, cellarium, secretarium, cunctaque habitacula sortita es in unum' (*Liber*, p. 78).[61] This casts it as a professional place, not a domestic space. Eve must convert its raw working materials to her advantage through hard spiritual labour. Other earlier guides similarly acknowledge the existence of a bed, an altar and of windows only when they carry the significance of enclosure forward. Thus, Aelred and the *Ancrene Wisse* author and his revisers' recommendations of simple interior decoration – a crucifix, white altar covering, or picture of the Virgin – reinforce vocational virtues, notably 'castitatem … et simplicitatem' (*DII*, p. 657).[62] As Robertson suggests, the recluse's physical engagement with material objects 'including the [guide's own] manuscript, the walls of the anchorhold, and the curtains … replicate synergistically the primary object of her meditation'.[63] In typical Cistercian fashion, Aelred therefore rejects external luxury:

> Sed illam te nolim quasi sub specie deuotionis sequi gloriam in picturis uel sculpturis, in pannis auium uel bestiarum, aut diuersorum florum imaginibus uariatis. Sint haec illorum qui nihil intus in quo glorientur habentes, exterius sibi comparant in quo delectantur (*DII*, p. 657).[64]

In the tradition of earlier guidance, it is all but impossible to visualize the anchorhold under discussion in the later medieval guides; even more so, since these later texts dispense almost wholly with the daily reclusive regimen wherein, in earlier guides, the cell could (rarely) be glimpsed. Focus is firmly on the recluse's interior, contemplative potential, indeed even the structural device of inner and outer, favoured by earlier guidance, is largely absent.[65] Earlier medieval guides note the basic geographical position, contents and decoration of the cell and regulate its daily routine, but in later guidance even the sense of a hypothetical enclosure – of one cell standing for all cells – is gone. Aelred's Bodley redaction does retain some of his practical recommendations, including material on simple interior decoration, which the recluse is still encouraged to read for its symbolic significances of chastity and purity (*DII*, MS Bodley 423, p. 15). The cell's icons should continue to inspire her. Yet, this guide is the exception. Powell Harley's conclusion that *Myrour* 'serves reasonably well as an outer rule', misses the point.[66] Location, for later guidance writers, does not matter at all, for as Hilton argues, it is not in the cell, but in 'thyn owen soule, where he [God] is hid' (*Scale I*, p. 87).

Safeguarding anchoritic enclosure

Earlier guidance suggests many strategies to safeguard enclosure, all of which trade in fear and imply that enclosure is, paradoxically, an experience of fundamental insecurity. Aelred writes: 'nunquam uolo esse securam, sed timere semper' (*DII*, p. 654).[67] Goscelin anticipates that Eve may 'oblitam petite patrie tedeat aliquando solitudinis, captiuitatis et clausule' (*Liber*, p. 69).[68] She should resist sadness and 'accidia' or sloth and also 'somnum, torporem, mestitiam, fastidia' (*Liber*, p. 88).[69] She should take enclosure one day at a time and invert temporal time schemes, thereby experiencing enclosure as temporary: 'Totam uitam tuam unam diem cum eternitate' (*Liber*, p. 88).[70] As will be explored in chapter 3, all the earlier guidance writers recommend the limitation of social interaction combined with sensory shutdown, particularly focusing on sight, as a means of safeguarding enclosure (*Liber*, p. 51; *DII*, pp. 644–5 and *AW*, Corpus, p. 18).[71] Other weapons in the earlier medieval recluse's spiritual arsenal also include reading, ascetic practice and contemplative experience.[72] Goscelin, uniquely, advises Eve to take the Eucharist: 'cotidianum uiaticum celestis alimonie' (*Liber*, p. 90), daily, as a pre-emptive strike against despair, reflecting on Cyprian's arguments that if sin is diurnal then so must its remedy be.[73] Goscelin links this diurnal communion specifically to the reinforcement of enclosure: 'Tali cibo ... nec foris mente uagabunda, sed intus ... intenta, iam non eris solitaria, nec patieris mortalia tedia' (*Liber*, p. 90).[74] This advice is unusual for this time; Otter notes its rarity 'in practice and even as an ideal' (Otter, p. 11, n. 128).

The later guides continue to argue that no recluse can be saved simply by virtue of her enclosure. Anchoritic fixity of place is still rendered insufficient, in itself, to ensure salvation. The experience of enclosure, codified in the earlier medieval shape-shifting of the cell as metaphorical signifier, remains one of spiritual insecurity. The earlier guidance writers use fear as a form of social control, seeking to render the recluse constantly fearful of compromising her enclosure. The later writers prefer to use love; the inculcation of the contemplative love of God, confident that this will preserve the boundaries of enclosure as securely as fear was formerly thought to do. For later medieval guidance anticipates that contemplative experience (the purpose of anchoritism) will naturally safeguard enclosure. It will inculcate in the recluse a love of God that automatically lessens her attachment to humanity. It seeks, therefore, not so much to safeguard the vocation in the minds of its exponents as to protect it against its opponents. Rolle's defence is robust: 'we haue more ioy ... in oon day þan þei haue in þe worlde al har lyfe ... If þei saw þat, many of ham wold forsake al þat þei haue for to folow vs' (*Form*, p. 6). For the later writers operate with an inevitable awareness of the spiritual validity of other ways of life. As chapter 5 will show, their guidance reacts to the idea that contemplation may not require the anchorhold for its achievement, although they still declare that it provides the best conditions for contemplation for those individuals for whom they write, and Hilton remarks that anchoritic contemplation has the potential to be far more sophisticated than that of actives (*Scale I*, p. 37). Yet, he also implies that it is possible, with grace, for an active to recreate in her heart contemplative conditions which earlier guidance claimed was attainable only in the anchorhold (*Scale I*, p. 36). The later writers do not condemn anchoritism, or explicitly argue that it is outdated – the very act of writing their *anchoritic* guides implies their continued support for the vocation (and Rolle also defends it as a solitary himself). Yet, they do not elevate it as the wisest of vocations for all (as did earlier guidance). Since enclosure is now only the wisest choice for some, the later writers do not devote the same energy as their earlier counterparts to its protection or its glorification.

3

Anchoritic Solitude and Sociability[1]

The idealisation of solitude

Barratt notes that 'enclosure is not enough by itself to make a true solitary'; it must be accompanied by the renunciation of 'the company of the good as well as … evil'.[2] Anselm compares the heart to a vessel which cannot be filled with oil if already partly full of water: 'tanto minus capit oleum: ita cor, in quantum occupatur alio amore, in tantum excludit istum' (Anselm, 'Letter 112', vol. 3, p. 246).[3] Goscelin argues: 'Vt solum accipias, sola huc intrasti. Clama, eiula, pulsa, ut aperiatur tibi. Luctare cum Domino donec superes: uim fac regno celorum ut intres' (Liber, p. 28).[4] Ancrene Wisse is emphatic: 'Hu god is to beon ane … Godd his dearne runes ant heouenliche priuitez schawde his leoueste freond nawt i monne floc, ah dude þer ha weren ane bi ham seoluen' (AW, Corpus, p. 60).[5] It argues that solitude fosters contemplative (here, visionary) potential: 'Engel to mon i þrung ne eadewede neauer ofte' (AW, Corpus, p. 62).[6] Solitude, like the enclosure which facilitates it, is occasioned only by the sinfulness of the world. In heaven there is 'iunctissima contubernia; nusquam solitudo' (Liber, p. 115).[7] Eternity is constructed as sociable in direct proportion to anchoritic seclusion: 'Tanto gaudentius in perhenni mansione ueros dilectos colliges, quanto hic uulneratius in Deo dilexeris' (Liber, p. 42).[8]

The earlier guides are rich in solitary role models. Their lineage of solitude is the recluse's by right. This familia, with Christ at its head, banishes earthly loneliness (Liber, pp. 87–8).[9] He himself passed through 'Per loca horroris et uaste solitudinis' (Liber, p. 47).[10] He is now Eve's constant companion: 'Esto cum Domino, iam non eris solitaria' (Liber, p. 69).[11] Hayward has shown that Goscelin adapts Jerome's Letter 22, To Eustochium to offer Eve 'a new [paradoxical] imagined community' of solitude.[12] It includes St John the Baptist, St Paul (admired for sixty years of solitude), St Mary of Egypt (for forty-six years) and Moses and Elijah (Liber, pp. 75–6).[13] Mary, sister of Lazarus, personifies solitary contemplative experience (Liber, pp. 73–4).[14] Ancrene Wisse also idealizes the Virgin as recluse: 'Ne fond te engel hire in anli stude al ane? … biloken feste' (AW, Corpus, p. 62).[15] Recluses whose solitude was unbroken in the face of worldly resistance are also admired, notably she who refused to speak with St Martin; praised for that silence both by Aelred (DII, p. 642) and Ancrene Wisse (AW, Corpus, p. 26).[16]

Silence is highly prized as a solitude reinforcement strategy (AW, Corpus, p. 41).[17] Aelred's recluse is advised to organize her silence and speech according to the liturgical calendar (DII, pp. 643–6) and told that 'sola sedeat et taceat ore, ut spiritu loquatur'

(*DII*, p. 641).[18] The desirability of female silence has its roots in long-established spiritual tradition. Nancy Bradley Warren argues that in medieval monastic houses the penalties for female speech were more severe and the expectation of regular female verbal transgression more pronounced: 'a system of social relations' in which male authorities can speak, 'while female hearers are commanded to keep silent'.[19] Yet, this does not imply, as Patricia J. F. Rosof argues, that the recluse is 'in a totally passive position'.[20] She is constructed as an active spiritual combatant, not a docile victim. *Ancrene Wisse* likens her, in her solitude, to a wild animal (*AW*, Corpus, p. 74).[21] All the earlier writers depict the female recluse as potentially powerful in her silence. Worldly silence fosters a creative spiritual dialogue: 'Sola sis cum Domino solitaria. Orando cum Domino loquere, legendo tecum loquentem Dominum attende' (*Liber*, p. 80).[22] Solitude is a medium for communicative interaction, but crucially, with God, not mankind.

The purpose of the death metaphor analysed in chapter 2 is to communicate the solitude of anchoritism as a social death.[23] The recluse can have no 'tibi cum relicta seculi decipula' (*Liber*, p. 40).[24] Goscelin declares: 'Qui ergo amat ascendere in montem cum Domino uerum, et turrim edificare in celum' (*Liber*, p. 62), must separate himself from the crowd.[25] Solitude is cast as martyrdom; horrifying and viscerally painful, it drives the recluse's habits and thoughts into rhythms of life incompatible with the outside world, as self is swallowed up by cell. Aelred, quoting Matthew, urges: 'Nescias te esse in hoc mundo, quae ad illos qui in caelis sunt et Deo uiuunt, tuum transtulisti propositum. *Vbi est thesaurus tuus, ibi sit et cor tuum*' (*DII*, p. 676).[26] *Ancrene Wisse* uses eremitical anecdote to make the same point. The relative who comes to a recluse for aid is directed to one who is dead: '"... Ich", quoð þe hali mon, "am dead gasteliche. Na fleschlich freond ne easki me fleschlich froure"' (*AW*, Corpus, p. 160).[27]

This does not mean that the earlier guides wish the recluse to abandon all her social responsibilities. Paradoxically, it is precisely because of her solitude that they construct her as able to intercede for the world she seeks to reject. *Ancrene Wisse* states: 'þe treowe ancre þet is ... riht ihud – he hereð ant 3eteð hire alle hire benen, ant sawueð þurh ham muche folc. Monie schulde beo forloren þe beoð þurh þe ancre benen iborhen' (*AW*, Corpus, p. 65).[28] Goscelin consequently counsels Eve: 'in caritate diffusa Dei et proximi' (*Liber*, p. 32).[29] In prayer, the recluse may safely wander the world, interacting with the poor, the orphaned, the widowed, the pilgrim and the traveller (*DII*, p. 661 and *AW*, Corpus, p. 12).[30] Aelred casts good will, prayer and pity as the only acceptable forms of reclusive almsgiving: 'Itaque totum mundum uno dilectionis sinu complectere, ibi simul omnes qui boni sunt considera et gratulare, ibi malos intuere et luge. Ibi afflictos conspice et oppressos, et compatere' (*DII*, p. 661).[31] This passage influences *Ancrene Wisse* directly:

> gederið in ower heorte alle seke ant sarie ... [þe wa þet pouere] þolieð, þe pinen þe prisuns habbeð ... habbeð reowðe of þeo þe beoð i stronge temptatiuns. Alle hare sares setteð in ower heorte ant sikeð to ure Lauerd, þet he neome reowðe of ham ant bihalde toward ham wið þe ehe of his are (*AW*, Corpus, p. 12).[32]

Later medieval guidance also constructs solitude as an important anchoritic ideal. Rolle argues: 'The state þat þou art in, þat is solitude, þat is most able of al othre to reuelaciouns of þe Holy Goste' (*Form*, p. 6), for 'þe lasse speche þou [hast] of men, þe mor is þi ioy afor God' (*Form*, p. 5). Recluses should still 'hold ham fro mych speche of men

... so þat har holynesse were more sene in Goddis eigh þan in mannys' (*Form*, p. 5). Rolle concludes: 'If we be about to hide vs fro speche or preisynge of þe world, God wol shewe vs to his praysynge and oure ioy' (*Form*, p. 5). Silence is still prized as a method of preserving solitude, in a tradition that also began in earlier medieval guidance. Hilton couples his suggestion that the recluse stop her own activities to attend to visitors with the commendation of silence as protective strategy, advising that conversations be short and broken off entirely if the caller seeks only to gossip: 'answere hym not but litil, ne feede not his speche ... of alle thynges kepe silence as moche as thou mai, and thou schal have litil prees in schort tyme that schal lette thee' (*Scale I*, pp. 124–5).Yet, less space is devoted to solitude's perpetuation; later medieval guidance is on as unworldly a plane as its recluses should be. Contemplative experience is expected now to dictate anchoritic solitude naturally. Hilton concludes: 'Whoso hath this gift of God [i.e. contemplative ability] ferventli, hym bihoveth for the tyme flee presence and cumpanye of alle men and to be alone that he be not lettid' (*Scale I*, p. 62).

The later guides' encouragement of the recluse to the contemplative love of God is best read as their implicit encouragement of anchoritic solitude. In this, they follow the far earlier exhortations of guidance writers like Anselm, who declares, God 'non quaerit nisi amorem ... Da ergo amorem et accipe regnum: ama, et habe' (Anselm, 'Letter 112', vol. 3, p. 245).[33] Their insistence on the development of a contemplative bond with God is insistence on the natural exclusion of the world for, as the *Speculum* author argues: 'Dum enim solitario contemplanti fervens amor Dei dulcessit, omnis secularis leticia nimirum marcessit' (*Speculum*, p. 114).[34] Rolle, of all the later writers the most interested in love, unites it firmly with solitude in this description of his own eremitism:

> And I haue loued for to sit, for no penaunce ne for no fantasie þat I wold men spake of me, ne for no such þynge, bot only for I knewe þat I loued God more, and langer lested with me comfort of loue, þan goynge or standynge or knelynge. For syttynge am I in most reste, and my hert most vpward (*Form*, pp. 23–4).

Rollian love is constructed in three degrees: 'insuperabile', essentially stable for the recluse's will is in accord with God; 'inseperabile', where the presence of God is constant throughout everything except sleep and 'synguler', which is in a close relationship with solitude, for the outside world is abandoned and the soul is 'Ihesu louynge, Ihesu thynkynge, Ihesu desyrynge ... of hym brennynge, in hym restynge' (*Form*, p. 17). Such love is 'a rightwise turnynge fro al erthly thynges' (*Form*, p. 19), which both reinforces and is reinforced by enclosure and solitude. This, too, echoes Anselm's earlier argument that 'ama deum plus quam te ipsum, et iam incipis tenere quod ibi perfecte vis habere ... Hunc vero amorem non poteris habere perfectum, nisi evacuaveris cor tuum ab omni alio amore' (Anselm, 'Letter 112', vol. 3, pp. 245–6).[35] Yet, it is the *love* prompted by anchoritism's enclosure and solitude, not enclosure and solitude per se, that is to be admired. It is love itself that is now as 'stalworth as deth' (*Form*, p. 21).

Qualifying solitude: acceptable anchoritic interaction

Solitude is constructed as an absolute anchoritic ideal by the earlier guides, but even they construct it as absolute only in theory. Anchoritic guides do not, as Licence argues, 'mislead us into thinking that a recluse did nothing but pray and occupy her time with psalms'.[36] Acceptable levels of social interaction are built into the guidance tradition from its very beginning. The guides acknowledge that without human contact the recluse will simply die, unconfessed, in a state of sin. In a study of claustrophilia, Howie argues that for Aelred 'there is no such thing as complete enclosure, no ultimately impermeable wall'.[37] Aelred certainly concedes: 'Quibus quia perpetuum ne cum uiris loquantur indicere non possumus silentium, cum quibus honestius loqui possint uideamus' (DII, p. 642).[38] Anselm also envisages the recluse in conversation: 'Colloquia vestra semper sint munda et de deo' (Anselm, 'Letter 230', vol. 4, p. 135).[39] It is solitude of the mind that the earlier medieval guides encourage the recluse to seek, an aspiration which their later medieval counterparts most certainly share. Georgianna writes: 'the anchorhold is *not*, after all, either a desert or a grave, nor can it ever be'.[40] The cell is the world in miniature; every urge which exists outside it is present within. The guides imply that it is in the tension between social temptation and solitary aspiration that the recluse can learn the full meaning of the choice she has made.

As early as 1914, Clay conceded: 'The solitary was not condemned to a ... life of utter separation and silence' for 'to live entirely apart from human converse was positively dangerous to the soul'.[41] Darwin noted later, in 1944, that a recluse 'can hardly have known the meaning of real physical solitude from year's end to year's end', for 'true ... "solitude" was to be found in a state of spiritual rather than physical loneliness'.[42] Yet, while important work on earlier medieval anchoritism by critics including Watson, Georgianna, Warren and Robertson has usefully focused on transgressive anchoritic sociability, less has been written about acceptable interaction. The exception to this is the work of Anneke B. Mulder-Bakker. She argues, in terms of continental anchoritic hagiography, that the sociability and spirituality of recluses are not mutually exclusive. She casts continental anchorholds as potential centres of learning, linking a growth in female anchoritic literacy to later medieval urbanization. Recluses are an unthreatening source of learning, attractive to the laity, central 'mediators between the Lord and the faithful ... between ecclesiastical learning and lay culture'.[43] She even argues that 'solitary contemplation served social ends'.[44] Her conclusions are made in terms of the lowlands of north-west Europe between 1100 and 1311 and the hagiographic, textually constructed lives of five female anchorites. Of these women, specifically, she is able to conclude: 'Living in their anchorholds in the midst of their fellow citizens', they were not isolated, but 'strong, self-assured believers ... at the heart of the community', serving God 'in a way that included service to their fellow human beings'.[45] She argues that such hagiography reveals anchoritism as part of a 'living community'.[46] Clearly, these hagiographers admired these five exceptional, continental recluses for their social functions and, if read as evidence, not of the reality of continental anchoritism as it was lived, but of contemporary ideological perceptions of the vocation as they were recorded, then Mulder-Bakker's conclusions are important. Her study shows us what key writers of continental twelfth- and thirteenth-century hagiography believed the continental anchoritic vocation should be admired for. In that specific context, she is right to encourage scholars to stop interpreting the medieval recluse as simply a silent, restricted, secretive figure. She is right to conclude that over-reliance upon patristic constructions of the solitary ideal potentially keeps scholarship 'on the wrong track when interpreting the phenomenon of medieval anchoritism'.[47]

Yet, her conclusions are made in terms of a very specific group of recluses, in a very specific geographical location and in terms of a very specific tradition of (hagiographical) writing. They cannot be applied wholesale to the recluses of medieval Europe, or of medieval England, without a basis in similarly widespread and conclusively sociable hagiographical material.

Nonetheless, it cannot be as simple as Jocelyn Price's conclusions that English anchoritism 'must not have a story in or to it', that it can have 'a structure but not a plot'.[48] Anchoritic guides construct anchoritic lives with the potential for complex plots, based on acceptable, not just transgressive, social interaction. The earlier guides do not construct sociability solely as an aberration. Instead, they site the recluse at the heart of their communities, interacting with it (albeit, ideally, infrequently) and through such contact, as part II of this book will demonstrate, they construct their recluses as potentially capable of transmitting anchoritic spiritual aspirations and ideals to the outside world. Herbert McAvoy acknowledges that anchoritic guidance: 'on the surface ... constructs the anchorhold as a place of silent ... tranquil[lity]', yet 'from beneath ... bubbles up a veritable bustle of activity and interaction'.[49] Goscelin is freer than Aelred or the *Ancrene Wisse* author and his revisers on the subject of this activity:

> te ... hic populus colligit, ... huius piissime matris cunctarumque sororum affectus in te redundant ... te patrum et pontificum dignitas uisitat ... hec benedicta domina, que tibi hunc locum parauit ... nunc est uerius comitissima, te colit et affectat (*Liber*, p. 92).[50]

This is conjecture on his part, but conjecture that implies his belief in the potential for the recluse to retain a post-enclosure public status at this time and to command respect from (male) visitors and the wider community.

Anselm, Aelred and *Ancrene Wisse* are more reluctant than Goscelin to permit vital interaction, but all, nonetheless, permit it. Aelred and *Ancrene Wisse* do discourage contact with religious figures, even the confessor, and seek to limit interaction with the anchorhold's servants. Yet, this is contact that, they concede, nonetheless liberates the recluse from wider worldly interaction; social interaction which – ironically – seeks to preserve solitude. Regular contact represents regular risk to the earlier writers, but all of them legislate for its acceptability. *Ancrene Wisse* surmises interaction with the religious to present the gravest threat precisely because it may not appear to be so: '"monie cumeð to ow ischrud mid lombes fleos, ant beoð wedde wulues"' (*AW*, Corpus, p. 28).[51] The recluse is warned: 'Worltliche leueð lut, religiuse 3et leas' (*AW*, Corpus, p. 28).[52] Reinforcing her claim that the guide is of Dominican origin, Millett notes that two additions to the Corpus text qualify this with 'warm recommendation of ... friars ... exempting their visits from the special permission required for other male visitors'.[53] *Ancrene Wisse* warns the recluse not to teach or preach to men, although her devotions may match the rhythm of the priesthood which surrounds her at a distance (*AW*, Corpus, p. 18).[54] Recluses may, however, counsel women (*AW*, Corpus, p. 29),[55] although contact with female religious continues to be discouraged (*AW*, Corpus, p. 26).[56]

Earlier anchoritic guidance constructs the anchorhold as a household like any other. *Ancrene Wisse* is more detailed than Aelred in its treatment of the anchoritic servants, although both guides envisage the need for two women – one older, one younger, and each with distinct roles.[57] The older woman is expected to supervise access to the anchorhold as its doorkeeper and controller of the boundary line between both worlds

– a powerful role. The young girl's corruptive potential is especially feared, for her errands will take her in and out of the world.[58] The earlier guides suggest that the inevitable dependence created by the practical powerlessness of the recluse, occasioned by geographical fixity, will forge an unusually intimate bond between these women. This acceptable social interaction therefore represents, for every earlier medieval guidance writer apart from Goscelin, the gravest of all potential vocational threats.[59] The uneasy solution to this problem, for Aelred and *Ancrene Wisse*, is for each woman to operate within a triangle of fiercely protected virtue; each safeguarding the other through self-protection. Goscelin, however, has no qualms about encouraging Eve to enlist the regular services of a helper, chiefly to facilitate her reading. He suggests: 'Ipsa quoque ut possit admittere bibliotecam tam capacem, in longum esse uelim huius celle fenestram, aut per fenestram te legere posse a foris ap(p)ositam. Recita' (*Liber*, p. 80).[60] Goscelin's advice that Eve read aloud and visibly at the window would strike horror into Aelred and the *Ancrene Wisse* author, who both urge their recluses to cover and avoid their windows as much as possible.

Yet, even *Ancrene Wisse* implies that anchoritic servants may facilitate acceptable sociability, in its case involving indirect interaction between recluses. The Nero text refers to the 'Wummen ant children þet habbeð iswunken uor ou', in the advice: 'hwatse 3e sparieð on ou: makieð ham to etene' (*AW*, Nero, p. 190).[61] These women are constructed as the lifeblood of an anchoritic support network by the Corpus text. It stipulates that these 'ancre meidnes' (*AW*, Corpus, p. 157) may make visits between anchorholds and are to be welcomed.[62] More detailed regulations governing 'hu longe 3e edheolden' (*AW*, Corpus, p. 160)[63] are now required: 'Hwen ower sustres meidnes cumeð to ow to froure, cumeð to ham to þe þurl earunder ant ouerunder eanes oðer twien ant gað a3ein sone … swa þet hare cume beo na lure of ower religiun ah gastelich bi3ete' (*AW*, Corpus, p. 164).[64] Whether these visits were actually made in practice is not the point. That they are permitted in theory demonstrates an ideological qualification: a widening of the anchoritic ideal of solitude. Sauer argues that, paradoxically, in rejecting the outside world, the recluse 'draws herself tighter into the anchoritic community'.[65] The community envisaged by the Corpus text is far larger than this guide's original sisterhood of three:

> 3e beoð þe ancren of Englond, swa feole togederes (twenti nuðe oðer ma …), þet meast grið is among, meast annesse ant anrednesse ant sometreadnesse of anred lif efter a riwle, swa þet alle teoð an, alle iturnt anesweis ant nan frommard oðer, efter þet word is (*AW*, Corpus, p. 96).[66]

The Corpus text implies a wider, virtual network of anchorites, living out their vocation separately and yet united in the pages of the guide that they potentially use and given permission therein to encourage visits which connect one anchorhold with another literally, as well as metaphorically. Millett describes them as 'members of a spiritual rather than a literal cloister'.[67] Thus, this earlier medieval guide legislates for acceptable communication and, in advice that mirrors (although it does not match) Goscelin's, even legislates for book-loaning between anchorholds (*AW*, Corpus, p. 94).[68]

Less vital interaction, including contact with friends, family or some of the local community, is anticipated with greater reluctance by the earlier guides, but it is still permitted. *Ancrene Wisse* mentions the recluse's fear at a 'freondes deað, secnesse oðer on ham oðer o þe seoluen' (*AW*, Corpus, p. 69), although this is still regarded as a temptation sent by God to test the recluse's devotion to him.[69] Aelred forbids his sister to give material alms and *Ancrene Wisse* discourages it. Anselm admires 'paupertatem, laborem, subjectionem' (Anselm, 'Letter 112', vol. 3, p. 246).[70] Yet the 'Scribe B' (or C2) revisions to the Cleopatra text of *Ancrene Wisse* envisage, in their treatment of almsgiving, a greater share of reclusive interaction. The recluse can now receive gifts beyond those required by necessity and bestow them with permission: 'Ne makie ȝe nane purses forte freondin ow wið, bute to þeo þet ower meistre ȝeueð ow his leaue' (*AW*, Corpus, p. 160).[71] Dobson argues that this concession to sociability arises from 'a response to the needs of a larger community' of individual anchorites without the stable patronage arrangements of the guide's original audience.[72] This new direction nonetheless represents a further qualification of the ideology of solitude. The Corpus text also incorporates another passage which permits the recluse to agree to practical assistance when pressed: 'ne pleainin ow of na wone, bute to sum treowe freond þet hit mei amendin ... priueiliche ... þet ȝe ne beon iblamet ... ȝef he easkeð ȝeornluker, þonkið him ȝeorne, ant seggeð, "Ich ne dear nawt lihen o me seoluen; wone Ich habbe"' (*AW*, Corpus, p. 99).[73] Such contact must be negotiated in secrecy, but it is nonetheless permitted: 'Ha nis nawt husewif, ah is chirch-ancre. ȝef ha mei spearien eani poure schraden, sende ham al dearnliche ut of hire wanes' (*AW*, Corpus, p. 156).[74] Within circumscribed boundaries, then, the earlier guides legislate for the recluse as an increasingly and acceptably social being.

Warren proposes that 'save for servants, the anchorite's confessor was his or her only routine contact with the world'.[75] This chapter has shown that this is not the ideological picture suggested by earlier medieval guidance and it is certainly not the case in the later guides. They illustrate a growing tension between the ideal of solitude and the emergence of even greater levels of acceptable reclusive sociability. The later medieval recluse is still admired for relative solitude, yet her increased involvement in the surrounding community is also celebrated, although Aelred's Bodley redaction retains some of Aelred's original advice about limiting social interaction, regulating speech and letter-writing and recommends the supervision of additional witnesses and the security measure of the veil during essential contact (*DII*, MS Bodley 423, pp. 2–3). Yet, surprisingly for guides that demonstrate an increased focus on acceptable social interaction (with the exception of the Bodley redaction), little specific mention is made of those individuals with whom even the earlier medieval writers permitted their recluses to interact. No mention is made of the anchorite's patron, beyond *Myrour*'s reference to 'her souereyns wyl' (*Myrour*, p. 13). Little mention is made of contact with religious, of a reclusive network, or of the servants which were so vital and yet so potentially problematic to some earlier guidance writers.

The later guides do return, however, to the subject of almsgiving. Material poverty continues to be an ideological aspiration: the livery which marks the recluse out as God's. The later writers still urge their recluses, as did their earlier medieval counterparts, to become neither housewives nor businesswomen. Yet, in the tradition of earlier medieval guidance, which, as has been noted above, does allow a measure of alms distribution, the later medieval recluse is encouraged to distribute practical aid. Rolle goes much further than his earlier medieval counterparts, legitimizing almsgiving as a method of regaining spiritual purity (*Form*, p. 20). Neither the Bodley redactor nor the *Speculum* author share Rolle's wholehearted approval but, still, they permit almsgiving.

In a passage not in *Speculum*, *Myrour*'s recluses are discouraged from aiding relatives and yet concurrently encouraged to look after them, something which *De institutione* and *Ancrene Wisse* condemn: '3e be moore hoolden to releue 3oure blood, 3if he be vertuous þan an-oþer strange persone, þou3 it be virtuous ant meritorie to releue hem bothe' (*Myrour*, pp. 6–7). Aelred's redactor reiterates his belief that a recluse should be so poor that she can have no surplus to distribute (*DII*, MS Bodley 423, p. 16). Yet, even he reluctantly concedes a correct method of gift giving via the servants (*DII*, MS Bodley 423, pp. 2–3).

The later medieval recluse actually finds God in 'mutua caritate fraterna' (*Speculum*, p. 90).[76] Hilton therefore advises her to welcome visitors:

> be soone redi with a good wille for to wite what his wille is. Be not daungerous, ne suffre him stonde longe for to abide thee ... And though thou be in preiere or in devocioun, that thee then-keth looth for to breeke of, for thee thenketh thou schuldest not leve God for mannys speche, me thenketh it is not so ... for yif thou be wise, thou schal not leve God, but ... fynde Hym and have Hym and see Him in thyn evene Cristene as wel as in praiere (*Scale I*, p. 124).

Anne Clark Bartlett argues that by this time, visitors were 'a matter of institutional protocol and vocational obligation'; the focus is 'on the community's need for the read-er's spiritual instruction, rather than on [the recluse's] ... need for protection'.[77] Rolle encourages the recluse to teach those that come to the reclusorium and Hilton is more emphatic: 'as moche as thou conceyvest that schulde profite thyn evene Cristene goostli, mai thou seie yif thou can and he wil take it' (*Scale I*, p. 125). While all guidance writers agree that it is still unacceptable for a recluse to preach to or teach priests, even here Hilton offers a caveat: 'it falleth not to thee for to teche a preest, *but in nede*' (*Scale I*, p. 125). This sets a new precedent for the guidance tradition's constructions of acceptable reclusive sociability.[78] Fiona Somerset acknowledges similar contemporary conces-sions, in terms of the Lollard preacher Walter Brut, tried for heresy from 1391–3. Brut concedes 'that women, while capable of performing the offices of priesthood, should not do so when there are men available', yet asserts 'that women *have* stepped in as substitutes ... where male priests have not performed [their preaching adequately]'.[79] Rolle and Hilton do not construct their female anchorites as spiritually equal to men, but they do permit them to communicate spiritual precepts to others. They construct a later medieval recluse who can potentially disseminate anchoritic ideology and contempla-tive theology into the surrounding community.

Later medieval guidance's construction of the recluse as emergently social grows out of the (admittedly more reluctant) earlier medieval negotiations of acceptable soci-ability explored above; it is not a sharp departure from it. The later guides simply encourage the recluse more than their earlier counterparts did to continue to see herself as part of the world she has rejected. Hilton echoes Aelred's and *Ancrene Wisse*'s earlier legislation for prayerful intercession: 'though thu be stoken in an hous with thi bodi, nevthelees in thyn herte, where the stide of love is, thou schulde mow have part of siche love to thyn even Cristen' (*Scale I*, p. 110). This is a natural progression from the earlier guides' aforementioned encouragement of the recluse's intercessionary prayers, not a rejection of it. By now, that prayer's supplicatory tone has altered from humble request to emphatic demand: 'Pro his omnibus inclusus frequencius *viscera miseri-cordis Dei* pulsabit gemitibus, lacrimis exorabit et suspiriis provocabit misericordiam, graciam et succursum' (*Speculum*, p. 112).[80] Even Aelred's redactor now envisages his far more insistent intercessionary recluse 'wailyng and wepynge' (*DII*, MS Bodley 423, p. 17) as she beseeches God's aid on behalf of the world outside her window.

Yet the later guides construct the vocation as both increasingly sociable and increasingly contemplative. This is the paradox: the cell, textually speaking, is constructed as the focal point for a community that is to be made welcome there, yet it houses an occupant whose primary aim is to leave the world utterly behind, through contemplative fusion with God. There is a tension between these two seemingly incompatible positions and the later guides are demonstrative of the transition between them. This is perfectly encapsulated in Rolle's list of these social impulses as sins of the heart:

> fleishly affeccioun ... ioy in any mannys ilfare, sorowe in har welfare ... despit of pouer or of synful men ... sorow of þe world ... loue to plese men, dred to displese ham ... shame with pouer frendes, pride of ryche kyn (*Form*, p. 11).

and his concurrent conception of social involvement as spiritual purification:

> The thynges þat clenseth vs ... ben þre ... sorowe of hert ayeyns þe synnes of thoght ... shrift of mouth agayn þe syn of mouth ... satisfaccioun, þat hath þre parties, fastynge, prier, and almysdede; nat only to gyf pouer men met or drynke, bot for to foryeve ham ... and enfourme ham how þei shal do þat ben in poynt to perisshe (*Form*, p. 13).

Love both widens and narrows the divide between anchoritic solitude and sociability. Later guidance deliberately brings the outside world not only into the mind, but into the cell of its recluse and yet it envisages her more tightly bound to God through a sophisticated contemplative practice that inevitably excludes others. Love of God in contemplation demands the recluse's distance from the community, but love of God in mankind binds her more closely to it.

Safeguarding solitude: demonizing anchoritic sociability

Earlier anchoritic guidance deliberately sets the unattainable standard of total isolation as an ideal against which the recluse will find herself wanting. This is part of a wider rhetorical strategy intended to encourage the recluse to aspire continually to greater things, counting her best actions as inadequate and herself in consequent need of divine grace (and, of course, the anchoritic guidance writer's advice). Even though the earlier guides legislate for acceptable sociability, they concurrently condemn it, privileging anchoritic solitude by vivifying its allegedly widespread contemporary abuse. Earlier guidance qualifies this by claiming that its own readership knows nothing of such sin. Nonetheless, Anselm warns his women against admitting sinful notions into their heads in the first place, judging, as do all the earlier guidance writers, that mental rumination occasions active transgression (Anselm, 'Letter 414', vol. 5, p. 361).[81] He exhorts them: 'Nolite igitur considerare tantum quid faciatis, sed quid velitis ... quae sit voluntas vestra' (Anselm, 'Letter 414', vol. 5, p. 360).[82] The recluse is to second-guess herself continually, and the rhetoric of social corruption is intended to horrify her, to unsettle her in every respect, so that she will cleave even more closely to God in the geographical permanency of her enclosure and its facilitation of comparative solitude. The demonization of anchoritic sociability, therefore, is intended to safeguard comparative solitude.

Goscelin consequently devotes substantial space to the chilling story of St Alexander, who, in the privacy of his rural cell, sexually abuses the girl whom the Devil brings to him as a baby to raise (*Liber*, pp. 103–6).[83] Aelred, as a Cistercian, evinces similar (and predictable) mistrust of eremitism's paradoxical freedoms.[84] By the end of his life, his own coenobitism was to assume an eremitic cast, yet in this guide he constructs anchoritic solitude as an excellent refuge for corruption, constructing the anchorhold (as do most earlier writers) as uniquely vulnerable precisely because of its comparative secrecy. His condemnation of masturbation as a solitary vice is founded on the argument that even in solitude 'uehementior aestus carnem concutiens, uoluntatem sibi subdiderit, et rapuerit membra' (*DII*, p. 651).[85] His guide opens with dire warnings about the supposed need for increasingly strict social segregation: 'Illi uero qui nec hoc sibi securum, propter solitudinis libertatem et uagandi potestatem, arbitrabantur, includi potius et intra cellulam obstruso exitu contineri tutius aestimabant' (*DII*, pp. 637–8).[86] Fond also of the rhetoric of the alleged contemporary abuse of anchoritism, *Ancrene Wisse* concludes: 'sum unseli ancre: went into hole of ancre-hus to bifule þet stude, ant don dearnluker þrin fleschliche fulðen þen ha mahte 3ef ha were amidde þe worlde' (*AW*, Corpus, pp. 51–2).[87] It surmises: 'hwa haueð mare eise to don hire cweadschipes þen þe false ancre?' (*AW*, Corpus, p. 52).[88]

Corrupt reclusive sociability is constructed by earlier guidance as so marked by the thirteenth century that *Ancrene Wisse* cites a proverbial saying: 'From mulne ant from chepinge, from smiððe ant from ancre-hus me tidinge bringeð' (*AW*, Corpus, p. 36).[89] The proverb is glossed: 'Wat Crist, þis is a sari sahe, þet ancre-hus, þet schulde beon anlukest stude of alle, schal beon ifeiet to þe ilke þreo studen þet meast is in of chaffle' (*AW*, Corpus, p. 36).[90] The early guides depict a morally degenerate anchorhold, beseiged by gossips, widows, cuckolding wives, whores and amorous men (*DII*, p. 638).[91] This is sadly bemoaned: 'We hit habbeð – weilawei! – iherd of inohe' (*AW*, Corpus, p. 26).[92] The recluse is warned to remain ever vigilant, for the 'totilde ancre … þe beakeð eauer utward as untohe brid i cage' will be dragged from the anchorhold by the 'þe cat of helle' (*AW*, Corpus, p. 40).[93] Even interaction with children and animals is constructed as potentially dangerous in this context. Goscelin simply advises Eve to keep no creatures: 'Non cata, non altilia, non bestiola, non omnis irrationabilis anima sit tibi condomestica, nec tua exinaniant tempora auolantia' (*Liber*, p. 80).[94]

Later revisions of the lost original of *Ancrene Wisse* expand significantly on the apparent deterioration of earlier medieval reclusive spirituality: 'Þe gastelich lif bigunnen i þe Hali Gast beoð bicumene al fleschliche – lahinde, lihte ilatet … bittre ant attrie wið heorte tobollen' (*AW*, Corpus, p. 43).[95] The anchorhold is threatened by external as well as internal forces which cast the recluse as a captive target (*AW*, Corpus, p. 63).[96] For this reason Eve is 'uitulam cum canibus demoniacis inclusam' (*Liber*, p. 49).[97] Aelred describes those who play upon the recluse's powerlessness to flee (*DII*, pp. 638–40).[98] *Ancrene Wisse* depicts the surrounding churchyard as a hive of activity, envisaging this hypothetical confession from a non-reclusive onlooker: 'Ich … e[o]de o ríng i chirch3ard; biheold hit … spec þus … biuoren [religiuse], in ancre-hus' (*AW*, Corpus, p. 121).[99] It reminds its recluses that some visitors will deliberately seek them out precisely because of the strange beauty of their inviolability.[100] Purity is shown to call corruption forth.

Goscelin argues that the death of salvation enters 'per fenestras nostras' (*Liber*, p. 77), that is, by our eyes, because knowledge of the world enters thereby.[101] This is a train of thought much developed by Aelred and the *Ancrene Wisse* author. *Ancrene Wisse* states: 'al þe wa þet nu is, ant eauer 3ete wes, ant eauer schal iwurðen, al com of sihðe' (*AW*, Corpus, p. 21).[102] These arguments stem from an ancient tradition which reinforces the pre-eminence of sight in theological constructions of sensory danger. Christopher M. Woolgar links this to 'the notion that there was direct contact, effectively touch, between the seen and the seer', a sensory relationship with grave 'moral or spiritual consequences'.[103] This is certainly echoed in earlier guidance, which renders the eyes as vulnerable as the windows of the cell itself, for only they separate the recluse from the world's iniquity.[104] *Ancrene Wisse* instances numerous biblical women who have, through sight, caused humanity's downfall, fashioning a chain of transgressive females beginning with Eve and ending with the recluse. The white cross of *Ancrene Wisse*'s anchorhold window coverings signals both the problem (inherent female sinfulness) and its solution (the recluse's sensory segregation for the world's sake as much as for her own). To preserve the safety of all, the 'windows' of the soul (the five senses) must be similarly shut and secured. Part II of *Ancrene Wisse* is entirely devoted to showing the recluse how to shut down her senses to secure her solitude: 'Ne þunche hire neauer wunder, 3ef ha nis muchel ane, þah he hire schunie – ant swa ane þet ha putte euch worldlich þrung, ant euch nurð eorðlich, ut of hire heorte, for heo is Godes chambre' (*AW*, Corpus, p. 36).[105] In terms which foreshadow these words and those of Aelred, too, Goscelin warns Eve: 'Celle, lingue et aurium fenestre a fabulis et uaniloquiis ... sint obserate' (*Liber*, p. 80).[106]

Since later guidance encourages much higher levels of acceptable interaction, its rhetorically constructed fears of transgressive sociability are, in contrast with earlier guides, heavily minimized. Sociability is certainly still cast as dangerous, if it takes the recluse beyond the confines of the cell into 'patria contingentes' and 'varias fantasias' (*Speculum*, p. 70).[107] Hilton warns against crowding the contemplative mind with 'the folk of thy worldeli thoughtes' (*Scale I*, p. 88). The earlier medieval image of the garrulous old rumour monger, central to Aelred's guide, is retained in the Bodley redaction, although heavily condensed (*DII*, MS Bodley 423, pp. 1–2). Neither Rolle nor Hilton use this image explicitly, but it is adapted in *Myrour* and *Speculum* to include male as well as female gossips (*Speculum*, p. 70).[108] It is also adapted to signal anxieties about anchoritism's geographical demographics; configuring urban, not rural, corruption. Earlier medieval guides construct the corrupt cell as a largely rural phenomenon, but *Speculum* and *Myrour* construct a new kind of recluse: the urban degenerate.[109] It is her cell, rather than that of her rural counterpart, which is now under fire. These same anxieties also motivate the *Speculum* author and the *Myrour* translator's distrust of 'quibusdam nostri temporis inclusis, non in heremo sed in urbe ... largas elemosinas recipiant unde magnam familiam retineant, consanguineos at amicos ... iuvent et promoveant' (*Speculum*, p. 70).[110] This is part of a wider later medieval rhetorical tendency to construct urbanization as vice.[111] If, ideologically, the anchorhold has moved into the corrupt urban world, then, this later medieval guide and its translation suggest, rhetorically speaking, that the corrupt urban world has moved into the anchorhold.

Hilton writes that sinful social contact damages the boundaries of enclosure and solitude, constructing its threat, as did earlier medieval guidance, in terms of the senses. A neighbour may, for example, 'touch' the recluse with angry speech (*Scale I*, p. 109). In terms which echo Goscelin's almost word for word and which are also highly allusive of *Ancrene Wisse*, he declares: 'Deeth cometh in bi oure wyndowes ... oure fyve wittes, bi the whiche oure soule gooth out from himsilf and sicheth his delite and his feedynge in ertheli thynges' (*Scale I*, p. 120). Hilton also uses wider pollution metaphor, of the 'stinkynge welle' (*Scale I*, p. 93), to construct the insidious danger of corrupt social forces. Even if its streams (the seven deadly sins manifested in social contact) are stopped, the well's source (the anchorite) remains corrupt unless cleansed. Hilton reminds the recluse that 'comenynge with thyn evene Cristene is not moche agens thee, but helpith thee sumtyme *yif thou worche visili*' (*Scale I*, p. 124).[112] This admonition to engage in increased sociability in the right way demonstrates the continued implication, derived from earlier guidance, that the recluse requires protection not just from others but from herself. Yet, this is not done for the same reasons. The earlier and later guides draw different conclusions about exactly why transgressive reclusive social contact is dangerous. They are motivated by different fears. Earlier guidance, as the remainder of this chapter will demonstrate, is motivated by sexual anxieties. Later guidance demonstrates a divide between those guidance writers who still fear the loss of reclusive chastity and those, notably Rolle and Hilton, who fear the loss of reclusive spiritual orthodoxy far more.[113]

Anchoritic sociability and chastity

Earlier medieval guides fear transgressive social interaction because of the risk it carries of sexual misconduct. Chastity, the third vital anchoritic ideal upon which the vocation is ideologically founded, is cast in earlier guidance in a mutually referential relationship with the ideals of enclosure and solitude; breakdown in one means the breakdown of all. Utter collapse is shown to spring, potentially, from one seemingly innocent sociable impulse. Unlike enclosure and solitude, however, the earlier guides are clear: chastity is not open to negotiation or qualification. It must remain absolute in theory and in practice.

Otter argues that Goscelin is 'unlike his successors ... only marginally interested in the anchoress's ... untouched and unseen body'.[114] Curiously, although he exhibits less anxiety about Eve's chastity, he, of all guidance writers, has the most to prove. To protest Eve's purity is to protest his own. To exhort her to protect her continued virginity is to proclaim their relationship's innocence. It is not the case therefore that, as Hollis argues, Goscelin 'does not ... exhort [Eve] ... to defend' it.[115] He wants her to die a virgin (*Liber*, p. 99).[116] Yet his protestations are at odds with the erotically charged description of the *coup de foudre* of Eve's formal profession: 'Tamen te tolerabiliter forinsecus tantum in spe bona Christi dilexi' (*Liber*, p. 28)[117] changes to: 'pignus fidei diuine cum sacrata ueste induisti ... altius uiscera me percussere ... magis accenderunt uota mea' (*Liber*, p. 28).[118] For all Goscelin's attempts here to clothe the moment, literally and metaphorically, in spiritual discourse, we recognize, as Otter notes, 'perhaps better than he could, his half-acknowledged sexual desire' (Otter, pp. 12–13).

Despite his comparative lack of anxiety about Eve's ability to remain a virgin, Goscelin's depictions of sexuality, which focus on incest, rape and prostitution, are darker than those of his successors. His guide constructs the female body as expendable, violatable and wholly consumable in God's service. This is clear from the violence of the aforementioned tale of St Alexander (*Liber*, p. 104).[119] The close of the tale sees its menfolk appropriating this nameless girl's body for God's purposes. Rapist, king and guidance writer together interpret the violated female form as an emblem of God's power to direct men's spiritual destiny. Robert Mills proposes that tales of such martyred virgin bodies provide the strongest possible codification of spiritual 'order and invincibility', derived from 'the juxtaposition of violence and virginal impermeability'.[120] In this terrifying context, Eve can only hope that God will permit her to stay a virgin.

For the *Liber* reads God's will as more savage than any other earlier guide: 'multe, uolentes perseuerare, nec precibus id obtinuere, multe, nolentes, aut flagellis aut disciplina sunt seruate' (*Liber*, p. 97).[121] It argues that God will strip proud, thoughtless, chaste females of both beauty and chastity, by force (*Liber*, pp. 95–6).[122] God's will: 'Turbat et confundit ... Ruit uirgo, surgit meretrix, uiolatur pudica, castificatur prostituta' (*Liber*, p. 93).[123] In terms that foreshadow Aelred's, Goscelin writes of 'infirmitate carnis nostre', 'limum nostrum et carnem nostram' and 'fertur ad precipitia' into which Eve may be driven by 'fornicationem, immunditiam, luxuriam' (*Liber*, pp. 52, 54, 56).[124] Anselm writes similarly that: 'Secundum carnem enim ambulare est: carni voluntate concordare' (Anselm, 'Letter 414', vol. 5, p. 361).[125] Consequently: 'edomanda carnalia desideria, excidenda uitiorum capita' (*Liber*, p. 51).[126] Goscelin paraphrases St Ambrose's *De Virginibus*: 'melius est ... mori martyrem' than 'uiuere scortum' (*Liber*, p. 98). He continues: 'O grauior metus stupratoris quam tortoris, o maiora discrimina pudicitie quam uite!' (*Liber*, p. 99).[127]

Aelred and the *Ancrene Wisse* author exhibit greater anxiety than Goscelin about their recluses' ability to remain pure.[128] Sarah Salih concludes: 'it is hard to imagine how [*Ancrene Wisse*] ... could be any more erotically preoccupied'.[129] Gunn is right to argue that some of its sexualized material is intended for a wider (lay) audience and that the author's 'assumption of sexual purity on the part of the anchoresses was of great importance'.[130] Yet, this guidance writer nonetheless must anticipate that his recluses will reflect on this material. Aelred regards desire as the most disruptive worldly force and considers waging war against the flesh to be the vocation's central purpose: 'Virginitas aurum est, cella fornax, conflator diabolus, ignis tentatio' (*DII*, p. 650).[131] His guide is explicit in its denunciation of heterosexual and homosexual licentiousness. Of same-sex desire, he argues: 'Nec sic hoc dictum aestimes, quasi non uir sine muliere, aut mulier sine uiro possit foedari, cum detestandum illud scelus quo uir in uirum, uel femina furit in feminam, omnibus flagitiis damnabilius iudicetur' (*DII*, p. 651).[132] He also condemns wet dreams and masturbation and, in a passage that rejects arrangements like those of Eve and Hervé, reduces syneisaktism, the practice of chaste co-habitation amongst those devoted to lives of sexual purity, to sordidity:

> Vnde non parum pudet quorumdam impudentiae, qui cum in sordibus senuerint, nec sic suspectarum personarum uolunt carere consortio. Cum quibus quod dictu nefas est eodem lectulo cubantes, inter amplexus et oscula de sua castitate se dicunt esse securos ... Videat tamen utrum uerum dicat an mentiatur inquitas sibi, et dum nititur uelare unum, duplex in se prodat flagitium (*DII*, p. 654).[133]

Barratt suggests that the devotion of four chapters to sexuality is 'inappropriate and unnecessary for a woman in her sixties'.[134] Yet this guidance is given in the context of the long-term struggle against sexual desire of 'a certain monk' that some, notably

MacPherson, have speculated may be Aelred himself.[135] Aelred writes: 'Nemo se palpet
... nunquam ab adolescentibus, sine magna cordis contritione at carnis afflictione
castitas conquiritur uel seruatur, quae plerumque in aegris uel senibus periclitatur' (DII,
p. 653).[136] Moreover, the guidance tradition casts desire as a threat to the recluse at any
age and Aelred writes also for others who surround his sister. Anke Bernau argues for a
communal claim to virginity at this time, citing the disgraced nun of Watton, forced by
her community to castrate her lover and to cram his severed genitals into her mouth: a
horrific distortion of the penetration which preceded her condemnation.[137] She must do
this precisely because, Bernau argues, the loss of the individual's virginity is 'understood by the other[s] ... as well as by Aelred ... as a communal affront and crime',
requiring communally witnessed retribution.[138] Ancrene Wisse's personification of
woman as a pit into which the hapless male may fall (AW, Nero, p. 25) also has a
communal significance.[139] The conclusion that: 'þu unhelest þesne put þu þat dest eni
þing hwar of þet mon is fleschsliche ivonded ofðe. þauh þu hit nute nout dred þesne dom
swuð' (AW, Nero, p. 25) is truly intended to terrify, for it renders man's fall entirely
woman's responsibility and also implies that any breakdown in reclusive chastity has
communal consequences, just as it did for Watton's coenobitic community.[140] If 'Cella
vertitur in prostibulum' (DII, p. 638),[141] then, as Karma Lochrie argues: 'The sealed
body ... becomes the sign not only of virginity but of the integritas of all'.[142]

Christ is the ultimate chaste role model of earlier anchoritic guidance. He is 'uirginis
uiginitas', at the centre of a virginal trinity of Mary, Christ and John: 'iuxta crucem tres
uirgines ... trina uirginitas' (Liber, p. 31).[143] Phyllis G. Jestice suggests that 'In the early
Middle Ages, there is little emphasis on the life and activities of Christ ... little stress on
Jesus' human[ity]'.[144] Yet Goscelin vivifies the dying Jesus commending his mother to
John's care because of the virginity which rendered him his favourite disciple (Liber,
p. 31).[145] Aelred focuses chiefly on virginity, but Goscelin's guide also praises formerly
sexualised females, again by virtue of their intimate bond with Christ. He assures Eve:
'celibes et coniugati ... omnes saluari ... uirgo genuit, uidua baiulauit ... meretrix
presum[p]sit, pedes ... lauit' (Liber, p. 101).[146] This willingness to exalt the formerly
sexual widow sets his guide apart from Aelred's. Its most surprising argument is that a
widow can join the virgins in heaven if she seeks virginal chastity, albeit after suffering
the wounds of sexual activity. John Chrystosom's teaching on Mary Magdalene corrob-
orates this: 'Inuenit meretricem et uirginibus coequauit' (Liber, p. 98).[147] Ancrene Wisse
also invests those recluses who choose chaste cleanness after their virginity's destruction, with a spiritual valence, addressing itself to virgin and non-virgin alike, provided
that both have now renounced sexual intimacy (AW, Corpus, pp. 63–4).[148]

The later guides demonstrate a split in their conception of how grave a threat sexualized transgression is to the vocation in ideological terms. The Bodley redaction and
Speculum (and its translation Myrour) express continued concern about anchoritic chastity, while Rolle and Hilton focus on it very little. It would be logical to expect all later
medieval guidance to demonstrate even greater anxiety about anchoritic chastity, since
it permits increased social interaction. Yet, the later guides, as a group, focus upon sexualized transgression far less than their earlier counterparts.

Nonetheless, the Bodley redaction continues Aelred's obsessive sexualized focus,
still regarding the five senses as inevitable pathways to sexualized sin and retaining
Aelred's notion of the gradual descent into concupiscence, triggered by one seemingly

innocent gesture. Aelred's image of the earlier medieval anchorhold as brothel is retained and the redaction continues to link food with sexual desire and idleness with lust (*DII*, MS Bodley 423, pp. 8, 6). Aelred's assumption that the recluse will be, not just chaste, but a virgin, persists. The cell remains the crucible in which the gold of reclusive 'maydenhood' is refined (*DII*, MS Bodley 423, p. 10). The anchorhold's iconography continues to reinforce virginity and there is an increased focus on Christ as bridegroom, which casts enclosure as 'weddynge days ... praienge after ... thy loue and thy louyer' (*DII*, MS Bodley 423, p. 8). Sexual sin continues, frequently, to be gendered feminine in the Bodley redaction and also in *Speculum* and *Myrour*. In the tradition of earlier guidance, numerous anti-feminist examples of transgressive women are given (*Speculum*, pp. 77–8).[149] Yet the Bodley redaction concurrently increases the number of virtuous women used as positive reclusive role models (*DII*, MS Bodley 423, p. 11) and the impression is consequently stronger in the redaction of Aelred's text that some women are capable of great, chaste virtue.

At times, *Speculum* and *Myrour* go beyond the Bodley redactor, who issues general warnings about sexual transgression (*DII*, MS Bodley 423, pp. 10, 12) rather than Aelred's original explicit rejections of homosexuality and masturbation, syneisaktism and wet dreams. While the Bodley redaction maintains a new silence on these subjects, both *Myrour* and *Speculum* comment specifically on masturbation, characterizing it as a sin to which solitaries are particularly susceptible because of their seclusion (*Myrour*, p. 14).[150] Referred to in *Speculum* as 'mollicies' (*Speculum*, p. 79) and as 'luxurie species contra naturam' (*Speculum*, p. 79),[151] *Myrour* preserves the Latin 'molicies' (*Myrour*, p. 14), which could potentially preserve the modesty of a vernacular audience ignorant of its meaning. Although etymologically the links are groundless, John Boswell argues for a similarity between the terms for masturbation, 'mollitia' or 'mollicies', and those for sodomy, 'mollis' meaning 'soft' or 'effeminate', arguing for their synonymity in medieval writing.[152] There is no reason to read fear of sodomy into *Speculum* and *Myrour*, however; indeed Powell Harley proposes that the translator's deliberate omission of the Latin gloss: 'ubi dicit quod "neque molles, neque masculorum concubitores regnum Dei possidebunt"' (*Speculum*, pp. 79–80), is precisely intended to avoid confusion between them.[153] Nonetheless, it is clear that some later medieval guides still see the anchorhold as a potential place of sexualized danger. *Speculum* recalls *Ancrene Wisse* in conclusions that: 'Ulterius adhuc auditus suggerit de spurciciis peccati et illecebris quicquid audit ... verba detraccionis et invidie' (*Speculum*, p. 79).[154] The wider world is still characterized as sexually lax: 'O felix auris hominis, que sic prudenter disponitur quod contra voces illicitas non aperitur, contra voluptuosas seculi melodias clauditur' (*Speculum*, p. 79).[155]

In contrast, Rolle and Hilton write almost nothing about sexual transgression and sociability. They prefer to explore sin in general and regard a breakdown in any virtue as symptomatic of a wider hypocritical mindset. Rolle is simply concerned lest anchoritism's solitude afford his recluse the opportunity to seem virtuous even if she is generally corrupt: 'whate wrechednesse hit is for to have þe name and þe habite of holynesse and be nat so, bot couer pride, wreth, or envy vndre þe cloþes of Cristes childhode' (*Form*, p. 5). Hilton, too, focuses on virtue and vice in general and seeks to prevent the reclusive counterfeit of the appearance of holiness. Clothing metaphor is used to illustrate general duplicity, rather than the nuptial chastity of earlier guidance such as Aelred's. In Rolle's guide, we see the most marked departure from the earlier medieval anticipation of inevitable feminine sexualized transgression, for he does not suggest that women are naturally predisposed to sexual sin, but rather that all mankind is sinful and in need of protection and correction.

It is only as a reflection of the diseased nature of the contemplative relationship between recluse and God that sexual transgression alarms these two later guidance writers. The later medieval anchorhold houses, not a recluse who disrupts her spiritual practice to gossip with women of easy virtue, but one who suspends her contemplation to impart spiritual and material guidance to those that seek her wisdom. She is a figure of potential spiritual authority, not of sexual laxity. This move on the part of two later guidance writers, away from an earlier medieval focus on reclusive sexualized sin and towards a focus on mankind's general culpability, alongside the wider, general move of all the later medieval guidance writers (apart from the Bodley redactor) towards the recluse as even more acceptably social, suggests that the ideology of the vocation is in transition. The book has thus far focused on the English anchoritic guidance tradition in isolation. In so doing it has established the ideological foundations of the vocation as grounded in the four key ideals of enclosure, solitude, chastity and orthodoxy. It now moves, in part II, to contextualise insular anchoritic theological practice, notably the practices of asceticism and contemplative experience, within Christian theologies of wider Medieval Europe. It seeks, thereby, to determine the extent to which transitional, anchoritic ideology is in sync with the theological transitions of the wider medieval world.

II

Anchoritic Spirituality in Context:
English Anchoritism and the Wider Medieval World

4

Anchoritism and Asceticism[1]

The history of asceticism

Definitions of asceticism are seldom attempted by modern scholars. Henry Chadwick does not define it in his survey of the history of ascetical ideals.[2] Conrad Leyser does not gloss it in his survey volume *Authority and Asceticism from Augustine to Gregory the Great*, but instead conflates 'ascetic', 'mystic' and 'religious' and synonymizes the 'ascetic' with the 'monastic movement'.[3] Such synonymizations are common.[4] The absence of ascetical definition results in extremely broad contemporary applications of the term, often too inclusive to be useful.[5] These may focus on austerity and abstemiousness, but can obscure, through ambiguity, the precise nature of medieval asceticism, which the anchoritic guides reveal as a rigorous set of practices; a circumscribed form of devotional worship commanding a specialized vocabulary. In an age where violence was comparatively commonplace, medieval asceticism is best understood, not as the church's legitimization of self-harm or punishment, but as an intellectualized and disciplined devotional system intended to sublimate bodily desires to spiritual purpose.[6] Asceticism uses the body to 'get at' the soul or, rather, it uses the body to reveal the state of an ascetic's spiritual health and improve it. Its purificatory power ultimately remains an expression of God's strength, however, not mankind's.

Medieval writing does not imply that its society reads every aspect of the monastic life as ascetic, or any type of medieval penitential activity, including the penance which follows confession, as ascetical in nature, simply because they involve pain and deprivation. The anchoritic guides understand the term 'ascetic' to refer to an individual who engages in mortificatory and deprivatory practices for the purpose of regaining spiritual purity. This chapter therefore does not use the term 'ascetic' to denote any kind of religious, but recognizes a distinction between the ascetical life and the monastic life. The latter is held to be ascetical only when its coenobites are themselves engaged in ascetic practices. The ascetical directives, in particular of earlier anchoritic guidance, may well be made against a backdrop of generally punitive imagery. The frequently brutal register of earlier guidance may well render suffering a central tenet of the Christian life as a whole and certainly synonymizes anchoritism and suffering. Aelred constructs Christian suffering in all its gruesomeness using an extended linen-production metaphor which depicts starkly the maceration, pounding and threshing of the cloth (*DII*, p. 658).[7] *Ancrene Wisse* argues, of anchoritism specifically: 'Al is penitence, ant strong penitence, þet 3e eauer dreheð … Al … þet 3e þolieð, is ow martirdom i se derf ordre, for 3e beoð niht ant dei upo Godes rode' (*AW*, Corpus, p. 132).[8] In wider explorations of confession, this guide uses an image derived from Psalms 101.7, to liken the recluse to a pelican who slaughters her young (i.e. her good works) and revives them through blood drawn from her own breast (*AW*, Corpus, p. 48).[9] Goscelin uses this same image but, extraordinarily for the guidance tradition, to construct not the recluse's torment, but his own private sorrow, rendering vivid thereby the slaughtered creativity of this guidance writer (*Liber*, p. 27).[10] Yet, all this is not the stuff of ascetic practice. The guides deliberately distinguish asceticism from general suffering, from general anchoritic suffering and from penitential (i.e. penance-driven) pain, no matter how graphically it depicts all of these in their shared experience of affliction. They construct penance as a punishment motivated by sin, one which expiates transgression. They construct asceticism as a pre-emptive method of avoiding that sin. Otter argues for this as a creative and performative process, for ascetics: 'do not only deprive themselves ... they also create ... they actively stage and enact their way of being in the world'.[11] The guides construct anchoritic asceticism as a positive transformative process which creates precisely because it destroys, thereby cleansing the spirit through its purification of the flesh. Asceticism offers the recluse the means of reconstructing the unity between God and mankind shattered in the Fall; thereby transforming her body from a state of sin to the site of potential purity.

Asceticism is not, however, specifically Christian, medieval or eremitic in origin. Etymologically the term is derived from the Greek adjective ἀσκητικός (asketikos), from the noun ἄσκησις or askesis, meaning 'exercise, training or practice'.[12] From ancient times, men and women chose asceticism as a path to virtue and inner strength. Its influence extended from the Pythagoreans to Pachomius, from Sufi mysticism to Buddhist withdrawal. Yet, Christianity particularly embraced this notion of sanctity proven upon the body. The medieval writings to be explored in the remainder of this chapter all approve of asceticism as a form of spiritual training; a method of acquiring and exercising the qualities essential in a pious Christian. Although actives can espouse asceticism, these writings construct professional contemplatives as inherently ascetically predisposed. Eremitic asceticism is acknowledged as particularly sophisticated. Its capability to tolerate its harshest forms is rooted in the desert solitude of the early Christian ascetics of Egypt and Syria, whose extraordinary ascetical experiences are recorded in the *Vitas Patrum*. Anchoritic guides focus particularly upon St Antony, reputedly the first anchorite, an Egyptian landlord who renounces the world to dwell alone in the desert. Desert ascetics are, as C. Leyser puts it, part of an ascetical 'narrative of continuity' into which every Christian can locate themselves, but in which anchorites can regard themselves (in the earlier medieval period especially) as high achievers.[13] Anchoritic guidance encourages the recluse seeking to fulfil the vocation's increasingly contemplative goals to use asceticism as a vital tool in the fight to maintain relative spiritual purity; asceticism is shown to facilitate contemplation.

Traditionally, two main ascetical approaches exist: one passive, one aggressive.[14] Passive practices involve renunciation or deprivation, for example, of food, sexual desire or sleep. Aggressive asceticism involves the use of an external force upon the body, or the ingestion of a noxious substance. Both approaches are accounted useless unless accompanied by the correct devotional mindset. Jerome Kroll and Bernard Bachrach, in their study of the psychology of medieval asceticism, argue: 'When we hurt ourselves ... we are doing more than just causing pain, or fulfilling some symbolic function of cultural significance. We are altering our brain state in significant ways'.[15]

One ensuing mental alteration, greatly to be feared, is, as this chapter will show, the production of ascetical spiritual arrogance, derived from an ability to withstand harsh ascetical acts. From the earliest times, therefore, the notion of discretion or ascetical moderation is debated. Giles Constable argues that from the time of St Basil, St Benedict, Daniel the Stylite and Gregory of Tours, the importance of ascetical moderation is understood.[16] Guidance on discretion is woven into spiritual legislation from the time of the Persian councils of the late fifth century onwards.[17] The early discretionary movement is not intended to be anti-ascetical, but rather promotes asceticism, crucially, within a framework of supervision. Much emphasis is placed upon the individual's responsibility to recognize and remain within their own capabilities. The *Vitas Patrum*, for example, contain references to Abba John who sought the accomplishments of an angel but had to learn to act like a man.[18]

Medieval asceticism derives much of its authority from three patristic writers, all of whom believed the body had a vital role to play in devotional piety: Augustine of Hippo (*c*.354–*c*.430), John Cassian (*c*.360–*c*.435) and Jerome (*c*.347–*c*.419). Cassian's *De institutis coenobiorum* and *Collationes* promote the authority of the desert solitaries (the latter text is a hypothetical conversation with the desert fathers). His work influences the Rule of St Benedict, which in turn plays an important part in shaping medieval ascetical attitudes. Cassian constructs asceticism as a highly technical, uniform and disciplined undertaking involving both body and mind. It eschews inadequacy and excess alike. He rewrites the drive of the desert fathers, so that the community appears to renounce the ascetic rather than vice versa.[19] In this way he fosters notions of an ascetical elite and strengthens public perceptions of accomplished eremitic asceticism. His *Collationes* (Book II, Chapter 23) actually supports moderation: 'quotidianam panis refectionem quotidiana comitetur esuries, in uno eodemque statu animam pariter corpusque conservans; nec jejunii fatigatione concidere, nec gravari mentem saturitate permittens'.[20] Yet, Cassian's work also calls for a return to advanced forms of asceticism and is therefore inevitably appropriated by those medieval writers who wish to justify ascetical severity. This renders him an obvious choice for earlier anchoritic guidance writers intrigued by the possibilities asceticism holds for their accomplished recluses.

Augustine of Hippo's ascetical teachings also influence medieval thought, although, unlike Cassian, Augustine favours a communal life of charity and poverty and links solitude and dangerous ascetical extremes together. He concludes that the renunciations of the desert solitaries are worthy of admiration not emulation. This finds widespread support amongst medieval writers who believe in the potential of asceticism, but concurrently fear its tendency to foster an elitism which breeds division and dissent. Yet, Augustine constructs asceticism as a source of strength, not debilitation, in *De Doctrina Christiana*, Book I, Chapter 24.[21] He writes also in his *Confessiones*, Book 10, Chapter 31: 'et quotidianum bellum gero in jejuniis, saepius in servitutem redigens corpus meum [I Cor. 9: 27]; et dolores mei voluptate pelluntur. Nam fames et sitis quidam dolores sunt; urunt, et sicut febris necant'.[22] His support for moderation clearly does not erode his belief in the need for asceticism. Yet, since he argues vehemently against flesh-hatred, his work attracts those who seek an authority for increased ascetical discretion.

Jerome also advocates ascetical moderation, arguing that the adequately nourished body fights temptation more securely.[23] The second book of *Ad Jovinium* states: 'Adesse ergo debet ratio, ut tales ac tantas sumamus escas, quibus non oneretur corpus, nec libertas animae praegravetur; quia et comedendum est, et deambulandum, et dorm-iendum, et digerendum'.[24] The Benedictine Rule displays a similar concern about asceticism's divisive nature, fearing eremitism's extremism, which, in terms reminis-cent of Augustine, it constructs as worthy of admiration and not emulation.[25] Yet, the Rule's ascetical perspective is ambiguous, not anti-ascetical; much is left to the indi-vidual's discretion. It therefore lends itself to the manifold monastic interpretations made of it later by various religious orders. All of its ascetic expositions, for example those entitled 'Abnegare semetipsum sibi ut sequatur Christum', 'Corpus castigare' and 'ieiunium amare' (all subheadings from Chapter 4, 'Quae sunt instrumenta bonorum operum'), are open to different degrees of interpretation.[26] The Rule demonstrates a familiarity with the language of suffering and trades in ascetical imagery. For instance, Chapter 30, 'De pueris minori aetate, qualiter corripiantur', argues: 'aut ieiuniis nimiis affligantur aut acris verberibus coerceantur'.[27] Chapter 28 in particular authorizes the abbot to act harshly under certain circumstances. Benedict also recommends: 'ustionem excommunicationis vel plagarum virgae'.[28] Yet the Rule characterizes the role of phys-ical pain in monastic life as often the result of penance prompted by transgression rather than the pre-emptive product of ascetical practice.

Anchoritism and earlier medieval asceticism: waging ascetical war

Constable notes: 'the approval of almost all [earlier medieval Christians] of voluntary … physical mortifications'.[29] Aggressive asceticism is especially popular in the earlier medieval world, facilitated by a Christocentric piety which fosters the desire to emulate, not just admire, Christ's Passion. Earlier medieval anchoritic guidance sets great store by ascetical accomplishment and reflects wider society's expectations of sophisticated ascetical reclusive achievement. Goscelin constructs the anchorhold itself as an aggres-sive ascetical force, to be used actively upon the body of the recluse: 'Lapis puluinar, terra lectica, cilicium toga, crassa pellis frigori obuia' (*Liber*, p. 78).[30] The need for her accomplished asceticism is strongly linked to the sinfulness of the world. As with anchoritism itself, Goscelin argues that, in the afterlife, there will be no further need for it: 'sicut nulla preuaricatio, ita nulla correctio' (*Liber*, p. 114).[31] Otter regards the *Liber* as 'a textbook of asceticism' (Otter, p. 11). Goscelin certainly calls Eve to ascetic warfare, citing Prudentius' *Cathemerinon*: 'Et ad astra doloribus itur' (*Liber*, p. 48),[32] waxing lyrical about the ingestion of noxious substances and about food deprivation. Eve is to follow a strict regime of bread, vegetables and water, which are pure 'cum munda conscientia' (*Liber*, p. 78).[33]

Yet, if it is a textbook, the *Liber* is surprisingly lacking in specifics. It contains little detail about Eve's known capabilities to withstand pain or her pre-enclosure ascetical tendencies. Much of Goscelin's narrative focuses on pain, to be sure, but on his pain and not Eve's. It is only in general, not specific, terms, that Goscelin vivifies asceticism, as, for example, a justified amputation: 'si mortificauerimus facta carnis, si carnem nostram crucifixerimus cum uitiis et concupiscentiis, si omnes passiones et incentiua carnis iugulauerimus, si crucifigamur mundo et mundus nobis' (*Liber*, p. 58).[34] His meaning is not always metaphorical. Eve is reminded of ancient ascetics who 'seruire libidini execrantes, ipsa sibi arma nequitie amputauere' (*Liber*, p. 74).[35] The silent approval of castration is implied by Goscelin's juxtapositional condemnation of only those ancients who plucked out their eyes, thinking to strengthen their souls through self-mutilation. Only these individuals are condemned as 'insanius progressi' (*Liber*, p. 74).[36] The impression that this gives of Goscelin's unwillingness to condemn extremism is not entirely assuaged by the later proviso: 'Nec uero lex Christi tam dira est, ut oculos nostros eruamus, sed ne uideant uanitatem auertamus' (*Liber*, p. 74).[37] Goscelin may say that 'Nec iubet membra nostra mutilari, se uitia amputari, ed [*sic*] a uitiis et concupiscentiis castrari, circumcidi, crucifigi' (*Liber*, p. 74),[38] but elsewhere the *Liber* demonstrates his approval of extreme asceticism. He references his own ascetical desire (*Liber*, p. 34),[39] linking passive asceticism with an increased ability to concentrate spiritually, fearful: 'corpus uero a luxu coercerent, ne mentem ad sublime nitentem pondere pinguedinis obrueret' (*Liber*, p. 73).[40] Aelred shares Goscelin's brutality, advising ascetical abstinence to the point of debilitation: 'Quid enim interest utrum absentia an languore caro superbiens comprimatur, castitas conseruetur? ... certe si languet, si aegrotat, si torquentur uiscera, si arescit stomachus, quaelibet deliciae oneri magis erunt quam delectationi' (*DII*, p. 655).[41] Both writers understand, as Otter rightly acknowledges, that 'for anchorites, psychological wholeness and personal fulfilment is not the goal' (Otter, p. 13). The earlier medieval recluse's ability to wage ascetical war is tied to her rejection of the world. Yet it is not the victory, but the battle itself that is the ascetical anchorite's glorious prize (*Liber*, p. 57).[42] Its violence triggers God's: 'teque rebellante seuos dentes inimicorum conterit in ore ipsorum hasta crucis sue' (*Liber*, p. 49).[43]

Earlier medieval anchoritic guidance on asceticism is closely connected with guidance on chastity, for both: 'Spurcitiis quoque inimici exterminatis' (*Liber*, p. 102).[44] Aelred enlists asceticism chiefly as a powerful weapon in his crusade against lust. Reinforcing the ancient link between food and sexual arousal, he accepts the directives of the Benedictine Rule only in the case of elderly or sick anchorites (*DII*, p. 648), discouraging even the most basic food intake.[45] His recluse must associate all eating and drinking with guilt, humiliation and a sense of weakness and failure: 'ad eius perfectionem suspirans cibos fastidiat, potum exhorreat. Et quod sumendum necessitas iudicauerit, aut ratio dictauerit cum dolore ac pudore aliquando cum lacrymis sumat' (*DII*, p. 651).[46] Warren concludes that '*Ancrene Riwle* is gentler than Aelred ['s guide]', and Clay even refers to *Ancrene Wisse*'s perspective as one of 'tender leniency'.[47] This is not so: *Ancrene Wisse* shares Aelred's enthusiasm for ascetical severity and his conception of bodily sickness as spiritually desirable: 'Betere is ga sec to heouene þen hal to helle' (*AW*, Corpus, p. 72), for 'Secnesse makeð mon to understonden hwet he is, to cnawen hím seoluen, ant as god meister, beat forte leorni wel hu mihti is Godd' (*AW*, Corpus, p. 69).[48] This guide's ascetic litany includes frequent fasting, vigil and flagellation and its recommendations are at times more detailed than Aelred's, not less so. The gruesome wording of the graphic list of aggressive ascetic practices in Part VIII details the use of holly, nettles, hedgehog skins, leaded scourges, belts and knives on the body (*AW*, Corpus, p. 158).[49] The conclusion of this passage has traditionally been interpreted as proof of the guidance writer's disapproval of severe asceticism, yet it does not forbid ascetic practices outright; it simply regulates their usage 'þurh scriftes leaue' (*AW*, Corpus, p. 158).[50] Millett notes, rightly, the 'general tendency of the Part 8 [Corpus] revisions ... to temper the asceticism recommended in the original'.[51] *Ancrene Wisse* does not so much disapprove of aggressive asceticism as support its enactment in a care-fully controlled environment. Its anchorites are both metaphorically and literally 'a folc tolaimet ant totoren' (*AW*, Corpus, p. 137).[52] As such, they are actively encouraged to share Christ's sufferings: 'his folhere mot wið pine of his flesch folhin his pine' (*AW*, Corpus, pp. 138–9).[53] Directions about self-flagellation are discernibly influenced by Benedictine thought: 'nim þe aleast forð Sein Beneites salue – þah ne þearf hit nawt beon se ouer-strong as his wes ... al o gure-blode. Ah lanhure 3ef þe seolf hwen þe strongest stont a smeort discipline, ant drif as he dude þet swete licunge into smeor-tunge' (*AW*, Corpus, p. 112).[54] The correctly ascetically disposed recluse understands that: 'We ahen him blod for blod' (*AW*, Corpus, p. 119).[55] As a fragment of Christ's flesh, the recluse's limbs should ache in tandem with his: 'His lím þenne nis he nawt þe naueð eche under se sar akinde heaued' (*AW*, Corpus, p. 136).[56]

The earlier medieval guides' expectation of ascetical sophistication on the part of their female recluses reflects wider contemporary social admiration for the ascetical achievements of women and the emergence of the female as ascetical role model. That Aelred is willing to admire women's ascetical potential is especially significant, since many Cistercians were unwilling even to acknowledge their nuns or supervise their spirituality.[57] The guides reflect society's increasing investment in female sanctity, even as they concurrently continue to imply female sinfulness. Caroline Walker Bynum reports that: 'bodily occurrences associated with women ... either first appear in the twelfth and thirteenth centuries or increase significantly in frequency'.[58] She argues that women were the creators of the most distinctive features of earlier medieval asceticism and that asceticism and female spirituality are so closely associated at this time that men's ascetical experiences should be regarded as feminized.[59] She notes that self-starvation as a demonstration of piety is reported only of women for most of the Middle Ages.[60] At its most extreme, this develops into an aversion to all food apart from the Eucharist, termed 'holy anorexia' by Rudolph M. Bell; a tendency not mentioned explicitly in earlier anchoritic guidance.[61] Walker Bynum argues that earlier medieval writings about women construct the 'flesh ... fertile and vulnerable ... [as] the occasion for salvation', for women's 'flesh could do what [Christ's] could do: bleed, feed, die and give life to others',[62] although Sandi J. Hubnik reminds us that asceticism only falsely entices 'the recluse with the possibility' of empowerment, for 'ecclesiastical codes effectively (re)shape her body and keep it bound and constituted by the markers of sex'.[63] Nonetheless, the guides imply a model of female sanctity constructed and medi-ated through ascetical suffering as part of a wider spiritual trend. It sees earlier medieval women suffer well and suffer because they have to.[64] We see anchoritic asceticism, and indeed anchoritism itself, are not cut-off from the outside world, but instead are reflec-tive of wider social developments.

Goscelin argues that women can use this practice to transcend the limitations of their inherently sexually transgressive bodies, restoring themselves to a unity with God shat-tered by the first Eve. He uses the example of a captive woman, who engages in vigils, fasting and in wearing a hair shirt (*Liber*, pp. 64–7).[65] She channels her God-given ascetical power as a system of devotional veneration (*Liber*, p. 65).[66] Mary of Egypt is also favoured (for ascetical exposure to the elements): 'quadraginta sex fere hiemes et estates egit sub diuo solitaria ... Uictus illi abstinentia ... Caput serpentis contriuit' (*Liber*, pp. 75–6).[67] The suffering of St Perpetua and her sister Felicitas involves graphic focus on Perpetua's ladder which exalts many instruments of pain: 'Cruces, eculei, lancee, gladii, crates, ignes, ungule, fustes, plumbati, scorpiones, bestie' and an immense, sleepless, dragon (*Liber*, p. 50).[68] Goscelin also exalts Deborah, Jael, Judith (*Liber*, p. 64)[69] and glosses the life of Saint Blandina, doubly marginalized as both a woman and a slave, whose story is recounted by Eusebius of Caesarea in his *Historia ecclesiastica* as striking in her ability to outstrip her torturers in stamina (*Liber*, pp. 63–4).[70] Goscelin deliberately aligns anchoritism, asceticism and female martyrdom, arguing: 'Non uocatur martir qui persecutorem non tulit, sed martyribus participatur qui martyrialiter uixit' (*Liber*, p. 98).[71] All three states require the body for the completion of their meaning and all three transform the sinful body into a signifier of sanctity and spiritual power. For this reason, Amy Hollywood argues: 'medieval texts emphasize women's association with embodiment ... in ways that exhibit the body's power to be divinized through its share in Christ's suffering ... Women as body, through suffering, redeem both themselves and the men around them'.[72] Goscelin believes Eve concurrently capable of inherent feminine weakness and of greater courage and ascetical capability than him (*Liber*, p. 63).[73] He admits that his accounts of ascetical women chill him, but advises Eve: 'sicut Dominus aspirauerit tibi exequenda' (*Liber*, pp. 63–4).[74]

Notable amongst celebrated earlier medieval female ascetics are the continental *mulieres sanctae*: Mary of Oignies (1157–1228), Lutgard of Aywières (1182–1246) and Christina the Astonishing (1150–1224).[75] Mary's asceticism is constructed in her Latin *vita* as particularly aggressive. She fasts, holds frequent vigils and her corpse is so emaciated at her death that her spine can be seen through her stomach.[76] Of Mary at her most extreme, James of Vitry writes: 'Fervore enim spiritus quasi inebriata, prae dulcedine Agni Paschalis carnes suas fastidiens; frustra non modica cum cultello resecavit'.[77] The excesses of Christina the Astonishing also render her similarly visible to her contemporaries. Thomas of Cantimpré records her tendency to creep into fiery ovens, thrust her feet and hands into flames and immerse herself in cauldrons of boiling water.[78] While most Christians would not have been encouraged, or able, to emulate these extreme ascetical acts, the sophisticated ascetic practice of the *mulieres sanctae* is an important spiritual context within which the anchoritic guidance tradition must be read.

Earlier medieval anchoritic guides also imply that it is not only female solitaries who are famed ascetics at this time. Goscelin fashions a male ascetical line, which includes Moses who emerges 'quadraginta dierum inedia leuigatus', in comparison with the Israelites who remain 'in infimis cum terrenis desideriis' (*Liber*, p. 62).[79] David, Daniel and especially Silvanus, bishop of Toulouse, are admired, the latter for the forty years that he 'pane et uino prorsus abstinuisse' (*Liber*, p. 63).[80] Germaine of Auxerre lived on 'pane locio confecto', and Genoveva 'a quinto decimo usque ad quinquagesimum annum nunquam preter dominicam et Vtam feriam cibum ullum uel potum pregustasse, qui cibus erat pisa uel fabe post coctionem quindecim dierum fere reposite' (*Liber*, p. 63).[81] The martyr-like end of Brithric, the recluse burnt to death in the cell he would not leave, is constructed as nourishment: his corpse filled out, not with food, but with the molten lead from the cell roof which kills him (*Liber*, pp. 67–8).[82] Contemporary historical examples of known male ascetics, including Roger of Markyate (d.1122), Wulfric of Haselbury (*c*.1090–1155), Godric of Finchale (*c*.1070–*c*.1170), Bartholomew of Farne (c.1120–c.93) and Henry of Coquet (d.1127/8), all demonstrate the extent to which one man's asceticism inspires 'communities' of solitaries to form, attracted, just as Cassian had envisaged, by notions of an ascetical elite and motivated by asceticism as a cohesive force.[83] The legendary ascetical abilities of Dominic Loricatus (995–1060), the hermit-monk whose name was derived from his fondness for hanging metal plates upon his body, attracted a considerable following.[84] His self-flagellations were reputed to have reached 'a total of fifteen thousand blows and a thousand *metanea* for each full recitation of the Psalter'.[85] Eremitical groups gathered in the forests of Brittany and Maine, where Robert of Abrissel founded Fontevrault (c.1100), and in Burgundy. More institutionalized hermit-monk communities also developed, including the Camaldolese, a community-in-solitude founded c.1022 by Romuald of Ravenna, which was particularly ascetically severe. Its monks manipulated the Benedictine Rule into a daily routine of passive and active ascetic practices, with particular emphasis upon flagellation. They combined coenobitism with eremitism, but their foundation's spatial layout potentially reflected their belief in the supremacy of solitude; the hermits resided in huts above the rest of the community. Similar communities developed at Vallombrosa, founded by John Gualberto of Florence, and at Fonte Avellana, a foundation associated with the famed ascetic, St Peter Damian. Lawrence reports that at Fonte Avellana when a monk died, the other brethren were 'enjoined to fast for seven days on his behalf, [and] to receive the whip seven times'.[86] Here, asceticism is a form of commemoration and a signifier of memory, of tradition and of a literal and metaphorical community in pain.

It is also within the context of monastic reform based upon a renewal of interest in harsh ascetical practices that the ascetical material of the earlier anchoritic guides is best understood. For asceticism plays a pivotal role in the identification, creation and shaping, not just of anchoritism, but many religious vocations, until the Fourth Lateran Council of 1215 forbade the creation of new orders and rules.[87] Differences in ascetical approach separated one community from another and certainly motivated the creation of new ones. Some were inspired by Augustinian ideas of one community fostering different levels of ascetical ability. Others, particularly those noted above with eremitical links, were inspired by the elitist notions like Cassian's and hoped to reinvent desert asceticism within a semi-communal context. Such desires could, on occasion, be manipulated. The Grandmontine *conversi* were given far greater powers over the temporal affairs of their abbey than was customary, ostensibly in order to facilitate the ascetic rigour of the choir monks. Yet, ultimately, that very rigour was used against them when they were forced to abstain unwillingly after their *conversi* chose to restrict their food further. Here, the Grandmontine interest in pursuing ascetical extremes renders them vulnerable to caprice and attitudes towards asceticism reveal discontent not just between, but within, emergent orders.

The split between the Cluniacs and Cistercians is also relevant here. Daniell notes their emergence in England as part of the impact made on post-Conquest mainland Britain by four new orders: 'Tiron [in Scotland and Wales], Savigny [subsumed into the Cistercian order in 1147], Cluny (the Cluniacs) and Citeaux (the Cistercians)'.[88] Less overtly ascetical than the hermit-monk communities, they nonetheless displayed renewed interest in ascetical discipline. The Cluniac monastic system was founded in the tenth century on the Burgundian estates of Duke William of Aquitaine under the supervision of Abbot Berno, motivated by a desire to revive the observance of the Benedictine Rule. Individual Cluniacs, such as Abbot Hugh, were famed ascetics and ascetic practice played a large part in Cluniac daily life. Cluniac silence, which gave rise to the development of a complex system of non-verbal communication, was constructed as an ascetical abstinence from communication and formed an important part of their ascetical recommendations, just as it does in earlier medieval anchoritic guidance.[89]

The Cistercians had their origins in conflict with a Cluniac authority which they began to perceive as outdated, even dissolute. Chief amongst the critics was the monk, Bernard of Clairvaux. In 1098, a group of like-minded coenobites, led by Abbot Robert of Molesme, settled at Cîteaux, later establishing further foundations elsewhere, for example at Clairvaux in 1115. At the time of their foundation, the Cistercians advocated the simplicity of the Benedictine Rule, seeking to interpret it to the letter and to exchange splendour and luxury for physical discipline and simple poverty; similar goals to those of earlier medieval anchoritic guidance. This led the Cistercians to their famed abandonment of the traditional black Benedictine habit in favour of undyed wool, which provoked criticism of them as an elitist group of malcontents. When the anchoritic guidance writer, Aelred, died at Rievaulx in 1167, there were 500 lay brothers and 140 choir-monks, living in what Lawrence calls 'social apartheid', maintaining distance from and subordinate to those that they served.[90] Southern argues that the Cistercian ideal involved 'complete self-abnegation, poverty, simplicity, retirement, purity', although some of their contemporaries, evidently threatened by such a formidable reformative group, recast their reputation as one of 'aggression, arrogance, military (or ... militant) discipline, outstanding managerial qualities, and cupidity'.[91] They would later fall prey to the very vices that they sought to reject, accruing great wealth and gaining a worse reputation for greed than the Cluniacs, but, at this time at least, the Cistercians were chief amongst the coenobites who sought ascetical authority and it is this tradition that is reflected in Aelred's guide for his sister.[92]

Anchoritism and ascetical discretion

The earlier guidance writers' promotion of ascetical discretion or moderation is slight in comparison to that of their later medieval counterparts. Goscelin reminds Eve that: 'qui sine beneficio conditoris est nullus, nil suis arroget uiribus' (Liber, p. 93),[93] but marks out as 'dementia' those who 'damnent continentiam, abstinentiam' (Liber, p. 82).[94] He says little about ascetical discretion directly, however, although he does cite the careful distinction of Eph. 6:11: 'non est nobis colluctatio aduersus carnem at sanguinem ... sed aduersus principes et potestates' (Liber, p. 56),[95] a perspective drawn on more fully in later medieval anchoritic guidance. Aelred is more detailed about ascetical moderation, but he never resolves the tension between his obvious enthusiasm for severity and his understanding, derived at least in part from the Benedictine Rule and also from the Church Fathers, of the need for ascetical regulation. Aelred recommends both moderation and extremism. He argues that both foster virtue. He pays lip service to discretion, but for him asceticism reads not simply as a means to an end, but as an end in itself. For Aelred, asceticism equals flesh-hatred, not sin-hatred. He praises the man who 'in hoc solo nimius uideretur ... Talibus armis gloriosum retulit de tyranno triumphum' (DII,

p. 655).[96] At times he appears defensive: 'Nec hoc dico ut discretioni, quae omnium uirtutum et mater et nutrix est, derogem … saepe falso nomine discretionis palliamus negotium uoluptatis' (*DII*, p. 656).[97] Yet, his subsequent definition of discretion is clearly a rejection of it: 'vera enim discretio est animam carni praeponere, et ubi periclitatur utraque … pro illius utilitate istam negligere' (*DII*, p. 656).[98]

Ancrene Wisse's treatment of discretion knows no such ambiguity. While deeply ascetical individuals are still admired, the guide takes greater pains to stress that asceticism is a means to an end, admirable only for what can be achieved through it – a perspective that the later guides apply not just to asceticism but to the very vocation of anchoritism itself. Incorrectly motivated aggressive ascetical acts are counted as 'homicide, ant morðe of hire seoluen' (*AW*, Corpus, p. 77).[99] The recluse is reminded that: 'al þet heard þet we þolieð o flesch … nis to luuien bute for-þi, þet Godd te reaðere þiderward lok[eð] mid his grace, ant makeð þe heorte schir' (*AW*, Corpus, p. 144).[100] She must understand that:

> Þah þe flesch beo ure fa, hit is us ihaten þet we halden hit up. Wa we moten don hit, as hit is wel ofte wurðe, ah nawt fordon mid alle; for hu wac se hit eauer beo, þenne is hit swa icuplet ant se feste ifeiet to ure deorewurðe gast, Godes ahne furme, þet we mahten sone slean þet an wið þat oþer (*AW*, Corpus, p. 55).[101]

Yet, *Ancrene Wisse*'s conceptualization of discretion is not anti-ascetical. Some revisions, such as those in the Cleopatra text, demonstrate an increasing tendency towards discretion, but do not criticize asceticism outright, as the later medieval guides do. Neither do they circumvent discretion as Aelred does. They simply promote it within a framework of supervision; its anchorites are encouraged to express their ascetical drive only as sanctioned by the church. Aelred writes from the perspective of flesh-hatred, but the author of *Ancrene Wisse* and his revisers operate from a sin-hatred. This involves the body but is not restricted to it. Therefore, *Ancrene Wisse* concludes: 'Sum wummon inohreaðe wereð þe brech of here ful wel icnottet … Me is leouere þet ȝe þolien wel an heard word þen an heard here' (*AW*, Corpus, p. 159).[102] Making time to eat, sleep and attend to the 'ground' of her body is part of this guide's definition of discretion. The recluse is warned that: 'Euch þing þah me mei ouerdon; best is eauer mete' (*AW*, Corpus, p. 109).[103] The desire to weaken the spirit through bodily annihilation is attributed to the Devil and ascetic practice is advised not, as it was in Aelred's guide, in order to destroy the flesh, but in order to balance it. *Ancrene Wisse*'s ascetical perspective differs from Aelred's not in a desire to spare the body, but from a desire to see physically expressed asceticism as only part of the ascetical response. The importance of the mortification of the spirit, which this chapter will show is developed at length in later guidance, is beginning to emerge.

Ancrene Wisse is, then, here in terms of its asceticism, a text in transition. This is informed by the rediscovery of the Augustinian Rule in the eleventh century, the subsequent development of the ordinary Augustinian canons, the independent congregations of, often stricter, Augustinian canons, including the Premonstratensians and Victorines, and the advent of the mendicant friars. The Augustinian rule lent authority to those who wished to broaden their devotional responses. A composite document, it comprises a letter written by Augustine to his sister's conventual foundation and an *ordo* for a monastery.[104] Ambiguously phrased and therefore widely applicable to the very different

groups and orders who espoused it as their 'rule', it accepts each individual's differing
ascetical abilities, although it argues that those requiring concessions are only to be
pitied: 'Carnem uestram domate ieiuniis et abstinentia escae et potus, quantum ualetudo
permittit. Quando autem aliquis non potest ieiunare, non tamen extra horam prandii
aliquid alimentorum sumat, nisi cum aegrotat' (*Regula Sancti Augustini*, Chapter 3, ll.
74–9).[105] Like *Ancrene Wisse*, then, and in marked contrast to *De institutione*, this 'rule'
puts the demands of health before the demands of asceticism.

During the earlier Middle Ages, activities such as silence, reading, writing, contemplation, almsgiving and the adoption of poverty, increasingly began to be regarded as
ascetic if they inculcated the same virtues as more traditional passive or aggressive
practices. The widening of the ascetic drive does not imply its weakening: medieval
writings imply that old and newer practices coexist; indeed, Cassian himself invests
mundane activities with an ascetical power if they result in the subjugation of the flesh.
Lawrence argues that voluntary poverty appealed only to the rich: 'it could have little
meaning for those for whom poverty and deprivation were the normal condition'.[106] Yet
poverty could potentially be significant to all and ascetical, if offered up as a form of
devotional self-abasement. This is reflected in the emergence of orders such as that of
Prémontré, founded by St Norbert (*c*.1115) and of the Franciscan and Dominican
friars.[107] In this context the (possibly Dominican) author of *Ancrene Wisse* expresses the
widening of the ascetical drive and the understanding that ascetical acts are only expressions of inner virtue and therefore subordinate to it. This increasing focus on the virtue
produced by asceticism, rather than on ascetical acts per se, is in keeping with the spirituality of the mendicants. Yet that harsher, more traditional, forms of asceticism also
continue at this time is equally illustrated by the development of the Carthusians.[108]
Bruno of Cologne is credited with having established them at the end of the eleventh
century, but it was Guigo who relocated them to the Grande Chartreuse in 1132. In
Carthusian life, solitude and community are united, not, as with other hermit-monk
groups, through the formulation of two separate communities, but through the concurrent combination of coenobitism and eremitism. Guigo's *Consuetudines Cartusiae*
argues that the brethren should meet once a day for Vespers and eat together on Sundays
and festivals. Alone for much of the rest of the time in individual cells (boasting both
garden and lavatory), the monks are attended to by their *conversi*, relatively uncon-
strained by the demands of a strict communal timetable and freer to pursue a more
flexible life which can include ascetic practice. Jessica Brantley terms this a 'novel
attempt to combine an eremitic ideal with a coenobitic structure ... [a] double emphasis
on solitude within community'.[109] Their renewed stress on interiority and resurgence of
interest in the individualized response to God accessed through solitude echoes earlier
anchoritic guidance. Yet their concessions to the varying needs of each monk, belief in
self-regulation and espousal of poverty as an ascetical response, foreshadow later medieval anchoritic ascetical thought.

Anchoritism and later medieval asceticism: sin-hatred not flesh-hatred

Later guides continue to explore earlier medieval links between spiritual corruption and
bodily sickness. The fallen anchorite is still 'a soule in bodi of synne' (*Scale I*, p. 41),

encumbered with herself, 'as ful of synne as the hide is full of fleisch' (*Scale I*, p. 129). Sin, as it disfigures the soul, is still mapped out on the body in deformity and Christ's image in mankind rendered a distortion of itself. The later guides discuss at length what defiles and what purifies mankind. Rolle's *Form* opens with an emphatic description of the wretchedness that leads unrepentant sinners to hell unless they 'turne ham and rise to penaunce' (*Form*, p. 3). Rolle writes: 'preir, gretynge, fastynge, wakynge ... putteth away synne and filthe from þe soule, and maketh hit clene' (*Form*, p. 7). *Speculum* exhorts its readership to visualize their corruption in the guide itself as a mirror, echoing *Ancrene Wisse*'s constructions of the power of self-knowledge. Every recluse's spiritual journey to self-knowledge still inevitably involves this self-reckoning and asceticism continues to be one method whereby the recluse may see herself accurately: 'Hoc modo vocacionem suam commutare poterit, Dei gracia mediante, de malo in bonum, de sinistra in dexteram et de viciis ad virtutes' (*Speculum*, p. 69).[110] Rolle concludes: 'if þou ... punysshe þi body skylwisly ... for þis trauaille þou shalt cum to reste þat lesteth euer, and sit in a seet of ioy with angels' (*Form*, pp. 21–2). *Speculum* articulates this struggle in an ascetical vocabulary highly allusive of Aelred's. The recluse takes up 'arma milicie spiritualis' (*Speculum*, p. 76); a life 'assumpta[m] in oracionibus, vigiliis ieiuniis at aliis sanctis observanciis quibuscunque' (*Speculum*, p. 77).[111] The recluse is still aligned with a tradition of penitent desert-sainthood, 'contritis et consciencciosis' (*Speculum*, p. 67), implying the continued tradition of positive ascetical role models.[112]

Hilton, although notably punitive, nonetheless problematizes asceticism more than any other guidance writer, but even he concludes: 'bodili peyne ... sumtyme letteth not the fervour of love to God in devocioun but often encresith it' (*Scale I*, p. 118). Even he believes that ascetic practice transforms potential transgression into spiritual achievement. Yet, he reinterprets the significance of the ancient eremitical asceticism of the desert fathers, so important to the earlier guidance writers: 'Lereth of me, he [God] seith, not for to goo baarfoot ne for to goo into desert and faste fourti daies, ne for to cheese yow disciplis, but lerith of me mekenesse' (*Scale I*, p. 89). He constructs mankind's natural post-lapsarian state as one of transgression, often terming this the 'ground' of sin. He implicitly embodies sin (simply because it is therefore easier for the recluse to conceive of and combat it). This creates the impression that the body requires surveillance and control. Hilton believes that it should be the goal of every Christian, but especially a recluse, to reform themselves to the image of Christ in which humanity was fashioned in pre-lapsarian times. This is an arduous task, carrying the implication of disunity and distress, of enormous pain and conflict. Hilton identifies two levels of rehabilitation: reforming in faith alone and reforming in faith and feeling, which is harder to achieve. This latter reformative process brings the understanding that soul and body have been separated, in the Fall, by a sin located first and foremost in the body. Original sin is shown to occasion all subsequent sin and the degenerate process is gradual, developing from a 'foryetynge of God and unknowynge of him, and into beestli likynge of thisilf' (*Scale I*, p. 78). The only cure for this, for the recluse for whom Hilton writes, is to 'Take this bodi of synne and doo hym on the cros' (*Scale I*, p. 127) of the anchoritic vocation. Yet, Tarjei Park rightly notes that 'Hilton does not ... advocate bodily negation, the body is to be correctly ordered'.[113] He argues that this 'goes further than a neat anti-flesh, pro-spirit dualism', for 'Hilton is not against flesh as flesh, but flesh as sin laden'; the soul is affected 'not by the physical, but by the fallenness of the physical'.[114] Certainly, Hilton does not allow his embodiment of sin to lead him to the same potential flesh-hatred manifested by Aelred. In fact, at his most daring, Hilton argues that sin, like the soul itself, is 'no bodili thynge' (*Scale I*, p. 43). Ultimately, he characterizes sin as an absence of good, of what is known and perceived; a 'merkenesse of unknowynge' (*Scale I*, p. 91), frequently referred to simply as this 'nothynge' (*Scale I*, p. 91). The new implication that this has for asceticism is clear: if sin, for Hilton at least, is not really located in the body, its remedy cannot be born of it.

For the ascetical drive is now firmly mediated, not through Aelred's flesh-hatred, but through the sin-hatred which had its beginnings in *Ancrene Wisse*. Ascetical discretion, only emergent in earlier guidance, has developed fully into the suggestion that ascetic practice is only one means amongst many of safeguarding spiritual purity and not necessarily the most effective. Rolle, in a style reminiscent of earlier guidance, states: 'Fastynge and wakyng letteth nat goostly goodes, bot helpeth, if þei be done with discrecioun; withouten þat, þei ben vices' (*Form*, pp. 4–5). He continues: 'I hold þe neuer of þe lasse merite if þou be nat in so mych abstinence as þou hast be, ne of þe more merite þogh þou take þe to moor abstinence' (*Form*, p. 11). The *Speculum* author advises his recluses to govern themselves: 'iuxta discretionis arbitrium sic corpus castigetur alternis vicibus et alatur, ut et imperio spiritus sit subditum et sufficiens perficere laborem iniunctum' (*Speculum*, p. 76).[115] Despite their seeming divergence, this later medieval position builds on earlier medieval anchoritic guidance, especially *Ancrene Wisse*'s recommendation that the body be sustained to facilitate its spiritual potential.[116] With the exception of *Scale*, later medieval ascetical perspectives are best read as the continuation, not wholesale rejection, of earlier guidance.

Constable proposes that in the later Middle Ages, ascetical austerities spread outside monastic circles, becoming more, not less, severe.[117] Pietro Camporesi writes of a blood pact between Christ and his ascetics, sited in 'a purificatory bath of spilled blood'.[118] He argues that late medieval flagellants 'celebrate … salvation anxieties in rites of violence and blood'.[119] It is the case that the fourteenth century saw increased severity in some ascetical forms, as, for example, among the Italian flagellant confraternities, which gave rise to a wider penance-driven movement intended to atone for the transgressions thought to have provoked the Black Death. Maiju Lehmijoki Gardner has shown that some later medieval Italian women brought excessive ascetical devotions into their domestic setting, just as Mary of Oignies did in the earlier period.[120] Later medieval hagiography demonstrates that sanctity continues to be constructed ascetically and continues to invest accomplished ascetics with considerable power. Such accounts approve of Catherine of Siena (1347–80), who develops her own extreme ascetic practices in the face of what she considers to be insufficient spiritual advice. Flora of Beaulieu (1309–47) manifests similar discontent with the apparent laxity of her confessors. Peter of Luxembourg's lists of his own grievous faults are discouraged by his advisors, yet he continues to attempt to wake them frequently, demanding confession. Bridget of Sweden (1303–c.73) assumes a semi-autonomous role in directing her own spirituality, discerning the gravity, not just of her own sin, but of that of others through sensory manifestations such as bitter taste and odour when sin is committed in her presence. Pope Urban V, as a young man, constructs his ascetic perspective as a secret challenge to authority, covering his bed with sand when forbidden to sleep on rocks. Clare Gambacorta disobeys her family by concealing a hair shirt beneath her finery as a challenge to those who would force her to assume the traditional female roles of marriage and motherhood. Egotism, even envy, can be read into Gonsalvo Sancii's desire to see only himself as worthy of ascetic penance. Upon seeing others beaten he is reputed to have cried out: 'Alas for me, who should be hit and punished as a miserable sinner – but what have these innocent ones done?'[121]

Their examples demonstrate the continued admiration of medieval society for accomplished ascetics and concurrently configure the uneasy power balance between the ascetic and her spiritual advisors. Pope Innocent III was especially anxious to supervise the solitary ascetic, and anchoritic guidance is similarly uneasy about the relationship between asceticism and heresy.[122] Peter Biller writes of the authority of the heretical Waldensians: 'Their asceticism set them apart … in this rested their power'.[123] Yet, if harnessed correctly, the ascetic's power could support, not subvert, the church, as in the thirteenth-century fight against Cathar dualism.[124] Yet, these (potentially unruly) ascetical accounts are the revelation of God-granted ascetical extremes gifted to a few, not a wholesale call to ascetical arms for the many. The guides argue that if the later medieval recluse requires a mind uninterrupted by the aggressive demands of an indulged body, she also requires freedom from the disruption of a suffering one. Discretion is the tool that best equips her to balance herself between overindulgence and insufficiency. The cautious reservations of later medieval guidance about hypocritical ascetical extremists who assume only the outward appearance of sanctity, its fears and warnings against losing the self in ascetical practice without understanding its real purpose are all more influenced by the Augustinian Rule than Cassian. *Ancrene Wisse*'s hair shirt warning, implying that aggressive asceticism is an easier undertaking than simple love, has developed into Hilton's belief that:

> It is no maistrie for to wake and faste til thyn heed wirke and thi bodi waike … But it is a greet maistrie for a man to kunne love his even Cristene in charité, and viseli hate the synne of him and love the man (*Scale I*, p. 69).

It is discernible, too, behind Rolle's judgement that the hypocrite may 'wake and faste and suffre peyne more þan any creature may, bot mekenesse and loue may he nat haue' (*Form*, p. 21). Real spiritual strength comes from virtue itself, not from the ascetical acts that may inculcate it. Without the comprehension of the bond of love that asceticism generates between sinner and saviour, even the boldest of aggressive late medieval ascetics is shown to be spiritually powerless.

Later anchoritic guidance and wider contemporary theological writings imply that the emulation of aggressive ascetical acts should give way to an admiration for them and, even then, only if they inculcate love. Severer forms of asceticism are increasingly seen as exceptional and asceticism presented as a vocation for a minority, not an occupation for the majority.[125] Fourteenth-century ascetics Gerard Cagnoli (1270–1345) and Henry Suso (c.1295–1366) did not recommend to others the torments that they endured. Richard Kieckhefer argues that Suso implies: 'it is better to practice only moderate austerities … if it is difficult to determine what constitutes moderation, it is preferable to stop short rather than to venture too far'.[126] Later guidance constructs an ascetically inspired recluse who is zealous, emotional and unstable, prompted by flesh-hatred not sin-hatred; rendered thereby vulnerable, not invincible. She has, Rolle argues, 'vnþanke' for her deeds (*Form*, p. 5). Hilton is even more condemnatory: 'unskilful peyne of hungir wilfulli taken, or sikeness in the stomac ... in ony ... partie of the bodie for the defaute of thisilf bi to moche fastynge ... schal ... lette the spirit and ... hyndre him' (*Scale I*, p. 118). As with earlier guidance, the Devil's influence is found to foster such 'vnstable and vnwise' individuals 'begiled with ouer mych abstynence', for too much penance has rendered them 'so feble þat þei may nat loue God as þei sholden do' (*Form*, pp. 4–5, 1). Ascetical extremes now sever the very bond between God and mankind that asceticism seeks to facilitate. To withhold bodily necessities or do it 'outrage' continue to be counted as sins; a clear development of *Ancrene Wisse*'s ideas about self-slaughter, which it terms 'desesperance ... unhope ant an unbileaue forte beon iborhen' (*AW*, Corpus, p. 3).[127] *Speculum* develops this into specific recommendations about a system of probation for the ascetically inspired recluse. Behind its year-long supervision by up to three persons is the implicit suggestion that the judgement of such an individual requires corroboration, even validation, by those not similarly driven.

The instability of excess is implicitly criticized in the *vitae* of several later medieval ascetics, attesting to the fine line between acceptable mortification and self-harm. Suso, breaking his abstinence from meat after several years, reportedly prompted a 'devil-beast' to punish him by driving a gimlet into his mouth, wounding him so badly that 'he could eat only by sucking through his teeth'.[128] The ascetic's swift degeneration into self-destruction is illustrated in Caesarius of Heisterbach's tale of the knight Baldwin who attempts suicide following excessive mortifications of the flesh.[129] Caesarius (*c*.1170–1240) was an earlier medieval Cistercian monk at the monastery of Heisterbach, but his *Dialogue on Miracles*, printed five times between 1475 and 1605, gathered much popularity in the later Middle Ages. Of Baldwin it reports: 'excessive vigils and labours affected his brain, and he incurred such violent headaches' that one night he tied the church bell rope round his neck and jumped, thus 'the vice of *accidie* is born of indiscreet fervour'.[130] Ironically, here asceticism, intended, pre-emptively to combat transgression, triggers a chain of events that results in the mortal sin of suicide.[131] Caesarius recounts another tale of a new monk who treated himself 'so severely and was so solitary, that the abbot feared for him and ... reproved him for his indiscreet zeal'.[132] Here, solitude is implicitly constructed as part of the problem. We later learn that this monk died after only a year, slain by his own fervour. The later anchoritic guides clearly reflect these kinds of contemporary fears about the relationship between solitude, asceticism and self-slaughter.

Later anchoritic guidance, building on the emergent earlier medieval approval of discretion, now advocates the complete harmony of body and soul. Aelred's advice that the recluse associate only over-consumption with shame has evolved into Hilton's suggestion that 'it cometh to thi mynde bitynge in conscience that thou has eaten too much *or to litil*' (*Scale I*, p. 82).[133] Rolle states: 'Rightwisnesse is neþer in fastynge ne in etynge, bot þou art rightwise if al ilike be to þe, dispite as praysynge ... hungre and need as delites or dayntees' (*Form*, p. 14). Hilton argues: 'the fervour of lust in contemplacion' may be had 'in gret reste of bodi and soule. Forthi ... kepe thi bodili kynde up resoun ... eschew to moche as wel as to litil' (*Scale I*, p. 82). It is now part of the recluse's duty to self-sustain. This can be traced back to *Ancrene Wisse*'s demand that she come down to the 'ground' of her body and eat and drink, yet it clearly moves beyond it. Hilton's perspectives are markedly different at times from the earlier guidance tradition, but his advice – 'For be a man nevere so hooli, hym bihoveth ete and drynke and slepe' (*Scale I*, p. 79) – still recalls *Ancrene Wisse*'s emergent concern that the recluse should sometimes sustain herself. Yet, by now Hilton has reversed Aelred's position, concluding that hunger is a sickness of nature and food the medicine for it, while Rolle suggests that when ill, the recluse must recuperate. The Bodley redaction of Aelred's guide signals the shift between earlier and later ascetical attitudes most clearly. It renders it shameful now not, as formerly, to succumb to the body's needs, but to fail to meet them.

The vocabulary of the anchorhold has shifted in accordance with changing ascetical ideals. In the later guides the language of satiety and not of deprivation now prevails. The exemplary recluse goes, not hungry, to bed, but 'replet and fedde with deuocion' (*DII*, MS Bodley 423, p. 6). Exemplary ascetics are less of a focal point and Aelred's redactor states explicitly that bodily temptations are to be overcome by reading, prayer and meditation on the Passion. The body is no longer pitted physically against itself. Aelred's paradoxical definition of discretion has been reworked: 'If it be discrecion to put the soule aboue the body in reuerence, then is it discrecion to put the body bynethe the soule by subieccyon' (*DII*, MS Bodley 423, p. 13). There is little suggestion that this involves either passive or aggressive asceticism. Aelred's formerly gruesome linen metaphor is almost unrecognizable, functioning now to connote confession, not wider human suffering (*DII*, MS Bodley 423, p. 15).[134]

Yet, it is only Hilton who advocates a completely new ascetical direction. His concurrent arguments are that the body is a problem that can never be overcome and that sin is not really located in the flesh, consequently sin is body-less; an absence of good, a 'nothingness' which cannot be combated physically (although its embodiment may render it easier for the reclusive mind to fight). This leads him to the conclusion that asceticism's focus on the body actually encourages the ascetic to lose sight of both spiritual purpose and perspective. He reasons, again in tones reminiscent of *Ancrene Wisse*: 'stryve not to moche as thou wolde distroie it uttirli, for it is not for to doo. Thou schal never brynge it so aboute' (*Scale I*, p. 82). If controlling the flesh through ascetic practice remains central to the recluse's spirituality, then Hilton believes that the recluse will never advance further than that flesh. It is asceticism itself that keeps the problem of body alive. Body-consciousness is a prison from which the recluse can never escape through contemplation, which the later guides in particular construct as her life's work. Hilton's treatment of discretion therefore assumes an anti-ascetical tone. Humility and charity will profit the contemplative more in one year of their pursuit than would seven years of aggressive asceticism 'though he stryve … contynueli and bete himself eche dai with scourgis from morwe til evesong tyme' (*Scale I*, p. 82).

Rolle writes: 'men and wommen þat most hath of Goddis loue, wheþer þei don penaunce or none, þei shal be in þe heghest degre in heuyn' (*Form*, p. 15). In the highest state of Rollian 'synguler loue', the recluse thinks only of Jesus, not of the flesh. The fire of this love (*Form*, p. 17) is constructed as real and as purificatory as any literal fire utilized by accomplished earlier medieval ascetics like Christina the Astonishing. Love, not fear, occupies the central place in a theology that seeks to move the recluse beyond the problem of body. Passive and aggressive ascetic practices and their production of purificatory pain are, in the context of love, simply signifiers of human limitation not an imitation of divine freedom. Hilton does not simply re-locate sin away from the flesh, he seeks to de-locate it. He alone of all the later medieval guidance writers seeks to liberate his recluse from an ascetic practice that ties her reductively to her flesh and her flesh to the world.

Purity without pain: ascetical meditation[135]

Earlier medieval guidance proposes an asceticism of the mind as well as the body. All the earlier writers recommend meditation upon ascetical subjects, such as human sinfulness, bodily corruption and eternal judgement. They advise the contemplation of pain – either the anchorite's or, more usually, Christ's – as a potentially purificatory process. They focus upon the Passion in gruesome detail, upon the healing properties of Christ's blood and the ascetical significance of the Eucharist.[136] Such meditative material is so abundant in the three earlier guides that the examination of just one type, of meditation upon the sufferings and particularly the blood, of Christ's Passion, the most important example of physical suffering for the anchoritic tradition, must stand here as a model for their utilization of all ascetically meditative material.

Goscelin centralizes the Passion as the recluse's ultimate source of ascetical devotional inspiration, drawing frequent attention to Christ's 'passiones, dolores et supplicia corporis, opprobria, sputa, flagella, crucem, uulnera cum acerbitate mortis, ac sepulture exequiis' (*Liber*, pp. 52–3).[137] Through the savagery of such suffering, Christ redeems the recluse 'suo sancto sanguine' (*Liber*, p. 55).[138] Goscelin is not as bloodthirsty as Aelred, yet Eve is encouraged to focus on the Passion in minute detail. The Passion is central to her devotional hours and Eve should use each of its pain-filled stages as a devotional inspiration, weaving pain and praise together: 'Omnes horas Christi passionibus consecra. Media nocte adora captum et carceratum, mane flagellatum' (*Liber*, p. 83).[139] Christ's wounds, like the wounds of all martyrs, will remain for all eternity upon Him as 'quinque sensuum redemptrices' (*Liber*, p. 110).[140] Since Christ's human capacity to endure pain is best rendered visible by the Passion, so the recluse's sufferings are best rendered visible in Christ's (*Liber*, p. 55).[141] The tendency of the *Liber* to intersect Christ's divinity and humanity, which Southern calls 'the greatest triumph of medieval humanism', is part of a new earlier medieval drive to render God mortal, epitomized by Anselm's famous work, *Cur Deus Homo* (1098).[142] This demonstrates, as Jestice argues, an emphasis beginning 'in the late tenth century … on suffering with Christ … a figure marked by willing suffering', a Christian response in which 'God is wrapped up in the human condition'.[143]

Goscelin's ascetical construction of the Passion is not, however, focused wholly on savagery and pain, but also on the love in which the crucifixion is grounded: 'Aspice ergo ut affectuosa brachia extendat in cruce, ea benignitate, qua nos redemit, inuitans ad se' (*Liber*, p. 107).[144] Eve's visualization of Christocentric pain, because it is affective, will break down, in love, the barriers between herself and the God she contemplates: 'Qui sedet super cherubim, potest etiam puer teneri desiderantibus et ulnis et gremio' (*Liber*, p. 107).[145] In this and in his emotive style, Goscelin is aligned with the later medieval guidance writers, whose narratives are far more stylistically fervent than their earlier counterparts. Love, for Goscelin, becomes an affective devotion: 'Hinc indulgentie tue presumptione licentius effluo, quia nec dilectio tam … composite loquitur quam affectuose' (*Liber*, p. 35).[146] Describing Eve's submission to her anchoritic destiny as being wounded by love (*Liber*, p. 68),[147] Goscelin urges her to use her meditative ascetical practice to love God zealously, engaging with Him not in remote detachment in tones highly reminiscent of those that Rolle later emulates: 'non sensu frigido ... sed cum incensu amoris flagrantissimo' (*Liber*, p. 28).[148] He writes of the fire of love, citing St Gregory's construction of the contemplation of eternity as inner fire: 'inardescit animus, iamque illic cupit assistere' (*Liber*, p. 62).[149] He encourages Eve: 'Induere fortes animos eternorum gaudiorum amore et contemplatione' (*Liber*, p. 48),[150] yoking both love and contemplative experience together, as will his later medieval counterparts.

Both Aelred's guide and *Ancrene Wisse* are significantly more bloodthirsty than this. They urge the recluse to visualize the five deep streams of blood from Christ's five wounds, from the sharp crown of thorns and from the gashes delivered during the violent scourging. The cross runs with blood and Christ, as wounded lover, writes love letters in it. The recluse is to imagine entering Christ's wounds, mingling his blood with hers (*DII*, pp. 670–1).[151] Aelred also draws on the bloodier aspects of birth imagery; the recluse is enclosed within the walls of Christ's bleeding flesh and drinks His blood as if it were milk. Visualized blood is thereby rendered an ascetical tool, used to increase love through the inculcation of virtue. In this context, Aelred fosters his sister's horror at the scourging: 'Scio non potes ulterius sustinere, nec dulcissimum dorsum eius flagellis atteri, nec faciem alapis caedi, nec tremendum illud caput spinis coronari' (*DII*, p. 670).[152] *Ancrene Wisse* is even more graphic: 'Ouer all oþre þohtes, in alle ower passiuns þencheð eauer inwardliche upo Godes pinen ... schendlakes: hokeres, buffez, spatlunge, blindfeallunge, þornene crununge þet set him i þe heaued swa þet te blodi strundes striken adun ant leauden dun to þer eorðe' (*AW*, Corpus, p. 71).[153] Yet, instead of shying away from this horror, as Aelred anticipates his recluse may do, *Ancrene Wisse*'s readers must visualize directly the heavily bleeding flesh 'þenche o Godes rode, ase muchel as ha eauer con mest oðer mei, ant of his derue pine' (*AW*, Corpus, pp. 13–14).[154]

This is reflected in the thinking of the wider medieval world. By the thirteenth century the crucifix had superseded representations of the living Christ in popularity.[155] Constable terms this, at its most extreme, a 'crucifixion complex', linked to the phenomenon of stigmatization. This begins with St Francis himself and is manifested in 300 cases from the twelfth century onwards, the majority of whom are women.[156] None of the anchoritic guides refer to stigmatization, but they do reflect a dramatic interest in the contemplation of Christ's Passion wounds. Bettina Bildhauer notes the same fascination with bleeding and with Christ's blood in the wider medieval world: 'Water and blood prove that Christ had a human body ... that Christ had blood during his lifetime'; it 'connects blood with "the truth" ... [of] the incarnation of Christ ... because bleeding means being human'.[157] She continues: 'Blood reveals secrets', arguing that in, for instance, Eucharistic and crucifix miracles, blood 'uncovers a violation of the body', simultaneously rendering Christ's divinity a public expression, not a private pact.[158] Earlier medieval guidance's Christocentric ascetical focus upon the meditation on Christ's blood and wounds is borne out in historical accounts of contemporary contemplative experience. Elisabeth of Schönau (*c*.1129–*c*.64) frequently witnesses the crucified Christ: 'I saw ... the Lord on the cross ... His neck was curved, His loveable head fell down, His knees were bent and all of His limbs'.[159] Similarly, Mary of Oignies is granted the graphic vision of Christ crucified, although James of Vitry writes that she (potentially like Aelred's recluse) can scarcely endure it.[160]

Later medieval anchoritic guidance builds on the earlier guides' meditative focus on Christ's Passion agonies, the healing properties of his blood and the torments of the Christian martyrs. Yet, while earlier guidance wishes its recluses both to think about pain and experience it, later guidance encourages them to think about pain more than they experience it. There is a relationship between its decreased interest in aggressive ascetical acts and increased interest in aggressively ascetical meditation. Later guidance constructs a recluse capable of suffering as greatly, mentally, through ascetical medita- tion, as the earlier medieval recluse was capable of suffering bodily. Asceticism has become more a psychological than a physical battleground. This mental struggle is articulated in later guidance in an ascetical vocabulary reminiscent of the earlier guides' focus on aggressive ascetical acts. Hilton urges the recluse to take, not her body, but the vice of pride and 'hit ... take in thi mynde and rende it, breke it, dispice it, and doo al the schame that tho mai therto. Loke that thou spare it not' (*Scale I*, p. 94). It is the soul, not the body, that is now contaminated by the 'ground of synne' (*Scale I*, p. 75). In this context only, the recluse must 'arise up in thyn owen herte agens thisilf, for to hate and deme in thisilf al maner of synne' (*Scale I*, p. 48); precisely the kind of language with which earlier guidance vivified physical mortification. The language of physical torment is no longer utilized to inspire physical ascetic emulation, but to foster a mental, contem- plative, ascetical response in the recluse.

The examination of (now later medieval) ascetical meditation upon Christ's Passion must again stand here as a model for the later guides' treatment of all ascetically medita- tive material. Later guidance depicts its torments in even more gruesome detail than earlier guidance, yet its interest in the harrowing nature of Christ's suffering is a clear continuation of earlier perspectives. Through an increased appeal to the visual, the later writers aim to redirect the energies expended by earlier medieval writers upon encour- aging acts of asceticism in order to relocate the recluse's focus safely upon Christ. *Speculum* consequently echoes, but moves beyond, *Ancrene Wisse*'s visible interest in blood to a veritable delight in it, releasing an outpouring of eulogized emotion in its honour. The streams and rivers of blood that flow from the wounded Christ now have seven, not just five, sources and the sight of such blood purifies the recluse in the same way as the literal production of blood through, for example, flagellation was held to do in earlier guidance:

> O visio salutaris, o medicina sufficiens ad salutem ... que quoslibet percussos ab ignitis serpen- tibus temptacionis perfectissime sanas ... Hanc Passionem frequenter aspicias ... hic succursum quere, hic pete, hic pulsa ... non desinas ... dicas Domino fiducialiter ... 'Ab occultis meis munda me Domine. Et iterum Sana me Domine et sanabor, salva me' (*Speculum*, p. 110).[161]

The later medieval recluse is thereby freed from subjection to her own flesh, finding spiritual fulfilment in the visual meditation of another's. The contemplation of this pain is now thought to afford a more constructive, intimate bond than the physical experi- ence of it ever could. *Speculum* urges the recluse to visualize Christ's body in the 'eye' of her soul:

> quod fuit nodosis flagellis asperrime cesum, alapis illusum, crucifixum, lancea, clavis atque spinis undique perforatum, et a planta pedis usque ad verticem sanguinolentum, primitus tamen brachiis atque tibiis per cordas in longum et latum extractis, corpus sanctissimum affixum est

cruci penaliter, et tam crudeliter elevabatur in altum et iterum ad terram corruit violentur, quod omnes vene atque nervi corporis rumpebantur (*Speculum*, pp. 94–5).[162]

The crown of thorns bursts through his scalp: 'coronam spineam sustinuit, impressam suo capiti usque ad ipsius cerebri contaminacionem, et ex omni parte distillantes preciossimas guttas sanguinis' (*Speculum*, p. 110).[163]

This same graphic register is reflected in contemporary contemplative meditations and visions of the passion, such as those of Julian of Norwich, who received sixteen visions in May 1373 and may have spent the next twenty years contemplating their significance and whom Santha Bhattacharji calls 'the foremost representative of the female visionary tradition in England'.[164] Denise Baker argues that similarities between the theologies of anchoritic guidance and Julian's text are so great that she must have read *De institutione*, *Ancrene Wisse*, *Form* and *Scale*.[165] Jonathan Hughes goes so far as to observe that the 'remarkable congruity of thought between … Hilton and Julian … suggests that Hilton had a direct influence on the Norwich anchoress (he may have met her)'.[166] This is conjecture. While Julian's theology is not identical to that of later guidance and her assertions about universal salvation, in particular, run contrary to Hilton's teaching about the damnation of certain souls, notably heretics and hypocrites (*Scale I*, pp. 61–3), it is clear that all these texts negotiate similar spiritual territory, especially in their graphic revelation of the Passion.[167] Julian shares *Speculum*'s graphically visual intensity.[168] Just as the seven rivers of blood flowing from head, heart, hands, whip lacerations, genitalia, feet and even from Christ's pores, are seen in *Speculum* (pp. 96–7),[169] so Julian vivifies:

> The grete dropis of blode … from under the garland like pellots semand as it had cum out of the veynis … full thick, and … bright rede … the bleding continuid till many things were seene and understondyn … it were like to the scale of heryng in the spreadeing on the forehead.[170]

The later medieval guides share with other contemporary spiritual texts a continued focus on the broken body as the ultimate symbol of Christ's humanity. His crucified pose is one of defeat, of human fallibility. It calls salvation forth. God-as-man continues to reach out to mankind from the cross, united briefly in temporary willingness to embrace mortality through suffering. *Speculum* depicts the crucified Christ stretching out his head to kiss, his arms to embrace, his heart to love, surrendering his hands and feet to the cross (p. 98).[171] Yet, concurrently, it is clear that the contemplation of Christ's humanity has increasingly become a means to access his divinity. Hilton writes: 'a man schal not come to goostli delite in comtemplacioun of His Godhede, but yif he come first in ymaginacion … of His manhede' (*Scale I*, p. 68). This is echoed in other contemporary writings. Julian argues: 'the onyng of the God-hede gave strength to the manhode', for 'where Jesus appereith the blissid Trinite is understond'.[172] Christ's incarnation is, as Ellen M. Ross terms it, 'the critical restorative act in the God–human relationship' and as such is alien, terrible and almighty.[173] Ross observes a shift, certainly borne out in later anchoritic guidance, from a twelfth-century emphasis on the humanity of Christ's suffering to a fourteenth-century glorification of its majesty, ascribing to this the later medieval emergence of the pietà, a devotional image of the dead Christ in his mother's arms.[174] Jeffrey F. Hamburger's survey of the influence of works of art upon the contemplative experience of nuns, argues that devotional images can be read as texts that not only reflect but shape contemplative culture: 'the images came to life. The visions of female mystics ... brim over with accounts of nuns standing before works of art, exchanging love vows with Christ, sharing embraces, kissing his wounds, and ... receiving the stigmata'.[175]

The fifteenth-century manuscript, London, British Library, MS Harley 1740, contains a lengthy vernacular Passion narrative; one of many such narratives that vivify the sufferings of Christ in gruesome severity.[176] The appendix to this narrative is a letter written to a woman addressed as 'Mother', entitled 'Item de passione Christi bona contemplacio'. Its author and addressee remain unknown, although its editor, C. W. Marx, proposes her a religious. Its sublimation of the physical experience of pain into its contemplation is strikingly similar to that of later medieval guidance. If read in the context of increased later medieval interest in the contemplation, rather than enactment, of pain, it is not the 'puzzle' Marx makes it.[177]

It begins by encouraging the contemplative, as Rolle does, to kindle the 'fier of Goddis loue ... in thyn herte' ('Item de passione Christi', ll. 6–7). She must abandon the world's concerns and 'beilde a fare honest chapell amyddes þine awne hert' ('Item de passione Christi', ll. 22–3), the centrepiece of which is Christ crucified. She must contemplate the 'grysely woundes all fresch bledynge' ('Item de passione Christi', ll. 27–31). This is in keeping with the contemporary tradition of affective piety constructed in texts such as Nicholas Love's *The Mirrour of the Blessed Lyf of Jesu Christ*, a Middle English translation of the *Meditationes vitae Christi*. It also has parallels with the allegorical construction of works such as the fourteenth-century *Abbey of the Holy Ghost*. It encourages the contemplative to build an inner 'chapel', each component of which is invested with spiritual significance and associated with specific virtues.[178] It then venerates the instruments of the Passion in the *Arma Christi* tradition.[179] The contemplation of each instrument is constructed as the remedy for a specific sin; action has truly become subordinate to contemplation.[180] The author seeks to inspire only the desire to emulate Christ's suffering, recommending a mental, not a physical, 'scourging'; a contemplative participation in self-purification, although one constructed so graphically that it is easy to forget it is metaphorical construct, not literal instruction:

> And þat þou may suffre ... in þe ende of þe awter set þe piller þat our lord was bounde to and ... take þe oþer ende of þe corde ... and bynde þe ... In þe other side of þe crosse hange þe two scourges and when ony temptacion of þe flesch commyth to the, scourge þe well all aboute and make þe a reed cote to þi lordes leuerey till þe temptacion be voyded frome the ('Item de passione Christi', ll. 40–8).

Such mental scourging is a purgative performance, to be used ascetically to calm the rebellion of the flesh. Contemplation here is an ascetic practice through which the individual assumes an ascetical disposition not an ascetical position; the ascetic-contemplative is not constructed as inferior to the aggressive ascetics of former days. This text is only one among many later medieval passion narratives that exemplify a contemporary interest in the contemplation of bodily suffering as contemplative inspiration. It frees the contemplative from the demands of her own body, to which the earlier medieval was firmly tied. It does not, however, go as far as Hilton would wish and advocate bodily transcendence.

This chapter has shown that the anchoritic guidance tradition reinforces the significance of asceticism to the vocation. In the earlier period, acts of asceticism are encouraged, both passive and aggressive, although an increasing interest in discretion is demonstrated, in particular by the time of *Ancrene Wisse*. Earlier guidance displays some interest in rendering pain vivid to the recluse through ascetical meditation, notably on Christ's Passion torments. The later guides show awareness of and some interest in the continuation of ascetical acts, but they demonstrate much greater interest in discretion. In the case of Hilton, these recommendations of moderation tend towards anti-asceticism. The later guides demonstrate an increased interest in ascetical meditation as a purificatory practice, building on the earlier guides' comparatively less graphic interest in meditation on pain. The later texts do not require the physical production of pain from their recluses and instead use increasingly gruesome ascetical contemplation to produce the same kinds of purification countenanced in earlier guidance's focus on aggressive ascetical acts. These developments in anchoritic ascetical ideology have been shown to resonate with those of the wider medieval world. Anchoritism has begun to emerge as a vocation in theological transition and anchoritic ideals and practices – here of asceticism – have been shown not to remain constant, but to be subject to the same fluctuations and trends as wider medieval spiritualities. It remains to be seen whether, in chapter 5's contextualization of anchoritic contemplative experience, this picture of an eremitic vocation which develops in tandem with the world outside the anchorhold will continue to be borne out.

5

Anchoritism and Contemplative Experience

Earlier anchoritic guidance is devoted to the exploration of asceticism, precisely because its central purpose is to equip the recluse contemplatively. Anselm advises his recluses: 'Exceptis iis quae fragilitas humanae naturae ad suam exigit sustentationem ... angelicam in omnibus considerate et imitamini conversationem. Haec contemplatio sit magistra vestra, haec consideratio sit regula vestra' (Anselm, 'Letter 230', vol. 4, p. 135).[1] Goscelin argues that anchoritism 'animam relaxat ab exterioribus curis, uocans in libertatem sue contemplationis' (*Liber*, p. 89),[2] which he describes as a means whereby 'ut de plurimis uenias ad unum, in quo sunt omnia' (*Liber*, p. 89).[3] Many famed, non-anchoritic ascetics, including Peter Damian and Mary of Oignies, were concurrently and, precisely because of their asceticism, famed contemplatives. Hence, Otter can argue that Goscelin's guide is a textbook of asceticism and at the same time 'a textbook of meditation' (Otter, p. 11): the two are not mutually exclusive. Mary Edsall links them together implicitly in her demand for the critical revaluation of *Ancrene Wisse* in the face of scholarly rejections of it as contemplative: '[by collapsing] the image of the body of the bird in flight ... with the concept of the anchoress spreading her spiritual wings in ... self-denial', she believes, the guide depicts 'a contemplative life ... [where] asceticism and spiritual purgation merge with ascent and union'.[4] Undoubtedly, the earlier anchoritic guides deal chiefly with asceticism as a preparation for contemplation, whereas later guides focus upon the experience and rewards of that contemplation and touch comparatively little on its ascetical preparations. Yet, Aelred still devotes half his guide to a systematic threefold meditation on Christ, for a contemplative he constructs as on fire with love (*DII*, p. 676).[5] *Ancrene Wisse*'s focus upon devotion, confession and penitence is structured to lead to the culmination of its inner rule; a chapter, again, on love. The boundaries between asceticism and contemplative experience are not distinct in the guides themselves; it may be more accurate to think of asceticism as a form of contemplative experience. Yet, criticism of earlier anchoritic guidance tends to regard these practices as mutually exclusive and casts the early guides as purely ascetic. This implication drives Watson's description of Rolle as the earliest vernacular exponent of later medieval mystical spirituality on the basis that earlier guides 'envisage the spiritual life not as ... ascent but as ascesis'.[6] Warren identifies the earlier guides as ascetic and only the later ones as contemplative.[7] Similarly, Gerard Sitwell argues that in *Ancrene Wisse*, 'of contemplation ... the highest form of union with God that the soul can attain on earth ... there is nothing'.[8] This chapter problematizes such assertions. It challenges Shepherd's conclusion that 'there is little point in speaking of *Ancrene Wisse* as a mystical work', and argues instead for a clear tradition of anchoritic contemplative guidance that begins with Goscelin.[9]

The vocabulary of contemplation

The modern study of medieval contemplative experience is hampered by the lack of a shared critical vocabulary. Many terms exist, including 'mystic', 'mysticism', 'visionary', 'contemplative' and even 'clairvoyant', but they are often synonymized or undefined and can obscure, not clarify, meaning.[10] Warren conflates 'mysticism' and 'contemplation' and argues: 'The word *contemplative* has many meanings', but writes of 'the achievement of the mystical moment' without defining it.[11] Other conclusions may be too inclusive, for instance Laurie A. Finke's, plausible, suggestion that mysticism is 'a set of cultural and ideological constructs that both share in and subvert orthodox religious institutions'.[12] The concept of mysticism dominates contemporary critical discussion and yet, as Baker remarks (of Dean Inge's 1899 conclusion in his *Christian Mystics*), 'no English word has been employed more loosely'.[13] Marion Glasscoe centres her own definition upon veracity: '[Mysticism is] an ultimate spiritual reality experienced both within the … human personality and as a transcendent power'.[14] Watson concludes: 'Mystical writing fuses subjective experience and expression with absolute declarations as to the nature of truth … it is thus … potentially uncontrollable'.[15] He rightly argues that mysticism is so complex that it is hard even to determine 'what is being said', let alone 'to decide whether it is consistent with orthodoxy'.[16] Evelyn Underhill writes of the confusion of 'the inexperienced student, who usually emerges from his struggle with the ever-increasing mass of … literature possessed by a vague idea that every kind of super-sensual theory … is somehow "mystical"'.[17] Her attempts to dispel such confusion result in the, rather broad, definition that mysticism is 'the science of ultimates'.[18] Rosalynn Voaden recalls Cuthbert Butler's 1926 conclusion that 'there is probably no more misused term in these our days than … "mysticism"' and remarks that 'The situation has not improved a great deal since'.[19] Her definition usefully separates it from visionary experience, proposing the former as an intellectual and the latter as a 'spiritual or imaginary' union with God, but nonetheless it must carry the caveat: 'The two categories … are not mutually exclusive'.[20] William F. Pollard and Robert Boenig rightly problematize 'Efforts to reduce mysticism to one paradigm', noting aptly that the output of diverse medieval theologians 'leave[s] us with disparate mysticisms rather than some central concept lionized as "Mysticism"'.[21] Another valuable definition is Gunn's, for whom mysticism is 'union with God achieved through asceticism, devotional practices and contemplation: a foretaste of the beatific vision … after death'.[22] This admits the 'mystical' nature of diverse spiritual practices including asceticism and rejects the reductive synonymization of mysticism with visionary experience.

The terms 'mysticism' and 'mystic' are problematic not only because their definition is subjective, but because their usage was not prevalent in the Middle Ages. Butler remarks that although the term 'mystic' was originally used in connection with the Greek mysteries and its Christian usage began in relation to the fifth-century pseudo-Dionysius, '"contemplation" is the word that will be met with in St Augustine, St Gregory, and St Bernard'.[23] Baker argues that even in the later Middle Ages the texts we identify as mystical 'would have been referred to as contemplative and placed in the Christian tradition of spiritual practices reserved for those in contemplative not active life'.[24] *The Middle English Dictionary* records the usage of 'mystic' as early as 1382 (in the Wycliffite Bible).[25] Yet, it is not until later that its meaning approaches its contemporary synonymity with 'contemplative', for instance in the 1552 conclusion that 'The haly kirk is callit the mistike bodye and spouse of Christ'.[26] Watson questions the term's 'protective enclosure':

> the phrase 'Middle English mystics' is anachronistic in its application of a Counter-Reformation category to the medieval period ... the phrase 'mystick theology' is first recorded in 1639 and 'mystic' and 'mysticism' are eighteenth-century terms; while the Latin *theologica mystica* attains its present sense only in the sixteenth century.[27]

He believes that 'the canon of "Middle English mystics" and the term "mysticism" ... have largely outlived their usefulness'. The 'heterogeneous club' of five: Rolle, Hilton, Julian, the author of *The Cloud of Unknowing* and Margery Kempe, is, he argues, 'reductively exclusive'.[28] He mistrusts the motives of the critics who gave this group prominence at the turn of the twentieth century as inspired by their own faith agenda.[29] Others, such as Lochrie, have gone still further, demanding the large-scale revision of the language currently used to study medieval contemplation.[30]

This chapter prioritizes the contemplative terminology of the anchoritic guides themselves, but also uses the terms 'contemplative experience' and 'contemplative activity' to describe any stage of contemplative experience and refers to individuals engaged in such practices as 'contemplative'.[31] Earlier guidance refers usually to 'meditation' not contemplation. Aelred declares that 'affectus salutari meditatione nutritur' (*DII*, p. 662) and avows at its conclusion: 'meditatio affectum excitet ... ut sint tibi lacrymae tuae panes die ac nocte' (*DII*, p. 681).[32] He constructs meditation as not only the practice of thinking about spiritual matters but also of reading and praying about them, practices that can blend together and all tend towards spiritual visualization.[33] In this, he follows Goscelin, who endeavours to train Eve's mind to blend reflective, ruminative, reading with prayer and visualization into one affective whole (*Liber*, p. 82).[34] At the heart of imaginative spiritual rumination is, for Goscelin, a text, which functions as a contemplative trigger. It is not simply read but, as Otter argues, generatively thought through (Otter, p. 11). Anselm similarly recommends the blending of spiritual practices, binding 'orationibus ... et cogitationibus' (Anselm, 'Letter 112', vol. 3, p. 246).[35] *Ancrene Wisse* also refers to 'meditation', but favours terms relating to this kind of spiritual thinking. The *Concordance to 'Ancrene Wisse'* notes four usages of 'meditatiuns' but sixty-six usages of words relating to thought.[36] The term 'contemplatiun' is found only once, in a passage which may be its first recorded usage in Middle English,[37] a metaphorical construction of the contemplative anchorite as a bird: 'Alswa schal ancre fleon wið contemplatiun (þet is, wið heh þoht) ant wið hali bonen bi niht toward heouene, ant bi3eote ... hire sawle fode' (*AW*, Corpus, p. 56).[38] This passage also implies the shared belief of all earlier medieval guidance writers that contemplation unites many restorative, spiritual activities together and cannot be understood as a signifier for one alone.

In contrast with the contemplative vocabulary of earlier guidance, the later writers freely use terms which equate to 'contemplate', 'contemplation' and 'contemplative'. Warren notes a similar trend in contemporary episcopal registers and court rolls.[39] Rolle writes: 'in contemplacioun ... haue þi delite' (*Form*, p. 9). For him, the anchoritic life is 'contemplatif lif', which has 'two parties', the lower is in meditation on holy writing and 'good thoghtes'; the higher is the soul's 'biholdynge ... of þe þynges of heuyn ... a wonderful ioy of Goddis loue' (*Form*, p. 24). Hilton refers to 'the staat of contemplatif liyf' (*Scale I*, p. 133), noting that: 'Thre meenys there ben whiche men most comonli use that yyven hem to contemplacioun: redynge ... of hooli techynge, goosteli meditacion, and besi praeris with devocioun' (*Scale I*, p. 45). He identifies three levels of contemplative experience: knowledge of God, affection for God, and knowledge and affection for God. *Speculum* identifies 'Dei contemplacioni ... fructum ... vite contemplative ... videlicet ... oracione, meditacione et leccione' (*Speculum*, p. 81).[40] Aelred's Bodley redactor refers to 'meditacion and praier and contemplacion' (*DII*, MS Bodley 423, p. 2), inserting the term 'contemplacion', absent from Aelred's original, although the threefold meditation continues to be called a meditation (*DII*, MS Bodley 423, p. 17). Evidently the later guides use some terminology from earlier guidance to reference the same kinds of contemplative experience favoured by them, including ruminative thought, visualization through prayer, reading and meditation. Yet, as the remainder of this chapter will show, the later texts also focus far more on experiences only hinted at by the earlier guides.

The three stages of contemplation: meditation, vision, fusion

Meditation

Most anchoritic guidance writers construct meditation as the primary stage in a contemplative ascent. Goscelin urges Eve: 'ad tam bonum Dominum toto animo propera' (*Liber*, p. 108).[41] Contemporary devotional sources also reflect this upward contemplative progress. An illustrated copy of *La Sainte Abbaye* (*c.*1300) depicts a Cistercian nun progressing upwards through each phase and Hamburger notes her 'ecstatic posture' as she attains the ultimate contemplative state, passing 'from visible to invisible things'.[42] Earlier anchoritic guidance argues that meditation can involve the deliberate imagination of a spiritual subject (for instance a period in the life of Christ, or the recluse's own mortality) or focus on an inanimate object (such as an altar cloth) or on the ruminative reading of a spiritual text. Meditation fosters a cognitive relationship with God, more apt to be comprehended intellectually than felt experientially. Otter differentiates between meditative revelations engaged in by an 'imaginer' and actual visions, gifted to a 'visionary', calling the former 'deliberate imaginings, meditation work, the "craft of thought"'.[43] During meditation, the guides suggest that the recluse remains aware of her temporal surroundings, conscious of her meditation as a devotional exercise. Anselm anticipates that this may be disrupted and disruptive:

> Cum autem vultis ... aliquam bonam meditationem intendere: si vobis tunc importunae sunt cogitationes quas non debetis suscipere, numquam propter illarum importunitatem bonum quod incepistis velitis dimittere ... sed eo quem dixi modo illas contemnendo superate (Anselm, 'Letter 414', vol. 5, p. 361).[44]

The earlier medieval recluse is not constructed by the guides as a full participant in her imaginary world, although some, notably Aelred's, encourage the suggestion, using the present tense to convey meditative immediacy. Aelred's meditation upon the past casts the recluse as Christ's companion, one who runs, laughs, weeps and suffers, touches and is touched: 'insta, ora, et grauidos lacrymis oculos attolle, imisque suspiriis inenarrabilibusque gemitibus extorque quod petis' (*DII*, pp. 665–6).[45] Such descriptions are affective; intended to foster the recluse's sensory and emotional involvement. Yet, the scene remains a tableau: an imaginary landscape, intensely visual, but cognitively intellectualized nonetheless, despite all attempts to draw the recluse literally into it. Frequent exhortations to 'call to mind', 'contemplate', 'consider' and 'meditate' only serve to disrupt the illusion (*DII*, p. 665).[46] Aelred's controlling presence as meditative orchestrator is asserted so strongly at times that it seems more his meditation than hers, one in which the recluse remains forever an onlooker, enclosed by her own self-awareness and silence in the face of this guidance writer's speech. In this, Aelred follows Goscelin, whose *Liber* casts Eve as onlooker, even when engaging in a passionate contemplative practice which uses her tears as a creative form of worship described in the most affective of terms (*Liber*, p. 106).[47]

Comparatively little material is devoted to meditation in the later medieval guides. Yet, they certainly continue to expect their contemplatives to meditate on subjects evocative of earlier guidance, including human mortality and eternal judgement. Rolle's suggestions for meditation on hell's torments are as dark as any earlier medieval ones, while the *Speculum* author's meditations upon Judgement Day (*Speculum*, pp. 101–2; *Myrour*, pp. 30–1) are cast in a tradition deeply allusive of Goscelin's and Aelred's. The later guides continue to regard meditation as the first of the three stages in a contemplative ascent, but meditation is now recommended, for instance in *Speculum* (p. 90), when disrupted prayer is ineffective.[48] This is a significant shift from earlier medieval guidance founded upon narrative meditation as its central contemplative focus. Yet, *Speculum*'s later position has parallels with Goscelin's earlier advice that Eve persist in contemplative reading, praying and meditative visualization even when the mind is 'sine fructu' (*Liber*, p. 60), for it can still refresh the spirit.[49]

The later guides anticipate that greater physical extremes will be manifested during such experience, including weeping, writhing, babbling, shaking, singing (peculiarly Rollian), physically sensed burning and sweetness, trance-like stillness and an inability to speak. This is not entirely new. Goscelin described contemplative experience as a trigger for affective piety, in keeping with contemporary accounts of visionary experience, such as that of Ademar of Chabannes (989–1034) who, Frassetto argues, saw 'Jesus on the cross, the color of fire and blood … shedding many tears'.[50] Goscelin had advised Eve, in terms very similar to the later guide *Speculum*, that purificatory tears would cleanse her of her sinfulness:

> eternis amoribus rapiaris … recogitans semper et preterita et futura … ut de profundo cordis … in omni genere compunctionis facias aqueductum lacrimarum, quibus lota et candidata ueste … Habes magnam materiam lacrimarum … exultes' (*Liber*, p. 106).[51]

Vision

The anchoritic guidance tradition constructs vision as the second stage of contemplative experience. The later guides focus on it in most detail, but the earlier guides certainly explore its significance. The *Liber* casts meditative rumination as one visionary trigger. The Virgin 'Canticum graduum inter surgendum timpanizaret … ingressum fuisse Gabrielem arc(h)angelum' (*Liber*, p. 83).[52] Goscelin describes a visionary who may not be able to interpret her own experience: 'quia … si nos non intelligimus que de ore nostro proferimus, ille tamen uirtutes que nobis assistunt intelligunt, et uero quodam carmine in uirtute adesse se nobis, et ferre auxilium delectantur' (*Liber*, p. 60).[53] Goscelin undoubtedly believes in the spiritual possibilities of vision and frequently focuses upon the inspirational examples of Christian visionaries, such as St Gertrude's appearance to the abbess Modesta: 'Huic uirgo gloriosa, ea hora qua animam celo reddidit, oranti in ecclesia uisibiliter apparuit, et … presentialiter se ac si in corpore exhibuit, atque ita infit: "quam scias hac hora ad Dominum de ergastulo migrasse corporali"' (*Liber*, p. 44).[54] Gertrude appears at the moment she dies, but the visionary power of the living is also vivified: 'Plerumque etiam spiritus sanctorum adhuc in corpore mortali degentium in remotas terras uisibiliter ac si corporaliter apparere at colloqui hominibus fecit' (*Liber*, p. 44).[55] Peter Brown argues, in the context of the cult of the saints which dominated Europe in the sixth and seventh centuries, that Christian writers in the period leading up to the year 1000 validate 'the closeness of invisible guides and protectors'.[56] While Anselm's encouragement, 'Angelos vestros … semper vobis praesentes et actus et cogitatus vestros considerantes cogitate … velut si eos visibiliter inspiceretis, semper vivere curate' (Anselm, 'Letter 230', vol. 4, p. 135),[57] implies that his recluses cannot actually see their celestial companions, he nonetheless believes that they exist. Goscelin cites the examples of St Nicholas, St Martin, St Benedict, St Ambrose of Milan (*Liber*, p. 45)[58] and the Jewish convert to Christianity, who appears to his brothers to urge their baptism prior to their imminent death (*Liber*, p. 108).[59]

Jane Schulenburg argues that at this time vision and prophecy give women 'a voice, visibility, power and authority within … society'.[60] Mulder-Bakker argues, in terms of the twelfth- and thirteenth-century lowlands, that 'Everything off-limits to a woman because of her socially inferior status, God could impart to her in a vision', which 'legitimizes her with a personal order for prophetic proclamation'.[61] Goscelin, as writer of the *Vita* and *Translatio* of Edith of Wilton, would have been aware of the various posthumous visionary appearances of the convent's patron saint and of the wider visionary potential of women.[62] Yet, his primary motivation in insisting on its potential is, unlike any other guidance writer, to reassure himself that vision may yet unite him with Eve miraculously, rather than to construct her as a visionary by virtue of her gender or even her vocation. Nonetheless, he declares of Eve: 'merearis … et hunc saluatorem tuum perpetuo uidere modo in anima, deinde in duplici corporis et anime stola' (*Liber*, p. 116).[63]

Ancrene Wisse validates the visions of others, authenticating visionary experience as the medium for the dissemination of knowledge impossible to obtain by other means (*AW*, Corpus, p. 90).[64] It describes a state in which, unlike meditation, all sense of temporal reality is suspended; vision becomes reality, albeit only temporarily. A vague awareness of the temporal body may be retained: vision, even etymologically, is ultimately grounded in and experienced through the bodily senses, especially sight, and is often recounted retrospectively in embodied terms by visionaries themselves. From the time of St Paul onwards, contemplatives have bemoaned their inability to relate experiences which are beyond the body in language that cannot escape it.[65] Elzéar of Sabran (1285–1323) writes: 'Oh how badly and imperfectly I speak! I do not know and cannot formulate what I saw, or express in speech what I learned by experience'.[66] The thirteenth-century visionary contemplative, Hadewijch of Brabant, demonstrates the discontent of the visionary upon returning to the lower contemplative stage of meditation:

I was taken up in the spirit. There I saw a very deep whirlpool … I saw the forms of many different souls … I received interior knowledge about some, and also exterior knowledge … Then I saw coming as it were a bird … Then I heard a voice like thunder.[67]

She complains: 'afterwards I returned to myself, where I found myself poor and miserable, I reflected on this [vision] … which I had attained. I was not contented'.[68]

Walker Bynum relates the body-conscious example of Mechthild of Magdeburg (1207–82):

Then the maid [i.e. Mechthild] went up to the altar with great love … John the Baptist took the white lamb with the red wounds and laid it on the mouth of the maid. Thus the pure Lamb laid itself on its own image in the stall of her body and sucked her heart with its tender lips.[69]

Marguerite of Oingt (c.1240–c.1310) also articulates her vision in embodied terms: 'I approach and take out the nails and then I carry him on my shoulders down from the cross and put him between the arms of my heart'.[70] Some female contemplatives such as Gertrude of Helfta (1256–c.1301/2) and Mechthild of Hackeborn (c.1240/1–c.1298/99) were granted visions of Christ both as mother and babe.[71] Gertrude was gifted with the sight of 'the immaculate womb of the glorious virgin, as transparent as the purest crystal'; she saw 'the little blossoming boy … nurse avidly in delight at the heart of his virgin mother'.[72] This trope concurrently connotes birth and death and Christ's birth foreshadows his crucifixion. In this tradition, Aelred concludes: 'expansis brachiis ad suos te inuitet amplexus, in quibus delecteris, nudatis uberibus lac tibi suauitatis infundat quo consoleris' (DII, p. 658).[73]

Yet, Ancrene Wisse focuses far more than Goscelin on the potential dangers of visions, debating the problem of 'lease swefnes, false schawunges, dredfule offearunges' (AW, Corpus, p. 102).[74] It warns the recluse not to credit visions on her own authority. The Devil may enter the cell as an 'angel of light': 'Na sihðe þet 3e seoð, ne i swefne ne waken, ne telle 3e bute dweole' (AW, Corpus, p. 86).[75] This may be read as a discouragement of all visionary activity, but it could also simply be specific to the construction of the devil-angel preceding it. It may be his visions, rather than all visions, that are to be discredited. Such warnings are part of a tradition of scepticism about personal contemplative inspiration which also prompts Aelred's insistence that all thought be grounded in scripture to prevent spiritual falsity: 'Nihil enim magis cogitationes excludit inutiles, uel compescit lascivas quam meditatio uerbi Dei' (DII, p. 654).[76] Hollywood argues that fear of female visionaries was so pronounced that it led to the 'denigration of mysticism, and particularly those affective, visionary and ecstatic forms … most often associated with women'.[77] She points particularly to the repudiation, in the writings of Jean Gerson (1363–1429), chancellor of the University of Paris from 1395, of 'women's visionary, auditory and sensory experiences of the divine' and 'the teaching, preaching and writing that these experiences authorized'.[78] David A. Salomon argues: 'The … inscription of the body' shifts 'to the page as the printed work becomes the only physical manifestation of the mystical experience'.[79] Ancrene Wisse's reaction to this atmosphere of fear regarding the recording and veracity of visionary experience is reflected in the wider anxieties of contemporary non-anchoritic contemplatives. Elisabeth of Schönau, in a letter to Hildegard of Bingen (1098–1179), states that she was beaten into revelation by an angel, while Gertrud of Helfta speaks out only when Jesus himself commands it and Mechthild of Magdeburg complains that a priest who had written as she had done would, in all likelihood, not have had his books burnt.[80]

Later anchoritic guidance continues, as earlier guidance did, to validate visionary experience as a medium for spiritual knowledge not acquirable by other means but, rather than chiefly recount the visionary experience of others as reclusive inspiration (as the earlier guides did), the later guides now fully anticipate that their own recluses may be visionaries. *Speculum* acknowledges 'devotam meditacionem ... visiones seu revelaciones de rebus occultis' (*Speculum*, pp. 82–3),[81] constructing vision as an imperfect, brief foretaste of heavenly reward, the revelation of future things gifted by grace to very few (*Speculum*, p. 130).[82] Vision is, for Hilton, also partial, a 'lyvynge bi a schadewe in contemplacion' (*Scale I*, p. 132), existing 'half in derkenesse' (*Scale I*, p. 38). It continues to involve the temporary suspension, not the total abandonment, of the temporal world and senses. It continues to be articulated through language that is inherently embodied. Visions continue to be mistrusted. The same atmosphere of fear that surrounded visionary experience in earlier guidance persists in the later guides. In terms reminiscent of *Ancrene Wisse*'s treatment of the same passage, *Myrour* still warns against 'angelus sathane in lucis angelum se transfigurans', charging the anchorite-visionary to fear the 'magnitudo revelationis' of God, lest it results in spiritual arrogance (*Speculum*, pp. 114–15).[83] This is also reflected in the experiences of contemporary contemplatives, such as Margaret Porete, whose visionary experiences are recorded in *The Mirror of Simple Souls*. Her failure to gain episcopal approbation saw her burnt at the stake as a heretic in Paris in 1310 and her book suppressed.[84]

Yet, the later guides imply that visionaries of whom the church approves will be gifted with a greater measure of contemplative authority.[85] Contemporary sources echo the later medieval guides' constructions of the visionary recluse as potentially powerful. One of the lives of St John of Bridlington (1320–79) notes the example of an anchorite at Richmond who had a vision of an eagle bearing a parchment in its beak declaring 'Jesus is my love', although the saint himself is said to have discounted this.[86] The aforementioned fifteenth-century anchorite, Emma Rawghton, of All Saint's Church, North Street, York was esteemed for her visions of Mary. The Rous roll records that in 1421, the year of King Henry VI's birth, the Virgin appeared seven times to Emma, informed her of the impending death of Henry V, of the coronation of Henry VI in France and advised her that Richard Beauchamp would have the rule of the young king until he came to the age of sixteen. Her second vision predicted that he would father an heir if he founded a chantry in the chapel of the hermitage of Guy's Cliff.[87] An image of Rawghton, featuring both her visions of Beauchamp, appears in the *Pageants of Richard Beauchamp*.[88]

Contemporary historical records also suggest that later medieval anchorites were implicated as authority figures in the visions of others, in ways which potentially endangered them. Elizabeth Barton, whose predictions about Henry VIII's downfall were he to marry Anne Boleyn led to Barton's execution for treason in 1534, tried to draw Christopher Warner, a Dominican recluse at Canterbury, into her situation.[89] Clay notes that in 1533: 'Cromwell tried to get ... [Warner] to incriminate the nun, but he would only say that he was never of counsel with her, never saw her in a trance, nor heard her say aught against the King'.[90] Warner was powerful enough to complain that being questioned disrupted his contemplative experience and therefore his anchoritic vocation.[91] Julian understood the continuing dangers involved in identifying as a contemplative in the later medieval period: 'at that tyme I cowde tell it no preist. For I thowte, how should a preist levyn me?'[92] Fear potentially motivates her self-identification as a simple, unlearned creature, despite her evident theological sophistication, education and her ability both to describe and interpret her visionary experience.[93] Finke suggests that visionaries like Julian, Hildegard of Bingen and Angela of Foligno (1248–1309) were 'not nearly as disingenuous as they had to appear', having 'the power to shape the meaning and form of their experiences'; their 'words and their bodies ... sites of struggle to redefine the meaning of female silence and powerlessness'.[94] Julian may write: 'god for bede that ye schulde saye or take it so that I am a techere ... For I am a womann, leued, febille, and freyll', yet she continues: 'Botte I wate wele this that I saye: I hafe it of the schewynge of hym thas es soverayne techare'.[95] Kathryn Kerby-Fulton reminds us that Julian is 'extremely well informed about the theological arguments supporting female teaching, or even preaching – arguments usually discreetly buried in Latin scholastic discussions and not well advertised to the laity'; yet here Julian makes 'a *de facto* claim for the gift of [women's] prophetic vision ... a deft reminder of the spiritual equality of men and women'.[96]

The later anchoritic guides express a greater expectation of bodily transcendence through vision than did their earlier counterparts. Although the later writers continue the earlier medieval tradition of focus on vision's traditional relationship with the five senses, there is also a focus on what Rolle terms 'þe egh of þyn hert' (*Form*, p. 13) and Hilton 'the mynde of thyn herte' (*Scale I*, p. 65).[97] The *Mirror of St Edmund* (*c*.1390) states that 'Contemplaciun is ... þe goodnesse of god for to seo'.[98] Yet it is not always connected with physical sight in the later guides or other contemporary writings.[99] The *Book to a Mother* (*c*.1400) constructs thought as sight: 'Blessid ben the clene of herte, for thei schulen see God ... by contemplacioun, that is to seye, by goode thou3tes and desyres and goode undurstondynges'.[100] Margery Kempe (*c*.1373–*c*.1438) locates her visions in the soul. She 'cowd nevyr telle the grace that sche felt, it was so hevenly, so hy aboven hyr reson and hyr bodyly wyttys ... that sche myth nevyr expressyn it wyth her word lych as sche felt it in hyr sowle'.[101] Hilton locates vision both 'in cognicion and in affeccion' (*Scale I*, p. 37), yet, nonetheless, just as with sin that he believes erroneously drives the ascetic to focus upon the body, so vision 'is neither bodili, ne is it bodili feelid. A soule may fele it ... whiche soule is in the bodi, but he felith it not bi no bodili witt' (*Scale I*, p. 59). Rolle locates contemplation only in the body by virtue of its relationship with the soul. It 'is in þe soule, and for aboundance of ioy and swetnesse hit ascendeth in to þe mouth ... þe hert and þe tonge accordeth in on, and body and soule ioyeth in God' (*Form*, p. 25).

Fusion
Fusion is constructed in anchoritic guidance as the highest and rarest of contemplative states, in which the senses are entirely overcome, the recluse fused to God: two rendered one. No guidance writer can lead the recluse to this grace-given experience, or even describe it adequately (certainly not in embodied language, for it is far beyond the body). Meditation and vision are not its prerequisites and even the most experienced contemplative may never achieve fusion. Its biblical precedent is St Paul's Damascus road conversion in Cor. 2, 12:2–4:

> scio hominem in Christo ante annos quattuordecim sive in corpore nescio sive extra corpus nescio Deus scit raptum eiusmodi usque ad tertium caelum et scio huiusmodi hominem sive in

corpore sive extra corpus nescio Deus scit quoniam raptus est in paradisum et audivit arcana verba quae non licet homini loqui.[102]

Fusion is far more of a focus for later anchoritic guidance, but is nonetheless anticipated by the earlier guides. Goscelin hints at it in his synonymization of three contemplative experiences of contemplation with the biblical books of Proverbs, Ecclesiastes and the Song of Songs. The first two experiences and books, which focus on discipline and the eradication of vanity, are only necessary 'ut ad tertium gradum ... appetitu nos rapiat ... in pace conditoris mens contemplatiua pertendat' (Liber, p. 39).[103] He describes heavenly, not earthly, union with God in terms of ravishment. The soul 'tunc mirabitur et obstupescet, ultra se ipsam rapta a tam inseparabili claritate et letitia' (Liber, pp. 39–40).[104] Full contemplative fulfilment then, for Goscelin, is reserved for heaven. Aelred's construction of the recluse's meditation on the Magdalene's meeting with Jesus hints at bodily transcendence: 'Nam plura dicere lacrymae prohibent, cum uocem occludat affectus, omnesque animae corporisque sensus nimius amor absorbeat' (DII, p. 672).[105] Aelred also implies fusion in his description of meditative ascent: 'quotiens orantem in quoddam ineffabile desiderium sui rapiebat, quotiens mentem tuam a terrenis subtractam ad caelestes delicias et paradisiacas amoenitates transportabat' (DII, p. 676).[106] He continues: 'quotiens aestuanti prae amore ipse se tuis uisceribus infundebat' (DII, p. 676).[107] It necessitates the rejection of the temporal sphere: 'Non has delicias tuas somnus interpolet, nullus exterior tumultus impediat' (DII, p. 673).[108]

Warren argues that earlier guides 'approach the ascent of [the contemplative] ... ladder only in a tentative and furtive manner' and that 'the achievement of the mystical moment is mentioned only in passing ... cloaked in obscure language'.[109] Yet, Ancrene Wisse does more than just approach it in passages that focus on contemplation as a soaring upwards in flight (AW, Corpus, p. 56).[110] The Eucharist is central to this guide's construction of fusion. As soon as she awakes, the recluse should 'þencheð o Godes flesch ant on his deorewurðe blod, þet is abuue þe hehe weoued, ant falleð adun þertowart' (AW, Corpus, p. 7).[111] The host is rendered the embodiment of Christ: 'euche dei he kimeð forð ant schaweð him to ow fleschliche ant licomliche ínwið þe Messe – biwrixlet þah on oþres lite, under breades furme, for in his ahne ure ehnen ne mahten nawt þe brihte sihðe þolien. Ah swa he schaweð him ow (AW, Corpus, p. 100)'.[112] Fusion comes in a moment of ecstasy inspired by this host: 'Efter þe measse cos, hwen þe preost sacreð – þer for3eoteð al þe world, þer beoð al ut of bodi, þer i sperclinde luue bicluppeð ower leofmon, þe into ower breostes bur is iliht of heouene' (AW, Corpus, p. 13).[113] Christ literally and figuratively assumes the body of the recluse: 'as þe preoste measseð – þe meidene bearn ... licomliche lihteð oðerhwiles to ower in, ant inwið ow eadmodliche nímeð his herbearhe' (AW, Corpus, p. 102).[114] Hamburger describes this as the mimicry of the priest's kiss of peace, yet the anchorite journeys far beyond a simple embrace.[115] It is as brief as it is rare and the demands of the body swiftly reassert themselves: 'þe gode ancre, ne fleo ha neauer se hehe, ha mot lihten oðerhwiles dun to þer eorðe of hire bodi, eoten, drinken, slepen, wurchen, speoken, heren of þet hire neodeð to of eorðliche þinges' (AW, Corpus, p. 53).[116]

Ancrene Wisse's construction of fusion in the mass through spousal metaphor recalls Goscelin's construction of Eucharistic intimacy, where, Goscelin argues, Eve and God: 'non sunt duo, sed una caro' (Liber, p. 90).[117] He intersects sexualized and maternal imagery, safely channelling Eve's potentially sexual impulses into spiritual desire: 'totis uisceribus illum concupisce, illum concipe, illum amplectere ... parturi, gigne, enutri' (*Liber*, pp. 106–7).[118] The Eucharist binds God and the recluse together in spirit and flesh. Transformed into an expectant bride, potentially fertile and ardent, yet firmly solitary, the recluse enters: 'nouum testamentum corporis et sanguinis, eterna memoria passionis, eterno federe dilectionis, quo in ipso manerent et ipse in eis contradidit' (*Liber*, p. 30).[119] In the tension of anticipation, the earlier guides construct their recluses awaiting their submission to Christ as master-husband in death. Aelred declares: 'Cogitet sine intermissione ad cuius ornatur thalamum, ad cuius praeparatur amplexum' (*DII*, p. 651).[120] Yet, *Ancrene Wisse* also implies the potential of fusion as spiritual consummation on earth. Nonetheless, its eroticized description demonstrates the limitations of a language doomed to communicate the very transcendence of the flesh in terms of embodiment; the body rendered conspicuous especially in its absence.

Rachel Fulton argues, in terms of Bernardine writing, that contemplative spousal metaphor renders the divine 'beloved ... visible and thus thinkable ... [providing] the lover, the bride, with a way to ascend from the lower stages of love to the higher'.[121] It implies, as Jenifer Sutherland argues, the possibility of an 'approach to the divine presence' which 'draws past and future into a transformative present; the future union in death of soul and God is subsumed in the present union of the virgin [contemplative] ... with the Virgin Mediator'.[122] Wider medieval contemplative writings, such as those of Gertrude of Helfta, also reflect an increased tendency to fashion Jesus as lover. Gertrude writes:

> You are the delicate taste of intimate sweetness.
> O most delicate caresser,
> Gentlest passion,
> Most ardent lover,
> Sweetest spouse,
> Most pure pursuer.[123]

Mechthild of Magdeburg argues: 'We each have a bridegroom; / He is the priest of the blessed maids / Who looks so lovingly on them'.[124] Mary of Oignies lies in bed with Christ for three days: 'cum de Sponsi labiis lac ant mel manducaret'.[125] One of Catherine of Siena's many contemplative experiences sees her spiritually married to Christ.[126] While Julian writes chiefly of 'our pretious Moder Jesus',[127] she also utilizes spousal imagery: 'in the knittyng and in the onyng He is our very trewe spouse, and we His lovid wif and His fair maiden with which wif He is never displesid'.[128] Angela of Foligno sexualizes Christ, kissing the breast of his corpse, then his mouth: 'she drew her cheek to Christ's and Christ placed his hand on her other cheek, clutching her to him. In that moment she heard these words: "before I was laid in the tomb I held you this tightly to me"'.[129] Mechthild of Hackeborn counsels a nun that 'the cross is a couch on which she should consummate her love for Christ'.[130] Gertrude of Helfta locates fusion in the Eucharist, as does Beatrice of Nazareth (1200–68) who is described as having 'lost the use of her outward senses ... Her spirit melted before the deifying sacrament, and her body before the spiritual joy flowing out from her interior'.[131] Hadewijch of Brabant uses imagery and language allusive of *Ancrene Wisse*'s mass-kiss:

> He came himself to me, took me entirely in his arms, and pressed me to him; and all my members felt his in full felicity ... Then it was to be as if we were one without difference ...

> After that I remained in a passing away in my beloved, so that I wholly melted away in him and nothing any longer remained to me of myself.[132]

Georgianna may conclude that *Ancrene Wisse* 'fall[s] short of ... otherworldly mysticism', and Watson may argue that *Ancrene Wisse*'s contemplative material 'clearly lies outside the main development of late-medieval mysticism',[133] but evidently these earlier medieval guides echo wider medieval contemporary negotiations of contemplative union in their anticipation of contemplative fusion.

Later anchoritic guidance reverses the earlier medieval contemplative position. The earlier guides' central focus on meditation and brief acknowledgement of vision and fusion evolves into the later guides' centralization of fusion and brief acknowledgement of meditation and vision. Every later guide defines fusion as the ravishing of the soul, which for Rolle particularly, is 'rauist in loue' (*Form*, p. 25). For him, fusion is the highest of the three states of love, involving the exclusion of all other thought. Only the most loving of contemplatives can experience it. Rolle argues that even fusion, however sophisticated, can only indicate the state of love in a soul, it cannot increase it. For him, contemplation is not, in itself, an act of love; consequently love cannot be located in, or intensified by it, but only revealed thereby (*Form*, p. 20). The *Speculum* author echoes this Rollian perspective (*Speculum*, p. 130) and describes ravishment thus: 'quando usus sensuum est ligatus, vel quasi in raptu, quando mens non considerat res sensibiles circumstantes' (*Speculum*, p. 83).[134] Contemporary contemplative revelations echo this: 'me thoght I was rauyshed into purgatory, and ... saw al þe peynes ... and ... thre grete fyres'.[135] Both Hilton and the *Speculum* author liken fusion to being ravished 'into the thridde hevene' (*Scale I*, p. 84), as was Paul. *Speculum* glosses Paul's experience: 'sicut beatus Paulus raptus usque ad tercium celum, utrum in corpore vel extra corpus fuerat, ignoravit' (*Speculum*, p. 83), and 'Hoc autem omnes non extra corpora raptos, sed in corporibus estimo talem consolacionem divinitus habuisse' (*Speculum*, p. 129).[136] Aelred is tied explicitly into this fusion tradition:

> narrat sanctus Alredus ... quibus orantibus mira quedam suavitas superveniens omnes mundanas cogitaciones et carnales affectus extinxit. Moxque rapti quasi ad tercium celum cum beato Paulo et incomprehensibili luce perfusi, quadam beatifica visione Dei, licet inperfecta, vel saltem quodam excellenti ac inenarrabili gaudio perfusi, sic inebriati sunt, quod ab aliis pulsati, cum difficultate ad corporales sensus, quos reliquerant, redire valebant (*Speculum*, p. 129).[137]

The body is transcended: 'we overpasse oure bodili wittes to God in contemplacion' (*Scale I*, p. 38), as love 'bi grete violence and maistrie breketh doun alle ... ertheli thinges, and ... woundeth the soule' (*Scale I*, p. 62), and 'the bodi faileth and falleth doun and mai not bere it' (*Scale I*, p. 62). This is the highest point of the contemplative ascent, constructed by Hilton as marriage between God and the soul (*Scale I*, p. 38). The *Speculum* author's language is reminiscent of the Song of Songs, similarly recalling earlier guidance's material on the Eucharist and spousal metaphor, in his communication of the love between God and contemplative:

> cantabitis ... 'Osculetur me osculo oris sui', tanquam spiritualiter amorosi sponso vestro Christo dicentes corditer ... 'trahe me, post te curremus in odorem unguentorum tuorum' (*Speculum*, p. 135).[138]

This is echoed by other contemporary sources. John Lydgate's *Secreta Secretorum* describes Aristotle thus: 'He was Ravysshed, Contemplatyff of desir, Vp to the hevene lyk a dowe of ffyr', locating contemplation through the same images of heat, fire and ascent.[139] The progress to fusion is similarly likened by Rolle to fire which burns 'euer vpward' (*Form*, p. 9). Putter argues that 'About the climax of contemplation [Hilton] ... has little to say, and ... union with God figures as a distant prospect rather than an immediate objective', yet Hilton casts fusion as both fire and as a consummatory union in terms allusive of *Ancrene Wisse*.[140] The contemplative will be 'ravysschid out of the bodili wittes ... with a soft swete brennande love', for 'the soule is ooned for the tyme ... thanne God and a soule aren not two but bothe oon' (*Scale I*, p. 38). Ascent is also implied through the later medieval development of the image of the scale, or ladder, also focused on in *Ancrene Wisse* (*AW*, Corpus, p. 134).[141] Rolle concludes: 'I wil þat þou be [euer] clymynge to Ihesuward, and echynge þi loue ... in hym' (*Form*, p. 10), while *Speculum* constructs contemplatives as people who 'ad gradum maximum perfeccionis anhelant' (*Speculum*, p. 72).[142] Such imagery is echoed in texts such as the *Abbey of the Holy Ghost*, which defines contemplation as 'a deuote rysynge of herte, with byrnynge lufe, to God'.[143] Contemplative accounts sometimes intersect metaphorical and literal ascent. Flora of Beaulieu is reputedly 'carried into rapture and raised up more than two cubits from the ground by angels' and Gerard Cagnoli and Catherine of Siena are similarly affected.[144]

The later guides do not always construct fusion as brief and momentary. Rolle believes the contemplative who achieves it may remain in such love until death: 'þat soul ... til þe deth cum is syngynge gostly to Ihesu *and in Ihesu*' (*Form*, p. 17).[145] Yet, for Hilton, such an achievement is so rare as to be virtually non-existent: 'I not whether ther be ony siche man lyvande in erthe' (*Scale I*, p. 42). Paradoxically, fusion is also constructed as insecure; God may withdraw it at any time. Desire for fusion is consequently often expressed in later guidance as an addiction that cannot be satisfied. Yet, all the later medieval guides agree, in an idea which recalls Goscelin (*Liber*, pp. 39–40),[146] that fusion offers the fortunate few a (comparatively imperfect) foretaste of the true fusion deferred until heaven. This is also implied by Julian: 'I saw a mervelous, hey privitye hid in God, which privity He shall openly make knowen to us in Hevyn, in which knowyng we shal verily see ... in which syte we shall endlesly joyen in our Lord God'.[147] Baker observes that this type of 'Union with God, contemplative as well as beatific, forms the nucleus of Julian's revelations'.[148] Julian writes of the 'onyng' of God and the soul through the contemplation of both the humanity and divinity of Christ.[149] It is foregrounded as compassion: 'Here saw I a gret onyng betwyx Christe and us, to myn understondyng. For whan He was in payne, we were in peyne'.[150] Her own contemplative experience seems to have been one in which she moves beyond her body, where meditation, vision and fusion intersect. She is returned to her body afterwards:

> I had no greife ne disese, as long as the fifteen shewings lestid folowand. And at the end al was close, and I saw no more ... and anon my sekenes cam agen, first in my hede with a sound and a dynne; and sodenly all my body was fulfillid with sekeness like as it was aforn ... And as a wretch I moned and hevyed for felyng of my bodily peynes and for fayling of comfort, gostly and bodily.[151]

Henry Suso and Catherine of Siena similarly experience liberation from their bodies during fusion, so much so that Catherine's companions attempt to test her contemplative authenticity by attacking her physically. They found that she: 'lost the use of her bodily senses, and her extremities ... became quite paralysed. Her clenched fingers would press so tightly into the palms of her hands that … it would have been easier to break them than force them open'.[152]

Anchoritic contemplation and the active/contemplative debate

Earlier anchoritic guidance is best understood as part of society's admiration for professional contemplatives. While the earlier Middle Ages gave rise to a new awareness of the variety of religious experience and new forms of spiritual life became classed as contemplative, the guides and other contemporary writings concurrently reinforce the continued importance of traditional contemplative lives.[153] Contemplative privacy facilitated by solitude is cited as a primary motivation for anchoritic enclosure (e.g. *AW*, Corpus, pp. 64–7). Mary, sister of Lazarus, is celebrated as the archetypal contemplative role model, cast by Aelred as silent, submissive and solitary: 'Denique non ambulans … non cura rei familiaris distenta … Haec pars tua … quae saeculo mortua atque sepulta (*DII*, p. 660).[154] *Ancrene Wisse* concludes: 'Marie dale is stilnesse ant reste of alle worldes noise, þet na þing ne lette hire to heren Godes steuene' (*AW*, Corpus, p. 156).[155] The guides prefer the contemplative over the active life, the scriptural foundation for which is the story of Martha and Mary (John 12:1–18; Luke 10:38–42). Although other contemplative role models exist, including Jacob's wives Leah and Rachel, the sisters of Lazarus particularly captured the medieval imagination. Luke's gospel states:

> Factum est autem dum irent et ipse intravit in quoddam castellum et mulier quaedam Martha nomine excepit illum in domum suam. Et huic erat soror nomine Maria quae etiam sedens secus pedes Domini audiebat verbum illius. Martha autem satagebat circa frequens ministerium quae stetit et ait Domine non est tibi curae quod soror mea reliquit me solam ministrare dic ergo illi ut me adiuvet. Et respondens dixit illi Dominus Martha Martha sollicita es et turbaris erga plurima. Porro unum est necessarium Maria optimam partem elegit quae non auferetur ab ea.[156]

Constable notes that the sisters' lives were not always contrasted 'as alternatives' or read as mutually exclusive.[157] Yet, earlier medieval anchoritic guidance represents them as polarities. Aelred argues:

> sedebat ad pedes Iesu, et audiebat uerbum illius. Haec pars tua, carissima, quae saeculo mortua atque sepulta, surda debes esse ad omnia quae saeculi sunt audiendum et ad loquendum muta … Exequatur partem suam Martham quae licet non negetur bona, Mariae tamen melior praedicatur (*DII*, p. 660).[158]

Tradition suggests that Jesus himself conferred Mary's contemplative superiority, although Constable notes the ambiguity of his words.[159] Whether misread or not, much medieval writing reiterates this received interpretation and by the time of Aelred's guide, the tradition of contemplative supremacy had long been established, reinforced by the works of Ambrose, Jerome, Augustine and Gregory, and disseminated in many different genres of religious writing, notably anchoritic guidance.[160]

Later medieval guidance continues to construct its recluses as highly accomplished professional contemplatives and to synonymize anchoritism with contemplation. Contemplation is still the inevitable territory of the professional solitary. Hilton considers it an inward pilgrimage into the soul (*Scale I*, p. 53), and declares: 'thy staat asketh to be contemplatif' (*Scale I*, p. 33). The need for silence, solitude, relative privacy and freedom from social obligation to facilitate contemplation persists, in ideological terms. *Speculum* states: 'labor corporalis ... impedit seu remittit opera contemplacionis' (*Speculum*, p. 83). Contemplation occurs 'soli Deo vacantibus et pro amore Dei multum laborantibus, in secretis oracionibus, sanctis meditacionibus' (*Speculum*, p. 129).[161] Hilton now constructs the contemplative bond in the same kind of terms in which the earlier medieval writers constructed enclosure itself. It is contemplation itself, as the goal of anchoritism, which is now the anchorite's grave, not the cell per se: 'thou schalt in plenté of gode bodili werkes and goostli vertues entre thi grave, that is reste in contemplacioun' (*Scale I*, p. 46).

Yet, the later guidance writers delineate their contemplative positions in an increasingly complicated dispute about the efficacy of the contemplative vocation. The acknowledged supremacy of the professional contemplative has given way to an increased interest in and approval of the contemplative experience of actives. Anchoritism is no longer constructed as the only, or even the best, way to be a contemplative. It is simply the best way for some. Hughes casts fourteenth- and fifteenth-century recluses as influential communicators of their experiences of the contemplative life, who nonetheless suggest 'laymen could aspire towards these same experiences'.[162] Both Rolle and Hilton deliberately encourage their recluses to understand their vocation as only one path amongst many to a spiritual connection with God. Rolle warns that the unenclosed layman may know more of love than the solitary recluse. Contemplation is no longer the exclusive privilege of the few, but the expected portion of many. Some later guidance writers write as contemplatives themselves, not by virtue of any personal eremitic experience (although Rolle was certainly a solitary at various points in his life), but because they share in wider society's contemplative expectations.

Yet, taken to its logical conclusion, if actives can achieve contemplative sophistication, then the life of the professional contemplative is potentially rendered obsolete, no matter how much later guidance may still approve of and seek to bolster it. Rolle's and Hilton's guides in particular, while defending the vocational choices of the professional contemplatives for whom they were written, are frequently appropriated by the laity as part of their wider absorption of contemplative material.[163] Yet, the later guides' continued support for the vocation is, in an important sense, a vindication of the anchoritic contemplative life. They respond to the need to re-establish the territory of the anchoritic contemplative. Nonetheless, concurrently, their narratives inevitably, implicitly question the need for professional anchoritic contemplation. Other lives, only emergent in the earlier Middle Ages, formerly understood as active are now thought to afford a sophisticated contemplative connection with God.[164] They include the life of the vowess who, vowed to chastity, yet remained in the world, retaining property rights and the right to make a will.[165] The beguines, too, at least initially, were able to remain in the world, residing in an unenclosed spiritual community and yet espousing contemplation.[166] The mendicant friars espoused voluntary poverty without submitting to a conventual framework.[167] Hilton is particularly intrigued by the notion of the mixed life, intended chiefly for secular priests, but with a wider appeal. His *On Mixed Life*, part of what Watson has called Hilton's 'great project, the harmonisation of the "active" life of the laity with the devotional life of contemplatives',[168] argues:

þe þridde lyf, þat is medlet, longeþ speciali to men of holy churche, as to prelates or to oþur
curates ... to use werkes of active lyf ... and sum-tyme [forto] leue al bisynes outward and 3ive
hem for a tyme to preyers, meditacions, redynges ... ant to oþer gostly occupacions ... Also hit
longeþ generali to sum temporal men.[169]

The desire to capitalize on the best elements of both lives also inspired, as chapter 4
demonstrated, orders such as the Carthusians. The Bridgettines also sought to live in
separate enclosures but share one church.[170] Yet, while such lives remained essentially
religious, Hilton's mixed life, a secular phenomenon, utilizes the Mary/Martha
dichotomy differently: 'For þou schalt o tyme wiþ Martha be bisy ffor to ruile ant
gouerne þin houshold, þi children, þi seruauns ... A noþur tyme þou schalt with Marie
leue þe bisynes of þe world ant sitte doun at þe feet of vr lord ... in contemplacion of
him'.[171] This ideal life reflects both sisters. Yet, however much Hilton desires their amal-
gamation, he perpetuates their rhetorical division.[172]

Walker Bynum argues that lives such as that of the late fifteenth-century Catherine of
Genoa (1447–1510) reflect such a 'profound combination of action and contemplation
that the contrast between the[m] vanishes'.[173] Kempe's *Book* illustrates her extraordinary attempts to live the contemplative life in the world. Kempe, an active and a
laywoman, nonetheless seeks to live 'in devocyon of holy medytacyon of hy contem-
placyon'.[174] Despite being a wife and a mother to fourteen children, she constructs
herself as a contemplative visionary. She wears white (implicitly recalling Cistercian
simplicity described in chapter 4 above) and wanders the country in accordance with the
will of God. Ruth Evans rightly problematizes our conception of Margery as 'a single
sovereign author ... [controlling the *Book*'s] meaning', separating, in the tradition of
Lynn Staley, although not for Staley's reasons, 'the textual voice from the putative
author'.[175] Evans argues: 'we cannot ... claim with any confidence that [in the words of
Samuel Fanous] "Margery's voice rings clearly from the text"'.[176] Yet, while questions
of authorship should continue to trouble us, there is no doubt that the text seeks and,
arguably, succeeds in places to construct the 'creature' Margery as a sophisticated
contemplative. She seeks the approbation of reclusive authority, placing anchorites
below only 'worshepful clerkys ... archebysshopys ... bysshoppys, doctowrs of dyvy-
nytéé and bachelers'.[177] Kempe describes how 'the ankyr of the Frer Prechowrys in
Lenn', himself a visionary who 'be the spiryt of prophecye teld hir ... sche schuld have
mech tribulacyon ... and how owyr Lord schuld asayn hir scharply and prevyn hir ful
streytly', maintains the veracity of her contemplative experiences 'on charge of hys
sowle'.[178] Her faith in anchoritism's contemplative expertise is what motivates her
meeting with Julian. Kempe writes of the 'wondirful revelacyons whech sche schewyd
to the ankres ... for the ankres was expert in swech thyngys and good cownsel cowd
gevyn'.[179] Nicholas Watson and Jacqueline Jenkins call this a 'seductively pleasing
account of Julian's public reputation ... an idealized picture of a visionary anchorite, a
... specialist, in action, passing on what she has learned of God to one of her
"evenchristen" in the world'.[180] Kempe's welcome is not always constructed as this
warm. She describes herself, on her return from pilgrimage to Jerusalem, being sent
away from a York anchorhold because of her dangerous reputation.[181] Her unwillingness
to conform leads to wider accusations of heresy, although she maintains orthodoxy
under scrutiny. Nonetheless, Kempe's *Book* implies both society's respect for the
contemplative anchoritic vocation and concurrently claims authority for the contemplative experiences of the laity.

Julian's own text takes us a step further than this. Its existence implies that anchorites may have had a potential role in shaping, not just reflecting, contemporary spirituality. Herbert McAvoy points to Julian's contemplative anchoritism as the very source of her spiritual authority: 'As a result it is rendered proleptic … [and] serves to transform Julian into sibylline wise woman whose voice has … been privileged by God'.[182] The anchorhold potentially allows Julian to profit contemplatively from her experiences, providing her with a framework within which she can articulate and, more importantly, understand her visions and reflect on them in her writing. Although, admittedly, later than the later anchoritic guides, it is potentially in this professionally contemplative tradition that the London anchorite Simon Appulby crafts *The Fruit of Redempcyon* (1514), his popular translation of a series of affective meditations on Christ's life, from the anonymous Latin text *Meditationes de vita et beneficiis Jesu Christi, siue gratiarum actiones.*[183]

Other texts that demonstrate lay contemplative experience include the aforementioned *Abbey of the Holy Ghost*, which allegorizes the heart of an active as a convent inhabited by personified virtues. Similarly, Nicholas Love's fifteenth-century translation of the pseudo-Bonaventurian text *Meditationes Vitae Christi* into the *Myrrour of the Blessed Lyf of Jesu Christ* provides the laity with meditational material and identifies affective piety with acts of charity in the world.[184] Love's text nonetheless perpetuates the active/contemplative distinction, recognizing the highest state of contemplation as beyond the province of the lay audience for whom his text is intended.

Yet, some medieval writers sound a note of caution to the lay contemplative. The fourteenth-century *The Cloud of Unknowing* author discourages the idle and partial reading and copying of his book, seeking to limit its dissemination to a professionally contemplative audience.[185] For him, 'the contemplative … and active life are joined' as 'sisters after the example of Martha and Mary', yet he vindicates the contemplative life, warning that the active can advance no further than the second of three degrees of contemplation: 'do not meddle with contemplatives, you do not know what they are about'.[186] This message stands implicitly behind later anchoritic guidance's continued reinforcements of the value of professional contemplation. It persists in its continued focus on Mary, sister of Lazarus, for although the *Speculum* author and Hilton conflate her with Mary Magdalene (*Speculum*, p. 67), Hilton constructs Mary Magdalene as a hermit-contemplative, still strongly linking her diurnal visions with her solitude (*Scale I*, p. 42).[187] Rolle writes: 'Contemplatif lif is … lestynger and sykerer, restfuller, delitabeller, louelier and more medeful' (*Form*, p. 24).[188] Hilton remarks that an active's contemplation: 'lasteth not wel longe' (*Scale I*, p. 36), despite acknowledgments that, through divine grace, even an active may be granted the highest level of contemplative experience.[189] For Hilton, fusion is the likely province of the professional, reclusive contemplative:

> God yyveth where that he wole … but it is special and not comone … though a man which is actif have the yifte of it bi … grace, neverthelees the ful use of it … may no man have, but he be solitarie and in liyf contemplative (*Scale I*, p. 39).

Hilton believes that only anchorites and religious will have 'special' or 'accidental meede' in heaven above the 'sovereyn and principal' reward that is universal (*Scale I*, pp. 64–5). *Speculum* uses the same terminology but reverses Hilton's application of 'accidental' reward so that it becomes the portion of every Christian (*Speculum*, p. 125). *Speculum* makes largely the same point as Hilton, however: that the enclosed recluse will potentially know greater contemplative reward than other Christians. The later medieval contemplative anchoritic life is not constructed as passive in contrast to the business of actives, but continues to be an arduous existence, involving the constant manipulation of body and mind to spiritual advantage. It is a life of aspiration, not fulfilment: 'quia nunquam perficit artifex opus suum arduum et subtile' (*Speculum*, p. 140).[190] Hilton's text on the mixed life may seek a solution to the increasing fragmentation of the anchoritic contemplative vocation, but *Scale* (in its original eremitic conception, at least) continues, in common with other later guides, to assert the peculiar joy experienced by anchoritic contemplatives.

Anchoritic contemplation and contemplative orthodoxy

Contemplation is potentially subversive, for although its authority is ultimately God's, its power, as with asceticism, is mediated through the individual. Constable argues, in terms allusive of anchoritism, that the contemplative's potential spiritual autonomy is derived from cultural marginalization: 'outside ... society ... [they are not] bound by its standards'.[191] There is no doubt that the power of the contemplative was feared by some. Diane Watt argues, partly in terms of the furore surrounding Margery Kempe:

> churchmen ... were suspicious of [women contemplatives] ... who were being revered as saints, fearing that they would either overtly undermine the authority of the Church ... (claiming ... the voice of God), or more indirectly destabilize it through their popularity.[192]

Robertson's exploration of the post-Conquest background to earlier medieval anchoritism argues that some early Anglo-Norman women became recluses in order to gain exactly this kind of contemplative independence.[193] Anchoritic guidance problematizes the vocation's potential for devotional freedom and constructs contemplative orthodoxy as the fourth of the four anchoritic ideals upon which their constructions of the vocation are founded. Earlier guidance certainly is less anxious about orthodoxy than later medieval guidance, but it still betrays some concern, notably about the orthodoxy of visions, as discussed earlier in this chapter, and wider anxiety about general spiritual orthodoxy is also potentially implicit in the sheer amount of detail given on meditation guidance, particularly by Aelred.

Kathleen G. Cushing argues, of the great reformative periods, including the fourth, sixth, the sixteenth and twentieth centuries, that 'none ... has so dominated the discourse of reform as that of the eleventh'.[194] Daniell similarly suggests that between 1066 and 1215, England was characterized by the drive to reform the church, to centralize its hierarchical power and to foster the power of the papacy, thereby elevating 'the church in Rome' as the domain of 'Christ's representative on earth'.[195] Yet, Goscelin's concerns about spiritual orthodoxy centre on conflict with Christianity, not on reformative conflicts within Christianity. Goscelin fears the threat of pervasive, pagan perfidious influence, which for him renders Christian orthodoxy visible through conflict. Pagans are 'hostibus Christi' deserving 'proscripta dampnatio' (*Liber*, p. 111).[196] Similarly to the outlawed, these should be killed on sight, therefore Goscelin pits 'catholici contra ciuiles bellatores hereticos' (*Liber*, p. 111), predicting that on Judgement Day they will rise up against their pagan persecutors.[197] For him, the eternal damnation of the godless is set up in contrast to the salvation of the elect (*Liber*, p. 112).[198] As living (and dying) embodiments of orthodoxy, the Christian martyrs are to be highly admired. They stand in opposition to heretical and pagan persecution and anchorites like Eve live out the matryological tradition; likewise cast as orthodox role models for the faithful.

Schulenburg argues that heresy, at the time of the first millennium, is 'dangerous ... for anyone', but especially for women.[199] She argues that heretical thinkers seduced women with the promise of a prophetic voice. The writings of Ademar of Chabannes and his contemporaries render heretical women 'convenient scapegoats' in a larger pattern of social persecution.[200] Griffiths argues that the *cura monialium* develops from a desire to safeguard and supervise the women of the twelfth century, in sympathy with Southern's famous argument that the twelfth century 'solidified the equation between orthodoxy and the assertion of male authority'.[201] Unsupervised women, constructed implicitly as heretics, or 'witches, poisoners, and adulteresses', all cast as 'determined to undermine the order of society', were regarded as 'instruments of the devil ... deviant ... dangerous'.[202] Schulenburg argues that the turn of the eleventh century saw churchmen single out women for blame, synonymizing them with the wickedness of their age.[203] Yet, while Goscelin is certainly anxious to supervise Eve, he does not gender heresy as implicitly female. He trusts Eve, granting her a measure of spiritual autonomy unparalleled in any other anchoritic guide, urging her: 'Ipsa Deo sacerdos esto, te ipsam sacrificando, et ignis amoris diuini semper ardeat in altari cordis tui' (*Liber*, p. 80).[204] Eve, far from condemned as high-risk heretic, must instead inspire others to turn to the true faith. Goscelin favours the example of the captive woman who convinces her queen of God's power, vivifying a female network of spiritual orthodoxy (*Liber*, p. 66).[205] He pays homage to individual women who successfully confront pagan forces, including Augustine's own mother (*Liber*, p. 33).[206] Eve is to fashion herself in their image.

It is vital that Eve arm herself intellectually for the fight. She must 'hebetatam mentem cote librorum exacue' (*Liber*, p. 80); even commit intellectual gluttony: 'Itaque ... imploro, ut sacrorum uoluminum mensam sanctam auiditate et laudabili ingluuie peruadas, hanc ut uite panem ut uite fontem esurias et sitias' (*Liber*, p. 80).[207] Reading recommendations include Augustine's *Confessions*, his *De Civitate Dei*, Orosius's *De Ormesta Mundi* and Boethius's *Consolation of Philosophy* (*Liber*, pp. 80–1).[208] Goscelin gives Eve the freedom to interpret these texts herself, judging she may safely be handed the key to her own spiritual empowerment. Hayward and Hollis argue that he hands her these 'books ... not [as] an end in themselves, but ... a[s] means to salvation'.[209] Knowledge is (spiritual) power and Goscelin empowers Eve willingly. Far from being *Ancrene Wisse*'s pit, Eve as recluse is constructed as capable of holiness, justice, innocence, virginity, 'immaculate uite pulc(h)ritudo', for 'Ecce que erat septem demoniorum baratrum, totidemque principalium uitiorum cum suis agminibus receptaculum, eiectis demoniis facta est septiformis gratie sacrarium' (*Liber*, pp. 101–2).[210] Goscelin shows little interest in Eve's relationship to her transgressive namesake, referring more to mankind's guilt as a whole, as does Rolle (and to a lesser extent, Hilton). The biblical tales of David and Bathsheba and of Dina's tragic curiosity and rape, used in *Ancrene Wisse* to condemn womankind are recast, to suggest simply that all who are glorified will ultimately be humbled and rehabilitated: 'Domino sanante mox uenena excussere' (*Liber*, pp. 93–4, 97–8).[211]

Aelred and *Ancrene Wisse* exhibit far greater fear of the female contemplative. *Ancrene Wisse*'s constructions of inherent female sinfulness have sometimes been read as misogynistic. Sarah Maitland identifies its 'sadomasochistic relationship with a masculine God, which ultimately robs women of any kind of dignity'.[212] It certainly reiterates anti-feminist beliefs in woman's spiritual, physiological and intellectual inferiority. Yet, Gopa Roy argues persuasively that *Ancrene Wisse* should not be vilified for simply expressing contemporary prejudice.[213] Gunn reminds us that: 'To claim that *Ancrene Wisse* is misogynistic is … not to add any insight to a reading of the text'.[214] Catherine Innes-Parker urges us not to project our '"raised consciousness" onto the thirteenth-century'.[215] To castigate Aelred and the *Ancrene Wisse* author and revisers for misogyny is also to overlook their (admittedly less frequent) approbation of female contemplative spirituality. Nicholas Watson reminds us that *Ancrene Wisse* 'also addresses its readers … as tough-minded, ambitious descendants of the heroic solitaries of the early church, attempting something the author himself cannot'.[216] Earlier guidance's warnings about female transgression spring from a desire to help women overcome their apparently inherent weaknesses and deepen their spiritual practice, not from blind woman-hatred. Aelred often praises his sister's achievements, especially her chastity, above his own, while many texts of *Ancrene Wisse* praise the devotional fervour of their female readership. Herbert McAvoy argues that 'in spite of the warnings … an alternative discourse [emerges, which] … focuses on the chaste female body as the site of potential transcension and apotheosis'.[217]

Consequently, both Aelred's guide and *Ancrene Wisse* enlist their recluses, not in the fight between faiths, but in orthodox conflicts within the Christian faith. *Ancrene Wisse* is especially concerned that the recluse triumph over the danger of independent spiritual thought, or individual difference, termed 'singularite, þet is anful frommardschipe' (*AW*, Corpus, p. 97).[218] Anselm's notion of heaven similarly envisages a community united in love: 'omnes se invicem diligant … et quod unus volet, hoc volent omnes … Quapropter quidquid unusquisque volet, hoc erit et de se ipso et de omnibus aliis … Et sic singuli erunt perfecti reges, quia quod singuli volent, hoc erit' (Anselm, 'Letter 112', vol. 3, p. 245).[219] Aelred warns against the 'diabolicarum suggestionum' (*DII*, p. 654),[220] which lead anchorites astray theologically, but *Ancrene Wisse* writes of 'heresie' (*AW*, Corpus, p. 33). The Corpus text of *Ancrene Wisse* declares: 'Heresie, Godd haue þonc, ne rixleð nawt in Englelond' (*AW*, Corpus, p. 33).[221] Defined as poisonous speech, including lying, viciousness and flattery, 'heresie' is not used in Goscelin's sense or in its later medieval sense (to be defined below). *Ancrene Wisse*'s original audience is presented as small, remarkable in fidelity and confident in shared perfection, but the Corpus text's wider audience has a wider range of life experiences and the text reflects increased anxiety about its recluses' potential for spiritual individualism. Aelred's sister, although presented as spiritually continent, is surrounded by others, which increases the spiritual risk to all. Aelred consequently advises a scriptural basis for every thought and deed: 'Nihil enim magis cogitationes excludit inutiles, uel compescit lascivas quam meditatio uerbi Dei' (*DII*, p. 654).[222] *Ancrene Wisse*'s legitimization of a network of reclusive sociability, revealed in chapter 3, implies an increased potential for spiritual corruption; one anchorhold in error may infect many through (albeit limited) social contact but, as will be outlined below, the guide also offers a potential solution to the problem.

Earlier medieval guidance seeks to foster a sense of spiritual stability in its recluses, to ensure spiritual orthodoxy and to bring the power of the contemplative within that of the church. *Ancrene Wisse* focuses on the threefold nature of its anchoritic vow, which binds the recluse not just to fixity of place and chastity but, crucially, to obedience (*AW*, Corpus, p. 3).[223] Submission to the confessor/spiritual director sets the attractions of comparative contemplative spiritual autonomy firmly within his control. Anselm recommends the occupation of a mind molested with wicked thoughts: 'Numquam enim expellitur ... cogitatio vel voluntas, nisi alia cogitatione et alia voluntate' (Anselm, 'Letter 414', vol. 5, p. 361).[224] Anselm recommends constant vigilance: 'Si ergo bene vultis vivere, voluntatem vestram indesinenter custodite, in magnis et in minimis' (Anselm, 'Letter 414', vol. 5, p. 360).[225] Since the Devil tempts recluses secretly by lesser sins: 'minima quaeque nolueritis negligere. Qui enim in minimis servat diligentiam, non facile admittit in maioribus negligentiam' (Anselm, 'Letter 230', vol. 4, p. 135).[226] Devotional routines are detailed, particularly in *Ancrene Wisse*, to direct reclusive spiritual fervour into authorized patterns of devotion (*AW*, Corpus, p. 10).[227] The guide also inculcates in the recluse a sense of herself as part of a wider community-in-solitude, investing her with the security of communal, if virtual, surveillance. Left implicit in Aelred's guide in references to his sister's companions (*DII*, p. 642),[228] this notion is explored at length in *Ancrene Wisse*. Its recluses can not only style themselves part of the hypothetical order of St James (*AW*, Corpus, p. 4),[229] but as members of a community-in-separateness (*AW*, Corpus, p. 97).[230] Its members do not simply spy on and report on each other to their spiritual advisor, although this is recommended – they afford each other mutual strength. The lone individual cannot stray, unseen, from the treacherous path. Fellow recluses 'beoð tur ... treoweliche ant se feste ilimet wið lím of anred luue, euch of ow to oþer' (*AW*, Corpus, pp. 86–97).[231] The whole virtual community's orthodoxy is cloned from the 'hehe fame' and reputation of the 'moder-hus' (*AW*, Corpus, p. 97).[232] Where one anchorhold is orthodox, this guide implies that all have the potential to be.

Later medieval anchoritic guidance regulates orthodoxy with the same obsessive focus earlier guidance applied to chastity. Earlier medieval fears about individual spiritual difference have, by this time, developed into full-blown fear of religious dissent, against which all the later guidance writers attempt, textually, to fight. Bestul, pointing to the controversies surrounding the visions of Bridget of Sweden and Catherine of Siena, situates the urgency behind the need to authenticate contemplative experience far beyond medieval England, pointing to 'widespread European interest in the practice and techniques of contemplation and ... the recording of ... [such] experiences ... [and] concern, which can be found in Hilton, about the validity of such experiences and how they might be authenticated'.[233] He cites the example of the writings of Gerson as reflective of this wider medieval European desire to codify and calculate the authenticity of contemplative experiences and offer the faithful a set of categories by which they may judge such experience.

As this chapter cannot contextualize every single one of the many concerns later medieval anchoritic guidance demonstrates about contemplative orthodoxy, special focus is given to the relationships between anchoritic contemplation, orthodoxy and

Lollardy. Known as 'the English heresy', this was specific to England and embedded in controversy over the development of the vernacular and, in particular, the vernacular translation of the Bible. The Lollards pitted themselves against the most basic structures of the institutionalized medieval church, although Anne Hudson has written, rightly, of the dangers of constructing one homogenized view of the uniformity of Lollard belief and attributing all Lollard beliefs to John Wyclif (c.1324–84). Gordon Leff argues that the church's institutional structures rest at this time upon endowments, taxation, tithes and jurisdiction: 'Without them, it … had no visible identity or continuity'.[234] Lollard problematizations of lay giving therefore potentially threaten the church's very survival.[235] Bishop Arundel's Constitutions of 1407, although written after the composition of many of the later anchoritic guides, are nonetheless born from a desire to defend the church's most sacred (and most financially lucrative) institutions.[236] Their protection of the priesthood includes the prohibition of preaching without a licence (granted only to those regarded as orthodox) and the dissemination of Wyclif's heretical texts and translation of the Bible into the vernacular (which would liberate it from Latinate clerical control). The later anchoritic guides' vehement defence of the 'true' church implicitly reacts, as Arundel's Constitutions do, to demands for ecclesiastical reform, to heretical problematizations of papal authority, of the sacraments' inherent validity, of transubstantiation, of the authority of corrupt clerics, of the validity of the sacraments if celebrated by the corrupt, of excommunication, of the worship of images, of the efficacy of pilgrimage, the validity of oaths and the status of tithes. Such debates implicitly inform the later guides' reiteration of orthodox beliefs, motivating their negotiations of the sanctity of the priestly office, the infallibility of the papacy, the orthodoxy of the sacraments, the importance of the use of images as contemplative inspiration and the need for actives (not anchoritic contemplatives) to support the church financially.

A heretical anchorite ought, the later guidance writers imply, to be a contradiction in terms, but all fear that the recluse may easily lose sight of orthodox church doctrine, lost as she is in her own, comparatively solitary, contemplation. Historical records note accusations of anchoritic heresy. Clay refers to 'irregular life or belief' among solitaries from 1231, concluding that by 1334, 'heresy and schism are recorded both north and south'.[237] The same Anna Palmer of St Peter's Church, Northampton, accused of sexual incontinence, was also charged with permitting a group of (male) heretics to meet in her anchorhold secretly at night. Imprisoned during the winter of 1393–4 and then taken to London, nothing more is known of her.[238] More is known about Matilda of St Peter's Church, Leicester. A famed heretic, she was incarcerated following evasive responses under examination in 1389 and is explicitly referred to as a Lollard in the enquiry's documentation. Imprisoned, she subsequently retracted her errors and was re-enclosed.[239] Clay also mentions a rumoured heretic, a Dominican anchorite of Norwich, possibly Katherine Mann, influenced by the Protestant reformer Thomas Bilney, himself burnt for his beliefs in 1531, who lent her a copy of the Tyndale's New Testament and who attempted to clear her name before his death.[240]

Since all the later guides apart from the Bodley redaction anticipate that the recluse may interact with, or even advise those who come to her, potentially drawn by her contemplative prowess, the need to preserve her orthodoxy is vital. If she is in spiritual error herself, then the guides themselves effectively facilitate the promulgation of heresy through her to the community they encourage her to serve. Two protective strategies are recommended: the first is educative. Key orthodox spiritual beliefs are detailed and endorsed in the guides so the recluse can see clearly what she may safely believe and communicate. The second approach is darker and may be read as a continuation of earlier guidance's inculcation of fear (largely, then, about the loss of reclusive chastity). Later guidance writers, notwithstanding their primary focus upon contemplative love, concurrently seek to promote fear about the veracity of contemplative experiences, in order to safeguard reclusive orthodoxy. The passage about the transfiguration of the devil into an angel of light, referred to in *Ancrene Wisse* (*AW*, Corpus, p. 86), based on 2 Cor. 11:14, is intended by all the later writers to shock their recluses into seeking spiritual corroboration.[241] The increased problematization of reclusive spiritual autonomy concurrently safeguards the roles of spiritual director and confessor and also the role of anchoritic guidance writer. Hilton declares emphatically that anyone who engages in contemplation in any way contrary to that which he authorizes, be condemned 'as a theef' to be cast out (*Scale I*, p. 96).

Each later guide focuses on different heretical threats, according to when in the fourteenth century it was composed. Only the Bodley redaction, in its replication of Aelred's earlier medieval concerns, is comparatively silent on heresy; atypically for later guidance. It retains Aelred's recommendation of the use of imagery without mention of Lollard attacks on religious images (*DII*, MS Bodley 423, p. 15) and supports the right of the church to collect and distribute money, without reference to increasing anger on the part of dissenters dissatisfied with the church's increasing wealth at the laity's expense (*DII*, MS Bodley 423, p. 16). All the other later guides immerse themselves in contemporary spiritual controversies. Rolle's guide, which pre-dates the fiercest period of contemporary heretical debate, nonetheless problematizes dreams (identifying six different types), false visions, predestination and faith through works. It denounces 'il thoghtis', 'vnstablenesse of thoght', 'singulere witte' and 'dispute of good consaille and … techynge' (*Form*, p. 11), constructing the sleeping recluse as especially vulnerable. It interrogates the contentious issue of salvation through works and enters into the contemporary debate about salvation and predestination.

The Franciscan William of Ockham (*c*.1285–*c*.1347/9) argued that human will and endeavour should remain distinct from divine grace. Bishop Thomas Bradwardine (*c*.1290–1349), in his *De causa Dei*, articulates vehement opposition to this and argues that God's omniscient knowledge, not his will, predetermines all human thought and action, rendering 'merit, contrition, repentance, and absolution … the expressions of grace'.[242] Wyclif espouses a far less orthodox and more radical theology. Preaching faith and salvation through works, placing God, not beyond knowledge, but rather as its final and inexhaustible source, he argues that God's will and divine grace are open to mortal comprehension. The Bible, as the source of all knowledge of God, is therefore translated into the vernacular, increasing the laity's personal connection with biblical teachings. Notions of the predestined elect are rendered invalid; the priesthood and even the Pope himself, Wyclif argues, operate within the possibility of damnation. For Rolle, as for Wyclif, salvation and damnation are not gender- or status-specific but open to all. He echoes Bradwardine, however, in the belief that the amount of grace accorded to an individual is predestined. Rolle concedes that good works, while an expression of this grace, cannot, in themselves save mankind or alter predestination. Yet, he expends much effort on reclusive spiritual self-improvement, largely prompted by his interest in the individual relationship with God. Although good works cannot alter salvation substantially, Rolle implies that a greater understanding of that relationship may result in its greater enjoyment. *Speculum* and *Myrour* also argue, in line with Bradwardinian thought, that partial comprehension of God is possible; for them, the soul has a memory and an intellectual function (*Speculum*, p. 92).[243] They acknowledge, as did Rolle, that only some Christians are predestined to eternal Paradise but, although God's majesty is too great for mankind to articulate (*Speculum*, p. 98; *Myrour*, p. 29), the relationship with God may be improved 'per inspiracionem et per graciam perseverancie finaliter in caritate' (*Speculum*, p. 75).[244]

Hilton does not focus on these issues in his later and therefore even more detailed engagement with heresy. Three main commentaries in *Scale I* condemn it.[245] Building upon the anchoritic guidance tradition's long-standing synonymization of sight with sin, Hilton's heretic is often presented as blind. He is also wild, and animal metaphor communicates his sinful degeneration. Heretics 'gnawen upoun the drie bark withoutyn, but the swete kirnel of it and the inli savoure may he not come to' (*Scale I*, p. 52). Leff usefully reminds us that heresy springs 'from believing differently about the same things as opposed to holding a different belief'.[246] Hilton stresses the heretic's own intolerance of those with whom he disagrees theologically, frequently characterizing him as a lone individual with little support, which recalls *Ancrene Wisse*'s attempts to surround the lone anchorite with a virtual community to secure her orthodoxy. Hilton, severe in his judgement, affords heretics no freedom to make amends for transgression; his is a passionate denunciation. Hilton enjoins his recluse to 'love the man, be he nevere so synful' (*Scale I*, p. 104), but in the case of heretics he hates both sin and sinner, condemning those who 'preisen and thanken God with here lippes, but in her hertis ... stelen as theves the worschip ... from God' (*Scale I*, p. 52). Hilton shares Rollian concerns about dreaming (*Scale I*, p. 75) and salvation through works. His chief preoccupations, however, are with predestiny, grace and volition. He argues that good works are not sufficient in themselves to save souls (which can only be done through God's grace). They are therefore 'not ... nedeful to savacion, but ... spedeful' (*Scale I*, p. 56). He generates an atmosphere of considerable fear in passages which demonstrate that devoutly motivated and corruptly motivated contemplative experience can seem the same to the untrained eye (*Scale I*, p. 40). Yet, chiefly, he adopts a largely educative perspective and is more detailed than Rolle in his provision of spiritual material in which the recluse can safely believe. His threefold system of orthodox belief (*Scale I*, pp. 94–5) requires the renunciation of personal intellect and demands unquestioning faith in the validity of the sacraments, the articles of faith and obedience to 'the lawes and the ordenaunces maad bi prelates and rulers of hooli chirche, either in declarynge of the feith ... or in general governance of alle Cristen men' (*Scale I*, p. 53). Hilton urges: 'what thou feelist, seest, ... smellest or savour ... in ymagynynge or feelynge ... brynge hit al withynne the trowthe and rulis of hooli chirche' (*Scale I*, pp. 56–7). His authority is synonymized with that of the Catholic Church, in turn synonymized with God's will: 'God and holi chirche are so onyd and acordid togidere that whoso dooth ayen that oon, he dooth ayen that othir' (*Scale I*, p. 96). In this, Hilton makes the highest of spiritual claims for his work. The supremacy, not only of the church's belief systems, but of its bureaucratic structures is reinforced: 'prelatis and curates ... aren bounden bi there office ... to see and seke and deme rightfulli othere mennys defautis ... with drede of

God and in his name' (*Scale I*, p. 49). He safeguards his role as spiritual advisor, but concurrently shows his recluse how to recognize for herself where, in her contemplation, she most risks 'fals restynge' in personal will (*Scale I*, p. 96). He provides more detailed tests than Rolle, whereby she may judge her contemplative veracity. His heresy detection system is not foolproof and he stresses repeatedly that only God can know what truly motivates contemplation. He advises, therefore, that every Christian assume a God-given motivation in others unless heresy is openly proved. Hilton strikes a delicate balance in his guide, between increasing the recluse's awareness of heresy and educating her in its avoidance.

Rolle and Hilton both reinforce contemplative, reclusive orthodoxy using the purely later medieval phenomenon of the tradition of the Holy Name to bind the recluse to the humanity, rather than divinity, of Christ: 'this savacion bitokeneth this name Jhesu … for to have it … bi the mekenesse of his manhede and by the merite of his passioun' (*Scale I*, p. 81).[247] This tradition imbues Christ's very name with the same restorative and purificatory significances as the Eucharist itself. Hilton writes: 'For this name is not ellis for to seie upon Ynglisch but heelere or hele' (*Scale I*, p. 80). Rolle constructs it as a contemplative aid, in its purificatory function: 'If þou thynk Ihesu continuely and hold it stably, hit purgeth þi syn and kyndels thyn hert, hit clarifieth þi soule … hit openeth heuyn and maketh a contemplatif man' (*Form*, p. 18). He characterizes the highest contemplative state of 'synguler' love as complete fixation upon this name: 'Þan þe sowl is Ihesu louynge, Ihesu thynkynge, Ihesu desyrynge … þan may þou say "I sleep and my hert waketh"' (*Form*, p. 17).

Speculum and *Myrour* argue that the recluse cannot function 'si intellectus erret in fide catholica' (*Speculum*, p. 116).[248] They interrogate contemplative orthodoxy through a similar mixture of education and manipulation, but their central focus is on Eucharistic orthodoxy. They also reiterate the desirability of belief in 'articulis fidei ab ecclesia determinatis' (*Speculum*, p. 116), specifically in the Trinity, Incarnation, Passion and Resurrection and the Last Judgement.[249] Belief is also demanded in the Athanasian Creed, the writings of the apostles, the ideals espoused by the Lord's Prayer (*Speculum*, p. 116; *Myrour*, pp. 39–40) and 'oraciones ad quas homo tenetur ex ordinacione ecclesie vel superiorum suorum … iuxta modum et consuetudinem sui Ordinis sive status' (*Speculum*, p. 87).[250] Faith, located in the mind and in the soul and given an intellectual function, as in *Scale*, binds together a community of what *Myrour* calls 'þe ry3t byleeue' (*Myrour*, p. 40). This communal strategy of orthodoxy promotion recalls *Ancrene Wisse*'s reclusive network. Yet, it is belief in the veracity of the sacrament of the Eucharist that is the ultimate reinforcer of orthodoxy for this guide and its translation. It binds God to man and man to man in an orthodox community of the replenished: 'facta consecracione, est caro, sanguis, corpus, anima et ipsa deitas, totus Christus, verus Deus et homo' (*Speculum*, p. 117).[251] *Speculum* and *Myrour* are unique amongst the later guides for their preoccupation with this, exclaiming: 'O preciosissimum nutrimentum, o nobilissimum restaurativum, o efficacissimum confortativum' (*Speculum*, p. 119).[252] Yet, their perspectives build on the focus of earlier guidance on the Eucharist, which, as this chapter's focus on fusion has demonstrated, forms the ultimate concurrent symbol of Christ's humanity and divinity, and binds God to mankind (explicitly through the Eucharist from *Ancrene Wisse* onwards). Jestice argues for a movement, from the late tenth century on, to 'emphasize the real presence of Christ in the Eucharist' as part of the drive to humanize Christ.[253]

Unlike earlier medieval guidance, however, *Speculum* and *Myrour* react implicitly to Wycliffite and Lollard arguments that the Eucharistic elements of bread and wine retain their own substance and are not transubstantiated into the body and blood of Christ either at the words of institution or the elevation.[254] Hudson cites the fifteenth-century abjuration of one heretic as the typical Lollard view: 'the sacramente of the awter lyfte vp ouer the priestis hed is not to be wurshipped more than materyall brede lifte vp ouer myn hede'.[255] This is not a wholescale rejection of the validity of the Mass, which the majority of Lollards continued to attend. Some sought to evade detection, some attended because they retained a belief in its symbolically restorative significance.[256] *Speculum* defends transubstantiation: 'Christus corporaliter in altaris sanctissimo sacramento, ubi cotidie sub specie panis et vini pro nobis offertur eius anima in nostre redempcionis precium, corpus in spiritualem cibum, sanguis in salutis poculum' (*Speculum*, p. 98).[257] The author anticipates squeamishness on the part of the communicant: 'horror crudi corporis vel sanguinis' (*Speculum*, p. 117).[258] His secular metaphor of copper production (allusive, stylistically at least, of Aelred's linen-production metaphor at *DII*, p. 658),[259] argues for transubstantiation at the consecration of the elements, not in consumption or at digestion. He states: 'quod equaliter post consecracionem sicut ante manent accidentia, videlicet color, sapor et pondus panis et vini, quando nec est ibidem panis, nec vinum, nec ulla substancia nisi substancia corporis et sanguinis Ihesu Christi cum deitate' (*Speculum*, p. 117).[260] This equation of bread and wine with the suffering body and blood synonymizes the Eucharist with the divinity, not humanity, of God. Yet all are united: 'sanguis non separabitur a carne, nec anima a corpore, nec humanitas a divinitate, ideo sub utraque specie, videlicit tam panis quam vini, facta consecracione, est caro, sanguis, corpus, anima et ipsa deitas, totus Christus, verus Deus et homo' (*Speculum*, p. 117).[261]

This recalls Goscelin's conclusions that although the Eucharist is 'dominico corpori et sanguini' (*Liber*, p. 90), it remains 'Magnum sacramentum' (*Liber*, p. 90), uniting heaven and earth in 'Hunc panem uite, panem angelorum' (*Liber*, p. 90).[262] In *Speculum*, each tiny particle of this host is imbued with the vastness of God's power: 'in speculo fracto, quod in qualibet parte fracta relucet eadem ymago, que prius in integro speculo relucebat' (*Speculum*, p. 118).[263]

Speculum and *Myrour*'s Eucharistic piety is mirrored in contemporary contemplative spiritual writings. Baldwin of Ford declares the sacrament was instituted 'so that Christians could offer, eat and imitate Christ', while Bernard of Clairvaux constructs its ingestation as participation in the Passion.[264] It empowers contemplatives, for, as the fusion section of this chapter has shown, it fuses God's body to mankind's as the contemplative becomes 'tanquam eius membrum suo sanguine proprio vivificatum' (*Speculum*, p. 98).[265] The Eucharist is the focal point of extraordinary intimacy between Christ and some believers. In 1421, Konrad Kügelin of Waldsee (1367–1428) writes the life of Elisabeth Achler, a Franciscan nun, also known as Elisabeth of Reute (1386–1420), a stigmatic. The *vita* argues that Elisabeth receives the sacrament from Christ himself in a vision.[266] Mary of Oignies is given the power to tell an unconsecrated from a consecrated host and subsists entirely on the Eucharist at one stage of her life.[267] Walter Simons identifies beguine recluses as especially attracted to Eucharistic devotion, while

Ernest McDonnell attributes the beguine cult of Eucharistic devotion to 'Ardent love for the humanity and passion of Christ'.[268] Lateran IV's dictates that every Christian receive Communion at least once a year were confronted by some who, like Margery Kempe, desired it far more frequently. She asks the archbishop of Canterbury himself to permit this: 'prayng hym of hys gracyows lordshyp to grawnt hir auctoryté of chesyng hyr confessowr and to be howselyd every Sonday, yyf God wold dysposen hir therto, undyr hys lettyr and hys seel thorw al hys provynce'.[269] Eamon Duffy, who writes extensively on the significance of the later medieval Mass both for individual believers and society as a whole, argues nonetheless that such individuals were relatively unique: 'for most people, most of the time, the Host was something to be seen, not … consumed'.[270] Yet, from the time of *Ancrene Wisse* onwards, anchoritic guides stress the intimate proximity of the recluse to the Host, binding the Eucharist and sight together in their explorations of its visual significance.

This chapter has shown that every anchoritic guide at once informs and is informed by contemporary shifts in medieval contemplative spirituality, although three kinds of contemplative experience, namely of meditation, vision and fusion, remain important throughout the Middle Ages. The guides' constructions of each have been shown to be reflective of developing trends, such as the accentuation of Christocentric piety, the emergence of lay piety, lay negotiations of contemplative experience and, in particular, increasing anxieties about heresy. The guides have been shown to reflect society's continued identification of anchoritic solitude with contemplation and also to evidence wider changes in the way the body, especially the body of Christ, is used as contemplative inspiration.

Conclusion

This book has revealed a tradition of anchoritic guidance writing in England in the Middle Ages; the product of overt and implicit relationships between many anchoritic guides. The eight guides upon which it has focused closely have been shown to negotiate four common anchoritic ideals: enclosure, solitude, chastity and orthodoxy, and two common spiritual practices: asceticism and contemplative experience. Yet, the emphasis placed upon each ideal, or spiritual practice, has been shown to vary from writer to writer, from period to period and, crucially, in tandem with wider changes in medieval culture. Each guide varies in its estimation of what constitutes the vocation's gravest threat. Earlier guidance gifts its attempts to safeguard the loss of reclusive chastity with the same obsessive focus the later guides devote to safeguarding her spiritual orthodoxy. Yet, all the writers agree that the place of the recluse on the 'sliding scale' of sin does not remain constant; her motivations and actions must be re-evaluated daily, even hourly; her gradual descent into corruption resisted again and again. All of these writers consequently trade in images of the idealized and demonized recluse. All construct their recluses in the grip of the opposing forces of good and evil; virtue and vice. These texts, then, generated by an anxiety that they can never fully quieten, construct a vocation of vulnerability and relentless spiritual threat, despite the potential sanctuary that they also imply the vocation can afford the faithful. All the guides are founded upon the understanding that anchoritism, if well lived, can bring untold spiritual reward and immeasurable contentment, even in the midst of wider, later medieval debates about the usefulness and purpose of the contemplative life.

This book argues that each of its anchoritic guides offers just one glimpse or 'snapshot' of the vocation in ideological terms. The tradition demonstrates mutable and shifting anchoritic ideologies; not a single ideological perspective set in stone. While the guidance tradition, at times, argues that all four of the anchoritic ideals of enclosure, solitude, chastity and orthodoxy, should be absolute in theory, this book has shown that enclosure and solitude are only ever intended to be relative in practice; they cannot even be iterated, textually, without qualification. In this context, it would be unwise to continue to allow one guide, or one part of the medieval period, to dominate critical conceptions of the vocation. The earlier medieval image of the anchorhold as a solitary death-cell is certainly striking, but it has been shown to be no more representative of the vocation, ideologically, than the construction of a busy later medieval reclusorium at the heart of the spiritual development of its community.

The book has demonstrated the extent to which later medieval anchoritic ideology develops from earlier perspectives. Ideological changes in the theology of the vocation have been revealed, not as sharp departures from earlier medieval positions, but gradual vocational developments. The perspectives of the later guides have been shown to grow, for the most part, out of the earlier ones, even where they appear, at first glance, to be markedly different. Earlier and later medieval anchoritic guides are cast in a mutually referential relationship. Later writers clearly diverge from and modify earlier material in their attempts to elucidate and resolve persistent problems and negotiate new territory. Nonetheless, the key developments in later medieval anchoritic ideology have been traced back to their roots in the earlier medieval texts. This has been particularly illustrated by the book's treatment of acceptable reclusive sociability. Chapter 3 has demonstrated that, although later guidance permits its recluses a greater social role, acceptable levels of sociability are anticipated and accepted by the earlier guides and sociability built into the vocation's ideological negotiations from its very beginning. A tension has been revealed, never fully reconciled by later medieval guidance, between the perpetuation of anchoritism as a vocation of relative solitude and the later medieval intensification of both anchoritic contemplative experience and the increasingly sociable identity of the reclusive life. Later guides have been shown to expect their recluses at once to maintain the relative social separation conducive to contemplation and yet to understand themselves as role models of orthodox spirituality in the wider communities of which they remain a part, despite their comparative physical isolation.

Whereas part I of this book focused solely on the guidance writing tradition, part II placed that tradition in its wider historical context in terms of two pervasive medieval spiritual phenomena: asceticism and contemplative experience. It demonstrated that shifts in the tradition's negotiations of these two practices were in sympathy with wider cultural and spiritual trends. Anchoritic spiritual practices and the meanings of those practices were shown to be continually susceptible to external cultural forces. Chapter 4 evaluated the ways in which anchoritic asceticism intersected with the asceticism of the unenclosed world. It demonstrated that as the wider medieval world moved away from an interest in the experience of physical pain towards an interest in ascetical contemplation, so too did the ideology of English anchoritism. Chapter 5 explored the intersections between anchoritic and non-anchoritic contemplative experience. It demonstrated that the contemplative models of the enclosed world echoed those of the unenclosed world. It found that anchoritic guides were reflective of exactly the same kinds of developing spiritual trends common to the wider world. Awareness of and interest in the contemplative experiences of meditation, vision and fusion were shown to remain constant both inside and outside the anchorhold, but the practice of meditation was shown to dominate earlier medieval perspectives to the same degree as the practice of fusion dominated those of the later Middle Ages. Crucially, the later guides revealed their potential awareness of the recluse as an inspirational spiritual role model and advisor and this was shown to inspire the urgent attempts of the later writers to educate them in vital, orthodox precepts. The later guides implied that the recluse has the potential to disseminate orthodox spirituality to the wider world. The anchoritic vocation has been shown to be all the more vulnerable and all the more glorious for that.

Despite the continued centrality of its comparative physical isolation, the guides have been shown to site the anchoritic vocation within the wider Christian community, in terms of shared spiritual ideals and practices. Just as the spirituality of the wider world was frequently renegotiated, so too was the spiritual ideology of the medieval anchorhold. In this context, the guidance tradition's ideological constructions are revealed as an intellectual currency which potentially passes into and, crucially, out of the English reclusorium. The guides reveal an anchoritic spirituality that is not only influenced by, but potentially influences, wider medieval piety.

Notes

Introduction

[1] Earlier medieval here denotes the period from 1000–1299; later medieval from 1300 to the end of the Middle Ages.

[2] This does not mean that individual guidance writers are not obsessed with individual ideals, e.g. Aelred of Rievaulx with chastity, but simply that as a group, all the guidance writers are interested in the fundamentals of enclosure and solitude.

[3] I am grateful to Dr Robert Hasenfratz for advice on this point (correspondence dated 11 March 2011).

[4] The *Vitas Patrum*, also known as the *Verba Seniorum*, do not constitute a single unified work in the Middle Ages. See Jacques-Paul Migne (ed.), *Patrologiae Cursus Completus: Series Latina*, 221 vols (Paris: Migne, 1841–64), vol. 73, cols 851–1052, and Benedicta Ward (ed. and trans.), *The Sayings of the Desert Fathers: The Alphabetical Collection* (rev. edn; Kalamazoo: Cistercian Publications, 2005). On ancient solitude, see Peter Brown, *The Body and Society: Men, Women and Sexual Renunciation in Early Christianity* (1988; New York: Columbia University Press, 2008), especially pp. 210–338, and Benedicta Ward, *Discernment in the Desert Fathers: Diakrisis in the Life and Thought of Early Egyptian Monasticism* (Eugene, Oregon: Wipf and Stock Publishers, 2007).

[5] Henry G. Liddell and Robert Scott, *A Greek–English Lexicon*, 2 vols (Oxford: Clarendon Press, 1843), vol. 1, p. 257.

[6] Taken from *Regula Sancti Benedicti*, online at, *http://www.intratext.com/IXT/LAT0011/_P2.HTM* (accessed 7 September 2011). Translated as: 'The second kind are the Anchorites or Hermits: those who, no longer in the first fervor of their reformation, but after long probation in a monastery, having learned by the help of many brethren how to fight against the devil, go out well armed from the ranks of the community to the solitary combat of the desert. They are able now, with no help save from God, to fight single-handed against the vices of the flesh and their own evil thoughts' (The *Rule of St Benedict* at, *http://www.osb.org/rb/text/rbejms1.html#1* (accessed 7 September 2011)).

[7] Ann K. Warren, *Anchorites and their Patrons in Medieval England* (Berkeley, Los Angeles and London: University of California Press, 1985), p. 8. This is one of the three works of anchoritic scholarship that has paved the way for all existing work in the field. See also Rotha Mary Clay, *The Hermits and Anchorites of England* (London: Methuen, 1914), and Francis D. S. Darwin, *The English Mediaeval Recluse* (London: SPCK, 1944).

Clay's monumental text is the first vital collection of information about English solitaries, focusing on wills, ecclesiastical and court documents, hagiography, enclosure ceremonials and the *Victoria County Histories* (then in an early stage of production). Edward A. Jones identifies Clay's biggest debt to the nineteenth-century county historians who came before the *VCH*, and her own correspondents: 'she seems to have sent out letters to all the librarians and archivists in the land' (E. A. Jones, personal correspondence dated 14 June 2004).

Warren's book is still the authoritative source for anchoritic statistical data and hers are the most recent figures to have been published en masse, therefore her text is currently the most influential of the three (although since she often relies on Clay, Clay dominates through her).

8   Edward A. Jones, 'Hermits and anchorites in historical context', in Dee Dyas, Valerie Edden and Roger Ellis (eds), *Approaching Medieval English Anchoritic and Mystical Texts* (Cambridge: D. S. Brewer, 2005), pp. 3–18 (pp. 7–8), and Edward A. Jones, 'Langland and hermits', *Yearbook of Langland Studies*, 11 (1997), 67–86.

9   See Henrietta Leyser, *Hermits and the New Monasticism. A Study of Religious Communities in Western Europe 1000–1150* (Basingstoke and New York: Palgrave Macmillan, 1984), pp. 4–8. See also Mari Hughes-Edwards, 'Anchoritism: the English tradition', in Liz Herbert McAvoy (ed.), *Anchoritic Traditions of Medieval Europe* (Woodbridge: Boydell and Brewer, 2010), pp. 131–52 (p. 135), on the fluidity of earlier medieval eremitism.

10   Tom Licence, *Hermits and Recluses in English Society: 950–1200* (Oxford: Oxford University Press, 2011), p. 15.

11   Clay, *Hermits and Anchorites*, pp. xvi–xvii.

12   Warren, *Anchorites and their Patrons*, p. 8.

13   Warren, *Anchorites and their Patrons*, p. 7.

14   Warren's *Anchorites and their Patrons*, p. 20, details 414 female solitaries, 201 males and 165 indeterminates (where gender is currently unrecoverable). See also Jones, 'Hermits and anchorites in historical context', p. 9, on this. Since female recluses outnumber males at every stage of the medieval period and most of the guides explored in this book were written for women, this book hereafter reads the default anchoritic gender as female.

15   Edward A. Jones, 'Ceremonies of enclosure: rite, rhetoric and reality', in Liz Herbert McAvoy (ed.), *Rhetoric of the Anchorhold: Space, Place and Body within the Discourses of Enclosure* (Cardiff: University of Wales Press, 2008), pp. 34–49, identifies their fourteen common elements. See also Warren, *Anchorites and their Patrons*, p. 76; Darwin, *The English Mediaeval Recluse*, pp. 71–8 and Clay's translation of the sixteenth-century ceremony in the Sarum manual: *Hermits and Anchorites*, appendix A, pp. 193–8.

16   See Warren, *Anchorites and their Patrons*, pp. 53–92.

17   See H. A. Wilson, *The Pontifical of Magdalen College*, Henry Bradshaw Society, 39 (1910), 243–4. Warren suggests that the door was only symbolically blocked (*Anchorites and their Patrons*, p. 98).

18   Jones, 'Ceremonies of enclosure', pp. 44–5.

19   Jones, 'Ceremonies of enclosure', pp. 45–6.

20   Warren, *Anchorites and their Patrons*, p. 190 (pp. 190–5 problematize anchoritic testamentary data).

21   Warren, *Anchorites and their Patrons*, pp. 163, 204.

22   See page 88 below for more information on Rawghton.

23   Clay, *Hermits and Anchorites*, p. 155. See also Warren, *Anchorites and their Patrons*, pp. 203–6.

24   Edward. A. Jones, 'Anchoritic aspects of Julian of Norwich', in Liz Herbert McAvoy (ed.), *A Companion to Julian of Norwich* (Cambridge: D. S. Brewer, 2008), pp. 75–87 (pp. 80–1, 82).

25   Jones, 'Anchoritic aspects of Julian', p. 82. Emphasis in the original.

26   We know that Christine fled her cell, but do not know for certain that she was re-enclosed, although the last letter that documents her case (dated November 1332) gives this or excommunication as her only options. See the episcopal register of John Stratford, Hampshire, Record Office, MS 21M65/A1/5, f. 46v and f. 76r. See also the leaflet, *Christine Carpenter, The Anchoress of Shere* (Guildford: Commercial Press, 1986); Liz Herbert McAvoy, 'Gender, rhetoric and space in the *Speculum Inclusorum, Letter to a Bury Recluse* and the strange case of Christina Carpenter', in *eadem* (ed.), *Rhetoric of the Anchorhold: Space, Place and Body within the Discourses of Enclosure* (Cardiff: University of Wales Press), pp. 111–27, and F. Donald Logan, *Runaway Religious in Medieval England, c.1240–1540* (Cambridge: Cambridge University Press, 1996), p. 267. Miri Rubin, 'An English anchorite: the making, unmaking and remaking of Christine Carpenter', in Rosemary Horrox and Sarah Rees Jones (eds), *Pragmatic Utopias: Ideas and*

Communities, 1200–1630 (Cambridge: Cambridge University Press, 2001), pp. 204–21, also focuses on the 1993 film *Anchoress*, which was loosely based on Christine's story.

27   Warren, *Anchorites and their Patrons*, pp. 182–3.

28   Warren, *Anchorites and their Patrons*, p. 81.

29   See Warren, *Anchorites and their Patrons*, pp. 64, 77–9, 268–9, and Clay, *Hermits and Anchorites*, pp. 50, 60, 85–6 and 159.

30   Warren, *Anchorites and their Patrons*, pp. 77–8.

31   Henry Mayr-Harting, 'Functions of a twelfth-century recluse', *History: The Journal of the Historical Association*, 60 (1975), 337–52 (337), which reveals Wulfric as potential conciliator, healer and scribe. Mayr-Harting's conclusions were updated in Susan J. Ridyard, 'Functions of a twelfth-century recluse revisited: the case of Godric of Finchale', in Richard Gameson and Henrietta Leyser (eds), *Belief and Culture in the Middle Ages: Studies Presented to Henry Mayr-Harting* (Oxford: Oxford University Press, 2001), pp. 236–50. See also Warren, *Anchorites and their Patrons*, pp. 110–11 and Clay, *Hermits and Anchorites*, p. 92.

32   Robert Hasenfratz (ed.), *Ancrene Wisse* (Kalamazoo: Medieval Institute Publications, 2000), Introduction, p. 6. This edition is also available via the *TEAMS Middle English Texts* webpage at, *http://www.lib.rochester.edu/camelot/teams/hasenfratz.htm* (accessed 7 September 2011); Licence, *Hermits and Recluses*, p. 108.

33   Licence, *Hermits and Recluses*, pp. 171, 163 (pp. 150–72 treat each element in turn).

34   Christopher Daniell, *From Norman Conquest to Magna Carta: England, 1066–1215* (London and New York: Routledge, 2005), p. 152.

35   Daniell, *From Norman Conquest*, p. 155.

36   Warren, *Anchorites and their Patrons*, p. 15.

37   Denis Renevey, 'Looking for a context: Rolle, anchoritic culture and the office of the dead', in G. D. Caie and D. Renevey (eds), *Medieval Texts in Context* (London and New York: Routledge, 2008), pp. 192–211 (p. 195).

38   Liz Herbert McAvoy, Introduction: place, space and the body within anchoritic rhetoric, in *eadem* (ed.), *Rhetoric of the Anchorhold: Space, Place and the Body within the Discourses of Enclosure* (Cardiff: University of Wales Press), pp. 1–16 (p. 7).

39   See Tom Licence, 'Evidence of recluses in eleventh-century England', in Malcolm Godden and Simon Keynes (eds), *Anglo-Saxon England*, 36 (2007), 221–34.

40   Licence, *Hermits and Recluses*, p. 87.

41   See Clay, *Hermits and Anchorites*, pp. 77–8, and Warren, *Anchorites and their Patrons*, pp. 157 and 288–9, on anchorholds in castles and religious foundations.

42   Roberta Gilchrist, *Contemplation and Action: The Other Monasticism* (London and New York: Leicester University Press, 1995), pp. 189–90.

43   Warren, *Anchorites and their Patrons*, p. 32.

44   See Warren, *Anchorites and their Patrons*, p. 29. H. Thackeray Turner, 'Notes on Compton Church, Surrey', *The Proceedings of the Society of Antiquaries*, 12 March 1908, 4–7 (5), suggests the Norman origin of the two-storied cell on the south side and argues that its doorway is a fourteenth-century insertion.

45   Gilchrist, *Contemplation and Action*, p. 187.

46   See Clay, *Hermits and Anchorites*, pp. 83, 214 (Clay records Chester-le-Street's named recluses from 1383 onwards). Warren notes that plural references to an anchorite's 'houses' are found in later medieval documentation but multi-roomed structures were exceptional (*Anchorites and their Patrons*, p. 32). See also Hasenfratz, *Ancrene Wisse*, Introduction, p. 9.

47   Warren, *Anchorites and their Patrons*, p. 50.

48   Clay, *Hermits and Anchorites*, p. 144, and Warren, *Anchorites and their Patrons*, p. 78.

49   Norman P. Tanner, *The Church in Late-medieval Norwich, 1370–1532* (Toronto: Pontifical Institute of Medieval Studies, 1984), p. 60.

50   See Clay's tabulated lists of cells (*Hermits and Anchorites*, pp. 203–63). Jones problematizes her classification of solitaries by site and county, proposing instead classification by individual. See Edward A. Jones, 'Christina of Markyate and the *Hermits and Anchorites of England*', in

Samuel Fanous and Henrietta Leyser (eds), *Christina of Markyate: A Twelfth-century Holy Woman* (London and New York: Routledge, 2005), pp. 229–53 (pp. 232, 235).

[51] Warren notes the gendered ratios of anchoritism as follows: in the twelfth century, five women: three men; in the thirteenth century, 4:1; in the fourteenth century, 5:2; in the fifteenth century, 5:3; in the sixteenth century, 3:2 (*Anchorites and their Patrons*, p. 19). See also Gilchrist, *Contemplation and Action*, pp. 183–9.

[52] Warren, *Anchorites and their Patrons*, p. 36.

[53] Gilchrist, *Contemplation and Action*, p. 183, and Edward A. Jones, 'A new look into the *Speculum inclusorum*', in Marion Glasscoe (ed.), *The Medieval Mystical Tradition in England, Ireland and Wales: Papers Read at Charney Manor, July 1999 (Exeter Symposium VI)* (Cambridge: D. S. Brewer, 1999), pp. 123–45 (p. 132). On medieval urbanization, see David M. Palliser, *Towns and Local Communities in Medieval and Early Modern England* (Aldershot: Ashgate, 2006), and Nigel Baker and Richard Holt, *Urban Growth and the Medieval Church: Gloucester and Worcester* (Aldershot: Ashgate, 2004).

[54] William Lyndwood, *Provinciale (seu constitutiones angliae) continens constitutiones provinciales quatuordecim archiepiscoporum cant' a Stephano Langtono ad Henricum Chichleium* (Oxford, 1679), III, 20.2., cited in Jones, 'A new look into the *Speculum inclusorum*', p. 132, and Warren, *Anchorites and their Patrons*, p. 40.

[55] Warren, *Anchorites and their Patrons*, p. 39.

[56] Current data implies that anchoritism then saw a 22:27 rural/urban ratio (Warren, *Anchorites and their Patrons*, p. 37).

[57] Rotha Mary Clay, 'Further studies on medieval recluses', *Journal of the British Archaeological Association*, 16 (1953), 74–86.

[58] Cottle's acknowledged revisions are incorporated into Jones's new data. For Jones's new findings to date, see his website *Hermits and Anchorites of England* at, *http://hermits.ex.ac.uk* (accessed 7 September 2011); his 'Christina of Markyate', pp. 240–50; his 'The hermits and anchorites of Oxfordshire', *Oxoniensia*, 63 (1998), 51–77 and his 'Rotha Clay's *Hermits and Anchorites of England*', *Monastic Research Bulletin*, 3 (1997), 46–8.

[59] Warren, *Anchorites and their Patrons*, p. 18. Bella Millett, drawing on the work of Brenda Bolton, Patricia Rosof and Warren, also argues this in '*Ancrene Wisse* and the life of perfection', *Leeds Studies in English*, 33 (2002), 53–76 (see especially 55).

[60] Warren, *Anchorites and their Patrons*, appendix 2, pp. 294–8, details thirteen extant English guides.

[61] Aelred's *De institutione inclusarum* and the *Speculum inclusorum* are both translated and revised in the later medieval period, and it would be useful to debate the extent to which these later texts, along with later revisions and translations of *Ancrene Wisse*, constitute new guides.

[62] Patricia Ranft, *Women and the Religious Life in Premodern Europe* (1996; New York: St Martin's Press, 1998), p. 44. Another, more minor, example of misreading the guides as evidence of practice centres upon *Ancrene Wisse*'s directions on keeping a cat, which have been so misapplied that some modern iconographic images of the (far later) anchorite, Julian of Norwich, depict her with a cat in her arms, e.g. as in Robert Lentz's image at, *https://www.trinitystores.com/store/art-image/julian-norwich-14th-century* (accessed 7 September 2011). There is no evidence to suggest that Julian kept such an animal, or even that the recluses of *Ancrene Wisse* did. Its author simply permits keeping them in theory.

[63] On fear as social control, see Robert Hasenfratz, 'Terror and pastoral care in *Handlyng Synne*', in Cate Gunn and Catherine Innes-Parker (eds), *Texts and Traditions of Medieval Pastoral Care: Essays in Honour of Bella Millett* (Cambridge: Boydell and Brewer, 2009), pp. 132–48, and Cynthia Kosso and Anne Scott (eds), *Fear and Its Representations in the Middle Ages and Renaissance* (Turnhout: Brepols, 2002).

[64] Bella Millett, *Ancrene Wisse: Guide for Anchoresses. A Translation* (Exeter: Exeter University Press, 2009), p. xv. All translations from *Ancrene Wisse* given in endnotes are taken from this translation, cited as '(Millett and page number)'.

[65] Mari Hughes-Edwards, 'The role of the anchoritic guidance writer: Goscelin of St Bertin', in Catherine Innes-Parker and Naoë Kukita Yoshikawa (eds), *Anchorism in the Middle Ages:*

Texts and Traditions (Cardiff: University of Wales Press, forthcoming 2012). Generative bonds between guidance writer and recluse generate the actual production of a guidance text; wider, or incidental, reclusive relationships unite a writer with a wider imagined (or sometimes unimagined) audience, but are not credited with textual generation.

66 This study excludes the following guides, all originally intended for male recluses (dating and attributions all taken from Warren, *Anchorites and their Patrons*, appendix 2, pp. 295–8, which also gives details of their editions and translations, where available): *Admonitiones*, around 210 lines long, composed *c*.1140–1215, by Robert, a priest, for Hugo; *The Dublin Rule* or *Regula reclusorum dubliniensis*, anonymous author, about 350 lines long, *c*.1220–1312 (probably earlier rather than later); *Walter's Rule* or *Regula reclusorum Walteri reclusi*, *c*.1280, about 930 lines long and, with the possible exception of Rolle's *The Form of Living*, the only known anchoritic guide composed for solitaries by a solitary (Walter was, by then, a 60-year-old man who had been solitary for ten years and, formerly, an Augustinian canon for thirty); the very short *Lambeth Rule*, a thirteenth-century vernacular guide for lay recluses; the manuscript, from which it takes its name, dates from the fifteenth; the later medieval *Letter to a Bury Recluse* or *The Reply of a Fourteenth-century Abbot of Bury St. Edmunds to a Man's Petition to be a Recluse*, fifty-five lines in length, undated and addressed to an unknown 'dominus L' by an abbot of Bury and finally Walter Hilton's *Epistola ad quendam solitarium*, for a censured priest who subsequently became solitary.

    Jones's conclusion that *Walter's Rule* is 'more or less entirely neglected' and that its dating and attribution should therefore 'be regarded as provisional' can be usefully applied to all these excluded guides, all of which deserve further critical evaluation. See Jones, 'Ceremonies of enclosure', p. 48, n. 37.

67 This book explores eight guides if Anselm's letters are counted as one (due to brevity), if Aelred's guide and its Bodley redaction are counted as two different guides (due to the differences between them, notably the redaction's removal of all personal references to Aelred's sister), if all *Ancrene Wisse*'s different texts are all held to constitute one guide but many texts, and if *Speculum* and *Myrour* are counted as one guide (because one is a faithful translation of the other, albeit with important omissions). In practice, this book analyses fourteen texts of its eight base guides; ten of the four earlier medieval guides, and four of the later medieval guides.

68 The Vernon manuscript certainly contains numerous texts originally written for anchorites. Yet, while John Ayto, Alexandra Barratt and Felicity Riddy, amongst others, have argued for its potentially female readership, Ayto and Barratt note that 'in the absence of any hard evidence it is pointless to speculate any further' and do not argue for an anchoritic audience. See John Ayto and Alexandra Barratt (eds), *Aelred of Rievaulx's 'De institutione inclusarum': Two English Versions*, Early English Text Society, original series, 287 (1984), Introduction, p. xviii. Their edition of the Vernon manuscript's text of *De institutione* is at pp. 26–60. See also Felicity J. Riddy, 'Women talking about the things of God: a late medieval sub-culture', in Carol M. Meale (ed.), *Women and Literature in Britain: 1150–1500* (Cambridge: Cambridge Studies in Literature, 1993), pp. 104–27 (pp. 106–7).

69 It is not, however, the intention of this book to read the anchoritic guidance tradition within the framework of contemporary gender or feminist theory, but in the context of the medieval ideological spiritualities of wider Europe. For a theorized feminist analysis, see Liz Herbert McAvoy's *Medieval Anchoritisms: Gender, Space and the Solitary Life* (Cambridge: D. S. Brewer, 2011).

70 The following guides, which have a relationship with the eight selected as the book's base guides have therefore been excluded: the later medieval texts of *De institutione inclusarum*, *Ancrene Wisse*, the *Scale of Perfection* and *The Form of Living* all extant in Oxford, Bodleian Library, MS Eng. poet.a.1 (the Vernon manuscript, *c*.1400); the *Ancrene Wisse* texts also extant in Cambridge, Magdalene College, MS Pepys 2498 (fourteenth century, possibly a Lollard redaction) and in London, British Library, MS Royal 8. C.i (fifteenth century) and Book II of Walter Hilton's *The Scale of Perfection*.

    For editions of these texts of *Ancrene Wisse*, see the bibliography to Millett's translation, *Ancrene Wisse*, especially pp. 281–94.

Book II of *Scale* is in Walter Hilton, *Walter Hilton: The Scale of Perfection*, ed. Thomas H. Bestul (Kalamazoo: Medieval Institute Publications, 2000), pp. 134–261. This book will only focus on *Scale I* which is also in this edition, at pp. 31–133; hereafter cited as '(*Scale I* and page number)'. Both books are also available via the *TEAMS Middle English Texts* webpage at, *http://www.lib.rochester.edu/camelot/teams/hilfr1.htm* (accessed 7 September 2011).

Bestul's edition is based on London, Lambeth Palace Library, MS 472, an early fifteenth-century vernacular form of the text in what appears to be 'a purposely assembled ... anthology of Hilton's work' (p. 7).

The Early English Text Society's critical edition of *Scale* is still in production. Two partial, unpublished editions exist: R. (Birts) Dorward, '*The Scale of Perfection* by Walter Hilton, Canon at the Augustinian Priory of Thurgarton Priory, Book I, chapters 38–52' (unpublished M.Litt diss., University of Oxford, 1956), and Stanley S. Hussey, 'An edition, from the manuscripts of Book II of Walter Hilton's *Scale of Perfection*' (unpublished Ph.D. diss., University of London, 1962).

For details of all editions of *Form*, see Sarah J. Ogilvie-Thompson (ed.), *Richard Rolle: Prose and Verse from MS Longleat 29 and Related Manuscripts*, Early English Text Society, original series, 293 (1988), Introduction, pp. xlix–l. All quotation from *Form* is taken from this guide's edition of it, at pp. 3–25, hereafter cited as '(*Form* and page number)'.

[71] The majority of the editions of these guides are detailed in chapter 1 and in the Appendix: Guidance Text Overview.

[72] Licence, *Hermits and Recluses*, p. 20.

[73] E.g. Warren, *Anchorites and their Patrons*, p. 103.

[74] Charlotte D'Evelyn, 'Instructions for religious', in J. B. Severs, A. E. Hartung and J. E. Wells (eds), *A Manual of the Writings in Middle English, 1050–1500*, 10 vols (New Haven: Connecticut Academy of Arts and Sciences, 1967–98), vol. 2, p. 21.

[75] Linda Georgianna, *The Solitary Self: Individuality in the 'Ancrene Wisse'* (Cambridge, Mass. and London: Harvard University Press, 1981), pp. 30–1 and pp. 8–32.

[76] Goscelin of St Bertin, *The Book of Encouragement and Consolation (Liber confortatorius). The Letter of Goscelin to the Recluse Eva*, trans. Monika Otter (Cambridge: D. S. Brewer, 2004), p. 12. All translations from the *Liber confortatorius* given in the endnotes are taken from this translation, cited as '(Otter and page number)'.

For another translation, see Stephanie Hollis (ed.), with W. R. Barnes, Rebecca Hayward, Kathleen Loncar and Michael Wright, *Writing the Wilton Women: Goscelin's Legend of Edith and Liber confortatorius*, Medieval Women Texts and Contexts, 9 (Turnhout: Brepols, 2004), pp. 97–212. This impressive text also contains a translation of Goscelin's *Legend of Edith* (at pp. 17–23) and a substantial body of critical work separated into: 'Part III: the Wilton women: subjects and audience' (pp. 217–340) and 'Part IV: the *Liber confortatorius*: the writer and the reader' (pp. 341–418).

[77] This criticism will be discussed fully in chapters 2 to 5, but examples of scholarship that focuses on a few guides or ideals in isolation include: Jocelyn Price, '"Inner" and "outer": conceptualizing the body in *Ancrene Wisse* and Aelred's *De institutione inclusarum*', in Gregory Kratzmann and James Simpson (eds), *Medieval Religious and Ethical Literature. Essays in Honour of G. H. Russell* (Cambridge: D. S. Brewer, 1986), pp. 192–208, and Tarjei Park, 'Reflecting Christ: the role of the flesh in Walter Hilton and Julian of Norwich', in Marion Glasscoe (ed.), *The Medieval Mystical Tradition in England V: Papers Read at Dartington Hall, July 1992* (Exeter: Exeter University Press, 1992), pp. 17–37.

[78] See Raymond W. Chambers, *On the Continuity of English Prose from Alfred to More and his School*, Early English Text Society, original series, 191A (1932, repr. 1966), and Tadao Kubouchi (ed.), *From Wulfstan to Richard Rolle. Papers Exploring the Continuity of English Prose* (Cambridge: D. S. Brewer, 1999). Since Rolle's and Hilton's guides have received considerable critical attention in terms of this theory and their role in the development of English contemplation, it is all the more surprising that so little has been written about their original anchoritic contexts. Even some editions of these guides, e.g. of *Form* in Rosamund S. Allen (ed.), *Richard*

Rolle: The English Writings (New York and Mahwah: Paulist Press, 1988), swiftly dispense with their anchoritic significance. Influential criticism, e.g. Marion Glasscoe's valuable text on contemplative spirituality (*English Medieval Mystics: Games of Faith* (London and New York: Longman, 1993)) and Michael Sargent's exhaustive survey of Rollian scholarship, make little mention of their anchoritic contexts (see Michael Sargent, 'Contemporary criticism of Richard Rolle', *Analecta Cartusiana*, 55 (1981), 160–205). As recently as 2004, Ad Putter classified the tradition of Hilton's *Scale* as 'that of the religious handbook for the layman'. See Ad Putter, 'Walter Hilton's *Scale of Perfection* and *The Cloud of Unknowing*', in A. S. G. Edwards (ed.), *A Companion to Middle English Prose* (Cambridge: D. S. Brewer, 2004), pp. 33–51 (p. 37). Two important exceptions to the neglect of the anchoritic aspects of Rolle's and Hilton's writing are, however, as will be shown below in chapters 2 to 5, the work of Denis Renevey (on Rolle) and Thomas Bestul (on Hilton).

[79] E.g. Robert Boenig, 'Contemplations of the dread and love of God, Richard Rolle and Aelred of Rievaulx', *Mystics Quarterly*, 16 (1990), 27–33 (especially 27).

[80] See Warren, *Anchorites and their Patrons*, p. 115. Warren's mutually exclusive binary influences, for instance, Jones's conclusion that *Speculum* 'has, in … its spirituality, a clear affinity with the works of Rolle and Hilton against the earlier anchoritic texts' (Jones, 'A new look into the *Speculum inclusorum*', p. 128).

[81] Warren, *Anchorites and Their Patrons*, p. 115.

[82] Quotation from the redaction of *De institutione inclusarum* extant in Oxford, Bodleian Library, MS Bodley 423 is from Ayto and Barratt, *Aelred of Rievaulx's 'De institutione inclusarum'*, pp. 1–25, hereafter cited as '(*DII*, MS Bodley 423 and page number)'.

[83] In 1999, Jones drew attention to its significance (Jones, 'A new look into the *Speculum inclusorum*', p. 130), but it has not yet generated the interest among scholars that it merits.

[84] All quotations from *Speculum inclusorum* are taken from P. Livario Oliger (ed.), '*Speculum inclusorum*', *Lateranum*, n.s., 4 (1938), 1–148, hereafter cited as '(*Speculum* and page number)'. Corresponding translations of the Latin guide are, where they match, given in endnotes and taken from the medieval vernacular translation of this guide: Marta Powell Harley (ed.), *The Myrour of Recluses* (Madison and Teaneck: Fairleigh Dickinson University Press, 1995), hereafter cited as '(*Myrour* and page number)'. Translations of passages from *Speculum* without corresponding vernacular translations in *Myrour* are my own and will also be given in the endnotes. I am grateful to Dr J. W. Binns for advice on this translation. Edward A. Jones is currently working on a parallel text edition of *Speculum* and *Myrour*, forthcoming 2013.

Unless otherwise stated, the book's analysis of the content of *Speculum* also implies matching content in *Myrour*. The book specifically clarifies those places where this guide and its medieval vernacular translation diverge (either when content is missing from *Myrour* and present in *Speculum*, or inserted material, for example about its wider audience, has been added to *Myrour* but is absent from *Speculum*).

This quotation is translated as: 'in accordance with the holy observances of your profession and the teaching of Aelred in his treatise on the instruction of a recluse and in accordance with the outstanding documents of other devout men' (my translation).

Chapter 1

[1] See the appendix to this book, entitled 'Appendix: Guidance Text Overview', page 159, below for a table that summarizes the key information about each of the eight base guides on which this chapter focuses.

[2] See Stephanie Hollis, 'Goscelin's writings and the Wilton women', in *eadem* (ed.), with W. R. Barnes, Rebecca Hayward, Kathleen Loncar and Michael Wright, *Writing the Wilton Women: Goscelin's Legend of Edith and Liber confortatorius*, Medieval Women Texts and Contexts, 9 (Turnhout: Brepols, 2004), pp. 217–44 (pp. 236–7), on the guide's manuscript hand, provenance and textual transmission.

³ Described as 'a cemetery church, dependent on the nunnery of Le Ronceray' in Hollis, 'Goscelin's writings', p. 229, and Irene van Rossum, '*Adest meliori parte*: a portrait of monastic friendship in exile in Goscelin's *Liber confortatorius*' (unpublished D.Phil. thesis, University of York, 1999), 47 and 64.

⁴ Goscelin of St Bertin, 'The *Liber confortatorius* of Goscelin of Saint Bertin', *Analecta monastica*, ed. Charles Hugh Talbot, series 3, *Studia Anselmiana*, fasc. 37 (Rome: Pontifical Institute of St Anselm, 1955), pp. 1–117, hereafter cited as '(*Liber* and page number)'. Pp. 24–5 also give Talbot's manuscript description. This quotation is translated as: 'May you receive all that your soul desires' (Otter, p. 150).

⁵ 'heads for the stars in a chariot' (Otter, p. 19).

⁶ Otter's essay: 'Inclusae exclusus: desire, identification and gender in the *Liber confortatorius*', closes her translation of the *Liber* at pp. 151–67. This quotation is at Otter, p. 161.

⁷ Hollis, 'Goscelin's writings', p. 237.

⁸ Hollis, Introduction, in *eadem* (ed.), with W. R. Barnes, Rebecca Hayward, Kathleen Loncar and Michael Wright, *Writing the Wilton Women: Goscelin's Legend of Edith and Liber Confortatorius*, Medieval Women Texts and Contexts, 9, pp. 1–13 (p. 2). Hollis speculates that Eve was Herman's niece ('Goscelin's Writings', p. 227).

⁹ Chronology taken from Stephanie Hollis, 'Strategies of emplacement and displacement: St Edith and the Wilton community in Goscelin's Legend of Edith and *Liber confortatorius*', in C. A. Lees and G. R. Overing (eds), *A Place to Believe In: Locating Medieval Landscapes* (Pennsylvania: The Pennsylvania State University Press, 2006), pp. 150–69 (p. 153).

¹⁰ Hollis, 'Goscelin's writings', p. 232.

¹¹ Hollis, 'Strategies of emplacement', p. 165 and n. 23; van Rossum suggests other factors, e.g. Norman political tensions, in her '*Adest meliori parte*', 61–5.

¹² Hollis, 'Goscelin's writings', p. 229 and n. 68. Eve's potentially shared anchoritic solitude with a member of her former blood family is in significant contrast to other earlier medieval guidance's discouragement of contact with relatives, for example as at page 42 below.

¹³ Dyan Elliott, 'Alternative intimacies: men, women and spiritual direction in the twelfth century', in Samuel Fanous and Henrietta Leyser (eds), *Christina of Markyate: A Twelfth-century Holy Woman* (London and New York: Routledge, 2005), pp. 160–83 (p. 168).

¹⁴ Elliott, 'Alternative intimacies', p. 177.

¹⁵ Daphne Stroud, 'Eve of Wilton and Goscelin of St Bertin at Old Sarum, *c*.1070–1078', *Wiltshire Archaeological and Natural History Magazine*, 99 (2006), 204–12 (205).

¹⁶ Hollis, 'Goscelin's writings', p. 227.

¹⁷ Biographical studies of Goscelin include: Frank Barlow (ed.), *The Life of King Edward Who Rests at Westminster* (Oxford: Clarendon Press, 1992); Hollis's introduction to *Writing the Wilton Women*, pp. 1–13 and her 'Goscelin's writings' (see pp. 217–31 on his literary career and relationship with Eve); Hollis, 'Strategies of emplacement', pp. 153–5. Hollis recommends Marvin L. Colker, 'Texts of Jocelyn of Canterbury which relate to the history of Barking Abbey', *Studia Monastica*, 7 (1965), 383–460 (383, n.1) for a bibliography of summaries of Goscelin's life and works (see 'Goscelin's writings', p. 218, n. 60).

Studies on Goscelin's works include: Tom Licence, 'Goscelin of St Bertin and the life of St Eadwold of Cerne', *Journal of Medieval Latin*, 16 (2006), 182–207; Linda Olson, 'Did medieval English women read Augustine's *Confessiones*? Constructing feminine interiority and literacy in the eleventh and twelfth centuries', in Sarah Rees Jones (ed.), *Learning and Literacy in Medieval England and Abroad* (Turnhout: Brepols, 2003), pp. 69–95; van Rossum's '*Adest meliori parte*'; Gopa Roy, '"Sharpen your mind with the whetstone of books": the female recluse as reader in Goscelin's *Liber confortatorius*, Aelred of Rievaulx's *De institutione inclusarum* and the *Ancrene Wisse*', in Lesley Smith and Jane H. M. Taylor (eds), *Women, the Book and the Godly: Selected Proceedings of the St Hilda's Conference 1993* (Cambridge: D. S. Brewer, 1995), pp. 113–22; Sharon K. Elkins, *Holy Women of Twelfth-century England* (Chapel Hill: University of North Carolina Press, 1988), especially pp. 21–7, and Brian Patrick McGuire, *Friendship and Community: The Monastic Experience, 350–1250* (Kalamazoo: Cistercian Publications, 1988), pp. 201–4.

On Eve and Goscelin, see also Therese Latzke, 'Robert von Arbrissel, Ermengard und Eva', *Mittellateinisches Jahrbuch*, 19 (1984), 116–54, and André Wilmart, 'Eve et Goscelin', *Révue Bénédictine*, 46 (1934), 414–38; and *idem*, 'Eve et Goscelin (II)', *Révue Bénédictine*, 50 (1938), 42–83.

18   Hollis, 'Goscelin's writings', p. 218.

19   Hollis, Introduction, *Writing the Wilton Women*, p. 12.

20   Joseph P. McGowan, 'An introduction to the corpus of Anglo-Latin literature', in Phillip Pulsiano and Elaine M. Treharne (eds), *A Companion to Anglo-Saxon Literature* (Oxford: Blackwell, 2001), pp. 11–49 (p. 42).

21   Hollis, Introduction, *Writing the Wilton Women*, p. 1, and Hollis, 'Strategies of emplacement', p. 153.

22   Hollis, Introduction, *Writing the Wilton Women*, p. 2. Barlow speculates that their age difference was thirty years (*The Life of King Edward*, p. 138), Hollis that Goscelin 'would have been only in his mid-to-late thirties when Eve was in her early twenties' ('Goscelin's writings', p. 226).

23   Rebecca Hayward and Stephanie Hollis argue that 'the text provides a space where they can be present' in 'The female reader in the *Liber confortatorius*', in Stephanie Hollis (ed.), with W. R. Barnes, Rebecca Hayward, Kathleen Loncar and Michael Wright, *Writing the Wilton Women: Goscelin's Legend of Edith and Liber confortatorius*, Medieval Women Texts and Contexts, 9 (Turnhout: Brepols, 2004), pp. 385–400 (p. 387).

24   See *Liber*, p. 33 (Otter, p. 31).

25   'I wanted this to happen elsewhere … and in a different way; I wanted you … a coenobitic pigeon, not a solitary mourning dove: or if that was what you preferred, a mourning dove in your own country … That we may suffer less desolation, with you near' (Otter, p. 36).

26   See pages 38 and 40 below for more information on later medieval anchoritic guidance and the validity of the active life.

27   Professor Robertson's remarks were made in response to my paper at 'Mapping the medieval anchorhold: dialogue between east and west', the Third International Conference for the International Anchoritic Society, Hiroshima Shudo University, Japan (15–17 September 2008).

28   Otter, 'Inclusae exclusus', p. 156.

29   'commend me, readmit me, receive me after the quarrel caused by your going away. Look at me as I sit with you; listen to me as I talk with you' (Otter, p. 33).

30   'the spewer of hot air and the dirty snickerer' (Otter, p. 19).

31   Emphasis mine, to stress that Goscelin's distress concurrently disarms him as a writer and a man: 'as I was writing this, my sorrow swelled up and could not be repressed. *My hand and my pen dropped*; a moaning and sobbing overcame me. I rushed before the altar of your St Lawrence … In a flood of tears, I called out again and again, as if buffeted and beaten by the Lord … and intoned … amidst sobs … "I am made like unto a pelican in the desert" … With loud wails … Now … I take up again my interrupted speech – interrupted by sorrow' (Otter, p. 22).

32   Otter, p. 1.

33   Otter, 'Inclusae exclusus', see especially pp. 158–61 (this quote is at p. 160).

34   Hollis, Introduction, *Writing the Wilton Women*, pp. 3–4.

35   Rebecca Hayward, 'Spiritual friendship and gender difference in the *Liber confortatorius*', in Stephanie Hollis (ed.), with W. R. Barnes, Rebecca Hayward, Kathleen Loncar and Michael Wright, *Writing the Wilton Women: Goscelin's Legend of Edith and Liber confortatorius*, Medieval Women Texts and Contexts, 9 (Turnhout: Brepols, 2004), pp. 341–55 (see especially pp. 348–9).

36   On these, see Elliott, 'Alternative intimacies', pp. 168–74.

37   Elliott, 'Alternative intimacies', p. 175.

38   Stroud, 'Eve of Wilton', 205.

39   H. M. Canatella, 'Long-distance love: the ideology of male–female spiritual friendship in Goscelin of Saint Bertin's *Liber confortatorius*', *Journal of the History of Sexuality*, 19, 1 (2010), 35–53 (36).

40 Hayward, 'Spiritual friendship and gender difference in the *Liber confortatorius*', p. 347. Pp. 341–7 give a critic-by-critic survey of academic attempts to define Eve and Goscelin's intimacy.

41 'And these torments of separation, which I deserved through my crimes' (Otter, p. 21).

42 'Everything has its season ... We, too, had our times ... we saw each other enough, we talked to each other enough, we had each other's company and ate together enough, we celebrated the holy rites together and rejoiced together enough – if anything could ever be enough for love ... Now indeed is the time to walk in tears' (Otter, pp. 43–4).

43 'How often I envied your friend Eadgyth, who not only loved you more intimately, but, since she shared your place and your sex, was able to warm herself in your presence! But now her rejoicing, too, has turned into mourning and solitude, though she was somewhat more fortunate in that she was able to say good-bye to you when you left' (Otter, p. 47).

44 Michael Frassetto (ed.), *The Year 1000: Religious and Social Response to the Turning of the First Millennium* (Basingstoke and New York: Palgrave Macmillan, 2002), pp. 1–8 (p. 3).

45 Canatella, 'Long-distance love', 36. He cites Colin Morris's theorizations in *The Discovery of the Individual, 1050–1200* (Toronto: University of Toronto Press, 1987).

46 Michael Frassetto, 'Heretics, antichrists, and the year 1000: apocalyptic expectations in the writings of Ademar of Chabannes', in *idem* (ed.), *The Year 1000: Religious and Social Response to the Turning of the First Millennium* (Basingstoke and New York: Palgrave Macmillan, 2002), pp. 73–84 (p. 75).

47 Hollis, Introduction, *Writing the Wilton Women*, pp. 9, 8.

48 On Anselm's life, see Eadmer's *The Life of St Anselm, Archbishop of Canterbury*, ed. and trans. Richard W. Southern (Oxford: Clarendon Press, 1972).

49 Richard Sharpe, 'Anselm as author: publishing in the late eleventh century', *Journal of Medieval Latin*, 19 (2009), 1–87 (43), which also details the manuscripts and editions of Anselm's *Monologion, Proslogion* and *Cur Deus Homo*, amongst other texts (see especially 1 and 15–17). On Anselm, see also Montague Brown, 'Augustine and Anselm on the essence of moral responsibility', *The Saint Anselm Journal*, 4 (2007), 1–10, and his 'Faith and reason in Anselm: two models', *The Saint Anselm Journal*, 2 (2004), 10–21, and Jeffrey E. Brower, 'Anselm on ethics', in Brian Davies and Brian Leftow (eds), *The Cambridge Companion to Anselm* (Cambridge: Cambridge University Press, 2004), pp. 222–56.

50 Richard W. Southern, *Saint Anselm: A Portrait in a Landscape* (Cambridge: Cambridge University Press, 1990), p. 475. See also M. R. James and C. Jenkins, *A Descriptive Catalogue of the Manuscripts in the Library of Lambeth Palace* (Cambridge: Cambridge University Press, 1930–2), pp. 91–6, on its manuscript and hand descriptions.

51 Colin Gale, 'Treasure in earthen vessels: treasures from Lambeth Palace library', *Fulcrum: Renewing the Evangelical Centre*, accessed via *http://www.fulcrum-anglican.org.uk/page.cfm?ID=542* (accessed 7 September 2011). Gale cites Walter Fröhlich (ed. and trans.), *The Letters of Saint Anselm of Canterbury*, 3 vols (Kalamazoo: Cistercian Publications, 1990–4), vol. 1, pp. 37–52 and Sally Vaughn, *Anselm of Bec and Robert of Meulan: The Innocence of the Dove and the Wisdom of the Serpent* (Berkeley, Los Angeles and London: University of California Press, 1987). While Gale's article is published on a website that is demonstrably biased towards Anglicanism, he nonetheless sets out the polarities of the debate about MS 59 with admirable clarity.

52 Gale here cites, Southern, *Saint Anselm*, pp. 459–81. See Gale, 'Treasure in earthen vessels', accessed via *http://www.fulcrum-anglican.org.uk/page.cfm?ID=542* (accessed 7 September 2011).

53 Licence, *Hermits and Recluses*, p. 160.

54 Licence, *Hermits and Recluses*, p. 83.

55 For Licence's cautious dating, see *Hermits and Recluses*, p. 73. An edition of Anselm's Latin letters is, Francis S. Schmitt (ed.), *Sancti Anselmi Cantuariensis Archiepiscopi, Opera Omnia*, 6 vols (Edinburgh: T. Nelson, 1946–63), hereafter cited as '(Anselm, letter no., vol. no., page no.)'. 'Letter 112' is in vol. 3, pp. 244–6; 'Letter 230' is in vol. 4, pp. 134–5 and 'Letter 414' is in

vol. 5, pp. 359–62. Their translations are given in the endnotes and taken from Fröhlich (ed. and trans.), *The Letters of Saint Anselm of Canterbury*, hereafter cited as '(Fröhlich, letter no., vol. no., page no.)'. 'Letter 112' is in vol. 1, pp. 268–71; 'Letter 230' is in vol. 2, pp. 199–200 and 'Letter 414' is in vol. 3, pp. 184–7.

Anselm's letter to Hugh is not, of course, an anchoritic guide, but has, unusually given the anchoritic rationale of this book, been included here as comparative context to his letters for female anchorites. This is not only because his anchoritic letters are so short that it is only of limited use to consider them in isolation but because the vocations of anchorite and hermit are far from distinct at this time.

56   'I … feel my spiritual fervour growing lukewarm, yet great joy springs up in my heart when I hear that others are burning with love of God' (Fröhlich, 'Letter 230', vol. 2, p. 199).

57   Southern, *Saint Anselm*, p. 396.

58   Latin quotation from *De institutione inclusarum* is taken from Aelred of Rievaulx, *Aelredi Rievallensis Opera Omnia: I Opera Ascetica*, in *Corpus Christianorum Continuatio Mediaeualis I*, ed. Anselm Hoste and Charles Hugh Talbot (Turnhout: Brepols, 1971), pp. 635–82, hereafter cited as '(*DII* and page number)'. Translations in modern English are given in endnotes and taken from Aelred of Rievaulx, 'A rule of life for a recluse', in *Aelred of Rievaulx: Treatises and Pastoral Prayer*, trans. Mary Paul MacPherson (Kalamazoo: Cistercian Studies Series, 1971), pp. 40–102, hereafter cited as '(MacPherson and page number)'.

59   Aelred Squire, *Aelred of Rievaulx: A Study* (London: SPCK, 1969), p. 119.

60   'I tell you, if you have more food and more clothes than you need for yourself, you are no nun' (MacPherson, p. 48).

61   'you also asked to receive something short written by me, with the help of which you could inspire the minds of the secular people who come to you to despise this world and love the eternal kingdom' (Fröhlich, 'Letter 112', vol. 1, p. 268).

62   'it was not for yourself alone that you wished me to write this rule, but also for the young girls who, on your advice, are eager to embrace a life like yours' (MacPherson, p. 52).

63   The anchoritism of Christina of Markyate (*c*.1096–*c*.1160) is constructed, in her *vita*, as demanded by necessity not adopted by choice, in order to facilitate her escape from an unwanted marriage. She takes no vow of enclosure and moves between anchoritism and hermitism and finally to reclusive coenobitism. See Charles Hugh Talbot (ed. and trans.), *The Life of Christina of Markyate, A Twelfth Century Recluse* (Oxford: Clarendon Press, 1959), pp. 144–5.

64   Alexandra Barratt, 'Small Latin? The post-Conquest learning of English religious women', in Sian Echard and Gernot R. Wieland (eds), *Anglo-Latin and its Heritage: Essays in Honour of A. G. Rigg on his 64th Birthday* (Turnhout: Brepols, 2001), pp. 51–65 (p. 53).

65   MacPherson, p. 59.

66   MacPherson, p. 56. See Bella Millett, '*Ancrene Wisse* and the book of hours', in Denis Renevey and Christiania Whitehead (eds), *Writing Religious Women: Female Spiritual and Textual Practices in Late Medieval England* (Cardiff: University of Wales Press, 2000), pp. 21–40 (p. 21).

67   'who are … incapable of grasping higher ideas' (Fröhlich, 'Letter 112', vol. 1, p. 268).

68   MacPherson, p. 62, n. 1.

69   All vernacular quotations from *Ancrene Wisse*, unless identified as being from a different text, e.g. the Nero text, are from Bella Millett (ed.), with Eric J. Dobson and Richard Dance, *Ancrene Wisse. A Corrected Edition of the Text in Cambridge, Corpus Christi College, MS 402, With Variants from Other Manuscripts*, vol. 1, Early English Text Society, original series, 325 (2005), hereafter cited as '(*AW*, Corpus and page number)'. Unless specified all *AW*, Corpus references indicate vol. 1 of Millett's EETS edition. References to vol. 2 (full details below) are cited specifically as (*AW*, Corpus, vol. 2 and page number).

Other editions include, J. R. R. Tolkien (ed.), *The English Text of the Ancrene Riwle: Ancrene Wisse: Edited from MS. Corpus Christi College Cambridge 402*, Early English Text Society, original series, 249 (1962) and Robert Hasenfratz (ed.), *Ancrene Wisse* (Kalamazoo: Medieval Institute Publications, 2000). See Bella Millett (ed.), with Eric J. Dobson and Richard Dance,

Ancrene Wisse. A Corrected Edition of the Text in Cambridge, Corpus Christi College, MS 402, With Variants From Other Manuscripts, vol. 2, Early English Text Society, original series, 326 (2006), Bibliography (pp. 305–33) for details of the many manuscripts, editions and translations of *Ancrene Wisse*.

    Translations include the aforementioned Millett, *Ancrene Wisse*; Hugh White (trans.), *Ancrene Wisse: Guide for Anchoresses* (London, New York, Victoria, Ontario and Auckland: Penguin, 1993) and Ann Savage and Nicholas Watson (trans.), *Anchoritic Spirituality: 'Ancrene Wisse' and Associated Works* (New York and Mahwah: Paulist Press, 1991).

[70] See Millett, '*Ancrene Wisse* and the book of hours', p. 22; Yoko Wada (ed.), *A Companion to 'Ancrene Wisse'* (Cambridge: D. S. Brewer, 2003), especially Yoko Wada, 'What is *Ancrene Wisse*? (pp. 1–28) and Bella Millett, 'The genre of *Ancrene Wisse*' (pp. 29–44). For a survey of critical work, see Millett's, *Ancrene Wisse, The Katherine Group and the Wooing Group: Annotated Bibliographies of Old and Middle English Literature*, vol. 2 (Cambridge: Boydell and Brewer, 1996), pp. 6–17.

[71] Barratt, 'Small Latin?', pp. 65, 51.

[72] Millett, '*Ancrene Wisse* and the book of hours', p. 26. Despite the increased involvement of the laity in the vocation, nuns continued to become anchorites throughout the Middle Ages. Ann K. Warren's 'The nun as anchoress: England 1100–1500', in John A. Nichols and Lillian Thomas Shank (eds), *Medieval Religious Women, Vol. One: Distant Echoes* (Kalamazoo: Cistercian Studies Series, 1984), pp. 197–212, proposes that medieval society nonetheless espoused 'the fundamental perception of the nun as quintessential anchoress' (p. 209). Mary Byrne argues that exactly this kind of awareness motivates thirteenth-century Latin literature to modify its perfect model of chastity from the nun to the recluse. See Mary Byrne, *The Tradition of the Nun in Medieval England* (Washington DC: Catholic University of America Press, 1932), especially pp. 56–67. See also Eileen E. Power, *Medieval English Nunneries: c.1275 to 1535* (Cambridge: Cambridge University Press, 1922).

[73] On *Ancrene Wisse*'s audiences, see *AW*, Corpus, pp. xix–xxiv and Millett, pp. xiv–xvi. See also Bella Millett, 'Woman in no man's land: English recluses and the development of vernacular literature in the twelfth and thirteenth centuries', in Carol M. Meale (ed.), *Women and Literature in Britain: 1150–1500* (Cambridge: Cambridge Studies in Literature, 1993), pp. 86–103.

[74] Millett, '*Ancrene Wisse* and the book of hours', pp. 25–6.

[75] The difficulties of dating *Ancrene Wisse*'s extant manuscripts foster different critical approaches, e.g. Geoffrey Shepherd simply places the earlier medieval texts in the category of 'thirteenth-century texts' in Geoffrey Shepherd (ed.), '*Ancrene Wisse': Parts Six and Seven* (1959; Exeter: Exeter University Press, 1985), p. xi.

    See *AW*, Corpus, vol. 2, pp. xi–xiii, which cites personal correspondence with Malcolm Parkes as the source of these, the most recent *Ancrene Wisse* dates (see especially p. xii). See also Millett, pp. xxxvii–xliii, on individual manuscripts' provenance and dates.

[76] Michelle M. Sauer, 'Privacy, exile and the rhetoric of solitude in the medieval English anchoritic tradition', in Liz Herbert McAvoy (ed.), *Rhetoric of the Anchorhold: Space, Place and Body within the Discourses of Enclosure* (Cardiff: University of Wales Press, 2008), pp. 96–110 (p. 99).

[77] Antonia Gransden believes that the later medieval anchoritic guide, *Letter to a Bury Recluse*, includes 'citations from common sources, notably Ailred of Rievaulx's *De Institutis Inclusarum*'. See Antonia Gransden (ed.), 'The reply of a fourteenth-century abbot of Bury St. Edmunds to a man's petition to be a recluse', *English Historical Review*, 75 (1960), 465–7 (465).

[78] Mabel Day (ed.), *The English Text of the Ancrene Riwle: Edited from Cotton MS. Nero A.xiv.*, Early English Text Society, original series, 225 (1952), hereafter cited as '(*AW*, Nero and page number)'. This quotation is at *AW*, Nero, Introduction, p. xvii.

[79] James Morton (ed.), *The Ancren Riwle: A Treatise on the Rules and Duties of Monastic Life* (London: Camden Society, 1853), hereafter cited as '(Morton, *Ancren Riwle* and page number)'.

[80] 'Each of you hath from one friend all that she requireth; nor need that maiden seek ... bread ... further than at his hall' (Morton, *Ancren Riwle*, p. 193).

[81] 'There is much talk of you, how gentle women you are; for your goodness and nobleness of mind beloved of many; and sisters of one father and of one mother; having, in the bloom of your youth, forsaken all the pleasures of the world and become anchoresses' (Morton, *Ancren Riwle*, p. 193).

[82] 'You are just a girl, an adolescent, the flower of life itself, and you have suddenly died' (Otter, p. 82).

[83] Shepherd, *'Ancrene Wisse'*, p. xi.

[84] Some critics refer only to the Corpus text as *Ancrene Wisse* and to all the others as *Ancrene Riwle*. Current scholarly practice is to refer to all extant texts as *Ancrene Wisse*, differentiating between them by manuscript name.

[85] Roger Dahood, 'The use of coloured initials and other division markers in early versions of *Ancrene Riwle*', in Edward D. Kennedy, Ronald Waldron and Joseph S. Wittig (eds), *Medieval English Studies Presented to George Kane* (Cambridge: D. S. Brewer, 1988), pp. 79–97 (p. 79).

[86] Millett, *'Mouvance* and the medieval author: re-editing *Ancrene Wisse'*, in Alistair J. Minnis (ed.), *Late-medieval Religious Texts and Their Transmission: Essays in Honour of A. I. Doyle* (Cambridge: D. S. Brewer, 1994), pp. 9–20 (p. 15).

[87] Millett, *'Mouvance'*, p. 16.

[88] Eric J. Dobson (ed.), *The English Text of the Ancrene Riwle: Edited from B.M. Cotton MS. Cleopatra C. vi.*, Early English Text Society, original series, 267 (1972), hereafter cited as '(*AW*, Cleopatra and page number)'.

[89] Millett, *'Mouvance'*, p. 15.

[90] *AW*, Cleopatra, Introduction, pp. ix–x.

[91] Dobson's first quotation is from *AW*, Cleopatra, Introduction, p. x; the second from Eric J. Dobson, *The Origins of 'Ancrene Wisse'* (Oxford: Clarendon Press, 1976), p. 259. Dobson argues that the passage referring to the original audience may have been overlooked by the Corpus reviser because it was unobtrusive.

[92] Millett, p. xxxviii.

[93] Millett uses C2 for Dobson's Scribe B (traditionally identified as the author of *Ancrene Wisse*) and C3 for Dobson's Scribe D, whom Millett argues was possibly a Dominican friar. See Millett, p. xxxviii.

[94] Frances M. Mack and Arne Zettersten (eds), *The English Text of the Ancrene Riwle, Edited from Cotton MS. Titus D. xviii, together with the Lanhydrock Fragment, Bodleian MS. Eng. th. c. 70.*, Early English Text Society, original series, 252 (1963), hereafter cited as '(*AW*, Titus and page number)'.

[95] See *AW*, Nero, Introduction, p. xiv on this.

[96] 'Much is said of you, how noble you are, who at such a young age became anchoresses and forsook the bliss of the world' (my translation).

[97] The significance of some textual alterations of *Ancrene Wisse* must not be over-interpreted. Passages in the original version forbidding anchoresses to preach are removed in some later texts. The passage at *AW*, Nero, p. 31 is not present at, for example, p. 12 of the Titus text (*AW*, Titus, Introduction, p. xv). Yet, this does not necessarily imply that such activity is now countenanced by the church.

[98] R. M. Wilson (ed.), *The English Text of the Ancrene Riwle: Edited from Gonville and Caius College MS. 234/120.*, Early English Text Society, original series, 229 (1954; repr. 1957), hereafter cited as '(*AW*, G&C and page number)'. On its scribe, see Dobson, *Origins of 'Ancrene Wisse'*, p. 359 and *AW*, G&C, Introduction, p. x.

[99] Yet, Aelred, writing in Latin, anticipates that his sister has read the *Vitas Patrum*. *Ancrene Wisse* also anticipates that its female audience will understand allusions to it.

[100] Millett, p. xlii.

[101] E.g. it retains anecdotes such as the Lord's rebuke to a female anchorite who failed to guard her senses (*AW*, G&C, p. 48).

[102] See Millett, Introduction, p. xii, n. 21 and also Hasenfratz, *Ancrene Wisse*, Introduction, p. 11.

[103] Dobson, *Origins of 'Ancrene Wisse'*, p. 113.

[104]   See Savage and Watson, *Anchoritic Spirituality*, p. 405, n. 30 which summarizes Dobson's solution to the supposed cryptogram. For Dobson's full hypothesis, see *Origins of 'Ancrene Wisse'*, pp. 343–5.

[105]   See Dobson, *Origins of 'Ancrene Wisse'*, pp. 174–237, 273 and 312–68.

[106]   Savage and Watson, *Anchoritic Spirituality*, Introduction, p. 10.

[107]   See Bella Millett, 'The origins of *Ancrene Wisse*: new answers, new questions', *Medium Aevum*, 60 (1991), 206–28 (219); Yoko Wada, 'Dominican authorship of *Ancrene Wisse*: the evidence of the introduction', in *eadem* (ed.), *A Book of Ancrene Wisse* (Suita, Osaka: Kansai University Press, 2002), pp. 95–110, and Millett, p. xix, which reiterates Dominican authorship.

[108]   Hasenfratz, *Ancrene Wisse*, Introduction, p. 15.

[109]   Millett, *Ancrene Wisse, The Katherine Group and the Wooing Group*, pp. 5–6 details all the texts in these groups, which have all been edited by the Early English Text Society. Selections are also edited in Millett and Jocelyn Wogan-Browne (eds), *Medieval English Prose for Women: Selections from the Katherine Group and 'Ancrene Wisse'* (Oxford: Clarendon Press, 1990).

[110]   Millett 'The *Ancrene Wisse* group', in A. S. G. Edwards (ed.), *A Companion to Middle English Prose* (Cambridge: D. S. Brewer, 2004), pp. 1–17 (p. 12).

[111]   Millett, *Ancrene Wisse, The Katherine Group and the Wooing Group*, p. 6; Millett, pp. ix–x.

[112]   Hasenfratz, *Ancrene Wisse*, Introduction, p. 14. On the guide's lay implications, see Cate Gunn, *'Ancrene Wisse': From Pastoral Literature to Vernacular Spirituality* (Cardiff: University of Wales Press, 2008); Gunn, *'Ancrene Wisse*: a modern lay person's guide to a medieval religious text', *Magistra: A Journal of Women's Spirituality in History*, 8 (2002), 3–25; Millett, *'Ancrene Wisse* and the book of hours'; Millett, *'Ancrene Wisse* and the life of perfection', *Leeds Studies in English*, 33 (2002), 53–76 (54–8); Roger Dahood, 'The current state of *Ancrene Wisse* group studies', *Medieval English Studies Newsletter*, 36 (1997), 6–14, and George R. Keiser, '"Noght how lang man lifs; bot how wele": the laity and the *Ladder of Perfection'*, in Michael G. Sargent (ed.), *De Cella in Seculum: Religious and Secular Life and Devotion in Late Medieval England* (Cambridge: D. S. Brewer, 1989), pp. 145–59.

[113]   Gunn, *'Ancrene Wisse'*, p. 1.

[114]   See Millett, *'Ancrene Wisse* and the book of hours', p. 32. See also Gunn, *'Ancrene Wisse'*, p. 69.

[115]   Gunn, *'Ancrene Wisse'*, p. 177.

[116]   Millett (*'Mouvance'*, pp. 12–13) discusses Paul Zumthor's *Essai de poétique médiévale* (Paris: Seuil, 1972).

[117]   Millett, *'Mouvance'*, p. 18. Millett here discusses Bernard Cerquiglini's *Éloge de la variante: Histoire critique de la philologie* (Paris: Seuil, 1989).

[118]   Millett, *'Mouvance'*, p. 9.

[119]   Millett, *'Mouvance'*, p. 13. Despite this acknowledged multiplicity of authorship, this book reflects current critical practice by referring only to the guide's original creator as the *Ancrene Wisse* author and to the writers who reworked his material as the revisers of their particular texts. Author and revisers alike are referred to as guidance writers.

[120]   Nicholas Watson, *Richard Rolle and the Invention of Authority* (Cambridge: Cambridge University Press, 1991), p. 229.

[121]   Ralph Hannah, 'Rolle and related works', in A. S. G. Edwards (ed.), *A Companion to Middle English Prose* (Cambridge: D. S. Brewer, 2004), pp. 19–31 (p. 20). Evidence suggests that, in 1357, Margaret moved from this enclosure to one at Ainderby Steeple (Clay, *Hermits and Anchorites*, pp. 142–3).

[122]   Hope E. Allen (ed.), *Writings Ascribed to Richard Rolle, Hermit of Hampole, and Materials for his Biography*, Modern Language Association Monograph Series, 3 (New York: Modern Language Association of America, 1927), p. 268.

[123]   *Form*, Introduction, pp. xxxvi–xliv detail *Form*'s manuscripts, and pp. xlix–l its printed editions.

[124]   *Form*, Introduction, pp. liii–lxv, pinpoint manuscript variations and construct a provisional stemma for manuscript recension.

[125]   *Form*, Introduction, p. lxii.

[126]   *Form*, Introduction, p. xv.

[127] See page 43 below for Rolle's separation of love into three degrees.

[128] David Knowles, *The English Mystical Tradition* (New York: Harper, 1961), pp. 50–4, and Ann K. Warren, *Anchorites and their Patrons in Medieval England* (Berkeley, Los Angeles and London: University of California Press, 1985), p. 298.

[129] Denis Renevey, 'Richard Rolle', in Dee Dyas, Valerie Edden and Roger Ellis (eds), *Approaching Medieval English Anchoritic and Mystical Texts* (Cambridge: D. S. Brewer, 2005), pp. 63–74 (p. 73).

[130] On Rollian love, see Denis Renevey, *Language, Self and Love: Hermeneutics in the Writings of Richard Rolle and the Commentaries on the Song of Songs* (Cardiff: University of Wales Press, 2001), especially pp. 66–121.

[131] Renevey, *Language, Self and Love*, p. 142.

[132] 'I am like the noncombatant trumpeter, who, even though he cannot fight, nonetheless can give much to the fight. He stirs up the strong ones, and strengthens them with the glory of victory' (Otter, p. 35).

[133] 'What I conceive about the rectitude of a holy life you achieve in your deeds; and what I can merely talk about, you savour by putting into practice' (Fröhlich, 'Letter 112', vol. 1, p. 268).

[134] Watson, *Richard Rolle and the Invention of Authority*, p. 19.

[135] Claire Elizabeth McIlroy, *The English Prose Treatises of Richard Rolle* (Cambridge: D. S. Brewer, 2004), p. 172.

[136] On Hilton's early life and his later 'conservative Augustinianism', see John P. H. Clark, 'Image and likeness in Walter Hilton', *The Downside Review*, 5 (1979), 204–5. See Michael Sargent, 'The organisation of *The Scale of Perfection*', in Marion Glasscoe (ed.), *The Medieval Mystical Tradition in England 1982: Symposium Proceedings* (Exeter: Exeter University Press, 1982), pp. 231–61 (pp. 231–4), on Hilton's scholasticism.

[137] Stanley S. Hussey in 'The audience for the Middle English mystics', in Michael G. Sargent (ed.), *De Cella in Seculum: Religious and Secular Life and Devotion in Late Medieval England* (Cambridge: D. S. Brewer, 1989), pp. 109–23, argues (at p. 116) that *Scale I* is extant in forty-one complete or partial vernacular manuscripts and that there are twenty-five manuscripts of *Scale II*, although Clark, Dorward and Hudson identify forty-five and twenty-six respectively. Hussey notes (at p. 116): 'the Latin translation was made before the end of the fourteenth century, possibly even within Hilton's lifetime, and therefore was capable of influencing the English of some English manuscripts'. See also Vivian K. Hudson, 'Clothing and adornment imagery in *The Scale of Perfection*: a reflection of contemplation', *Studies in Spirituality*, 4 (1994), 116–114 (p. 117). There are an additional twelve Latin manuscripts of *Scale I* and thirteen of *Scale II*.

Bestul's *Scale I*, Introduction, pp. 7–19, gives select detail about some of the forty-two extant manuscripts which contain one or both books of *Scale* and its printed editions.

[138] Michael G. Sargent, 'Walter Hilton's *Scale of Perfection*: the London manuscript group reconsidered', *Medium Aevum*, 52 (1983), 189–216.

[139] See page 25 below for Millett on the textual tradition of *Ancrene Wisse*.

[140] Sargent, 'Walter Hilton's *Scale of Perfection*', 196.

[141] Stanley S. Hussey, 'From *Scale* I to *Scale* II', *Analecta Cartusiana*, 130 (1995), 46–67 (50).

[142] E.g., Hudson, 'Clothing and adornment imagery' reads both *Scale* books as one text addressed to a primarily anchoritic audience. Minnis argues for a coenobitic audience, without reference to anchoritism, in 'Affection and imagination in *The Cloud of Unknowing* and Hilton's *Scale of Perfection*', *Traditio*, 39 (1983), 323–66 (351). M. F. Wakelin rejects *Scale*'s anchoritic audience in comparison with that of Rolle's *Form*: 'Hilton … writ[es] for a more general audience than … Rolle', in 'Richard Rolle and the language of mystical experience in the fourteenth century', *The Downside Review*, 5 (1979), 192–203 (194).

[143] 'to everybody alike' (Millett, p. 129).

[144] Stanley S. Hussey, 'Walter Hilton: traditionalist?', in Marion Glasscoe (ed.), *The Medieval Mystical Tradition in England: Papers Read at the Exeter Symposium, July 1980* (Exeter: Exeter University Press, 1980), pp. 1–16 (pp. 10–11), summarizes the evidence for an anchoritic audience for *Scale I* and a wider audience for *Scale II*.

[145] On this see Hudson, 'Clothing and adornment imagery', p. 117.

[146] John P. H. Clark and Rosemary Dorward (trans.), *The Scale of Perfection* (New York and Mahwah: Paulist Press, 1991), Preface, p. 10.

[147] William F. Pollard, 'Richard Rolle and the "Eye of the Heart"', in William F. Pollard and Richard Boenig (eds), *Mysticism and Spirituality in Medieval England* (Cambridge: D. S. Brewer, 1997), pp. 85–105 (p. 97).

[148] Clark and Dorward, *The Scale of Perfection*, Introduction, p. 24.

[149] See Denis Renevey, 'L'Imagerie des travaux ménagers dans *The Doctrine of the Hert*: spiritu-alité affective et subjectivité', *Micrologus: Natura, Scienze e Società Medievali*, 21 (2003), 519–53.

[150] Ayto and Barratt, *De institutione*, Introduction, p. xxix, attributes Dodesham's identification to A. I. Doyle.

[151] Ayto and Barratt, *De institutione*, Introduction, p. xviii.

[152] Ayto and Barratt, *De institutione*, Introduction, p. xiii.

[153] This manuscript, with corrections from the Oxford manuscript, forms the basis of Oliger's afore-mentioned edition of *Speculum*.

[154] *Speculum*, p. 106.

[155] Edward A. Jones, 'A new look into the *Speculum inclusorum*', in Marion Glasscoe (ed.), *The Medieval Mystical Tradition in England, Ireland and Wales: Papers Read at Charney Manor, July 1999 (Exeter Symposium VI)* (Cambridge: D. S. Brewer, 1999), pp. 123–45 (pp. 123–6).

[156] *Myrour* is named *Advice to Recluses* in Lillian E. Rogers's 1933 unpublished edition, at Oxford's Bodleian library. See her 'Edition of British Museum MS. Harley 2372 (Advice to Recluses) (B. Litt thesis, Oxford University, 1933). Rogers worked without knowledge of the Latin manu-scripts, as did Clay. Clay treats *Myrour*, referred to as *Book for Recluses*, as the only extant text of this guide (*Hermits and Anchorites*, p. 99). Even as recently as 1955, David Knowles did not recognize the link between *Speculum* and Rogers's *Advice*. See his *The Religious Orders in England, Volume II: The End of the Middle Ages* (Cambridge: Cambridge University Press, 1955), p. 121, n. 3. *Myrour* has also been referred to as *Speculum*, notably in J. B. Severs, A. E. Hartung and J. E. Wells (eds), *A Manual of the Writings in Middle English, 1050–1500*, 10 vols (New Haven: Connecticut Academy of Arts and Sciences, 1967–98), vol. 2, p. 480, and by no title at all in Peter S. Jollife's *A Check-list of Middle English Prose Writings of Spiritual Guidance* (Toronto: Pontifical Institute of Mediaeval Studies, 1974), p. 102, n. 28, p. 145, n. 40.

[157] Roger Ellis, 'The choices of the translator in the late Middle English period', in Marion Glasscoe (ed.), *The Medieval Mystical Tradition in England 1982: Symposium Proceedings* (Exeter: Exeter University Press, 1982), pp. 18–48 (p. 24).

[158] *Myrour*, Introduction, pp. xiii–xiv cites further examples.

[159] See Jones, 'A new look into the *Speculum inclusorum*', pp. 135–9.

[160] Jones, 'A new look into the *Speculum inclusorum*', p. 139.

[161] *Speculum*, p. 141.

[162] 'O benigne Ihesu … schew vn-to me what I schal telle on-to hem' (*Myrour*, p. 3).

[163] Jones, 'A new look into the *Speculum inclusorum*', pp. 138, 140–1.

[164] Jones himself concedes that there is, as yet, no proof of his hypothesis ('A new look into the *Speculum inclusorum*', p. 139).

Chapter 2

[1] 'stability of abode' (Millett, p. 3).

[2] 'all sorrows and pains, all the damages of death' (Otter, p. 35).

[3] 'Keep yourselves safely inside – not just the body, because that is the least important thing, but your five senses, and above all the heart … that is the life of the soul' (Millett, p. 67).

[4] 'They think it enough to confine the body behind walls while the mind roams at random, grows dissolute and distracted by cares, disquieted by impure desires' (MacPherson, p. 46). *Ancrene Wisse* echoes this at pp. 66–7 (Millett, pp. 66–7).

⁵   MacPherson, p. 55.

⁶   'þe lyf of moost perfeccion' (*Myrour*, p. 7) and 'in silence, in secret, and [in] derk places' (*Myrour*, p. 16).

⁷   'schal be kept vnto þe ende, on peyne of eternel and euere-lastinge dampnacion' (*Myrour*, p. 9).

⁸   *Myrour*, pp. 9–10.

⁹   'to lyue aftir þe arbitrement and doom of her owen wil, þei fleen fro her ordre as children of perdicion ant procuren and suen an exempcion or sum oþer liberte ... as to be þe popes chap-leyns or byscopes nullatenses' (*Myrour*, p. 5).

¹⁰ Ann K. Warren, *Anchorites and their Patrons in Medieval England* (Berkeley, Los Angeles and London: University of California Press, 1985), pp. 110–11.

¹¹ '[with] a little door for solemn exits' (Otter, p. 32).

¹² 'you, stripped of everything, can spread out and be more regal than a king' (Otter, p. 92).

¹³ 'Every anchoress has a commitment to this, both because of the name of "anchoress" and because she lives under the church, as if to prop it up ... she never stops; the anchor-house and her name are constantly proclaiming this commitment, even when she is asleep' (Millett, p. 56).

¹⁴ 'That is why the anchoress [*ancre*] is called an "anchor" [*ancre*], and anchored under the church like an anchor under the side of a ship ... Just so, all Holy Church (which is described as a ship) should anchor on the anchoress' (Millett, p. 56). The anchorite is also here rendered a bird shel-tering permanently under the eaves of Holy Church.

¹⁵ 'death ... night ... darkness' (Otter, p. 143).

¹⁶ 'It is your ship against the ocean of this wasteland, your shelter from the storms of the world, your refuge from the whirlwind of evil' (Otter, pp. 91–2). See Rebecca Hayward and Stephanie Hollis, 'The anchorite's progress: structure and motif in the *Liber confortatorius*', in Stephanie Hollis (ed.), with W. R. Barnes, Rebecca Hayward, Kathleen Loncar and Michael Wright, *Writing the Wilton Women: Goscelin's Legend of Edith and Liber confortatorius*, Medieval Women Texts and Contexts, 9 (Turnhout: Brepols, 2004), pp. 369–84 (pp. 376–7), on Goscelin's cell metaphor.

¹⁷ 'well-secured window' (Millett, p. 159). *Liber* and *Ancrene Wisse* both transform the recluse's chaste body (and her anchorhold) into a metaphorical castle under siege (*Liber*, pp. 50–1; Otter, p. 55; *AW*, Corpus, p. 146; Millett, p. 146). See Abigail Wheatley, *The Idea of the Castle in Medieval England* (Woodbridge: York Medieval Press, 2004), especially pp. 109–10; Catherine Innes-Parker, '*Ancrene Wisse* and *Þe Wohunge of Ure Lauerd*: the thirteenth-century female reader and the lover-knight', in Lesley Smith and Jane H. M. Taylor (eds), *Women, the Book and the Godly: Selected Proceedings of the St Hilda's Conference 1993* (Cambridge: D. S. Brewer, 1995), pp. 137–47.

¹⁸ 'Your portion is also this, your little cell, your shelter on your pilgrimage, and your pasture, that little eight-foot house' (Otter, p. 84).

¹⁹ 'I cannot tell you how often I have sighed for a little refuge similar to yours ... where I might escape the crowds ... where I might pray, read a little, write a little, compose a little; ... so that I could impose a law on my stomach and on this pasture feast on books rather than food' (Otter, pp. 32–3).

²⁰ 'You are safely in the harbor, I founder. You sit at home, I am shipwrecked. You have built your nest in a rock, I slide about in the sand' (Otter, p. 34).

²¹ Millett, pp. 3–4.

²² Emphasis mine.

²³ Nicholas Watson, 'The methods and objectives of thirteenth-century anchoritic devotion', in Marion Glasscoe (ed.), *The Medieval Mystical Tradition in England IV. The Exeter Symposium IV: Papers Read at Dartington Hall, July 1987* (Cambridge: D. S. Brewer, 1987), pp. 132–53 (p. 138). Hasenfratz gives a conjectural plan of *Ancrene Wisse*'s cell and church (Robert Hasenfratz (ed.), *Ancrene Wisse* (Kalamazoo: Medieval Institute Publications, 2000), Introduction, p. 11).

²⁴ Linda Georgianna, *The Solitary Self: Individuality in the 'Ancrene Wisse'* (Cambridge, Mass. and London: Harvard University Press, 1981), p. 32. *Ancrene Wisse* certainly contains many more worldly references than *De institutione*, but all the guides trade, at times, in worldly meta-phors for spiritual ends.

25   Georgianna, *The Solitary Self*, p. 50.

26   Janet Grayson, *Structure and Imagery in 'Ancrene Wisse'* (Hanover, NH: University Press of New England for the University of New Hampshire, 1974).

27   John A. Burrow, 'Fantasy and language in *The Cloud of Unknowing*', *Essays in Criticism*, 27 (1977), 283–98 (284). Emphasis in the original.

28   Cary Howie, *Claustrophilia: The Erotics of Enclosure in Medieval Literature* (Basingstoke and New York: Palgrave Macmillan, 2007), p. 4.

29   MacPherson, p. 97.

30   Watson, 'Methods and objectives', p. 141.

31   Otter, p. 13.

32   Christopher Cannon, 'Enclosure', in Carolyn Dinshaw and David Wallace (eds), *The Cambridge Companion to Medieval Women's Writing* (Cambridge: Cambridge University Press, 2003), pp. 109–23 (p. 113).

33   Barbara Newman, 'Liminalities: literate women in the long twelfth century', in Thomas F. X. Noble and John van Engen (eds), *European Transformations: The Long Twelfth Century* (Notre Dame, Ind.: University of Notre Dame Press, 2012), pp. 145–98 (p. 151). Accessed via *http:// northwestern.academia.edu/BarbaraNewman/Papers/1520025/Liminalities_Literate_Women_ in_the_Long_Twelfth_Century* (accessed 7 September 2011). See also Newman's 'Flaws in the golden bowl: gender and spiritual formation in the twelfth century', *Traditio*, 45 (1989–90), 111–46.

34   'Blessed are the dead who die in the Lord, with whom to die is to live' (Otter, p. 82).

35   'dying every day to the world and living for God' (Otter, p. 109).

36   'desiring to be hidden and unseen … dead as it were to the world and buried with Christ in his tomb' (MacPherson, p. 62). On Aelred and grave metaphor, see Amédée Hallier, *The Monastic Theology of Aelred of Rievaulx: An Experiential Theology* (Shannon: Irish University Press, 1969), pp. 159–60.

37   'what is the anchor-house but her grave?' (Millett, p. 43)

38   'is in a strange land here, put in a prison, confined in a death-cell' (Millett, p. 55).

39   'scrape up the earth every day from the grave in which they will rot' (Millett, p. 46).

40   Mary B. Salu (ed. and trans.), *The 'Ancrene Riwle'* (*The Corpus MS.: Ancrene Wisse*) (London: Burns and Oates, 1955), p. 51; Georgianna reads this literally in *The Solitary Self*, p. 5., on the basis that some recluses may indeed have dug and knelt daily in their own graves, as for example at St Anne's Church, Lewes. See also Roberta Gilchrist, *Contemplation and Action: The Other Monasticism* (London and New York: Leicester University Press, 1995), pp. 190–1.

41   Hugh White (trans.), *Ancrene Wisse: Guide for Anchoresses* (London, New York, Victoria, Ontario and Auckland: Penguin, 1993), p. 59. White's footnote to this translation is 'Anchorites were often buried in their cells' (p. 217, n. 56), but he does not force this reading onto the text. Millett translates this as: 'Certainly that grave does a great deal of good to many anchoresses' (p. 46).

42   'a fowl being fattened in a cage, but not in the flesh but in the soul' (Otter, p. 84).

43   'the tree … bears numerous offspring from its grave' (Otter, p. 93).

44   'luxuriate in the security of a narrow space' (Otter, p. 92).

45   'death is the beginning of eternal happiness, the goal of all your labours, the destroyer of vice' (MacPherson, p. 97).

46   MacPherson, p. 91. See pages 89–92 below on earlier medieval guidance and contemplative fusion.

47   'Burial does no harm to those who will rise again' (Otter, p. 93).

48   On the womb/tomb matrix, see Liz Herbert McAvoy and Mari Hughes-Edwards (eds), *Anchorites, Wombs and Tombs: Intersections of Gender and Enclosure in the Middle Ages* (Cardiff: University of Wales Press, 2005), and Hayward and Hollis, 'The anchorite's progress', p. 377.

49   'I have given birth to you and loved you for this, that you may pass into Christ's womb, and become totally Christ's sacrificial lamb' (Otter, p. 36).

50 'the first time he [Christ] emerged from a closed womb, the second time from a closed tomb' (Otter, p. 100).

51 'Mary's womb and this tomb were his anchor-houses' (Millett, p. 143).

52 MacPherson, p. 93, and 'Blessed the wombs in which the salvation of the whole world takes its origin, gloomy sadness is driven far away and everlasting joy foretold' (MacPherson, p. 81).

53 Miri Rubin, *Mother of God: A History of the Virgin Mary* (London, New York, Victoria, Ontario and Auckland: Penguin, 2009), pp. 131–2.

54 'both your anchor-houses … One is the body; the other is the outer house' (Millett, p. 142).

55 Victor Turner, *The Ritual Process: Structure and Anti-structure* (1969; New York: Aldine de Gruyter, 1995), p. 95.

56 'You have arrived at the door of paradise of true desire; be persistent and knock with tireless importunity, until the Lord comes' (Otter, p. 36).

57 'Now stand in the middle, not knowing to which company the Judge's sentence will assign you. O what a dreadful waiting. Fear and trembling have come upon me and darkness has covered me' (MacPherson, p. 99).

58 'you are dwellers in Paradise, we are wretched inhabitants of this world. You are at the gate of heaven, we are in deep mud. You exist in the mirror of truth and we in the darkness of falsity'.

59 See pages 94–8 below on anchoritism and the active/contemplative controversy.

60 Millett, p. 13.

61 'Here is your sanctuary, your oratory, your dining hall, your dormitory, your hall, your bedroom, your vestibule, your cellar, your office – you have merged all those living spaces into one' (Otter, p. 92).

62 'chastity and … simplicity' (MacPherson, p. 72). See also *DII*, pp. 658–9, and *AW*, Corpus, pp. 53–4 (MacPherson, pp. 73–4 and Millett, pp. 53–4).

63 Elizabeth Robertson, 'Savoring "scientia": the medieval anchoress reads *Ancrene Wisse*', in Yoko Wada (ed.), *A Companion to 'Ancrene Wisse'* (Cambridge: D. S. Brewer, 2003), pp. 113–45 (p. 130).

64 'I would not have you pursue, on the pretext of devotion, the glory which expresses itself in paintings or in carvings, in hangings decorated with birds or animals or flowers. Leave such things to people who have nothing in themselves and so must seek their pleasure in outward things' (MacPherson, pp. 71–2).

65 See Jocelyn Price, '"Inner" and "outer": conceptualizing the body in *Ancrene Wisse* and Aelred's *De institutione inclusarum*', in Gregory Kratzmann and James Simpson (eds), *Medieval Religious and Ethical Literature. Essays in Honour of G. H. Russell* (Cambridge: D. S. Brewer, 1986), pp. 192–208.

66 *Myrour*, Introduction, p. xix.

67 'I would have you never rest secure but always be afraid' (MacPherson, p. 68).

68 'forget the homeland you are seeking … depressed by your solitude, your imprisonment and your enclosure' (Otter, p. 81).

69 'sleepiness, sluggishness, sadness, depression' (Otter, p. 107).

70 'Regard your whole life as but one day compared to eternity' (Otter, p. 108).

71 Otter, p. 56; MacPherson, p. 55 and Millett, p. 18. See pages 49–50 below on earlier medieval guidance's limitation of social interaction. See also page 39 below on its regulation of sight.

72 See pages 62–7 below for recommendations about ascetic practice and pages 84–94 for their treatment of contemplative experience.

73 'take a daily viaticum of heavenly nourishment' (Otter, p. 110).

74 'If you dine on this food … with your mind not roaming outside but concentrated inward … you will not be lonely, and you will not suffer deadly depression' (Otter, p. 111).

Chapter 3

1   An earlier draft of some of the materials from this chapter formed the basis of Mari
    Hughes-Edwards, '"How good it is to be alone"? Sociability, solitude and medieval English
    anchoritism', *Mystics Quarterly*, 35 (2009), 31–61.

2   Alexandra Barratt, 'Anchoritic aspects of *Ancrene Wisse*', *Medium Aevum*, 49 (1980), 32–56
    (43).

3   'so, too, to the extent the heart is occupied by any other love, in the same measure it excludes this
    one' (Fröhlich, 'Letter 112', vol. 1, p. 270).

4   'You entered here alone to receive him alone. Shout, wail, knock, so as the door may be opened
    to you. Struggle with the Lord as long as you have life; push violently to enter the kingdom of
    heaven' (Otter, p. 24).

5   'How good it is to be alone … God revealed his hidden counsels and his heavenly secrets to his
    dearest friends not in a crowd of people, but where they were alone by themselves' (Millett,
    p. 60).

6   'An angel has rarely appeared to a human being in a crowd' (Millett, p. 62).

7   'an intimate companionship … nowhere solitude' (Otter, p. 148).

8   'The more you were wounded with love for your loved ones in Christ here on earth, the more
    joyfully will you gather them about you in the eternal mansion' (Otter, p. 43).

9   Otter, p. 107.

10 'places of horror and vast solitude' (Otter, p. 50).

11 'Be with the Lord, and you will not be alone' (Otter, p. 81).

12 Rebecca Hayward, 'Representations of the anchoritic life in Goscelin of Saint-Bertin's *Liber
    confortatorius*', in Liz Herbert McAvoy and Mari Hughes-Edwards (eds), *Anchorites, Wombs
    and Tombs: Intersections of Gender and Enclosure in the Middle Ages* (Cardiff: University of
    Wales Press, 2005), pp. 54–64 (p. 56).

13 Otter, p. 89.

14 Otter, p. 85. See page 94 and pages 96–7 below on the contemplative/active significance of Mary
    and her sister Martha.

15 'Did not the angel find her alone in solitude? … Strictly enclosed' (Millett, p. 62).

16 See MacPherson, p. 51; Millett, p. 26.

17 Millett, p. 41.

18 'she must sit alone, imposing silence on her tongue that her spirit may speak' (MacPherson,
    p. 50). See also MacPherson, pp. 54–7.

19 Nancy Bradley Warren, *Spiritual Economies: Female Monasticism in Later Medieval England*
    (Philadelphia: University of Pennsylvania Press, 2001), p. 37.

20 Patricia J. F. Rosof, 'The anchoress in the twelfth and thirteenth centuries', in John A. Nichols
    and Lillian Thomas Shank (eds), *Medieval Religious Women, Vol. Two: Peaceweavers*
    (Kalamazoo: Cistercian Studies Series, 1987), pp. 123–45 (p. 134).

21 Millett, p. 74.

22 'Be solitary, alone with the Lord. Speak to God in prayers, and in your reading hear God
    speaking to you' (Otter, p. 95).

23 See pages 35–8 above on enclosure and metaphorical constructions of death.

24 'further business … with the snares of the world you left behind' (Otter, p. 41).

25 'He who wishes to ascend the true mountain with the Lord and to build a tower to heaven' (Otter,
    p. 71).

26 'Forget that you are in this world, because you have shifted your interest to those who are in
    heaven and live for God. Where your treasure is, there let your heart also be' (MacPherson,
    p. 96).

27 '"I too", said the holy man, "am dead in a spiritual sense. No earthly friend should ask me for
    earthly help"' (Millett, p. 160).

28 'the true anchoress, who is … truly hidden – he [God] hears and grants her all her prayers, and
    through them she saves many people. Many who would otherwise be lost are saved through the
    anchoress's prayers' (Millett, p. 65).

29 'spread out in the love of God and of your neighbor' (Otter, p. 30).

30 MacPherson, p. 77 and Millett, p. 12.

31 'So embrace the whole world with the arms of your love and in that act at once consider and congratulate the good, contemplate and mourn over the wicked. In that act look upon the afflicted and the oppressed and feel compassion for them' (MacPherson, p. 77).

32 'gather into your heart all those who are ill and wretched ... the misery that the poor suffer, the torments that prisoners endure ... feel compassion for those who are attacked by strong temptations. Take all their sorrows into your heart and sigh to our Lord' (Millett, p. 12).

33 'asks for nothing but love ... Give love, therefore, and receive the kingdom; love and possess' (Fröhlich, 'Letter 112', vol. 1, p. 269).

34 'Truly to the solitary contemplative the burning love of God becomes sweet, every worldly joy assuredly withers' (*Myrour*, p. 37).

35 'love God more than yourself and you will already begin to hold what you want to have there in perfection ... But you shall not be able to possess this perfect love until you have emptied your heart of all other love' (Fröhlich, 'Letter 112', vol. 1, p. 270).

36 Tom Licence, *Hermits and Recluses in English Society: 950–1200* (Oxford: Oxford University Press, 2011), p. 109.

37 Cary Howie, *Claustrophilia: The Erotics of Enclosure in Medieval Literature* (Basingstoke and New York: Palgrave Macmillan, 2007), p. 39.

38 'Since it is impossible to impose a complete ban upon all converse with men, let us see to whom the recluse may justifiably speak' (MacPherson, p. 51).

39 'May your conversation always be pure and about God' (Fröhlich, 'Letter 230', vol. 2, p. 199).

40 Linda Georgianna, *The Solitary Self: Individuality in the 'Ancrene Wisse'* (Cambridge, Mass. and London: Harvard University Press, 1981), p. 53. Emphasis in the original.

41 Rotha Mary Clay, *The Hermits and Anchorites of England* (London: Methuen, 1914), p. 128.

42 Darwin's study may sometimes be whimsical in tone, but it rightly argues for the socialized identity of anchoritism far more than Clay or Warren's. See Francis D. S. Darwin, *The English Mediaeval Recluse* (London: SPCK, 1944) pp. 1–8, 8–20 and 20–42 (this quotation is at pp. 14–15).

43 Anneke B. Mulder-Bakker, 'The reclusorium as an informal centre of learning', in J. W. Drijvers and A. A. MacDonald (eds), *Centres of Learning: Learning and Location in Pre-modern Europe and the Near East* (Leiden: E. J. Brill, 1995), pp. 245–55 (pp. 251, 254).

44 Anneke B. Mulder-Bakker, *Lives of the Anchoresses: The Rise of the Urban Recluse in Medieval Europe* (Philadelphia: University of Pennsylvania Press, 2005), p. 179.

45 Mulder-Bakker, *Lives of the Anchoresses*, p. 12.

46 Mulder-Bakker, *Lives of the Anchoresses*, p. 175.

47 Mulder-Bakker, *Lives of the Anchoresses*, p. 179.

48 Jocelyn Price, '"Inner" and "outer": conceptualizing the body in *Ancrene Wisse* and Aelred's *De institutione inclusarum*', in Gregory Kratzmann and James Simpson (eds), *Medieval Religious and Ethical Literature. Essays in Honour of G. H. Russell* (Cambridge: D. S. Brewer, 1986), pp. 192–208 (p. 197).

49 Liz Herbert McAvoy, 'Gender, rhetoric and space in the *Speculum Inclusorum, Letter to a Bury Recluse* and the strange case of Christina Carpenter', in *eadem* (ed.), *Rhetoric of the Anchorhold: Space, Place and Body within the Discourses of Enclosure* (Cardiff: University of Wales Press, 2008), pp. 111–27 (p. 115). She argues this in terms of the later guide, *Letter to a Bury Recluse*, but this idea can also be usefully applied to earlier guidance.

50 'you ... are well received by the people there; ... the venerable mother and all the sisters shower you with love ... dignified fathers and bishops visit ... you ... the dear lady loves and cherishes you who prepared this place for you ... as ... a most kind friend to you in a truer way than before' (Otter, p. 113).

51 '"many people come to you wearing lambs' fleece, and are ravening wolves"' (Millett, p. 28).

52 'Trust seculars little, religious still less' (Millett, p. 28).

53 Bella Millett, '*Ancrene Wisse* and the book of hours', in Denis Renevey and Christiania Whitehead (eds), *Writing Religious Women: Female Spiritual and Textual Practices in Late*

Medieval England (Cardiff: University of Wales Press, 2000), pp. 21–40 (p. 27). These additions are at *AW*, Corpus, p. 28 (Millett, p. 28) and in the fourteenth-century French manuscript, London, British Library, MS Cotton Vitellius F.vii. A further reference to the friars, only in the Corpus manuscript, is at *AW*, Corpus, p. 157 (Millett, p. 157). These references to the friars date these two texts to after the arrival of the mendicants in England, *c*.1221 (Dominicans) and *c*.1224 (Franciscans).

54 Millett, p. 18.

55 Millett, p. 29.

56 Millett, p. 26.

57 On medieval servitude, see M. Kowaleski and P. J. P. Goldberg (eds), *Medieval Domesticity: Home, Housing and Household in Medieval England* (Cambridge: Cambridge University Press, 2008); Cordelia Beattie, *Medieval Single Women: The Politics of Social Classification in Late Medieval England* (Oxford: Oxford University Press, 2007), pp. 8, 33, 36 and especially pp. 75–6, and M. Goodich, '*Ancilla Dei*: the servant as saint in the late Middle Ages', in J. Kirshner and S. F. Wemple (eds), *Women of the Medieval World: Essays in Honour of John H. Mundy* (Oxford: Blackwell, 1985), pp. 119–36.

58 *DII*, p. 640 (MacPherson, p. 49) and *AW*, Corpus, pp. 161–4 (Millett, pp. 161–4).

59 *Ancrene Wisse*'s Titus text uses the word 'familiers' for servants, which potentially carries the etymological implication of close, regular domestic contact (see *AW*, Titus, p. 157). *The Middle English Dictionary* notes this as the first usage of this word in this context, arguing for its synonymous denotion of a member of the household retinue and 'a close … acquaintance … or friend'. See Hans Kurath et al. (eds), *The Middle English Dictionary* (Ann Arbor, Michigan: University of Michigan Press, 1956–2001), vol. E–F, pp. 396–7. The *MED* is also available online at, *http://quod.lib.umich.edu/m/med* (accessed 7 September 2011).

60 'I would like the window of your cell to be wide enough to admit a library of this size, or wide enough that you could read the books through the window if they are propped up for you there from outside. Read aloud' (Otter, pp. 95–6).

61 'Make women and children who have laboured for you to eat whatever food you can spare' (Morton, *Ancren Riwle*, p. 417).

62 'anchoresses' maids' (Millett, p. 157).

63 'how long you should have them to stay' (Millett, p. 160).

64 'When your sisters' maids pay you a visit, come to them at the window in the morning and afternoon once or twice, and go straight back to your spiritual duties … so that their visit may not mean the loss of any of your spiritual observances, but spiritual gain' (Millett, p. 164).

65 Michelle Sauer, '"Prei for me mi leue suster": the paradox of the anchoritic "community" in late medieval England', *Prose Studies*, 26, 1–2 (2003), 153–75 (169). See also Alexandra Barratt, 'Creating an anchorhold', in Miri Rubin (ed.), *Medieval Christianity in Practice* (Princeton, NJ: Princeton University Press, 2009), pp. 311–18, and Kevin J. Magill, *Julian of Norwich: Mystic or Visionary?* (London and New York: Routledge, 2006), pp. 36–66.

66 'You are the anchoresses of England, in such a large group (twenty now or more …), that most peace is among, most unity and unanimity and community of united life according to a rule, so that you all pull together, all turned one way and none away from each other, so it is said' (Millett, p. 96).

This does not necessarily imply a dramatic increase in the vocation's popularity, or a marked increase in the number of shared anchorages and the Corpus text does not refer here to a 'convent' of anchoresses: the conclusion, for example, of Cheryl Frost in 'The attitude to women and the adaptation to a feminine audience in the *Ancrene Wisse*', *AUMLA: The Journal of the Australasian Universities Language and Literature Association*, 50 (1978), 235–50 (240).

67 Bella Millett, '"He speaks to me as if I was a public meeting": rhetoric and audience in the works of the *Ancrene Wisse* group', in Liz Herbert McAvoy (ed.), *Rhetoric of the Anchorhold: Space, Place and Body within the Discourse of Enclosure* (Cardiff: University of Wales Press), pp. 50–66 (p. 55).

68 Millett, p. 94. Clay writes of literary recluses in Rotha Mary Clay, 'Further studies on medieval recluses', *Journal of the British Archaeological Association*, 16 (1953), 74–86 (74–80).

69 'the death of friends, their illness or your own' (Millett, p. 69). I am grateful to Professor Bella Millett for advice on this point (personal correspondence dated 5 October 2010).

70 'poverty, hard work and submission' (Fröhlich, 'Letter 112', vol. 1, p. 271).

71 'Do not make any purses to win friends, except for those people your director allows' (Millett, p. 160). Millett's edition and translation of *Ancrene Wisse* contain variants from other manuscripts, so although this reference abbreviation would appear to refer to the guide's Corpus text, in fact it refers to a variant from the Cleopatra text. Millett, p. 273, n. 84 notes this as an addition in both the Corpus text and in the hand of Scribe B (or C2) of the Cleopatra text; possibly the *Ancrene Wisse* author.

72 Eric J. Dobson, *The Origins of 'Ancrene Wisse'* (Oxford: Clarendon Press, 1976), p. 264.

73 'You should not ... complain about any shortage, except to some good friend who can put things right ... secretly ... so that you may not be criticized ... If he presses you ... thank him gratefully, and say, "I don't dare to lie about myself; I am in need"' (Millett, p. 99).

74 'She is not a housewife, but a church anchoress. If she can spare any poor scraps, she should send them with the utmost secrecy out of her house' (Millett, p. 156). My thanks to Professor Bella Millett for pointing out the link between these two passages (personal correspondence dated 5 October 2010).

75 Ann K. Warren, *Anchorites and their Patrons in Medieval England* (Berkeley, Los Angeles and London: University of California Press, 1985), p. 77.

76 'vertuous communycacion ant charytable speche ... wiþ his broþer' (*Myrour*, p. 23).

77 Anne Clark Bartlett, 'A reasonable affection: gender and spiritual friendship in Middle English devotional literature', in A. Clark Bartlett, T. H. Bestul, J. Goebel and W. F. Pollard (eds), *Vox Mystica: Essays on Medieval Mysticism in Honour of Professor V. M. Lagorio* (Cambridge: D. S. Brewer, 1995), pp. 131–45 (p. 142).

78 Emphasis mine. On this, see Gary Macy, *The Hidden History of Women's Ordination: Female Clergy in the Medieval West* (Oxford: Oxford University Press, 2008).

79 Fiona Somerset, 'Eciam mulier: women in Lollardy and the problem of sources', in Linda Olson and Kathryn Kerby-Fulton (eds), *Voices in Dialogue: Reading Women in the Middle Ages* (Notre Dame, Ind.: University of Notre Dame Press, 2005), pp. 261–78 (pp. 253, 254).

80 'For alle þese þinges, recluses schal often calle ant knokke on mercyable God, wiþ sorweful teres ant þoru3 sighynges prouoke and stire God to do mercy, grace ant socour' (*Myrour*, p. 36).

81 Fröhlich, 'Letter 414', vol. 3, p. 186.

82 'Do not therefore consider only what you do but what you intend to do ... what your intention is' (Fröhlich, 'Letter 414', vol. 3, p. 184).

83 Otter, pp. 130–3.

84 Aelred Squire, *Aelred of Rievaulx: A Study* (London: SPCK, 1969), pp. 168–70, details Aelred's quasi-eremitic seclusion.

85 'the flesh is set on fire by a strong heat which subdues the will and takes the members by surprise' (MacPherson, p. 64).

   Squire, *Aelred of Rievaulx*, p. 120, notes Aelred's sources on virginity. Thomas Renna traces Aelred's intertextual influences back to patristic sources, arguing that critics have over-interpreted Aelred's self-revelatory passages on sexual transgression (in 'Virginity in the life of Christina of Markyate and Aelred of Rievaulx's *Rule*', *American Benedictine Review*, 36 (1985), 79–92 (especially 89, 90–2)). One exaggerated reading of Aelred's sexualized material is John Boswell's: 'Aelred was gay and ... his erotic attraction to men ... a dominant force in his life'. See his *Christianity, Social Tolerance, and Homosexuality: Gay People in Western Europe from the Beginning of the Christian Era to the Fourteenth Century* (Chicago: University of Chicago Press, 1980), p. 222. A more balanced perspective is K. M. Yohe's 'Sexual attraction and the motivations for love and friendship in Aelred of Rievaulx', *Benedictine Review*, 46 (1995), 283–307.

86 'but there were others whose confidence was undermined by the very freedom inherent in the solitary life and the opportunity it affords for aimless wandering. They judged it more prudent to be completely enclosed in a cell with the door walled up' (MacPherson, p. 45).

87   'some wretched anchoress … goes into the cave of the anchor-house to foul the place, and to indulge in carnal filthiness there more secretly than she could if she were in secular life' (Millett, pp. 51–2).

88   'who has more opportunity to practise her vices than the false anchoress?' (Millett, p. 52).

89   'News is carried from mill and from market-place, from smithy and from anchor-house' (Millett, p. 36).

90   'This is a sad comment, to be sure, that the anchor-house, which should be the most solitary place of all, should be linked with these three places where there is most gossip' (Millett, p. 36).

91   MacPherson, p. 46.

92   'Regrettably, we have heard of plenty of cases of this' (Millett, p. 26).

93   'curious anchoress, always poking her nose out like an untamed bird in a cage' and 'the cat of hell' (Millett, p. 40).

94   'No cat, no chicken, no irrational animal of any sort should be your companion, lest your fleeting time be frittered away' (Otter, p. 95).

95   'Those who began spiritual life in the Holy Spirit have become altogether carnal – giggling, frivolous … bitter and venomous, with swollen hearts' (Millett, p. 43).

96   Millett, p. 63.

97   'a calf shut in by demonic dogs' (Otter, p. 53).

98   MacPherson, pp. 47–8. *Ancrene Wisse* also constructs burglary and fire as more dangerous because of anchoritic fixity of place (*AW*, Corpus, p. 92 and Millett, p. 92).

99   'I … joined in round dances in the churchyard; watched the dances … talked in such a way or joked in the presence of … religious, in the anchor-house' (Millett, p. 121).

100 *AW*, Corpus, p. 22–3; Millett, pp. 22–3.

101 'through our windows' (Otter, p. 91).

102 'all the misery that there is now, and ever has been up to now, and will ever be, came entirely from sight' (Millett, p. 21).

103 Christopher M. Woolgar, *The Senses in Late Medieval England* (New Haven and London: Yale University Press, 2006), p. 148. See also chapter 8, 'Vision' (pp. 147–89), and Sarah Stanbury, *The Visual Object of Desire in Late Medieval England* (Philadelphia: University of Pennsylvania Press, 2007).

104 See *AW*, Corpus, pp. 20–47 (Millett, pp. 20–47), and Alexandra Barratt's 'The five wits and their structural significance in Part II of *Ancrene Wisse*', *Medium Aevum*, 56 (1987), 12–24.

105 'She should not be at all surprised, if she is not alone a great deal, that he avoids her – and alone in such a way that she puts every worldly pressure, and every earthly disturbance out of her heart, because she is God's chamber' (Millett, p. 36).

106 'Let the windows of your cell, your tongue and your ears be locked to false tales and idle talk' (Otter, p. 95).

107 'diuerse contrees … diuerse fantasies' (*Myrour*, p. 6).

108 *Myrour*, p. 6.

109 Warren tabulates this shift (*Anchorites and their Patrons*, p. 38).

110 'of some recluses in þese dayes, nat in wildernesses but in þe citees, þat … þere receyue large almes, wher-of þei may holde greet meynee and helpe and promote more largely her kyn and her freendes' (*Myrour*, p. 6).

111 On this see Lutz Kaelber, *Schools of Asceticism: Ideology and Organization in Medieval Religious Communities* (Pennsylvania: The Pennsylvania State University Press, 1998), p. 82. See also Beth Allison Barr, *The Pastoral Care of Women in Late Medieval England*, Gender in the Middle Ages, vol. 3 (Woodbridge: Boydell and Brewer, 2008), especially pp. 94–120.

112 Emphasis mine.

113 See pages 101–7 below on later guidance and fears about spiritual orthodoxy.

114 Otter, p. 3.

115 Hollis, Introduction, in *eadem* (ed.), with W. R. Barnes, Rebecca Hayward, Kathleen Loncar and Michael Wright, *Writing the Wilton Women: Goscelin's Legend of Edith and Liber confortatorius*, Medieval Women Texts and Contexts, 9 (Turnhout: Brepols, 2004), pp. 1–13 (p. 9).

[116] Otter, p. 124.

[117] 'so far my love for you was only external, and bearable; it was love in the good hope of Christ' (Otter, p. 23).

[118] 'you put on the sacred vestment ... I was struck to the quick ... my desire was inflamed even more' (Otter, p. 23).

[119] Otter, p. 132.

[120] Robert Mills, *Suspended Animation: Pain, Pleasure and Punishment in Medieval Culture* (London: Reaktion Books, 2005), p. 117.

[121] 'Many women wished to persevere [in virginity] but could not obtain the gift even through prayers; others who did not wish to persevere were preserved in virginity by afflictions and chastisement' (Otter, p. 121).

[122] Otter, p. 119.

[123] 'disturbs and agitates ... The virgin falls ... the chaste is violated' and 'the prostitute made chaste' (Otter, p. 115).

[124] 'the frailty of our flesh' (Otter, p. 58); 'our filth and our flesh' (Otter, p. 60); 'the edge of the abyss' and 'fornication, uncleanness, luxury' (Otter, p. 63).

[125] 'to walk according to the flesh is to give in to the will of the flesh' (Fröhlich, 'Letter 414', vol. 3, p. 185).

[126] 'Carnal desires must be tamed; as soon as vices raise their heads, they must be crushed' (Otter, p. 55).

[127] 'it is better ... to die a martyr' than 'to live a whore' and 'O, the fear of rape is so much graver than the fear of torture! The danger to her chastity so much worse than threats to her life!' (Otter, p. 123).

[128] See Catherine Innes-Parker, 'Virgin, bride and lover: a study of the relationship between sexuality and spirituality in anchoritic literature' (unpublished diss., Memorial University of Newfoundland, 1992).

[129] See Sarah Salih, 'When is a bosom not a bosom? Problems with "erotic mysticism"', in Anke Bernau, Ruth Evans and Sarah Salih (eds), *Medieval Virginities* (Toronto and Cardiff: University of Wales Press and University of Toronto Press, 2003), pp. 14–32 (p. 20).

[130] Cate Gunn, *'Ancrene Wisse': From Pastoral Literature to Vernacular Spirituality* (Cardiff: University of Wales Press, 2008), p. 3.

[131] 'Virginity is the gold, the cell is the crucible, the devil is the assayer, temptation is the fire' (MacPherson, p. 63).

[132] 'Do not think that this means that a man cannot be defiled without a woman or a woman without a man, since that abominable sin which inflames a man with passion for a man or a woman for a woman meets with more relentless condemnation than any other crime' (MacPherson, p. 64).

[133] 'the effrontery of some who, grown old in uncleanness, will not even forego the company of undesirable persons. Dreadful as it is to say, they share the same bed with them, embrace them and kiss them, and yet declare they have no fear for their chastity ... Yet is what they say true, or is wickedness bearing false witness, showing up two sins in its efforts to conceal one?' (Macpherson, pp. 67–8).

[134] Alexandra Barratt, 'Small Latin? The post-Conquest learning of English religious women', in Sian Echard and Gernot R. Wieland (eds), *Anglo-Latin and its Heritage: Essays in Honour of A. G. Rigg on his 64th Birthday* (Turnhout: Brepols, 2001), pp. 51–65 (p. 54).

[135] See MacPherson, p. 66, n. 27.

[136] 'Let no one deceive himself ... the young never obtain or keep chastity without great contrition of heart and bodily affliction. Even in the sick and the aged it is not safe from danger' (MacPherson, p. 66).

[137] Aelred's own account of this controversy from the 1140s was recorded in his *De sanctimoniali de Wattun* or *De quadam miraculum mirabile, c.*1160. See Jacques-Paul Migne (ed.), *Patrologiae Cursus Completus: Series Latina*, 221 vols (Paris: Migne, 1841–64), vol. 195, col. 789–96. See also the translation: *A Certain Wonderful Miracle*, in Marsha L. Dutton (ed.), *The Lives of the Northern Saints*, trans. Jane Patricia Freeland (Kalamazoo: Cistercian Publications, 2006), pp.

109–22. Critical studies include Giles Constable, 'Aelred of Rievaulx and the Nun of Watton: an episode in the early history of the Gilbertine Order', in Derek Baker and Rosalind M. T. Hill (eds), *Medieval Women* (Oxford: Blackwell, 1978), pp. 205–26, and Sarah Salih, *Versions of Virginity in Late Medieval Europe* (Cambridge: D. S. Brewer, 2001), especially pp. 110, 154–5.

[138] Anke Bernau, *Virgins: A Cultural History* (London: Granta Books, 2007) pp. 38–9, and also her 'Virginal effects: text and identity in *Ancrene Wisse*', in Samantha J. E. Riches and Sarah Salih (eds), *Gender and Holiness: Men, Women and Saints in Late Medieval Europe* (London and New York: Routledge, 2002), pp. 36–48.

[139] Morton, *Ancren Riwle*, p. 59. Two folios are missing from the Corpus MS (after f. 14b, see J. R. R. Tolkien (ed.), *The English Text of the Ancrene Riwle: Ancrene Wisse: Edited from MS. Corpus Christi College Cambridge 402*, Early English Text Society, original series, 249 (1962), p. 33, where he notes, '*after* ah *two leaves lost*') at the point in part two where the image of woman as an uncovered pit would occur.

[140] 'You who uncover this pit, you who do anything so that a man is carnally tempted by you, even if you are unaware of it – be extremely afraid' (Millett, p. 23).

[141] 'what was a cell has now become a brothel' (MacPherson, p. 47).

[142] Karma Lochrie, 'The language of transgression: body, flesh and word in mystical discourse', in Allen J. Frantzen (ed.), *Speaking Two Languages: Traditional Disciplines and Contemporary Theory in Medieval Studies* (Albany: SUNY, 1991), pp. 115–41 (pp. 125–6).

[143] 'the virgin's virginity' and 'three virgins ... converging at the cross ... a triple virginity' (Otter, p. 29).

[144] Phyllis G. Jestice, 'A new fashion in imitating Christ: changing spiritual perspectives around the year 1000', in Michael Frassetto (ed.), *The Year 1000: Religious and Social Response to the Turning of the First Millennium* (Basingstoke and New York: Palgrave Macmillan, 2002), pp. 165–86 (p. 167).

[145] Otter, p. 28.

[146] 'the celibate and the married ... all can be saved ... a virgin gave birth to him, a widow carried him ... a whore presumed to wash his feet' (Otter, p. 126).

[147] 'He found a whore and made her equal to virgins' (Otter, p. 121).

[148] Millett, pp. 63–4. This contrasts with another work from the *Ancrene Wisse* group, *Hali Meiðhad*, devoted to persuading a woman against the permanent destruction of her virginity in wedlock: 'wedlac haueð hire frut þrittifald in heoune; widewehad, sixtifald; meiðhad wið hundretfald ouergeað baþe' ('marriage has its reward thirtyfold in heaven; widowhood sixty-fold; virginity, with a hundred-fold, surpasses both'). See Bella Millett and Jocelyn Wogan-Browne (eds), *Medieval English Prose for Women: Selections from the Katherine Group and 'Ancrene Wisse'* (Oxford: Clarendon Press, 1990), pp. 20–1.

[149] *Myrour*, p. 13.

[150] *Speculum*, p. 79.

[151] 'lecherie agayn kynde' (*Myrour*, p. 14).

[152] Boswell, *Christianity, Social Tolerance and Homosexuality*, pp. 76, 107 argues that 'mollis', originally used to denote weakness, was, through usage, corrupted into homosexual reference.

[153] *Myrour*, Introduction, p. xvi. On anchoritism and sodomitical practices, see Robert Mills, 'Gender, sodomy, friendship, and the medieval anchorhold', *Journal of Medieval Religious Cultures*, 36, 1 (2010), 1–27.

[154] 'Moore-ovyr, þe ere souketh and receyuyth al þat euyre he heryth of þe slym ant felþe of synne ... foul ant vnclene speches' (*Myrour*, p. 13).

[155] 'O blessyd is þe ere þat ys so prudently disposid þat he openeþ nat þe 3ates agayn suych vnleeful noyses; ant ys schyt ant spere agayn þe voluptuous or lusty melodyes of the world' (*Myrour*, p. 13).

Chapter 4

1 An earlier draft of some of the materials from this chapter formed the basis of Mari Hughes-Edwards, 'Hedgehog skins and hairshirts: the changing role of asceticism in the anchoritic ideal', *Mystics Quarterly*, 28 (2002), 6–25.

2 Henry Chadwick, 'The ascetic ideal in the history of the church', in W. J. Sheils (ed.), *Monks, Hermits and the Ascetic Tradition*, Studies in Church History, 22 (Oxford: Blackwell, 1985), pp. 1–23.

3 Conrad Leyser, *Authority and Asceticism from Augustine to Gregory the Great* (Oxford: Clarendon Press, 2000), p. 35.

4 E.g. Clifford H. Lawrence's seminal survey of medieval English monasticism synonymizes 'ascetical' and 'ascetic' with 'monastic'. See his *Medieval Monasticism: Forms of Religious Life in Western Europe in the Middle Ages* (London and New York: Longman, 1989), p. 120.

5 E.g. Chadwick's construction of the Greenham Common protest as ascetic (p. 2).

6 See R. W. Kaeuper (ed.), *Violence in Medieval Society* (Woodbridge: Boydell and Brewer, 2000), and M. Goodich, *Violence and Miracle in the Fourteenth Century: Private Grief and Public Salvation* (Chicago: University of Chicago Press, 1995).

7 MacPherson, p. 73.

8 'Everything that you have to bear ... is penance, and hard penance. Everything ... that you suffer, is martyrdom for you in such a harsh way of life, because you are on God's cross day and night' (Millett, p. 133).

9 Millett, p. 48.

10 Otter, p. 22.

11 Otter, p. 14.

12 Henry G. Liddell and Robert Scott, *A Greek–English Lexicon*, 2 vols (Oxford: Clarendon Press, 1843), vol. 1, p. 257.

13 Leyser, *Authority and Asceticism*, p. 42.

14 See Max Weber, *Essays in Sociology*, ed. and trans. H. H. Gerth and C. Wright Mills (New York: Oxford University Press, 1946), especially pp. 217–27, which categorizes ascetic acts as either 'passive' or 'active'. Chapter 4 utilizes 'aggressive' not 'active', to better connote the power of an external force used upon the body.

15 Jerome Kroll and Bernard Bachrach, *The Mystic Mind: The Psychology of Medieval Mystics and Ascetics* (New York and London: Routledge, 2005), p. 74.

16 Giles Constable, 'Moderation and restraint in ascetic practices in the Middle Ages', in Haijo J. Westra (ed.), *From Athens to Chartres: Neoplatonism and Medieval Thought. Studies in Honour of Edouard Jeauneau* (Leiden: E. J. Brill, 1992), pp. 315–27 (p. 316).

17 Constable, p. 316.

18 Jacques-Paul Migne (ed.), *Patrologiae Cursus Completus: Series Latina*, 221 vols (Paris: Migne, 1841–64), vol. 73, cols 851–1052.

19 Leyser, *Authority and Asceticism*, p. 46.

20 Migne, *Patrologiae Cursus Completus: Series Latina*, vol. 49, col. 554. An online translation of Cassian's work at, *http://www.newadvent.org/fathers/350802.htm* (accessed 7 September 2011), translates this as: 'daily hunger should go hand in hand with our daily meals, preserving both body and soul in one and the same condition, and not allowing the mind either to faint through weariness from fasting, nor to be oppressed by over-eating'.

21 See Migne, *Patrologiae Cursus Completus: Series Latina*, vol. 31, col. 797.

22 Migne, *Patrologiae Cursus Completus: Series Latina*, vol. 32, col. 797. This quotation from *Confessions*, book X, chapter 31, is translated at, *http://www.newadvent.org/fathers/110110.htm* (accessed 7 September 2011), as: 'I carry on a daily war by fasting. Oftentimes "bringing my body into subjection", and my pains are expelled by pleasure. For hunger and thirst are in some sort pains; they consume and destroy like unto a fever'.

23 See Elizabeth A. Clark, 'Perilous readings: Jerome, asceticism, and heresy', *Proceedings of the PMR Conference*, 19–20 (1994–6), 15–33.

24   Migne, *Patrologiae Cursus Completus: Series Latina*, vol. 23, col. 299. This quotation, from
     Against Jovinianus, Book II, is translated at, *http://www.newadvent.org/fathers/30092.htm*
     (accessed 7 September 2011) as: 'we may take food of such a kind and in such quantities as will
     not burden the body, or hinder the free movement of the soul: for it is the way with us that we eat,
     and walk, and sleep, and digest our food'.

25   See *Regula Sancti Benedicti* online at, *http://www.intratext.com/X/LAT0011.htm* (accessed 7
     September 2011). Translation: the *Rule of St Benedict*, online at, *http://www.osb.org/rb/text/*
     rbejms1.html#1 (accessed 7 September 2011).

26   See *Regula Sancti Benedicti*, online at, *http://www.intratext.com/IXT/LAT0011/_P5.htm*
     (accessed 7 September 2011). Translations of these subheadings are from chapter 4, 'The instru-
     ments of good works', taken from the *Rule of St Benedict*, available online at, *http://www.osb.*
     org/rb/text/rbejms2.html#4 (accessed 7 September 2011) are: 'To deny oneself, in order to
     follow Christ', 'To chastise the body', 'To love fasting'.

27   See *Regula Sancti Benedicti*, online at, *http://www.intratext.com/IXT/LAT0011/_PV.htm* the
     translation of which, in chapter 30, 'How young boys are to be corrected', taken from the *Rule of*
     St Benedict, available online at, *http://www.osb.org/rb/text/rbemjo1.html#30* (accessed 7
     September 2011) is 'let them be subjected to severe fasts or brought to terms by harsh beatings'.

28   See *Regula Sancti Benedicti*, online at, *http://www.intratext.com/IXT/LAT0011/_PT.htm*
     (accessed 7 September 2011). The translation, from chapter 28, 'On Those Who Will Not Amend
     After Repeated Corrections', taken from the *Rule of St Benedict*, available online at, *http://www.*
     osb.org/rb/text/rbemjo1.html#28 (accessed 7 September 2011) is 'the caustic of excommunica-
     tion and the blows of the lash'.

29   Giles Constable, *Attitudes towards Self-inflicted Suffering in the Middle Ages* (Brookline, Mass.:
     Hellenic College Press, 1982), p. 7.

30   'A stone is your armchair, the ground your bed, a hair shirt your dress, the fat under your skin
     protects you from cold' (Otter, p. 92).

31   'there will be no transgression, there will be no correction' (Otter, p. 146).

32   'And the stars are reached by way of suffering' (Otter, p. 51).

33   'to match your pure conscience' (Otter, p. 92).

34   'if we have mortified the things of the flesh, if we have crucified our flesh together with all its
     vices and desires, if we kill off all passions and incitements of the flesh, if we are crucified to the
     world and it to us' (Otter, p. 66).

35   'cursing the need to serve their lust, amputated the very instruments of crime' (Otter, p. 87).

36   '[acting] beyond sanity' (Otter, p. 87).

37   'Nor is Christ's law so severe that we must tear out our eyes: we must only avert them to avoid
     seeing vanity' (Otter, p. 88).

38   'Nor does he command us to mutilate our members or amputate our vices, or to be castrated of
     vices and desires, or to be circumcised, or crucified' (Otter, p. 88).

39   Otter, p. 33.

40   'lest the weight of fatness weigh down the mind that tends towards higher things' (Otter, p. 86).

41   'What difference does it make whether it be by fasting or by sickness that the pride of the flesh
     be tamed and chastity preserved? ... you may be sure that the man who feels weak, who is ill,
     whose bowels are wrung, whose stomach is dried up, will find pleasure more of a burden than a
     delight' (MacPherson, p. 69).

42   Otter, p. 64.

43   'if he sees you fight he will grind the enemies' savage teeth in their mouths with the lance of his
     cross' (Otter, p. 53).

44   'cuts away the "filth of the enemy"' (Otter, p. 127).

45   MacPherson, p. 59.

46   'in her longing for perfection let her have no appetite for food, a veritable loathing for drink.
     What necessity imposes let her take with pain and shame, at times with tears' (MacPherson,
     p. 64).

47   Ann K. Warren, *Anchorites and their Patrons in Medieval England* (Berkeley, Los Angeles and
     London: University of California Press, 1985), p. 107 and Rotha Mary Clay, *The Hermits and*
     Anchorites of England (London: Methuen, 1914), p. 124.

48 'It is better to travel in poor health to heaven than in good health to hell' (Millett, p. 72), and 'Illness causes a man to understand what he is, to know himself, and, like a good master, beats him to drive home the lesson of how powerful God is' (Millett, p. 69).

49 Millett, p. 158.

50 'with her confessor's permission' (Millett, p. 158).

51 Bella Millett, '*Mouvance* and the medieval author: re-editing *Ancrene Wisse*', in Alistair J. Minnis (ed.), *Late-medieval Religious Texts and Their Transmission: Essays in Honour of A. I. Doyle* (Cambridge: D. S. Brewer, 1994), pp. 9–20 (p. 17).

52 'A people dismembered and torn'(Millett, p. 137).

53 'his follower must follow his suffering with the suffering of his own flesh' (Millett, pp. 137–8).

54 'as a last resort bring out St Benedict's medicine for yourself – although it need not be as drastic as his was, when he was drenched with streaming blood … But at least give yourself a sharp scourging when you are most strongly under pressure, and drive that sweet delight into suffering as he did' (Millett, p. 112).

55 'We owe him blood for blood' (Millett, p. 119).

56 'Then no-one is part of his body who doesn't feel pain under a head that aches so badly' (Millett, p. 136).

57 See Eileen E. Power, *Medieval English Nunneries: c.1275 to 1535* (Cambridge: Cambridge University Press, 1922), and also S. Farmer and B. H. Rosenwein (eds), *Monks and Nuns, Saints and Outcasts. Religion in Medieval Society. Essays in Honor of Lester K. Little* (Ithaca, New York: Cornell University Press, 2000).

58 Caroline Walker Bynum, 'The female body and religious practice in the later Middle Ages', in her *Fragmentation and Redemption: Essays on Gender and the Human Body in Medieval Religion* (New York: Zone, 1992), pp. 181–238 (pp. 194–5).

59 Walker Bynum, 'The mysticism and asceticism of medieval women: some comments on the typologies of Max Weber and Ernst Troeltsch', in her *Fragmentation and Redemption: Essays on Gender and the Human Body in Medieval Religion* (New York: Zone, 1992), pp. 53–78 (p. 57).

60 Walker Bynum, 'The female body and religious practice', p. 186.

61 See Rudolph M. Bell, *Holy Anorexia* (Chicago and London: University of Chicago Press, 1985), especially pp. 54–83.

62 Walker Bynum, 'The body of Christ in the later Middle Ages: a reply to Leo Steinberg', in her *Fragmentation and Redemption: Essays on Gender and the Human Body in Medieval Religion* (New York: Zone, 1992), pp. 79–118 (p. 116), and Walker Bynum, 'The female body and religious practice', p. 222.

63 Sandi J. Hubnik, '(Re)constructing the medieval recluse: performative acts of virginity and the writings of Julian of Norwich', *The Historian*, 67, 1 (2005), 43–61 (49).

64 See Elizabeth A. Clark's 'Sane insanity: women and asceticism in late ancient Christianity', *Medieval Encounters: Jewish, Christian and Muslim Culture in Confluence and Dialogue*, 3 (1997), 211–30.

65 Otter, pp. 74–7.

66 Otter, p. 74.

67 'forty-six winters and summers alone under the open sky … Her food was abstinence … She crushed the head of the serpent', triumphing over 'the one who has vanquished Eve' (Otter, p. 89).

68 'Crosses, racks, lances, swords, grates, fires, hooks, whips, lead weights, scorpions, wild beasts' (Otter, p. 54).

69 Otter, p. 74.

70 Otter, pp. 73–4.

71 'We do not call someone a martyr unless he has suffered persecution; but one who lives in a martyr-like way partakes in martyrdom' (Otter, p. 121).

72 Amy Hollywood, *The Soul as Virgin Wife: Mechthild of Magdeburg, Marguerite Porete, and Meister Eckhart* (Notre Dame, Ind.: University of Notre Dame Press, 1995), p. 28.

[73] Otter, p. 72.
[74] 'as the Lord inspires you … follow them' (Otter, p. 73).
[75] For online Latin editions of James of Vitry and Thomas of Cantimpré's *vitae* of these women, see *http://www.peregrina.com/matrologia_latina/matrologia_latina.html* (7 September 2011). Translations include, Margot King (ed. and trans.), *The Life of Marie d'Oignies by Jacques de Vitry* (Toronto: Peregrina, 1986); *eadem* (ed. and trans.), *The Life of Christina Mirabilis, by Thomas de Cantimpré* (2nd edn; Toronto: Peregrina, 1999), and *eadem* (ed. and trans.), *The Life of Lutgard of Aywières, by Thomas de Cantimpré* (Toronto: Peregrina, 1987).
        Critical studies include, Louise Nelstrop, Kevin J. Magill and Bradley B. Onishi, *Christian Mysticism* (London: Ashgate, 2009), especially pp. 144, 148 and 170; Andrea Janelle Dickens, *The Female Mystic: Great Women Thinkers of the Middle Ages* (London: I. B. Tauris & Co., 2009), especially, pp. 39–55; John Wayland Coakley, 'James of Vitry and the other world of Mary of Oignies', in his *Women, Men, and Spiritual Power: Female Saints and their Male Collaborators* (New York and Chichester: Columbia University Press, 2006), pp. 68–88; Walter Simons, 'Reading a saint's body: rapture and bodily movement in the *vitae* of thirteenth-century Beguines', in Sarah Kay and Miri Rubin (eds), *Framing Medieval Bodies* (Manchester: Manchester University Press, 1994), pp. 10–23; J. Kowalczewski, 'Thirteenth-century asceticism: Marie d'Oignies and Lutgard of Awyières as active and passive ascetics', *Vox Benedictina: Women and Monastic Spirituality*, 3 (1986), 21–51, and Brenda M. Bolton, '*Vitae Matrum*: a further aspect of the Frauenfrage', in Derek Baker and Rosalind M. T. Hill (eds), *Medieval Women* (Oxford: Blackwell, 1978), pp. 253–73.
[76] On her corpse see section CIX of Mary's *vita* at, *http://www.peregrina.com/matrologia_latina/Marie_L1.html* (accessed 7 September 2011). Translated in King, *The Life of Marie d'Oignies*, p. 131.
[77] See section XXII of Mary's *vita* at, *http://www.peregrina.com/matrologia_latina/Marie_L1.html*. Translated as: 'From the fervour of her spirit and as if inebriated she began to loathe her flesh … she needlessly cut out a large piece of her flesh with a knife' (King, *The Life of Marie d'Oignies*, p. 54).
[78] See section XI of Christina's *vita* at, *http://www.peregrina.com/matrologia_latina/Christina_L.html* (accessed 7 September 2011). Translated in King, *The Life of Christina Mirabilis*, pp. 15–16.
[79] 'cleansed and lightened after forty days of fasting' and 'weighed down by earthly desires' (Otter, p. 70).
[80] 'completely abstained from bread and wine' (Otter, p. 72).
[81] 'bread made with urine' and 'from her fifteenth to her fiftieth year never ate or drank anything except on Sundays and Thursdays, and then her food was peas or beans left standing for about two weeks after cooking' (Otter, p. 72).
[82] Otter, p. 78.
[83] Clay, *Hermits and Anchorites*, pp. 4–5.
[84] Lawrence, *Medieval Monasticism*, pp. 128–9. See also Ludo J. R. Milis, *Angelic Monks and Earthly Men: Monasticism and its Meaning to Medieval Society* (Woodbridge: Boydell and Brewer, 1992).
[85] Constable, *Attitudes towards Self-inflicted Suffering*, p. 15.
[86] Lawrence, *Medieval Monasticism*, p. 155.
[87] Lateran IV also directed Christians to regular confession and penance. See Norman P. Tanner's translation of Giuseppe Alberigo's edition: Tanner (ed.), *Decrees of the Ecumenical Councils*, vol. 1, Nicaea I to Lateran IV (Washington and London: Georgetown University Press, 1990). See also David L. d'Avray, *The Preaching of the Friars: Sermons Diffused from Paris before 1300* (Oxford: Clarendon Press, 1985), and Jessalynn Bird, 'The religious's role in a post-Lateran world: James of Vitry's *Sermones ad Status* and *Historia Occidentalis*', in Carolyn A. Muessig (ed.), *Medieval Monastic Preaching* (Leiden: E. J. Brill, 1998), pp. 209–29.
[88] Christopher Daniell, *From Norman Conquest to Magna Carta: England, 1066–1215* (London and New York: Routledge, 2005), p. 144.

89   See Lawrence, *Medieval Monasticism*, especially pp. 98–103.

90   Lawrence, *Medieval Monasticism*, p. 178.

91   Richard W. Southern, *The Middle Ages*, The Pelican History of the Church, 10 vols (London, New York, Victoria, Ontario and Auckland: Penguin, 1970), vol. 2, p. 252.

92   David Knowles, *The Monastic Order in England: A History of its Developments from the Times of St Dunstan to the Fourth Lateran Council, 940–1216* (Cambridge: Cambridge University Press, 1963), p. 689.

93   'those who are nothing without their creator's gift should not attribute anything to their own powers' (Otter, p. 115).

94   'insane', 'condemn chastity, abstinence, keeping vigils' (Otter, p. 97).

95   'Our struggle is not against flesh and blood ... but against ... princes and powers' (Otter, p. 63).

96   'seemed to go to excess ... With arms such as these he won a glorious triumph' (MacPherson, p. 70).

97   'I do not say this in disparagement of discretion, the mother and nurse of all virtues ... But we often use discretion as a pretext to disguise the pursuit of pleasure' (MacPherson, p. 70).

98   'True discretion is to put the soul before the body and where both are threatened ... to neglect the body for the sake of the soul' (MacPherson, p. 70).

99   'homicide and suicide' (Millett, p. 77).

100 'all the physical pain and hardship we suffer ... is to be valued ... for this reason, that God looks towards it sooner with his grace, and purifies the heart' (Millett, p. 145).

101 'Although the flesh is our enemy, we are told that we should support it. We can make it suffer, as it very often deserves, but not destroy it completely; because however weak it may be, it is still so coupled and so closely linked to our precious soul, God's own image, that we might easily kill the one along with the other' (Millett, p. 55).

102 Millett translates this as 'A woman may perhaps wear drawers of haircloth tightly fastened ... but a mild and gentle heart is always best. I would rather have you bear a harsh word well than a harsh hair-shirt' (Millett, p. 159), but White's translation suggests the real delight with which some hypocrites relish ascetical acts while neglecting real Christian virtue (the true purpose of asceticism): 'Some women are ready enough to wear breeches of haircloth ... tightly laced ... I would rather you bore a harsh remark well than a harsh hairshirt' (Hugh White (trans.), *Ancrene Wisse: Guide for Anchoresses* (London, New York, Victoria, Ontario and Auckland: Penguin, 1993), p. 194).

103 'Anything, however, can be overdone; moderation is always best' (Millett, p. 109).

104 See George Lawless, *Augustine of Hippo and his Monastic Rule* (1987; Oxford: Clarendon Press, 1991) for a parallel text and translation of the Augustinian Rule. The translation of this Rule will hereafter be cited as '(Lawless, *Augustine of Hippo* and page number)'.

       The rule has generated great debate. Not all scholars think that the feminine version was the original text. Some, notably L. Verheijen, think that the masculine version was written first. See Thomas F. Martin, *Our Restless Heart: The Augustinian Tradition* (London: Darton, Longman & Todd, 2003), pp. 57–9. Lawless contextualizes Augustine's Rule and confronts key contentions about its authorship, audience and dating. See particularly pp. 135–48, 'Addressed to men, to women, or to both?'

105 Taken from *Regula Sancti Augustini*, online at, *http://www.thelatinlibrary.com/augustine/reg. shtml* (accessed 7 September 2011). Translated as: 'To the extent that your health allows, subdue your flesh by fasting and abstinence from food and drink. If anyone is unable to fast, let him at least take no food between meals, unless he is sick' (Lawless, *Augustine of Hippo*, pp. 84–5).

106 Lawrence, *Medieval Monasticism*, p. 48.

107 See Joseph A. Gribbin, *The Premonstratensian Order in Late Medieval England* (Woodbridge: Boydell and Brewer, 2001), and C. H. Lawrence, *The Friars: The Impact of the Early Mendicant Movement on Western Society* (London and New York: Longman, 1994), especially pp. 26–42, 65–88.

108 See Glyn Coppack and Mick Aston, *Christ's Poor Men: The Carthusians in England* (Stroud: Tempus, 2002), especially pp. 11–24; D. D. Martin (ed. and trans.), *Carthusian Spirituality: The*

Writings of Hugh of Balma and Guigo de Ponte (New York and Mahwah: Paulist Press, 1997); Robin B. Lockhart, *Halfway to Heaven: The Hidden Life of the Sublime Carthusians* (New York: The Vanguard Press, 1985), and E. M. Thompson, *The Carthusian Order in England* (London and New York: SPCK, 1930).

[109] Jessica Brantley, *Reading in the Wilderness: Private Devotion and Public Performance in Late Medieval England* (Chicago and London: University of Chicago Press, 2007), p. 43.

[110] 'In this manere by þe grace of God mai thei chaunge her clepynge from evyl in-to good, from þe wrong in-to ry3t, and fro vices into vertues' (*Myrour*, p. 5).

[111] 'þe armes of spiritual kny3thod' (*Myrour*, p. 11); 'labourynge and travaylynge in orisons, wakynges, fastynges, and … oþir obseruaunces' (*Myrour*, p. 12).

[112] 'contryt and wel consciencyd' (*Myrour*, p. 4).

[113] Tarjei Park, 'Reflecting Christ: the role of the flesh in Walter Hilton and Julian of Norwich', in Marion Glasscoe (ed.), *The Medieval Mystical Tradition in England V: Papers Read at Dartington Hall, July 1992* (Exeter: Exeter University Press, 1992), pp. 17–37 (p. 18).

[114] Park, 'Reflecting Christ', p. 23.

[115] 'aftir þe doom ant arbitrement of discrecion chastise ant nursche 3oure body in diuerse tymes, þat it be soget on þat o side to þe commaundement of 3oure spirites ant suffisaunt on þat oþir parte to performe ant fulfille þe labour enioyned to þe body' (*Myrour*, p. 11).

[116] On this later medieval shift in attitudes towards the body, see Tim Thornton, *Social Attitudes and Political Structures in the Fifteenth Century* (Stroud: Alan Sutton, 2001), and Miri Rubin, 'The body, whole and vulnerable, in fifteenth-century England', in B. A. Hanawalt and D. Wallace (eds), *Bodies and Disciplines: Intersections of Literature and History in Fifteenth-century England* (Minneapolis and London: University of Minnesota Press, 1996), pp. 19–28.

[117] Constable, *Attitudes towards Self-inflicted Suffering*, p. 15.

[118] Piero Camporesi, *Juice of Life: The Symbolic and Magic Significance of Blood*, trans. R. R. Barr (1995; New York: Continuum, 1998), p. 58.

[119] Camporesi, *Juice of Life*, p. 58. See also Bettina Bildhauer, *Medieval Blood* (Cardiff: University of Wales Press, 2005).

[120] Maiju Lehmijoki Gardner, *Dominican Penitent Women* (New York and Mahwah: Paulist Press, 2005), p. 260.

[121] Some of the hagiographical ascetical examples cited in this paragraph are drawn from accounts in Richard Kieckhefer's *Unquiet Souls: Fourteenth Century Saints and their Religious Milieu* (Chicago and London: University of Chicago Press, 1984). See especially pp. 124–9, 133, 142 and 148.

[122] On this see Brenda M. Bolton, 'Via ascetica: a Papal quandary', in W. J. Shields (ed.), *Monks, Hermits and the Ascetic Tradition*, Studies in Church History, 22 (Oxford: Blackwell, 1985), pp. 161–91 (p. 165).

[123] Peter Biller, '*Multum ieiunantes et se castigantes*: medieval Waldensian asceticism', in *Monks, Hermits and the Ascetic Tradition*, Studies in Church History, 22 (Oxford: Blackwell, 1994), pp. 215–28 (p. 224).

[124] Walker Bynum, 'The female body and religious practice', p. 196.

[125] See André Vauchez, *Sainthood in the Later Middle Ages*, trans. J. Birrell (Cambridge: Cambridge University Press, 1997), especially pp. 387–412, and Esther Cohen, *The Modulated Scream: Pain in Late Medieval Culture* (Chicago and London: University of Chicago Press, 2010), especially pp. 25–7.

[126] Kieckhefer, *Unquiet Souls*, pp. 148–9.

[127] 'despair … [to] lose hope and belief in being saved' (Millett, p. 3).

[128] Kieckhefer, *Unquiet Souls*, p. 142.

[129] On this see Constable, 'Moderation and restraint', p. 322.

[130] Caesarius of Heisterbach, *The Dialogue on Miracles*, trans. Henry von Essen Scott and Charles Cooke Swinton Bland, 2 vols (London: Routledge, 1929), vol. 1, p. 242.

[131] Such examples can arguably be read as the forerunners of modern notions of self-harm. Medieval society is being encouraged to reject such behaviour.

132 Heisterbach, *Dialogue*, vol. 2, p. 318.
133 Emphasis mine.
134 The earlier passage's brutal instruments are now simply: 'dyuerse temptacions', the purificatory fire, 'tribulacion' and the water, 'compunccyon' (*DII*, MS Bodley 423, p. 15).
135 Ascetical meditation is examined here, not in chapter 5, because it functions as an ascetic practice intended to have a purificatory effect.
136 On anchoritism and the Eucharist, see Kevin J. Magill, *Julian of Norwich: Mystic or Visionary?* (London and New York: Routledge, 2006), pp. 90–7.
137 'suffering, pain and physical tortures, taunts, spitting, scourging, the cross, wounds, even unto the bitter death and the rites of burial' (Otter, p. 58).
138 'with his holy blood' (Otter, p. 61).
139 'Sanctify all hours with Christ's suffering. In the middle of the night adore him captured and incarcerated, in the morning … flagellated' (Otter, p. 99).
140 'the five wounds that redeemed our five senses' (Otter, p. 140).
141 Otter, p. 61.
142 See Richard W. Southern, *Medieval Humanism and Other Studies* (Oxford: Blackwell, 1970), especially pp. 29–60 (p. 37).
143 Phyllis G. Jestice, 'A new fashion in imitating Christ: changing spiritual perspectives around the year 1000', in Michael Frassetto (ed.), *The Year 1000: Religious and Social Response to the Turning of the First Millennium* (Basingstoke and New York: Palgrave Macmillan, 2002), pp. 165–86 (pp. 171, 175).
144 'Look how he extends his affectionate arms on the cross, inviting us to come to him with his redeeming kisses' (Otter, p. 136).
145 'He who sits above the cherubim, can also be held as a baby in the arms and the lap of those who desire him' (Otter, p. 136).
146 'I let my speech flow forth uncensored. For love acts not so much … measuredly so much as affectively' (Otter, p. 34).
147 Otter, p. 79.
148 'not with a cold sense … but set ablaze by burning love' (Otter, p. 24).
149 'our mind catches on fire and wishes it were already there' (Otter, p. 71).
150 'In love and contemplation assume the inner strength of eternal joy' (Otter, p. 52).
151 MacPherson, pp. 90–1.
152 'I know you can bear it no longer, that you will not be able to look on while his most sweet back is torn with whips, his face struck, his majestic head crowned with thorns' (MacPherson, p. 89).
153 'Above all other thoughts, in all your sufferings always reflect devoutedly on God's sufferings … humiliations … insults, blows, spitting, blindfolding, crowning with thorns that pierced his head so that the streams of blood ran downwards and flowed down to the ground' (Millett, p. 71).
154 Millett translates this as 'meditate on God's cross, as far as she is able to or may, and on his cruel suffering' (Millett, p. 13), but White implies the image's graphic vehemence: 'think about God's cross as much as ever she knows how or is able, and of his terrible pain' (White, *Ancrene Wisse*, p. 18).
155 See Giles Constable, *Three Studies in Medieval Religious and Social Thought* (Cambridge: Cambridge University Press, 1995), p. 181.
156 Constable, *Three Studies*, p. 201.
157 Bildhauer, *Medieval Blood*, pp. 30–1.
158 Bildhauer, *Medieval Blood*, p. 46.
159 Constable, *Three Studies*, p. 210; John Wayland Coakley, 'Revelation and authority in Ekbert and Elisabeth of Schönau', in his *Women, Men, and Spiritual Power*, pp. 25–44, and Anne L. Clark, *Elisabeth of Schönau. A Twelfth-century Visionary* (Philadelphia: University of Pennsylvania Press, 1992).
160 For Mary's passion visions, see section LXXXVIII of King's online edition of her *vita* at, *http://www.peregrina.com/matrologia_latina/Marie_L1.html* (accessed 7 September 2011). Translated in King, *The Life of Marie d'Oignies*, pp. 112–13.

[161] 'O a hool-sum sy3te, O a suffisaunt medycyn of helþe … þat perfitly heelest alle þo þat be smerten or hurt of þe fyry serpentes of temptacion … bihold often þis passion; here seek þi socour; here aske; here knowe … stinte nat … seyinge feiþfully to Oure Lord … "Lord, purge or clense me of myn hid synnes … Hele me, Lord"' (*Myrour*, p. 35).

[162] 'was scharply beeten wyth knotty scorges, buffettid, crucified, ant with a spere and nayles ant þornes ant perside ouyral ant al forbleed, "fro þe sole of þe foot vn-to þe top of his heed", and his armes and his legges drawen out along with cordis and ropes, ant þan his holy ant blessid body peynfully ficchid to þe croys, and cruely was he reryd on hy and agayn þrowen adoun violently ant dispitously to þe erthe, þat alle þe veynes ant synwes of hys body were broken ant brosten' (*Myrour*, pp. 26–7).

[163] He 'baar a crowne of þorn on his heed, which stak scharply and sooree vn-to þe touchynge or þirlynge of [þe] brayn, and on euery part droppyd doun precious droopes of blood' (*Myrour*, p. 34).

[164] Santha Bhattacharji, 'Julian of Norwich', in Peter Brown (ed.), *Medieval English Literature and Culture, c.1350–c.1500* (2006; Oxford: Blackwell, 2007), pp. 522–36 (p. 522).

[165] See Denise N. Baker, 'Julian of Norwich and anchoritic literature', *Mystics Quarterly*, 19 (1993), 148–60 (158), where Baker notes she cannot prove or disprove this.

[166] Jonathan Hughes, *Pastors and Visionaries: Religion and Secular Life in Late Medieval Yorkshire* (Woodbridge: Boydell and Brewer, 1988), p. 225.

[167] Christopher Abbott, *Julian of Norwich: Autobiography and Theology* (Cambridge: D. S. Brewer, 1999), especially pp. 149–50, argues for Julian's conformity to the same orthodoxy as Rolle and Hilton. On Julian's doctrine of salvation, see Watson, 'Visions of inclusion: universal salvation and vernacular theology in pre-Reformation England', *Journal of Medieval and Early Modern Studies*, 27 (1997), 145–87.

[168] Julian's and the *Speculum* author's texts are so graphic, so experientially crafted, that in a sense they constitute visions in themselves. The boundaries are blurred, between the original vision Julian had, the textual reconstruction of the visionary experience that she seeks to recreate and the kind of visionary experience the *Speculum* author seeks to inculcate in his recluses. Thus this guidance writer is potentially through his guide, himself rendered, as Julian was, a visionary.

[169] *Myrour*, pp. 28–9.

[170] Julian of Norwich, *The Shewings of Julian of Norwich*, ed. G. Ronan Crampton (Kalamazoo: Medieval Institute Publications, 1994), pp. 46–7, hereafter cited as '(Julian, *Shewings* and page number)'. Also available via the *TEAMS Middle English Texts* webpage at, *http://www.lib. rochester.edu/camelot/teams/julianfr.htm* (accessed 7 September 2011). On Julian in this context, see Sarah A. Miller, 'Monstrous love: the permeable body of Christ in Julian's *Shewings*', in her *Medieval Monstrosity and the Female Body* (London: Routledge, 2010), pp. 93–135; Liz Herbert McAvoy (ed.), *A Companion to Julian of Norwich* (Cambridge: D. S. Brewer, 2008), especially pp. 1–18, and the essay in that volume by Laura Saetveit Miles, 'Space and enclosure in Julian of Norwich's *A Revelation of Love*', pp. 154–65; Edward A. Jones, 'A mystic by any other name: Julian (?) of Norwich', *Mystics Quarterly*, 33, 3–4 (2007), 1–18; Diane Watt, *Medieval Women's Writing: Works by and for Women in England, 1100–1500* (Cambridge: Polity Press, 2007), especially pp. 91–115; F. C. Bauerschmidt, 'Seeing Jesus: Julian of Norwich and the text of Christ's body', *Journal of Medieval and Early Modern Studies*, 27 (1997), 189–214; C. Abbott, 'His body, the church: Julian of Norwich's vision of Christ crucified', *Downside Review*, 115 (1997), 1–22; G. Brandolino, 'The "chiefe and principal Mene": Julian of Norwich's redefining of the body in *A Revelation of Love*', *Mystics Quarterly*, 22 (1996), 102–10; M. R. Lichtmann, '"I desyrede a bodylye syght": Julian of Norwich and the body', *Mystics Quarterly*, 17 (1991), 12–19, and Grace M. Jantzen, *Julian of Norwich: Mystic and Theologian* (London: SPCK Publishing, 1987), especially pp. 74–89.

[171] *Myrour*, p. 29.

[172] Julian, *Shewings*, pp. 64, 42.

[173] Ellen M. Ross, '"She wept and cried right loud for sorrow and for pain": suffering, the spiritual journey, and women's experience in late medieval mysticism', in Ulrike Wiethaus (ed.), *Maps of*

Flesh and Light: The Religious Experience of Medieval Women Mystics (Syracuse, New York: Syracuse University Press, 1993), pp. 45–59 (p. 50).

[174] Ross, 'She wept and cried', p. 46. See also D. Pezzini, 'The theme of the Passion in Richard Rolle and Julian of Norwich', in P. Boitani and A. Torti (eds), *Religion in the Poetry and Drama of the Late Middle Ages in England. The J.A.W. Bennett Memorial Lectures, Perugia, 1988* (Cambridge: D. S. Brewer, 1990), pp. 26–66.

[175] Jeffrey F. Hamburger, *The Visual and the Visionary: Art and Female Spirituality in Late Medieval Germany* (New York: Zone, 1998), pp. 79–80.

[176] See C. W. Marx, 'British Library, Harley MS. 1740 and popular devotion', in Nicholas Rogers (ed.), *England in the Fifteenth Century: Proceedings of the 1992 Harlaxton Symposium* (Stamford: Paul Watkins, 1994), pp. 207–22. 'Item de passione Christi bona contemplacio' is published as an appendix to this article at pp. 220–2, hereafter cited as '('Item de passione Christi' and line numbers)'.

[177] Marx, 'British Library, Harley MS. 1740', p. 217.

[178] Nicholas Love, *The Mirrour of the Blessed Lyf of Jesu Christ*, ed. James Hogg and Lawrence F. Powell, *Analecta Cartusiana*, 91 (1989). An edition of *The Abbey of the Holy Ghost* is in Norman F. Blake (ed.), *Middle English Religious Prose* (Evanston: Northwestern University Press, 1972), pp. 88–103. See also George G. Perry (ed.), *Religious Pieces in Prose and Verse*, Early English Text Society, original series, 26 (1867; rev. edn 1914; reprint 1973).

[179] See Mitchell B. Merback, 'Living image of pity: mimetic violence, peace-making and salvific spectacle in the flagellant processions of the later Middle Ages', in Debra Higgs Strickland (ed.), *Visualising the Middle Ages, Volume 1: Images of Medieval Sanctity: Essays in Honour of Gary Dickson* (Leiden: E. J. Brill, 2007), pp. 135–84; Søren Kaspersen and Ulla Haastrup (eds), *Images of Cult and Devotion: Function and Reception of Christian Images in Medieval and Post-medieval Europe* (Copenhagen: Museum Tusculanum Press, University of Copenhagen, 2004), and Robert N. Swanson, *Religion and Devotion in Europe, c.1215–c.1515* (Cambridge: Cambridge University Press, 1995), p. 221.

[180] Marx, 'British Library, Harley MS. 1740', pp. 214–15. Marx cites an unpublished Ph.D. thesis on the *arma christi* tradition: F. M. Lewis, 'Devotional images and their dissemination in English manuscripts, *c.*1350–1470', 2 vols (unpublished Ph.D. thesis, London, 1989), vol. 1, pp. 107–240.

Chapter 5

[1] 'Apart from those things which the weakness of human nature demands for its sustenance, consider and imitate … the angels so that your way of life may always be in heaven. May this contemplation be your mistress, this consideration your rule' (Fröhlich, 'Letter 230', vol. 2, p. 200).

[2] 'releases the soul from outward worries, calling it to the freedom of contemplating him' (Otter, p. 109).

[3] 'you come from the many to the one in which all things are contained' (Otter, p. 109).

[4] Mary Agnes Edsall, '"True anchoresses are called birds": asceticism as ascent and the purgative mysticism of the *Ancrene Wisse*', *Viator*, 34 (2003), 157–86 (164).

[5] MacPherson, p. 96.

[6] See Nicholas Watson, 'The methods and objectives of thirteenth-century anchoritic devotion', in Marion Glasscoe (ed.), *The Medieval Mystical Tradition in England IV. The Exeter Symposium IV: Papers Read at Dartington Hall, July 1987* (Cambridge: D. S. Brewer, 1987), pp. 132–53 (pp. 141, 146).

[7] Ann K. Warren, *Anchorites and their Patrons in Medieval England* (Berkeley, Los Angeles and London: University of California Press, 1985), p. 115. Jonathan Hughes, *Pastors and Visionaries: Religion and Secular Life in Late Medieval Yorkshire* (Woodbridge: Boydell and Brewer, 1988), pp. 83–4, paraphrases Warren's conclusions.

[8]   Mary B. Salu (ed. and trans.), *The 'Ancrene Riwle'* (*The Corpus MS.: Ancrene Wisse*) (London: Burns and Oates, 1955), pp. vii, ix–xi, where Sitwell's introduction both concedes that the author expected his recluses to be contemplatives (p. xi) and argues 'he mentions this only incidentally' (p. xii).

[9]   Geoffrey Shepherd (ed.), *'Ancrene Wisse': Parts Six and Seven* (London: Nelson and Sons, 1959; rev. edn, Exeter: Exeter University Press, 1985), p. lvvii.

[10] Warren calls the late medieval York recluse, Emma Rawghton, 'a clairvoyant', (*Anchorites and their Patrons*, p. 203), but it is problematic to conflate modern clairvoyancy with medieval visionary experience.

[11] Warren, *Anchorites and their Patrons*, pp. 100–1, 114–15, 347 and 362. Emphasis in the original.

[12] Laurie A. Finke, 'Mystical bodies and the dialogics of vision', in Ulrike Wiethaus (ed.), *Maps of Flesh and Light: The Religious Experience of Medieval Women Mystics* (Syracuse, New York: Syracuse University Press, 1993), pp. 28–44 (p. 29).

[13] Denise N. Baker, 'Mystical and devotional literature', in Peter Brown (ed.), *Medieval English Literature and Culture, c.1350–c.1500* (2006; Oxford: Blackwell, 2007), pp. 423–36 (p. 423).

[14] Marion Glasscoe, *English Medieval Mystics: Games of Faith* (London and New York: Longman, 1993), pp. 1, 3.

[15] Nicholas Watson, *Richard Rolle and the Invention of Authority* (Cambridge: Cambridge University Press, 1991), p. 1.

[16] Watson, *Richard Rolle and the Invention of Authority*, p. 1.

[17] Evelyn Underhill, *Mysticism: A Study in the Nature and Development of Spiritual Consciousness*, 2 vols (London: Methuen, 1912), vol. 1, p. 86.

[18] Underhill, *Mysticism*, vol. 1, p. 86.

[19] Cuthbert Butler, *Western Mysticism: The Teaching of SS Augustine, Gregory and Bernard on Contemplation and the Contemplative Life* (1922; London: Arrow Books, 1960), p. 3, and Rosalyn Voaden, *God's Words, Women's Voices: The Discernment of Spirits in the Writing of Late Medieval Women Visionaries* (Woodbridge: York Medieval Press, 1999), p. 9.

[20] Voaden, *God's Words, Women's Voices*, p. 10 and p. 10, n. 9.

[21] William F. Pollard and Richard Boenig (eds), *Mysticism and Spirituality in Medieval England* (Cambridge: D. S. Brewer, 1997), p. xi.

[22] Cate Gunn, '"Efter the measse-cos, hwen the preost sacreð": when is the moment of ecstasy in *Ancrene Wisse*?', *Notes and Queries*, 246 (2001), 105–8 (106, n. 2).

[23] Butler, *Western Mysticism*, p. 4. See also Brian Stock, *Augustine the Reader: Meditation, Self-knowledge and the Ethics of Interpretation* (Cambridge, Mass. and London: Harvard University Press, 1996), and Denys Turner, *The Darkness of God: Negativity in Christian Mysticism* (Cambridge: Cambridge University Press, 1995), especially pp. 252–74.

[24] Baker, 'Mystical and devotional literature', p. 423.

[25] Hans Kurath et al. (eds), *The Middle English Dictionary* (Ann Arbor, Michigan: University of Michigan Press, 1956–2001), vol. E–F, part M.5, 'Minten-Moliene', p. 596.

[26] This entry for 1552 is from A. B. P. Hamilton's *Catechism* (1884), as cited in J. A. Simpson and E. S. C. Weiner (eds), *The Oxford English Dictionary*, 10 vols (2nd edn; Oxford, repr. 1991), vol. 10, pp. 175–6.

[27] Nicholas Watson, 'The Middle English mystics', in David Wallace (ed.), *The Cambridge History of Medieval English Literature* (Cambridge: Cambridge University Press, 1999), pp. 539–65 (p. 544).

[28] Watson, 'The Middle English mystics', p. 539. Glasscoe's *English Medieval Mystics*, conforms to Watson's paradigm in its exclusive treatment of these five authors.

[29] Watson, 'The Middle English Mystics', pp. 542–3.

[30] Karma Lochrie, 'The language of transgression: body, flesh and word in mystical discourse', in Allen J. Frantzen (ed.), *Speaking Two Languages: Traditional Disciplines and Contemporary Theory in Medieval Studies* (Albany: SUNY, 1991), pp. 115–17. Watson proposes the term 'vernacular theology' instead. See Nicholas Watson, 'Censorship and cultural change in late

medieval England: vernacular theology, the Oxford translation debate, and Arundel's Constitutions of 1409', *Speculum*, 70 (1995), 822–64. See also Cate Gunn, *'Ancrene Wisse': From Pastoral Literature to Vernacular Spirituality* (Cardiff: University of Wales Press, 2008), pp. 175–89.

[31] This chapter is sympathetic to the continuities and the changes in the guidance tradition's contemplative terminologies but not wholly bound to them. It uses the terms 'contemplate' and 'contemplation' in references to both earlier and later guidance.

[32] 'the affections are nourished by wholesome meditation' (MacPherson, p. 79), and 'Meditation will arouse the affections ... so that your tears may be bread for you day and night' (MacPherson, p. 102).

[33] On Aelred's constructions of an emergent contemplative vocabulary, see John R. Sommerfeldt, 'The rape of the soul: the vocabulary of contemplation in Aelred of Rievaulx's *Mirror of Love*, Book II', in *idem* (ed.), *Erudition at God's Service. Studies in Medieval Cistercian History*, 11 (Kalamazoo: Cistercian Studies Series, 1987), pp. 169–74.

[34] Otter, p. 98. Some activities classed as contemplative in certain contexts are not in themselves inherently contemplative any more than the production of pain is inherently ascetic. An anchorite may read, for example, without having contemplative fusion as her ultimate goal. *Ancrene Wisse*'s recommendation that the recluse gather together in her mind all her daily transgressions (*AW*, Corpus, p. 27) is a penitential act, not a contemplative one and, although the two are not necessarily mutually exclusive, the guides recognize a difference of intent between this kind of exercise and that which is contemplative.

[35] 'prayers ... and meditations on heavenly things' (Fröhlich, 'Letter 112', vol. 1, p. 270).

[36] Jennifer Potts, Lorna Stevenson and Jocelyn Wogan-Browne (eds), *Concordance to 'Ancrene Wisse': MS Corpus Christi College, Cambridge 402* (Cambridge: D. S. Brewer, 1993). See p. 493 for 'meditatiuns' and pp. 751–2 for words relating to thought.

[37] Kurath et al., *The Middle English Dictionary*, vol. 2, pp. 555–6. The *MED* also records the first vernacular usage of the term 'meditatiuns' in *Ancrene Wisse*. See *The Middle English Dictionary*, vol. 6, pp. 255–6.

[38] 'In the same way, an anchoress should fly by night towards heaven with contemplation (that is, with elevated thought) and with holy prayers, and gain food for her soul' (Millett, p. 56).

[39] Warren, *Anchorites and their Patrons*, pp. 115–20, notes 'the word "contemplative" first appears here in the fifteenth century'.

[40] 'þe contemplacion of God' and 'þe fruyt of contemplatyf lyf ... þat is to seyn ... preyere, meditacion, and redynge' (*Myrour*, p. 15).

[41] 'fly to your good lord with your whole mind' (Otter, p. 138).

[42] Jeffrey F. Hamburger, *The Visual and the Visionary: Art and Female Spirituality in Late Medieval Germany* (New York: Zone, 1998), pp. 131–2.

[43] Monika Otter, 'Entrances and exits: performing the Psalms in Goscelin's *Liber confortatorius*', *Speculum*, 83, 2 (2008), 283–302 (291). Otter here cites Mary Carruthers, *The Craft of Thought: Meditation, Rhetoric, and the Making of Images, 400–1200* (Cambridge: Cambridge University Press, 2000).

[44] 'When you wish to ... engage in any good meditation, if thoughts which you ought not to entertain irritate you, never wish to give up the good you have started ... but overcome them by despising them ... do not submit to them' (Fröhlich, 'Letter 414', vol. 3, pp. 185–6).

[45] 'be insistent, beseech him, raise your eyes to him brimming with tears and extort from him with deep sighs and unutterable groanings what you seek' (MacPherson, pp. 83–4).

[46] MacPherson, p. 83.

[47] Otter, pp. 134–5.

[48] *Myrour*, p. 23.

[49] 'without fruit' (Otter, p. 69).

[50] Michael Frassetto, 'Heretics, antichrists, and the year 1000: apocalyptic expectations in the writings of Ademar of Chabannes', in *idem* (ed.), *The Year 1000: Religious and Social Response to the Turning of the First Millennium* (Basingstoke and New York: Palgrave Macmillan, 2002), pp. 73–84 (p. 75).

51 'let eternal love enrapture you ... Always reflect on the past and the future ... from the depths of your heart ... make an aqueduct of tears which will wash and whiten your dress ... You have enough material for tears ... rejoice' (Otter, pp. 134–5).

52 'intoned the gradual psalm ... at that very moment the Archangel Gabriel entered' (Otter, p. 100).

53 'even if we do not understand what comes from our mouths, these powers who assist us do understand, and will delight in being with us at the utterance of a song' (Otter, p. 68).

54 'At the moment when she gave back her soul to heaven, the glorious virgin ... visibly appeared ... as she was praying in church ... she showed herself present as if in the flesh; and she said ... "know that in this hour I have left the prison of my body and gone over to the Lord"' (Otter, p. 46).

55 'It also happens frequently that the spirits of saints who are still in the body appear in faraway places, visibly and as if corporeally, and speak to people' (Otter, p. 46).

56 Peter Brown (ed.), *The Rise of Western Christendom: Triumph and Diversity, A.D. 200–1000* (1996; Oxford: Blackwell, 2003), p. 19.

57 'Reflect that your angels are always with you and that they examine your actions and your thoughts ... take care so to live always as if you visibly perceived them' (Fröhlich, 'Letter 230', vol. 2, p. 200).

58 Otter, p. 47.

59 Otter, pp. 137–8.

60 Jane T. Schulenburg, 'Early medieval women, prophecy, and millenial expectations', in Michael Frassetto (ed.), *The Year 1000: Religious and Social Response to the Turning of the First Millennium* (Basingstoke: Palgrave Macmillan), pp. 237–56 (p. 238).

61 Anneke B. Mulder-Bakker, *Lives of the Anchoresses: The Rise of the Urban Recluse in Medieval Europe* (Philadelphia: University of Pennsylvania Press, 2005), p. 191.

62 Stephanie Hollis, 'Strategies of emplacement and displacement: St Edith and the Wilton community in Goscelin's Legend of Edith and *Liber confortatorius*', in C. A. Lees and G. R. Overing (eds), *A Place to Believe In: Locating Medieval Landscapes* (Pennsylvania: The Pennsylvania State University Press, 2006), pp. 155–8, details the dreams and visionary appearances related to Edith's conventual cult.

63 'May you be allowed to see your saviour eternally, first only in spirit, then in the double robe of body and soul' (Otter, p. 150).

64 Millett, p. 90.

65 Mari Hughes-Edwards, '"Wrapt as if to the third heaven": gender and contemplative experience in late medieval anchoritic guidance writing', in Liz Herbert McAvoy and Mari Hughes-Edwards (eds), *Anchorites, Wombs and Tombs: Intersections of Gender and Enclosure in the Middle Ages* (Cardiff: University of Wales Press, 2005), pp. 131–41, focuses on the gendered implications of this. See also Susannah M. Chewning, 'Mysticism and the anchoritic community: "a time ... of veiled infinity"', in Diane Watt (ed.), *Medieval Women in their Communities* (Cardiff: University of Wales Press, 1997), pp. 116–37.

66 Richard Kieckhefer, *Unquiet Souls: Fourteenth Century Saints and their Religious Milieu* (Chicago and London: University of Chicago Press, 1984), p. 160. Wolfgang Riehle, *The Middle English Mystics* (London, Boston and Henley: Routledge and Kegan Paul, 1981), explores medieval attempts to articulate contemplative ineffability. See especially pp. 67–89, which surveys the metaphors and technical terms used.

67 Hadewijch of Brabant, *Hadewijch: The Complete Works*, trans. Columba Hart (New York and Mahwah: Paulist Press, 1980), p. 290.

68 Hadewijch, *Hadewijch*, p. 290.

69 Caroline Walker Bynum, *Jesus as Mother: Studies in the Spirituality of the High Middle Ages* (Berkeley, Los Angeles and London: University of California Press, 1982), p. 237.

70 Walker Bynum, '"... And woman his humanity": female imagery in the religious writing of the later Middle Ages', in her *Fragmentation and Redemption: Essays on Gender and the Human Body in Medieval Religion* (New York: Zone, 1992), pp. 151–80 (p. 168).

71   Walker Bynum, *Jesus as Mother*, pp. 208–9. See also Susanna Greer Fein, 'Maternity in Aelred of Rievaulx's letter to his sister', in J. Carmi Parsons and B. Wheeler (eds), *Medieval Mothering* (New York and London: Garland, 1996), pp. 139–55; Marsha L. Dutton, 'Christ our mother: Aelred's iconography for contemplative union', in E. Rozanne Elder (ed.), *Goad and Nail*, Studies in Medieval Cistercian History, 10 (Kalamazoo: Cistercian Studies Series, 1985), pp. 21–45.

72   Walker Bynum, 'The female body and religious practice', p. 198.

73   'his outspread arms will invite you to embrace him, his naked breasts will feed you with the milk of sweetness to console you' (MacPherson, p. 73).

74   'misleading dreams, false visions, fearful terrors' (Millett, p. 102).

75   'You should not regard any vision that you see, whether in a dream or while you are awake, as anything but a delusion' (Millett, p. 86). The angel of light reference is an allusion to 2 Cor. 11:14. Rolle and Hilton also use the image of the good angel and bad angel as a source of authentic and inauthentic vision. Rolle's 'sathenas' passage appears in diffused form in *Scale*, which reveals 'the Enemy' who 'appears in a bodily form like an angel' (*Scale I*, pp. 84–5).

76   'nothing is better for preventing useless ideas or driving out impure imaginations than the study of God's word' (MacPherson, p. 68).

77   Amy Hollywood, *Sensible Ecstasy: Mysticism, Sexual Difference, and the Demands of History* (Chicago and London: University of Chicago Press, 2002), p. 9

78   Hollywood, *Sensible Ecstasy*, p. 8.

79   David A. Salomon, '*Corpus Mysticum*: text as body/body as text', in Susannah Mary Chewning (ed.), *Intersections of Sexuality and the Divine in Medieval Culture: The Word Made Flesh* (Hampshire: Ashgate, 2005), pp. 140–55 (p. 144).

80   See J. A. McNamara, 'The rhetoric of orthodoxy: clerical authority and female innovation in the struggle with heresy', in Ulrike Wiethaus (ed.), *Maps of Flesh and Light: The Religious Experience of Medieval Women Mystics* (Syracuse, New York: Syracuse University Press, 1993), pp. 9–27 (p. 11).

81   'vysyons or reuelacions of hyd þinges' (*Myrour*, p. 16).

82   *Myrour*, p. 37.

83   'the angel of Sathenas, transfygurynge hym in-to þe angel of ly3t' and 'þe gretnesse of reuelacion … or schewynge of God' (*Myrour*, p. 38).

84   Marguerite Porete, *The Mirror of Simple Souls*, trans. Edmund Colledge, J. C. Marler and J. Grant (Notre Dame, Ind.: University of Notre Dame Press, 1999), chapter 9, details the fifteen articles upon which Margaret's censure rested. See also Suzanne Kocher, *Allegories of Love in Marguerite Porete's 'Mirror of simple souls'*, Medieval Women: Texts and Contexts, 17 (Turnout: Brepols, 2008); Nicholas Watson, 'Melting into God the English way: deification in the Middle English version of Marguerite Porete's *Mirouer des simples âmes anienties*', in Rosalyn Voaden (ed.), *Prophets Abroad: The Reception of Continental Holy Women in Late Medieval England* (Cambridge: D. S. Brewer, 1996), pp. 19–51.

85   Hamburger cautions against making contemporary value judgements about contemplative experience, arguing, in terms of vision specifically, that whether validated as authentic by others or not, it is still 'a vital record of their author's and audience's spiritual aspirations' (Hamburger, *The Visual and the Visionary*, p. 115).

86   See L. P. Wenham and C. J. Hatcher, 'The anchoress of Richmond, north Yorkshire', in *A Richmond Miscellany*, North Yorkshire County Record Office Publications, 25 (1980), 46–55.

87   Rotha Mary Clay, *The Hermits and Anchorites of England* (London: Methuen, 1914), p. 155, and Warren, *Anchorites and their Patrons*, pp. 203–6.

88   William, earl of Carysfort (ed.), *The Pageants of Richard Beauchamp, Earl of Warwick* (Oxford: Roxburghe Club, 1908); John Rous, *Rows Rol* (London: Pickering, 1845), no. 50.

89   See Diane Watt, 'Reconstructing the word: the political prophecies of Elizabeth Barton (1506–1534)', *Renaissance Quarterly*, 50 (1997), 136–63. Watt argues for Barton's place in a tradition of political visionaries including Bridget of Sweden (1303–73) and Catherine of Siena (1347–80) and argues for the importance of vision and revelation to the political systems of the day. See also Watt's 'The prophet at home: Elizabeth Barton and the influence of Bridget of Sweden and

Catherine of Siena', in *Prophets Abroad*, pp. 161–77, and E. A. Petroff, 'The visionary tradition in women's writings: dialogue and autobiography', in Elizabeth A. Petroff (ed.), *Medieval Women's Visionary Literature* (New York and Oxford: Oxford University Press, 1986), pp. 3–59.

[90] Clay, *Hermits and Anchorites*, pp. 165–6.

[91] Warren, *Anchorites and their Patrons*, pp. 120–1.

[92] Julian of Norwich, *The Shewings of Julian of Norwich*, ed. G. Roman Crampton (Kalamazoo: Medieval Institute Publications, 1994), p. 132, hereafter cited as '(Julian, *Shewings* and page number)'.

[93] Julian, *Shewings*, p. 39.

[94] Finke, 'Mystical bodies', p. 44.

[95] Julian, *Shewings*, Appendix A: 'Two passages from the Short Text', pp. 207–9 (p. 207).

[96] Kathryn Kerby-Fulton, *Books Under Suspicion: Censorship and Tolerance of Revelatory Writing in Late Medieval England* (Notre Dame, Ind.: University of Notre Dame Press, 2006), pp. 302–3.

[97] See William F. Pollard, 'Richard Rolle and the "Eye of the Heart"', in William F. Pollard and Richard Boenig (eds), *Mysticism and Spirituality in Medieval England* (Cambridge: D. S. Brewer, 1997), pp. 85–105, on later medieval constructions of the notion of spiritual 'sight'.

[98] Carl Horstmann (ed.), 'The mirror of St Edmund', in *The Minor Poems of the Vernon MS, Part 1*, Early English Text Society, original series, 98 (1892), pp. 221–51 (p. 232).

[99] See for example: Margery Kempe, *The Book of Margery Kempe*, ed. Lynn Staley (Kalamazoo: Medieval Institute Publications, 1996), p. 18, hereafter cited as '(Kempe and page number)'. Also available via the *TEAMS Middle English Texts* webpage at, *http://www.lib.rochester.edu/camelot/teams/staley.htm* (accessed 7 September 2011).

[100] Adrian J. McCarthy (ed.), *Book to a Mother* (Salzburg: Institut für Anglistik und Amerikanistik, Universität Salzburg, 1981), p. 39.

[101] Kempe, p. 18.

[102] Taken from the Latin Vulgate Bible online at, *http://www.drbo.org/lvb/chapter/54012.htm* (accessed 7 September 2011). Translated (in the Douai-Rheims translation of the Latin Vulgate online) at, *http://www.drbo.org/chapter/54012.htm* (accessed 7 September 2011) as: 'I know a man in Christ above fourteen years ago (whether in the body, I know not, or out of the body, I know not; God knoweth), such a one [was] caught up to the third heaven. And I know such a man (whether in the body, or out of the body, I know not: God knoweth), that he was caught up into paradise, and heard secret words, which it is not granted to man to utter'.

[103] 'in order to ravish us to the third stage … where the contemplative mind may rush towards the peace of its maker' (Otter, p. 39).

[104] 'will be awestruck, stupified, ravished by this inseparable light and joy … Ravished beyond herself' (Otter, p. 40).

[105] 'Tears preclude any further utterance as the voice is stifled by emotion and excess of love leaves the soul dumb, the body without feeling' (MacPherson, p. 91).

[106] 'how often he carried you away with a certain unspeakable longing for himself while you were at prayer, how often he lifted up your mind from the things of the earth and introduced it into the delights of heaven and the joys of paradise' (MacPherson, p. 96).

[107] 'how often he infused himself into your inmost being when you were on fire with love' (MacPherson, p. 96). See Thomas H. Bestul, 'Antecedents: The Anselmian and Cistercian Contributions', in William F. Pollard and Richard Boenig (eds), *Mysticism and Spirituality in Medieval England* (Cambridge: D. S. Brewer), pp. 1–20 (p. 4) and Bernard McGinn, 'Contemplation in Gregory the Great', in John C. Cavadini (ed.), *Gregory the Great: A Symposium* (Notre Dame, Ind.: University of Notre Dame Press, 1995), pp. 146–167.

[108] 'Do not let these delights of yours be interrupted by sleep or disturbed by any tumult from without' (MacPherson, p. 92).

[109] Warren, *Anchorites and their Patrons*, p. 114.

[110] Millett, p. 56.

[111] 'think of God's flesh and his precious blood, which is above the high altar, and prostrate yourselves towards it' (Millett, p. 7).

[112] 'every day he comes out and reveals himself to you physically and bodily in the Mass – changed, however, into the appearance of something else, under the form of bread, because in his own our eyes could not tolerate the dazzling vision. But he reveals himself to you in this way' (Millett, p. 100).

[113] 'After the kiss of peace in the Mass, when the priest is taking communion – there forget all the world, there be quite out of the body, there in burning love embrace your lover, who has descended from heaven into the chamber of your breast' (Millett, p. 13).

[114] 'as the priest celebrates Mass – the child of a virgin ... sometimes comes down physically to your inn, and humbly takes up his lodging in you' (Millett, p. 102).

[115] Hamburger, *The Visual and the Visionary*, p. 108. Controversy exists over the timing of this moment of ecstasy. Gunn translates the verb 'sacreð' as 'communicates' rather than 'consecrates' and argues that ecstasy comes not at this kiss but at the priest's communion, which allows the reclusive contemplative 'a vicarious reception of the host' (Gunn, '"Efter the measse-cos"', p. 107).

[116] 'the good anchoress, however high she flies, must sometimes come down to the earth of her body, eat, drink, sleep, work, hear what she needs to about earthly matters' (Millett, p. 53).

[117] 'no longer two but one flesh' (Otter, p. 110).

[118] 'Desire him, conceive him, embrace him with all your insides ... give birth to him, engender, nourish him' (Otter, p. 135).

[119] 'in ... the new covenant of his body and blood ... in the eternal bond of love, he exhorted them to remain in him as he would give himself to them' (Otter, p. 27).

[120] 'Let her never cease to ponder for whose bridal chamber she is being embellished, for whose embrace she is being prepared' (MacPherson, pp. 63–4). Aelred describes the nuptial robe of woven gold/virtues at *DII*, p. 659 (MacPherson, p. 72).

[121] Rachel Fulton, *From Judgement to Passion: Devotion to Christ and the Virgin Mary, 800–1200* (New York and Chichester: Columbia University Press, 2002), p. 309.

Both Aelred and *Ancrene Wisse* owe much to Bernardine teachings, in particular his sermons on the Song of Songs, which state: 'Exigit ergo Deus timeri ut Dominus, honorari ut pater, et ut sponsus amari' (see Jacques-Paul Migne (ed.), *Patrologiae Cursus Completus: Series Latina*, 221 vols (Paris: Migne, 1841–64), vol. 183, col. 1183). From sermon 83 (lxxxiii), this is translated as: 'He should be feared as lord, honoured as Father, but as Bridegroom loved' (Cuthbert Butler, *Western Mysticism: The Teaching of SS Augustine, Gregory and Bernard on Contemplation and the Contemplative Life* (1922; London: Arrow Books, 1960), pp. 112–13).

[122] Jenifer Sutherland, 'Amplification of the virgin: play and empowerment in Walter of Wimborne's *Marie Carmina*', in Bonnie Maclachlan and Judith Fletcher (eds), *Virginity Revisited: Configurations of the Unpossessed Body* (Toronto, Buffalo and London: University of Toronto Press, 2007), pp. 128–48 (p. 132).

[123] Cited in Walker Bynum, *Jesus as Mother*, p. 188.

[124] Cited in Walker Bynum, *Jesus as Mother*, p. 240.

[125] See section LXXXVII of King's online edition of Mary's *vita* at, *http://www.peregrina.com/matrologia_latina/Marie_L1.html* (accessed 7 September 2011). Translated as: 'When she ate milk and honey from the lips of the bridegroom' (Margot King (ed. and trans.), *The Life of Marie d'Oignies by Jacques de Vitry* (Toronto: Peregrina, 1986), p. 111).

[126] Kieckhefer, *Unquiet Souls*, p. 158.

[127] Julian, *Shewings*, p. 124. On Julian's maternal imagery, see Kevin J. Magill, *Julian of Norwich: Mystic or Visionary?* (London and New York: Routledge, 2006), pp. 92, 103; Elisabeth M. Dutton, *Julian of Norwich: the Influence of Late-Medieval Devotional Compilations* (Cambridge: D. S. Brewer, 2008), pp. 129, 159; Liz Herbert McAvoy, '"The Moder's service": motherhood as matrix in Julian of Norwich', *Mystics Quarterly*, 24 (1998), 181–97. On *Ancrene Wisse* and Julian, see Elizabeth Robertson, 'Medieval medical views of women and female spirituality in the *Ancrene Wisse* and Julian of Norwich's *Showings*', in Linda Lomperis and Sarah Stanbury (eds), *Feminist Approaches to the Body in Medieval Literature* (Philadelphia: University of Pennsylvania Press, 1993), pp. 142–67.

[128] Julian, *Shewings*, p. 120.

[129] Rudolph M. Bell, *Holy Anorexia* (Chicago and London: University of Chicago Press, 1985), p. 109.

[130] Cited in Hamburger, *The Visual and the Visionary*, p. 124.

[131] Cited in Hamburger, *The Visual and the Visionary*, p. 127, and see also Walter Simons, 'Reading a saint's body: rapture and bodily movement in the *vitae* of thirteenth-century Beguines', in Sarah Kay and Miri Rubin (eds), *Framing Medieval Bodies* (Manchester: Manchester University Press, 1994), pp. 10–23 (p. 17).

[132] Hadewijch, *Hadewijch*, p. 281.

[133] Linda Georgianna, *The Solitary Self: Individuality in the 'Ancrene Wisse'* (Cambridge, Mass. and London: Harvard University Press, 1981), p. 73, and Watson, 'Methods and objectives', p. 134.

[134] 'a rauisschynge, whan þe herte or þe þou3t considereth nat þe sensible þinges standinge or beynge oboute' (*Myrour*, p. 17).

[135] Marta Powell Harley (ed.), *A Revelation of Purgatory by an Unknown, Fifteenth-century Woman Visionary* (Lewiston, New York: Edwin Mellen Press, 1985), p. 59.

[136] 'As Seynt Pouel, þat was "rauysschid in-to þe þrydde heuene," he wyste nat wheþir he was "with-ine his body" or "with-oute his body"' (*Myrour*, p. 17), and 'I think that men like these have such consolation ... not being wrapt out of their bodies but actually in their bodies'.

[137] 'holy Aelred says ... while certain people were praying a wonderful surpassing sweetness extinguished all worldly thoughts and all carnal affections. And soon, wrapt as if to the third heaven along with St Paul, infused with incomprehensible light and by a certain beatific vision of God, even though it is imperfect, they are so inebriated with an excellent and unspeakable joy that cannot be told, that they have to be struck by others and only with difficulty are they able to return to the bodily senses which they have left behind them'.

[138] 'you will sing ... "Let him kiss me with the kiss of his mouth" saying, amorous in a spiritual fashion, to Christ your bridegroom from the bottom of your heart ... "drag me, we will run after you towards the sweetness of your perfumes"'.

[139] Robert Steele (ed.), *Lydgate and Burgh's Secrees of Old Philisoffres*, Early English Text Society, extra series, 66 (1894; reprint 1973), p. 4.

[140] Ad Putter, 'Walter Hilton's *Scale of Perfection* and *The Cloud of Unknowing*', in A. S. G. Edwards (ed.), *A Companion to Middle English Prose* (Cambridge: D. S. Brewer, 2004), pp. 33–51 (p. 37).

[141] Millett, p. 134.

[142] 'folk þat desiren to ascende and clymbe to þe heyest degre of perfeccion' (*Myrour*, p. 8).

[143] George G. Perry (ed.), *Religious Pieces in Prose and Verse*, Early English Text Society, original series, 26 (1867; rev. edn 1914; reprint 1973), p. 53.

[144] Kieckhefer, *Unquiet Souls*, p. 155.

[145] Emphasis mine.

[146] Otter, p. 40.

[147] Julian, *Shewings*, p. 73.

[148] Denise N. Baker, 'Julian of Norwich and anchoritic literature', *Mystics Quarterly*, 19 (1993), 148–60 (155).

[149] Julian, *Shewings*, pp. 115–16.

[150] Julian, *Shewings*, p. 62.

[151] Julian, *Shewings*, p. 132.

[152] Kieckhefer, *Unquiet Souls*, p. 153.

[153] Walker Bynum, *Jesus as Mother*, p. 107, notes the 'many separate "callings" or "lives" ... possible in the [twelfth-century] church'. See also Sarah Spence, *Texts and the Self in the Twelfth Century* (Cambridge: Cambridge University Press, 1996), pp. 1–19; Constable's essays 'Past and present in the eleventh and twelfth centuries. Perceptions of time and change' and 'The ideal of inner solitude in the twelfth century', in his *Culture and Spirituality in Medieval Europe* (Aldershot: Variorum, 1996), pp. 135–70 and pp. 27–34 respectively, and Bernard Hamilton, 'Ideals of holiness: crusaders, contemplatives, and mendicants', *International History Review*, 17 (1995), 693–712.

[154] Millett, pp. 64–7. 'She did not walk about … was … not distracted by household worries … This is your portion … Dead and buried to the world' (MacPherson, p. 75).

[155] 'Mary's part is silence and peace from all the noise of the world, so that nothing can prevent her from hearing God's voice' (Millett, p. 156).

[156] Taken from Luke 10: 38–42, in the Latin Vulgate Bible online at, *http://www.drbo.org/lvb/chapter/49010.htm* (accessed 7 September 2011). Translated (in the Douai-Rheims translation of the Latin Vulgate online) at, *http://www.drbo.org/chapter/49010.htm* (accessed 7 September 2011), as: 'Now it came to pass as they went, that he entered into a certain town: and a certain woman named Martha, received him into her house. And she had a sister called Mary, who sitting also at the Lord's feet, heard his word. But Martha was busy about much serving. Who stood and said: Lord, hast thou no care that my sister hath left me alone to serve? speak to her therefore, that she help me. And the Lord answering, said to her: Martha, Martha, thou art careful, and art troubled about many things: But one thing is necessary. Mary hath chosen the best part, which shall not be taken away from her'.

[157] Giles Constable, *Three Studies in Medieval Religious and Social Thought* (Cambridge: Cambridge University Press, 1995), p. 5.

[158] 'She just sat at Jesus' feet and listened … This is your portion dearly beloved. Dead and buried to the world, you should be deaf to all that belongs to the world and unable to speak of it … Let Martha carry out her part; although it is admitted to be good, Mary's is declared better' (MacPherson, pp. 75–6).

[159] Constable, *Three Studies*, p. 5, argues that Jesus' comment that 'one or a few things were necessary … may even have applied to the number of dishes served by Martha', and that Jesus' judgement that Mary chose 'the best part' may be glossed instead as 'the good part', without implying superiority.

[160] See Constable, *Three Studies*, pp. 17–22, 30–1, and D. Jones, 'The tension in the psyche of the man of prayer between active and contemplative life', *Analecta Cartusiana*, 130 (1995), 15–39; Bestul, 'Antecedents: the Anselmian and Cistercian contributions', p. 4. Anne Savage notes Anselmian influence upon Aelred in 'The solitary heroine: aspects of meditation and mysticism in *Ancrene Wisse*, the Katherine Group, and the Wooing Group', in William F. Pollard and Richard Boenig (eds), *Mysticism and Spirituality in Medieval England* (Cambridge: D. S. Brewer, 1997), pp. 63–85 (p. 77).

[161] 'bodily labour … lettiþ ant sleutheeþ þe werkes ant deedes of contemplacion' (*Myrour*, p. 17), and 'only to … those who have time for God and labour greatly in secret prayers and holy meditations'.

[162] Hughes, *Pastors and Visionaries*, p. 78.

[163] Watson cautions that although works such as *Form* were indeed applicable to the laity, it may have been 'several decades' before his writings circulated fully among them, 'The Middle English mystics', pp. 548–9.

[164] On non-anchoritic female spiritual alternatives, see Brenda M. Bolton, 'Mulieres Sanctae', in Susan Mosher Stuard (ed.), *Women in Medieval Society* (1976; Philadelphia: University of Pennsylvania Press, 1993), pp. 141–58.

[165] See Jennifer Ward, *Women of the English Nobility and Gentry, 1066–1500* (Manchester: Manchester University Press, 1995).

[166] See Walter Simons, *Cities of Ladies: Beguine Communities in the Medieval Low Countries, 1200–1565* (Philadelphia: University of Pennsylvania Press, 2001); Penelope Galloway, '"Discreet and devout maidens": women's involvement in Beguine communities in northern France, 1200–1500', in Diane Watt (ed.), *Medieval Women in their Communities* (Cardiff: University of Wales Press, 1997), pp. 92–115, and Ernest W. McDonnell, *The Beguines and Beghards in Medieval Culture with Special Emphasis Upon the Belgian Scene* (New Brunswick, NJ: Rutgers University Press, 1954).

[167] See C. H. Lawrence, *The Friars: The Impact of the Early Mendicant Movement on Western Society* (London and New York: Longman, 1994), especially pp. 28–42.

[168] Watson, 'The Middle English mystics', p. 356.

[169]   'Walter Hilton's epistle on a mixed life', in Carl Horstmann (ed.), *Yorkshire Writers: Richard Rolle, an English Father of the Church, and his Followers*, 2 vols (London: Swan Sonnenschein, 1895–6; repr. Woodbridge: York Medieval Press, 1999), vol. 1, p. 268.

[170]   On St Bridget, see Julia Bolton Holloway (ed.), *Saint Bride and her Book: Birgitta of Sweden's 'Revelations'* (1997; Cambridge: D. S. Brewer, 2000), including her interpretative essay at pp. 111–37; H. Redpath, *God's Ambassadress: St Bridget of Sweden* (Milwaukee: Bruce Publishing Co., 1947); Bridget Morris, *St Birgitta of Sweden* (Woodbridge: Boydell and Brewer, 1999); Ingvar Fogelqvist, *Apostasy and Reform in the Revelations of St Birgitta* (Stockholm: Almquist and Wiksells International, 1993).

[171]   Horstmann, 'Walter Hilton's epistle on a mixed life', p. 267.

[172]   See Joseph E. Milosh, *'The Scale of Perfection' and the English Mystical Tradition* (Madison, Milwaukee and London: University of Wisconsin, 1966), especially chapter 2, 'The three Christian lives and levels of contemplation', on Hilton's perspective on each life and of his influence upon emergent thinking.

[173]   Walker Bynum, 'The mysticism and asceticism of medieval women: some comments on the typologies of Max Weber and Ernst Troeltsch', in her *Fragmentation and Redemption: Essays on Gender and the Human Body in Medieval Religion* (New York: Zone, 1992), pp. 53–78 (p. 69).

[174]   Kempe, p. 18.

[175]   Ruth Evans, 'The *Book of Margery Kempe*', in Peter Brown (ed.), *Medieval English Literature and Culture in Medieval England* (Cambridge: D. S. Brewer, 1997), pp. 507–21 (pp. 507–8).

[176]   Evans, 'The *Book of Margery Kempe*', p. 509, citing Samuel Fanous, 'Measuring the pilgrim's progress: internal emphases in *The Book of Margery Kempe*', in Denis Renevey and Christiania Whitehead (eds), *Writing Religious Women: Female Spiritual and Textual Practices in Late Medieval England* (Cardiff: University of Wales Press, 2000), pp. 157–76 (p. 171).

[177]   Kempe, p. 18.

[178]   Kempe, p. 54.

[179]   Kempe, p. 54.

[180]   Nicholas Watson and Jacqueline Jenkins (eds), *The Writings of Julian of Norwich: A Vision Showed to a Devout Woman and a Revelation of Love* (Turnout: Brepols, 2006), Introduction, p. 6.

[181]   Kempe, p. 120.

[182]   Liz Herbert McAvoy, *Authority and the Female Body in the Writings of Julian of Norwich and Margery Kempe* (Cambridge: D. S. Brewer, 2004), p. 215.

[183]   See Mary C. Erler, 'A London anchorite, Simon Appulby: his *Fruyte of Redempcyon* and its milieu', *Viator: Medieval and Renaissance Studies*, 29 (1998), 227–39.

[184]   Michael G. Sargent (ed.), *Nicholas Love's Mirror of the Blessed Life of Jesus Christ* (New York and London: Garland, 1992).

[185]   James Walsh (ed.), *The Cloud of Unknowing* (New York and Mahwah: Paulist Press, 1981), see especially the *Cloud* author's 'Prologue' at pp. 101–3. See R. Tixier, '"þis louely blinde werk": contemplation in the *Cloud of Unknowing* and related treatises', in William F. Pollard and Richard Boenig (eds), *Mysticism and Spirituality in Medieval England* (Cambridge: D. S. Brewer, 1997), pp. 107–37, and K. Greenspan, 'Stripped for contemplation', *Studia Mystica*, 1 (1995), 72–81.

[186]   *The Cloud of Unknowing*, pp. 164–5.

[187]   *Myrour*, p. 4. Such conflation was commonplace, Constable argues, 'until it was called into question by Lefèvre d'Etaples in the early sixteenth century' (Constable, *Three Studies*, p. 7). On the contemplative significance of the Magdalen, see Susan Haskins, *Mary Magdalen: Myth and Metaphor* (London: Riverhead, 1993), especially pp. 177–91, which argues that 'Like her sisters in prostitution, the medieval female mystic was often a product of the newly urbanised society' (p. 179), and that the example of the Magdalen as a working, urban woman who repented her life and dedicated herself to that penitence spoke to women with similar backgrounds such as Catherine of Siena, Angela of Foligno and Margaret of Cortona. See also Anneke B. Mulder-Bakker, 'Was Mary Magdalen a Magdalen?', in R. I. A. Nip et al. (eds), *Media Latinitas:*

A Collection of Essays to Mark the Occasion of the Retirement of L. J. Engels (Turnhout: Brepols, 1996), pp. 269–74.

[188] Rolle's articulation of his place within the active/contemplative debate comes at the close, not the beginning of his rule which prevents the reader from understanding exactly what he means by the two states until the close of his treatise. Hilton does the reverse.

[189] On the significance of both lives to Hilton, see John P. H. Clark, 'Action and contemplation in Walter Hilton', *Downside Review*, 97 (1979), 258–74. See especially 265–6 which argues that the ideal Christian life at this time contained elements of both. See also Stephen Medcalf, 'Medieval psychology and medieval mystics', in Marion Glasscoe (ed.), *The Medieval Mystical Tradition in England: Papers Read at the Exeter Symposium, July 1980* (Exeter: Exeter University Press, 1980), pp. 120–55, for a discussion of the effects of contemplative introspection on the medieval psyche.

[190] 'a craftsman can never complete his arduous and subtle work'.

[191] Giles Constable, *Attitudes towards Self-inflicted Suffering in the Middle Ages* (Brookline, Mass.: Hellenic College Press, 1982), p. 15. See also Patricia J. F. Rosof, 'The anchoress in the twelfth and thirteenth centuries', in John A. Nichols and Lillian Thomas Shank (eds), *Medieval Religious Women, Vol. Two: Peaceweavers* (Kalamazoo: Cistercian Studies Series, 1987), pp. 123–45 (pp. 135–6).

[192] Diane Watt, *Secretaries of God: Women Prophets in Late Medieval and Early Modern England* (Cambridge: D. S. Brewer, 1997), p. 36.

[193] Elizabeth Robertson, *Early English Devotional Prose and the Female Audience* (Knoxville: University of Tennessee Press, 1990), pp. 15–17.

[194] Kathleen G. Cushing, *Reform and Papacy in the Eleventh Century: Spirituality and Social Change* (Manchester: Manchester University Press, 2005), p. 29.

[195] Christopher Daniell, *From Norman Conquest to Magna Carta: England, 1066–1215* (London and New York: Routledge, 2005), p. 137.

[196] 'the enemies of Christ'; 'outright damnation' (Otter, p. 142).

[197] 'catholics against the heretics who fought civil wars' (Otter, p. 142).

[198] Otter, p. 143.

[199] Schulenburg, 'Early medieval women', p. 241.

[200] Schulenburg, 'Early medieval women', p. 251.

[201] Fiona J. Griffiths, '"Men's duty to provide for women's needs": Abelard, Heloise, and their negotiation of the *cura monialium*', in Constance Hoffman Berman (ed.), *Medieval Religion: New Approaches* (New York and London: Routledge, 2005), pp. 209–315 (p. 292), and Richard W. Southern, *Western Society and the Church in the Middle Ages* (London, New York, Victoria, Ontario and Auckland: Penguin, 1970), p. 310.

[202] Schulenburg, 'Early medieval women', pp. 250, 239–40.

[203] Schulenburg, 'Early medieval women', p. 249.

[204] 'You must be your own priest before God, sacrificing yourself, and the fire of divine love will always burn in your heart' (Otter, p. 95).

[205] Otter, p. 76.

[206] Otter, pp. 31–2.

[207] 'Sharpen your dulled mind with the whetstone of books' (Otter, p. 94); 'Therefore I ... implore you ... raid the holy banquet of the sacred volumes with eagerness, with a virtuous sort of gluttony; that you hunger and thirst for it as the bread and fountain of life' (Otter, p. 95).

[208] Otter, p. 96.

[209] Hayward and Hollis, 'The female reader in the *Liber confortatorius*', in Stephanie Hollis (ed.), with W. R. Barnes, Rebecca Hayward, Kathleen Loncar and Michael Wright, *Writing the Wilton Women: Goscelin's Legend of Edith and Liber confortatorius*, Medieval Women Texts and Contexts, 9 (Turnhout: Brepols, 2004), pp. 385–400 (pp. 387, 385).

[210] 'the beauty of immaculate life'(Otter, p. 127); 'Behold, she who was a pit that housed seven demons, the receptacle for the seven mortal sins with all their forces, has had her demons cast out and has become the sacred vessel for the sevenfold grace' (Otter, p. 127).

[211] See *AW*, Corpus, pp. 22–4, and Millett, pp. 22–4. Otter, pp. 116, 121. This quotation is 'the Lord
       cured them, expelling the venom' of the snake (Otter, p. 121). Hayward argues that Goscelin
       'edits out' of the story of Mary of Egypt the extent to which she reputedly succumbed to sexual-
       ized transgression ('Representations of the anchoritic life', in Liz Herbert McAvoy and Mari
       Hughes-Edwards (eds), *Anchorites, Wombs and Tombs: Intersections of Gender and Enclosure
       in the Middle Ages* (Cardiff: University of Wales Press, 2005), p. 57).

[212] Sarah Maitland, 'Passionate prayer: masochistic images in women's experience', in L.
       Hurcombe (ed.), *Sex and God: Some Varieties of Women's Religious Experience* (London and
       New York: Routledge and Kegan Paul, 1987), pp. 125–40 (p. 31).

[213] Gopa Roy, '"Sharpen your mind with the whetstone of books": the female recluse as reader in
       Goscelin's *Liber confortatorius*, Aelred of Rievaulx's *De institutione inclusarum* and the
       Ancrene Wisse', in Lesley Smith and Jane H. M. Taylor (eds), *Women, the Book and the Godly:
       Selected Proceedings of the St Hilda's Conference 1993* (Cambridge: D. S. Brewer, 1995),
       pp. 113–22 (p. 120).

[214] Gunn, '*Ancrene Wisse*: a modern lay person's guide to a medieval religious text', *Magistra: A
       Journal of Women's Spirituality in History*, 8 (2002), 3–25 (12).

[215] Catherine Innes-Parker, 'Fragmentation and reconstruction: images of the female body in
       Ancrene Wisse and the Katherine Group', *Comitatus: A Journal of Medieval and Renaissance
       Studies*, 26 (1995), 27–52 (p. 31).

[216] Nicholas Watson, '"With the heat of the hungry heart": empowerment and *Ancrene Wisse*', in
       Mary C. Erler and Maryanne Kowaleski (eds), *Gendering the Master Narrative: Women and
       Power in the Middle Ages* (Ithaca and London: Cornell University Press, 2003), pp. 52–70
       (p. 55).

[217] Liz Herbert McAvoy, '"Neb ... sumdeal ilich wommon ant neddre is behinden": reading the
       monstrous in the anchoritic text', in Edward A. Jones (ed.), *The Medieval Mystical Tradition in
       England: Papers Read at Charney Manor, July 2004 [Exeter Symposium VII]* (Cambridge: D. S.
       Brewer, 2004), pp. 51–69 (p. 55).

[218] 'singularity' in a recluse who 'does not follow the community' (Millett, p. 97).

[219] 'they shall all love each other ... and what one wills, all shall will ... whatever anyone individu-
       ally wills, shall come about for himself and for all the others ... And thus they shall each be
       perfect kings, because they shall all will one thing' (Fröhlich, 'Letter 112', vol. 1, p. 269).

[220] 'The devil's promptings' (MacPherson, p. 68).

[221] 'Heresy, thank God, is not prevalent in England' (Millett, p. 33).

[222] 'For nothing is better for preventing useless ideas or driving out impure imaginations than the
       study of God's word' (MacPherson, p. 68).

[223] Millett, p. 3.

[224] 'For no thought or intention is ever driven out ... except by some other thought or intention'
       (Fröhlich, 'Letter 414', vol. 3, p. 185).

[225] 'if you wish to live a good life, continually keep watch over your will in both great and small
       things' (Fröhlich, 'Letter 414', vol. 3, p. 185).

[226] 'do not neglect even the smallest faults. Whoever observes diligence in the smallest details will
       not easily permit negligence in more important things' (Fröhlich, 'Letter 230', vol. 2, p. 199).

[227] Millett, p. 10.

[228] MacPherson, p. 52.

[229] Millett, p. 4.

[230] Millett, p. 97.

[231] 'are a tower ... truly and firmly fixed together with the cement of shared love, each of you to the
       other' (Millett, pp. 86–7).

[232] 'high reputation' and 'mother-house' (Millett, p. 97).

[233] Thomas H. Bestul, 'Walter Hilton', in Dee Dyas, Valerie Edden and Roger Ellis (eds),
       Approaching Medieval English Anchoritic and Mystical Texts (Cambridge: D. S. Brewer, 2005),
       pp. 87–101 (p. 89).

[234] Gordon Leff, *Heresy in the Later Middle Ages: The Relation of Heterodoxy to Dissent, c.1250–
       1450* (Manchester: Manchester University Press, 1967), vol. 1, p. 10. See also: J. Patrick

Hornbeck, *What is a Lollard? Dissent and Belief in Late Medieval England* (New York: Oxford University Press USA, 2010), especially pp. 31–4, and Malcolm Lambert, *Medieval Heresy: Popular Movements from the Gregorian Reform to the Reformation* (1977; Oxford: Blackwell, 2002).

[235] See Anne Hudson, 'Lollardy: the English heresy?', in her, *Lollards and their Books* (London: Hambledon, 1985), pp. 141–63, especially p. 145 on the vernacular; pp. 125–39 on Lollard diversity and pp. 133–9 for the lists of questions put to Lollards. See also Shannon Gayk, *Image, Text, and Religious Reform in Fifteenth-century England* (Cambridge: Cambridge University Press, 2010), especially pp. 15–35; Richard Rex, *The Lollards* (Basingstoke: Palgrave Macmillan, 2002); Carolyn Dinshaw, 'It takes one to know one: Lollards, sodomites and their accusers', in her *Getting Medieval: Sexualities and Communities, Pre- and Postmodern* (Durham, NC and London: Duke University Press, 1999), pp. 55–99, and Peter Biller and Anne Hudson (eds), *Heresy and Literacy, 1000–1530* (Cambridge: Cambridge University Press, 1994). On Wyclif prior to his 1381 condemnation of the doctrine of the Eucharist, see Leff, *Heresy in the Later Middle Ages*, vol. 2, pp. 494–500.

[236] See Hudson, 'Lollardy: the English heresy?', pp. 146–9. See also Hughes, *Pastors and Visionaries*, pp. 125, 236 on Lollard heresy as 'an aspect of the eremitic movement'.

[237] Clay, *Hermits and Anchorites*, pp. 89–90.

[238] Warren *Anchorites and their Patrons*, pp. 79–80. On Palmer, see also A. K. McHardy, 'Bishop Buckingham and the Lollards of Lincoln diocese', in Derek Baker (ed.), *Schism, Heresy and Religious Protest,* Studies in Church History, 9 (Cambridge: Cambridge University Press, 1972), pp. 131–45.

[239] Warren, *Anchorites and their Patrons*, pp. 79–80, and Clay, *Hermits and Anchorites*, p. 143.

[240] Clay, *Hermits and Anchorites*, p. 184.

[241] Millett, p. 86. The *Speculum* author uses this metaphor twice, once, as Hilton and Rolle do, in warnings about false visions (*Speculum*, p. 114; *Myrour*, p. 38), and once to communicate caution when choosing the anchoritic vocation (*Speculum*, p. 72; *Myrour*, p. 8). See also *Form*, p. 7, where Rolle extends this image, giving anecdotal examples of recluses tempted by false visions of the Virgin. The passage appears in diffused form in *Scale* (*Scale I*, p. 40).

[242] Gordon Leff, *Bradwardine and the Pelagians: A Study of His 'Dei Causa Dei' and its Opponents* (Cambridge: Cambridge University Press, 1957), p. 79.

[243] *Myrour*, p. 24.

[244] 'by enspirynge ant grace of perseuerance fynaly in charite' (*Myrour*, p. 10).

[245] *Scale I*, chapter 4 (pp. 33–4), chapter 20 (pp. 51–3) and chapter 57 (pp. 95–6).

[246] Leff, *Heresy in the Later Middle Ages*, vol. 1, pp. 1–2.

[247] See Catherine A. Carsley, 'Devotion to the Holy Name: late medieval piety in England', *Princeton University Library Chronicle*, 53 (1992), 156–72; K. Ware, 'The Holy Name of Jesus in east and west: the Hesychasts and Richard Rolle', *Sobornos*, 4 (1982), 163–84; L. McAodha, 'The Holy Name of Jesus in the preaching of St Bernardine of Siena', *Franciscan Studies*, 29 (1969), 37–65.

[248] '3if þe vndirstandynge or reson inwardly erre in the feyth of Holy Cherche' (*Myrour*, p. 39).

[249] 'þe Artycles of the Feyth determynyd by Holy Cherche' (*Myrour*, p. 39).

[250] 'Preieres to þe which a man is holden of þe ordynaunce of Holy Cherche or of hys souereyns ... aftir þe custum of his ordre or his estat' (*Myrour*, pp. 20–1).

[251] 'whan þe consecracion is maad, yt ys flessch ant blood, body, soule and þat same Godhede, al Christ, verray God and man' (*Myrour*, p. 40).

[252] 'O most precious nourishment, O most noble restorative, O most efficacious comfort' (*Myrour*, p. 41).

[253] Phyllis G. Jestice, 'A new fashion in imitating Christ: changing spiritual perspectives around the year 1000', in Michael Frassetto (ed.), *The Year 1000: Religious and Social Response to the Turning of the First Millennium* (Basingstoke and New York: Palgrave Macmillan, 2002), pp. 165–86 (p. 175).

[254] Miri Rubin and Daniell argue that Eucharistic miracles increasingly intrigue Christian writers from the seventh century onwards, when the first transubstantiation miracle is recounted in the

Life of St Gregory the Great. See Daniell, *From Norman Conquest*, p. 159, and Miri Rubin, *Corpus Christi: The Eucharist in Late Medieval Culture* (Cambridge: Cambridge University Press, 1991). Maurice Keen, 'Wyclif, the Bible, and transubstantiation', in Anthony Kenny (ed.), *Wyclif in his Times* (Oxford: Clarendon Press, 1986), pp. 1–16, lists Wyclif's objections to the theories of Scotus and Ockham. Keen argues that Wyclif's attack on transubstantiation intersects with Wyclif's wider attacks on ecclesiatical abuses, but that 'Wyclif did not deny the importance of the mass, or the real presence of Christ at his Eucharist' (p. 14). See also Shannon McSheffrey, *Gender and Heresy: Women and Men in Lollard Communities, 1420–1530* (Philadelphia: University of Pennsylvania Press, 1995), especially pp. 142–9, which suggest that the sect did not have a widespread appeal and that 'women were less inclined ... to its creed' (p. 143).

[255] Hudson, 'A Lollard mass', in *Lollards and their Books*, pp. 111–23 (p. 117). Hudson cites the Stillington Register (Bath and Wells), opening 52 for 1475.

[256] Hudson, 'A Lollard Mass', p. 118.

[257] 'Crist schal duelle with vs bodyly in the holy and blisful sacrament of the autier, where euery-day, vndir þe figure or liknesse of breed and wyn, hys soule ys offred vn-to vs in-to þe þrys of oure redempcion – þe bodi in-to spirituel mete, þe blood in-to drynke of helþe' (*Myrour*, p. 29).

[258] 'dreede ... of a raw body or blood' (*Myrour*, p. 40).

[259] MacPherson, p. 73.

[260] 'in euen wyse aftir þe consecracion duellen as þer diden biforn accidentes (þat is to sey, colour, sauour, and wyghte) of breed and wyn whan þer is neyþer breed, ne wyn, ne noon oþir substance but substance of þe body and of þe blood of Ihesu Crist wiþ the Godhede' (*Myrour*, pp. 40–1).

[261] 'the blood schal nat be deseuered ne departid fro þe flessch, ne soule fro þe body, ne þe manhode fro þe deite of Godhede þerfor, vndir eyther lyknesse (þat ys to seyn, as wiel of breed as wyn), whan þe consecracion is maad, yt ys flessch ant blood, body, soule, and þat same Godhede, al Crist, verray God and man' (*Myrour*, p. 40).

[262] 'the Lord's body and blood' and 'a great mystery' (Otter, p. 110); 'This bread of life ... bread of angels' (Otter, p. 110).

[263] 'As ... in a broken myrour, in euery broken part of þe whiche þe same ymage schyneth and scewyth as yt dide fyrst in the hool myrrour' (*Myrour*, p. 41).

[264] Constable, *Three Studies*, pp. 192, 196.

[265] 'as a membre of hys qwykned wiþ his owen blood' (*Myrour*, p. 29).

[266] Hamburger, *The Visual and the Visionary*, p. 102. See also Caroline Walker Bynum, *Holy Feast and Holy Fast: The Religious Significance of Food to Medieval Women*, The New Historicism: Studies in Cultural Poetics (Berkeley, Los Angeles and London: University of California Press, 1987), p. 359, n. 160.

[267] James of Vitry, *Life of Marie d'Oignies*, pp. 126–7. See also Walker Bynum's essay 'Women mystics and Eucharistic devotion in the thirteenth century', in her *Fragmentation and Redemption: Essays on Gender and the Human Body in Medieval Religion* (New York: Zone, 1992), pp. 119–50; Walker Bynum, *Holy Feast and Holy Fast*, especially pp. 227–37, and Rubin's *Corpus Christi*, pp. 108–29, 316–19.

[268] Simons, *Cities of Ladies*, pp. 74–5; McDonnell, *The Beguines and Beghards*, p. 311. McDonnell notes that the Eucharistic ecstasies of some beguines were so extreme that they were forbidden to receive communion (p. 315).

[269] Kempe, p. 48.

[270] Eamon Duffy, *The Stripping of the Altars, Traditional Religion in England, c.1400–1580* (New Haven and London: Yale University Press, 1992), pp. 93, 95.

Appendix: Guidance Text Overview

An at-a-glance summary of the key features of each of the eight base guides focused on in this book

Name of guide	Date and language of original composition	Information on guidance writer	Information on reclusive readership	Information on key extant manuscripts	Edition used	Translation used (if used)	Structure and basic content
Liber confortatorius.	c.1080; Latin.	Goscelin of St Bertin (b.c.1040 in northern France; d.c.1107). Originally a monk at the Benedictine abbey of Saint-Bertin in Saint-Omer, he relocated to England pre-1065. He was part of the household of Bishop Herman and engaged to write the *Vita* and *Translatio* of the patron saint Edith. By c.1090 he was resident at St Augustine's, Canterbury.	The recluse Eve (perhaps b.c.1058; d.1120), possibly the English-born daughter of a Danish father and Lotharingian mother. She was perhaps Bishop Herman's niece and was dedicated as a child oblate to the Wilton community in 1065.	The guide is extant in one manuscript: London, British Library, MS Sloane 3103, of the Abbey of Saint-Sauveur-le-Vicomte in Normandy. It is the mid-twelfth-century work of more than one scribe.	Goscelin of St Bertin, 'The *Liber confortatorius* of Goscelin of Saint Bertin', in Charles Hugh Talbot (ed.), *Analecta monastica*, series 3, *Studia Anselmiana*, fasc. 37 (Rome: Pontifical Institute of St Anselm, 1955), pp. 1–117.	Goscelin of St Bertin, *The Book of Encouragement and Consolation (Liber confortatorius). The Letter of Goscelin to the Recluse Eva*, trans. Monika Otter (Cambridge: D. S. Brewer, 2004).	The guide is divided into a prologue and four books. Book I is on complaint and comfort. Book II is on spiritual battles against human sinfulness. Book III is on inspiring spiritual desires and conquering anchoritic dejection and doubt. Book IV is on humility, other virtues and the pleasures and pains of Judgement Day.

Name of guide	Date and language of original composition	Information on guidance writer	Information on reclusive readership	Information on key extant manuscripts	Edition used	Translation used (if used)	Structure and basic content
Three letters of St Anselm: 'Letter 112: Ad Hugonem'; 'Letter 230: Ad Rodbertum, Seit, Edit' and 'Letter 414: Ad Robertum eiusque moniales'.	Composed in Latin. 'Letter 112': between c.1078 and c.1093 (possibly c.1086); 'Letter 230': c.1102; 'Letter 414': c.1105).	St Anselm (b.1033; d.1109), author of the *Monologion*, the *Proslogion* and *Cur Deus Homo*; reluctant Benedictine monk; later prior and abbot of Bec and, in 1093, succeeded Lanfranc to archbishopric of Canterbury.	'Letter 112': for Hugh, the hermit of Caen; 'Letter 230': for Robert, Seitha and Edith, possibly recluses at Bury St Edmunds; 'Letter 414': for that same Robert, Seitha and Edith and also for Thydit, Lwerun, Dirgit and Godit. Robert seems to have been a spiritual advisor to this growing group of female solitaries. Licence (2011) speculates that he may have been an abbot at Bury St Edmunds.	The largest manuscript collection of Anselm's letters (composed from 1070–1109) is extant in London, Lambeth Palace Library, MS 59.	Francis S. Schmitt (ed.), *Sancti Anselmi Cantuariensis Archiepiscopi, Opera Omnia*, 6 vols (Edinburgh: T. Nelson, 1946–63). 'Letter 112' is in vol. 3, pp. 244–6; 'Letter 230' is in vol. 4, pp. 134–5; 'Letter 414' is in vol. 5, pp. 359–62.	Walter Fröhlich (ed. and trans.), *The Letters of Saint Anselm of Canterbury*, 3 vols (Kalamazoo: Cistercian Publications, 1990–4). 'Letter 112' is in vol. 1, pp. 268–71; 'Letter 230' is in vol. 2, pp. 199–200; 'Letter 414' is in vol. 3, pp. 184–7.	'Letter 112' advises Hugh on social interaction with visitors, synonymizes the Christian life with love and advises prayer, spiritual converse, heavenly meditation, poverty, industry and obedience as vital to the success of the solitary life. 'Letter 230' recounts Anselm's joy at this solitary group's inspirational spirituality. It advises diligence in the recognition of their most minute sinful flaws and seeks to regulate speech. 'Letter 414' rejoices at this same group's holiness. It focuses on the human will, on governing intention as well as action, on distinguishing good from bad thought and God's will from mankind's. It explores the vices of anger, envy and vainglory.

Name of guide	Date and language of original composition	Information on guidance writer	Information on reclusive readership	Information on key extant manuscripts	Edition used	Translation used (if used)	Structure and basic content
De institutione inclusarum.	c.1160–2; Latin.	Aelred of Rievaulx (b.c.1109; d.1167); abbot of the Cistercian foundation at Rievaulx.	Aelred's unnamed biological sister, evidently literate in Latin.	The guide survives in Latin in six complete manuscript versions and four partial manuscript versions. Its earliest complete Latin text is extant in the thirteenth century London, British Library, MS Cotton Nero A. III.	Aelred of Rievaulx, *Aelredi Rievallensis Opera Omnia: I Opera Ascetica*, in *Corpus Christianorum Continuatio Mediaevalis*, ed. Anselm Hoste and Charles Hugh Talbot (Turnhout: Brepols, 1971), pp. 635–82.	Aelred of Rievaulx, 'A rule of life for a recluse', in *Aelred of Rievaulx: Treatises and Pastoral Prayer*, trans. Mary Paul MacPherson (Kalamazoo: Cistercian Studies Series, 1971), pp. 40–102.	The guide comprises thirty-three sections. An overarching tripartite structure has been imposed on it by the guide's best-known modern English translator, MacPherson. Part I (sections II to XIII) focuses on outer issues, detailing diurnal practicalities and common reclusive problems. Part II (sections XIV to XXVIII) is on inner concerns, on virtue and safeguarding chastity. Part III (sections XXIX to XXXIII) offers a threefold meditation; on the past (the life of Christ), the present (Aelred and his sister's lineage) and the future (Judgement Day).

Name of guide	Date and language of original composition	Information on guidance writer	Information on reclusive readership	Information on key extant manuscripts	Edition used	Translation used (if used)	Structure and basic content
Ancrene Wisse.	Lost original composed c.1215–30; vernacular. Other key texts: Corpus: c.1230–80s (but after 1224); descended from a lost revision of the original guide; Nero and Titus: 1240s; Cleopatra: early 1230s; Gonville and Caius: third quarter of thirteenth century.	The guide's specific authorship is unknown. Contenders have included the hermit Godwine, Gilbert of Sempringham, Robert Bacon, Herbert Poor, Richard Poor and Simon of Ghent. Eric Dobson (1976) famously argued for Brian of Lingen, a secular canon of Wigmore Abbey. Bella Millett (1991) argues for Dominican authorship.	The guide's original audience was three well-born, probably lay, consanguineous sisters (mentioned in the Nero text), under the patronage of one man. They were known to the original author. Dobson (1976) hypothesized their location in the vicinity of Limebrook Priory. Their exact identity and location remains unknown. They were possibly only partially literate in Latin, but also in French.	Seventeen manuscripts are extant, containing material from the lost original, sometimes reworked or with added revisions. These include: nine vernacular, four Latin and four French manuscripts, of which London, British Library, MS Cotton Nero A. xiv and Cambridge, Corpus Christi College, MS 402 are the best known.	Bella Millett (ed.), with Eric J. Dobson and Richard Dance, *Ancrene Wisse. A Corrected Edition of the Text in Cambridge, Corpus Christi College, MS 402, With Variants From Other Manuscripts*, vol. 1, Early English Text Society, original series, 325 (2005). There are also individual Early English Text Society editions of each of the seventeen texts (see the Select Bibliography for full details).	Bella Millett, *Ancrene Wisse: Guide for Anchoresses. A Translation* (Exeter: Exeter University Press, 2009).	The Corpus text is split into a preface and eight parts. The Preface, Part I and Part VIII constitute the outer rule and Parts II to VII the inner. The Preface argues for threefold importance of anchoritic obedience, chastity and fixity of place. Part I details diurnal anchoritic devotions; Part II regulates the senses; Part III is on the inculcation of virtuous inner feelings, using bestiary motif; Part IV details specific spiritual problems and remedies; Part V focuses on confession; Part VI on penance; Part VII synonymizes the Christian life and the solitary vocation, with love.

Name of guide	Date and language of original composition	Information on guidance writer	Information on reclusive readership	Information on key extant manuscripts	Edition used	Translation used (if used)	Structure and basic content
			The Corpus text widens its audience to a group of twenty or more recluses scattered over a wide geographical area; identity unknown.				
			The Cleopatra text makes a direct address to a female audience; also reflects an audience division between a smaller and larger group of anchorites.				
			The Titus text is superficially widened to include male recluses (as is the Gonville and Caius text, partially). A mixture of gendered pronouns suggests a partial reversal of this in Titus.				

Name of guide	Date and language of original composition	Information on guidance writer	Information on reclusive readership	Information on key extant manuscripts	Edition used	Translation used (if used)	Structure and basic content
The Form of Living.	Lost original, composed c.1348; vernacular.	Richard Rolle, Hermit of Hampole, b.c.1290; d.1349.	Margaret Kirkby, recluse at East Layton and later (from 1357) at Ainderby Steeple.	The guide is extant in over forty vernacular manuscripts, including twenty-seven complete versions dating from the fifteenth to the sixteenth centuries. It was subsequently translated into Latin and adapted into English verse. Two main lines of manuscript descent, headed by two unrelated versions of the guide: Longleat, library of the marquess of Bath, MS 29, copied c.1430–50 and Cambridge, University Library, MS Dd. v. 64. III, copied c.1400.	Sarah J. Ogilvie-Thompson (ed.), *Richard Rolle: Prose and Verse from MS Longleat 29 and Related Manuscripts*, Early English Text Society, original series, 293 (1988), pp. 3–25.		The guide is not split into sections. It begins with an account of the three sins which most afflict humanity: lack of spiritual fervour, focus on fleshly desires and delight in temporality. It moves to an admiration of religious solitude. It then details a series of strategies for reclusive success. Four routes to spiritual purity are subsequently explored and three activities that purify the recluse interrogated. The rest of the guide is devoted to the inculcation (via contemplative experience) of spiritual love which is separated into three levels or degrees. The guide ends with an overview of the active and contemplative lives.

Name of guide	Date and language of original composition	Information on guidance writer	Information on reclusive readership	Information on key extant manuscripts	Edition used	Translation used (if used)	Structure and basic content
The Scale of Perfection, Book I only.	Book I begun *c*.1384–6. Book II completed *c*.1394–6. Sargent (1983) argues that a single authoritative version of the guide never existed; different versions circulated concurrently.	Walter Hilton (b.*c*.1340–5; d.1396), Augustinian canon, Thurgarton Priory, Nottingham.	Book I addresses itself to an unnamed, single, female anchorite in the early stages of her enclosure. The guide makes only four direct references to this 'ankir incluse' (*Scale I*, p. 79): in Chapters Forty-four, Sixty-one and Eighty-three, although wider allusions to her spiritual state of life or calling are made.	The guide is extant in forty-two manuscripts containing one or both books of *Scale*; a preponderance of Book I manuscripts exists. Nineteen vernacular manuscripts and two Latin manuscripts of either the whole of or part of *Scale I* on its own are extant, but only four vernacular and one Latin manuscript of *Scale II* on its own are extant. Sargent (1983) prioritizes the London MS Group.	Walter Hilton, *Walter Hilton: The Scale of Perfection*, ed. Thomas H. Bestul (Kalamazoo: Medieval Institute Publications, 2000).		Book I is divided into ninety-two chapters, each with separate title. Chapter 1 distinguishes between inner and outer spirituality. Chapters 2 to 9 focus on the three degrees of contemplative experience. Chapters 13 and 15 detail contemplative inspirations and occupations. Chapters 12, 46 to 51 and 91 offer strategies to accord the soul with God's will. Chapters 14 and 16 to 25 focus on the inculcation of virtue as vital preparation for understanding the fire of love (the focus of chapters 26,

Name of guide	Date and language of original composition	Information on guidance writer	Information on reclusive readership	Information on key extant manuscripts	Edition used	Translation used (if used)	Structure and basic content
							30 and 31). Prayer is the subject of chapters 27 to 30, 32 and 33. Meditation is the focus of chapters 34 to 36. The dangers which beset the contemplative are the subject of chapters 37 to 40 and 42. Sin is a central focus of the guide (for example, of chapters 53 to 60). The guide concludes with an exploration of its reclusive reader's contemplative state.
Vernacular redaction of Aelred's *De institutione inclusarum*, extant in Oxford, Bodleian Library, MS Bodley 423.	c.1430–40; vernacular translation of Aelred's original twelfth-century Latin text.	Unknown redactor.	The MS may possibly be Carthusian in provenance and therefore may even have been intended for a male readership, although this is unproven (the	Oxford, Bodleian Library, MS Bodley 423.	John Ayto and Alexandra Barratt (eds), *Aelred of Rievaulx's 'De institutione inclusarum': Two English Versions*, English Text Society, original series, 287 (1984), pp. 1–25.		Aelred's original thirty-three sections are compacted into sixteen. The overarching tripartite structure identified by MacPherson is still discernible. Aelred's initial focus on diurnal practicalities, subsequent focus on virtue and safeguarding chastity

Name of guide	Date and language of original composition	Information on guidance writer	Information on reclusive readership	Information on key extant manuscripts	Edition used	Translation used (if used)	Structure and basic content
	One of only two extant late Middle English translations of this Latin guide (the other is in the Vernon manuscript, c.1400).		original guide has a female audience). Precise audience is unidentified. All Aelred's original references to his sister and to their relationship are removed, notably from the meditation on the present.				(which is heavily condensed) and his final threefold meditation on the past, present and future are all retained.
Speculum inclusorum.	Its precise date of composition is unclear; possibly between c.1349 and c.1382, although Jones (1999) thinks it could be a further ten years later than this; Latin.	Its author is not known, but was probably a Carthusian.	It was composed for a group of unnamed male recluses, probably of considerable size; their exact identity and location is unknown.	It is extant in two fourteenth-century manuscripts of English provenance: London, British Library, MS Royal A.V and Oxford, St John's College, MS 177.	P. Livario Oliger (ed.), 'Speculum inclusorum', *Lateranum*, n.s., 4 (1938), 1–148.		The guide is split into fourteen chapters: a prologue, four parts and an epilogue. Part I contains five chapters; one is a preface and four that outline each of the four motivations for the anchoritic life in turn. Part II's three chapters focus on prayer, meditation and reading, and Part III returns to each spiritual practice in

Name of guide	Date and language of original composition	Information on guidance writer	Information on reclusive readership	Information on key extant manuscripts	Edition used	Translation used (if used)	Structure and basic content
							turn (again in three separate chapters), outlining their advantages and disadvantages. Part IV focuses on the rewards of the anchoritic vocation both in this life and in heaven.
The Myrour of Recluses.	The precise date of this medieval translation of the *Speculum inclusorum* is not known, but it is extant in a fifteenth-century manuscript (*c.*1450).	Unknown translator.	*Speculum's* original Latin text's audience of male recluses is widened to include females, probably a group of considerable size; their exact identity and location is unknown.	The guide is extant in only one, damaged mid-fifteenth-century manuscript: London, British Library, MS Harley 2372.	Marta Powell Harley (ed.), *The Myrour of Recluses* (Madison and Teaneck: Fairleigh Dickinson University Press, 1995).		*Myrour* contains only eight of *Speculum's* fourteen chapters, divided into only three of *Speculum's* four overarching parts. It lacks the first few lines of *Speculum's* preface; the third chapters from both Parts II and III (on edificatory reading) and the whole of Part IV ('The rewards of the contemplative life'). Where intact, it demonstrates great similarity to the Latin guide in form and content.

Select Bibliography[1]

Printed primary sources

Aelred of Rievaulx, 'A rule of life for a recluse', in *Aelred of Rievaulx: Treatises and Pastoral Prayer*, trans. Mary Paul MacPherson (Kalamazoo: Cistercian Studies Series, 1971), pp. 40–102.

——, *De institutione inclusarum*, in *Aelredi Rievallensis Opera Omnia: I Opera Ascetica*, in *Corpus Christianorum Continuatio Mediaeualis I*, ed. Anselm Hoste and Charles Hugh Talbot (Turnhout: Brepols, 1971), pp. 635–82.

Allen, Hope E. (ed.), *Writings Ascribed to Richard Rolle, Hermit of Hampole, and Materials for his Biography*, Modern Language Association Monograph Series, 3 (New York: Modern Language Association of America, 1927).

Allen, Rosamund S. (ed.), *Richard Rolle: The English Writings* (New York and Mahwah: Paulist Press, 1988).

Ayto, John and Alexandra Barratt (eds), *Aelred of Rievaulx's 'De institutione inclusarum': Two English Versions*, Early English Text Society, original series, 287 (1984).

Barlow, Frank (ed.), *The Life of King Edward Who Rests at Westminster* (Oxford: Clarendon Press, 1992).

Caesarius of Heisterbach, *The Dialogue on Miracles*, trans. Henry von Essen Scott and Charles Cooke Swinton Bland, 2 vols (London: Routledge, 1929).

Carysfort, William, earl of (ed.), *The Pageants of Richard Beauchamp, Earl of Warwick* (Oxford: Roxburghe Club, 1908).

Clark, John P. H. and Rosemary Dorward (trans.), *The Scale of Perfection* (New York and Mahwah: Paulist Press, 1991).

Day, Mabel (ed.), *The English Text of the Ancrene Riwle: Edited from Cotton MS. Nero A. xiv.*, Early English Text Society, original series, 225 (1952).

Dobson, Eric J. (ed.), *The English Text of the Ancrene Riwle: Edited from B.M. Cotton MS. Cleopatra C. vi.*, Early English Text Society, original series, 267 (1972).

Fröhlich, Walter (ed. and trans.), *The Letters of Saint Anselm of Canterbury*, 3 vols (Kalamazoo: Cistercian Publications, 1990–4).

---

[1] This is a select bibliography: it cites all the texts that have been quoted directly. It also cites some texts that have not been quoted, but are nonetheless noteworthy in the field and have been cited in endnotes. Essay collections from which multiple essays have been quoted are only given once (cited as the full collection); individual essay titles and paginations are given in the relevant endnotes.

Goscelin of St Bertin, *The Book of Encouragement and Consolation (Liber confortatorius). The Letter of Goscelin to the Recluse Eva*, trans. Monika Otter (Cambridge: D. S. Brewer, 2004).

——, 'The *Liber confortatorius* of Goscelin of Saint Bertin', *Analecta monastica*, ed. Charles Hugh Talbot, series 3, *Studia Anselmiana*, fasc. 37 (Rome: Pontifical Institute of St Anselm, 1955), pp. 1–117.

Gransden, Antonia (ed.), 'The reply of a fourteenth-century abbot of Bury St. Edmunds to a man's petition to be a recluse', *English Historical Review*, 75 (1960), 465–7.

Hadewijch of Brabant, *Hadewijch: The Complete Works*, trans. Columba Hart (New York and Mahwah: Paulist Press, 1980).

Hasenfratz, Robert (ed.), *Ancrene Wisse* (Kalamazoo: Medieval Institute Publications, 2000).

Hilton, Walter, *Walter Hilton: The Scale of Perfection*, ed. Thomas H. Bestul (Kalamazoo: Medieval Institute Publications, 2000).

Hollis, Stephanie (ed.), with W. R. Barnes, Rebecca Hayward, Kathleen Loncar and Michael Wright, *Writing the Wilton Women: Goscelin's Legend of Edith and Liber confortatorius*, Medieval Women Texts and Contexts, 9 (Turnhout: Brepols, 2004).

Horstmann, Carl (ed.), 'Walter Hilton's epistle on a mixed life', in *Yorkshire Writers: Richard Rolle, an English Father of the Church, and His Followers*, 2 vols (London: Swan Sonnenschein, 1895–6; repr. Woodbridge: York Medieval Press, 1999), vol. 1.

——, 'The mirror of St Edmund,' in *The Minor Poems of the Vernon MS, Part 1*, Early English Text Society, original series, 98 (1892), pp. 221–51.

Julian of Norwich, *The Shewings of Julian of Norwich*, ed. G. Ronan Crampton (Kalamazoo: Medieval Institute Publications, 1994).

Kempe, Margery, *The Book of Margery Kempe*, ed. Lynn Staley (Kalamazoo: Medieval Institute Publications, 1996).

King, Margot (ed. and trans.), *The Life of Christina Mirabilis, by Thomas de Cantimpré* (2nd edn; Toronto: Peregrina, 1999).

——, *The Life of Lutgard of Aywières, by Thomas de Cantimpré* (Toronto: Peregrina, 1987).

—— (ed. and trans), *The Life of Marie d'Oignies by Jacques de Vitry* (Toronto: Peregrina, 1986).

McCarthy, Adrian J. (ed.), *Book to a Mother* (Salzburg: Institut für Anglistik und Amerikanistik, Universität Salzburg, 1981).

Mack, M. Frances and Arne Zettersten (eds), *The English Text of the Ancrene Riwle, Edited from Cotton MS. Titus D. xviii, together with the Lanhydrock Fragment, Bodleian MS. Eng. th. c. 70.*, Early English Text Society, original series, 252 (1963).

Marx, C. W., 'British Library, Harley MS. 1740 and popular devotion', in Nicholas Rogers (ed.), *England in the Fifteenth Century: Proceedings of the 1992 Harlaxton Symposium* (Stamford: Paul Watkins, 1994), pp. 207–22.

Migne, Jacques-Paul (ed.), *Patrologiae Cursus Completus: Series Latina*, 221 vols (Paris: Migne, 1841–64).

Millett, Bella, *Ancrene Wisse: Guide for Anchoresses. A Translation* (Exeter: Exeter University Press, 2009).

—— (ed.), with Eric J. Dobson and Richard Dance, *Ancrene Wisse. A Corrected Edition of the Text in Cambridge, Corpus Christi College, MS 402, With Variants From Other Manuscripts*, vol. 2, Early English Text Society, original series, 326 (2006).

—— (ed.), with Eric J. Dobson and Richard Dance, *Ancrene Wisse. A Corrected Edition of the Text in Cambridge, Corpus Christi College, MS 402, With Variants from Other Manuscripts*, vol. 1, Early English Text Society, original series, 325 (2005).

—— and Jocelyn Wogan-Browne (eds), *Medieval English Prose for Women: Selections from the Katherine Group and 'Ancrene Wisse'* (Oxford: Clarendon Press, 1990).

Morton, James (ed.), *The Ancren Riwle: A Treatise on the Rules and Duties of Monastic Life* (London: Camden Society, 1853).

Nicholas Love, *The Mirrour of the Blessed Lyf of Jesu Christ*, ed. James Hogg and Lawrence F. Powell, *Analecta Cartusiana*, 91 (1989).

Ogilvie-Thompson, Sarah J. (ed.), *Richard Rolle: Prose and Verse from MS Longleat 29 and Related Manuscripts*, Early English Text Society, original series, 293 (1988).

Oliger, P. Livario (ed.), '*Speculum inclusorum*', *Lateranum*, n.s., 4 (1938), 1–148.

Perry, George G. (ed.), *Religious Pieces in Prose and Verse*, Early English Text Society, original series, 26 (1867; rev. edn 1914; reprint 1973).

Porete, Margaret, *The Mirror of Simple Souls*, trans. Edmund Colledge, J. C. Marler and J. Grant (Notre Dame, Ind.: University of Notre Dame Press, 1999).

Powell Harley, Marta (ed.), *The Myrour of Recluses* (Madison and Teaneck: Fairleigh Dickinson University Press, 1995).

——, *A Revelation of Purgatory by an Unknown, Fifteenth-century Woman Visionary* (Lewiston, New York: Edwin Mellen Press, 1985).

Rous, John, *Rows Rol* (London: Pickering, 1845), no. 50.

Salu, Mary B. (ed. and trans.), *The 'Ancrene Riwle' (The Corpus MS.: Ancrene Wisse)* (London: Burns and Oates, 1955).

Sargent, Michael G. (ed.), *Nicholas Love's Mirror of the Blessed Life of Jesus Christ* (New York and London: Garland, 1992).

Savage, Ann and Nicholas Watson (trans.), *Anchoritic Spirituality: 'Ancrene Wisse' and Associated Works* (New York and Mahwah: Paulist Press, 1991).

Schmitt, Francis S. (ed.), *Sancti Anselmi Cantuariensis Archiepiscopi, Opera Omnia*, 6 vols (Edinburgh: T. Nelson, 1946–63).

Shepherd, Geoffrey (ed.), *'Ancrene Wisse': Parts Six and Seven* (1959; Exeter: Exeter University Press, 1985).

Steele, Robert, (ed.), *Lydgate and Burgh's Secrees of Old Philisoffres*, Early English Text Society, extra series, 66 (1894; reprint 1973).

Talbot, Charles Hugh (ed. and trans.), *The Life of Christina of Markyate, A Twelfth Century Recluse* (Oxford: Clarendon Press, 1959).

The Abbey of the Holy Ghost, in Norman F. Blake (ed.), *Middle English Religious Prose* (Evanston: Northwestern University Press, 1972), pp. 88–103.

Tolkien, J. R. R. (ed.), *The English Text of the Ancrene Riwle: Ancrene Wisse: Edited from MS. Corpus Christi College Cambridge 402*, Early English Text Society, original series, 249 (1962).

Walsh, James, (ed.), *The Cloud of Unknowing* (New York and Mahwah: Paulist Press, 1981).

White, Hugh (trans.), *Ancrene Wisse: Guide for Anchoresses* (London, New York, Victoria, Ontario and Auckland: Penguin, 1993).

Wilson, R. M. (ed.), *The English Text of the Ancrene Riwle: Edited from Gonville and Caius College MS. 234/120.*, Early English Text Society, original series, 229 (1954; repr. 1957).

Online primary sources

Douai-Rheims Translation of the Latin Vulgate Bible, *http://www.drbo.org* (accessed 7 September 2011).

The Fathers of the Church, *http://www.newadvent.org/fathers* (accessed 7 September 2011).

Latin Vulgate Bible, *http://www.drbo.org/lvb/index.htm* (accessed 7 September 2011).

Matrologia Latina (includes the Latin *vitae* of Mary of Oignies and Christina the Astonishing), *http://www.peregrina.com/matrologia_latina/matrologia_latina.html* (accessed 7 September 2011).

Rule of St Benedict, http://www.osb.org/rb/text/rbejms1.html#1 (accessed 7 September 2011).

Regula Sancti Augustini, http://www.thelatinlibrary.com/augustine/reg.shtml (accessed 7 September 2011).

Regula Sancti Benedicti, http://www.intratext.com/X/LAT0011.HTM (accessed 7 September 2011).

TEAMS Middle English Texts, *http://www.lib.rochester.edu/camelot/teams/tmsmenu. htm* (accessed 7 September 2011).

Printed secondary sources

Abbott, Christopher, *Julian of Norwich: Autobiography and Theology* (Cambridge: D. S. Brewer, 1999).

Baker, Denise N., 'Julian of Norwich and anchoritic literature', *Mystics Quarterly*, 19 (1993), 148–60.

Baker, Derek and Rosalind M. T. Hill (eds), *Medieval Women* (Oxford: Blackwell, 1978).

Barr, Beth Allison, *The Pastoral Care of Women in Late Medieval England*, Gender in the Middle Ages, vol. 3 (Woodbridge: Boydell and Brewer, 2008).

Barratt, Alexandra, 'Creating an anchorhold', in Miri Rubin (ed.), *Medieval Christianity in Practice* (Princeton, NJ: Princeton University Press, 2009), pp. 311–18.

——, 'Small Latin? The post-Conquest learning of English religious women', in Sian Echard and Gernot R. Wieland (eds), *Anglo-Latin and its Heritage: Essays in Honour of A. G. Rigg on his 64th Birthday* (Turnhout: Brepols, 2001), pp. 51–65.

——, 'The five wits and their structural significance in Part II of *Ancrene Wisse*', *Medium Aevum*, 56 (1987), 12–24.

——, 'Anchoritic aspects of *Ancrene Wisse*', *Medium Aevum*, 49 (1980), 32–56.

Bartlett, Anne Clark, 'A reasonable affection: gender and spiritual friendship in Middle English devotional literature', in A. Clark Bartlett, T. H. Bestul, J. Goebel and W. F. Pollard (eds), *Vox Mystica: Essays on Medieval Mysticism in Honour of Professor V. M. Lagorio* (Cambridge: D. S. Brewer, 1995), pp. 131–45.

Bernau, Anke, *Virgins: A Cultural History* (London: Granta Books, 2007).

Bell, Rudolph M., *Holy Anorexia* (Chicago and London: University of Chicago Press, 1985).

Bildhauer, Bettina, *Medieval Blood* (Cardiff: University of Wales Press, 2005).

Biller, Peter and Anne Hudson (eds), *Heresy and Literacy, 1000–1530* (Cambridge: Cambridge University Press, 1994).

Boenig, Robert, 'Contemplations of the dread and love of God, Richard Rolle and Aelred of Rievaulx', *Mystics Quarterly*, 16 (1990), 27–33.

Boswell, John, *Christianity, Social Tolerance, and Homosexuality: Gay People in Western Europe from the Beginning of the Christian Era to the Fourteenth Century* (Chicago: University of Chicago Press, 1980).

Bradley Warren, Nancy, *Spiritual Economies: Female Monasticism in Later Medieval England* (Philadelphia: University of Pennsylvania Press, 2001).

Brantley, Jessica, *Reading in the Wilderness: Private Devotion and Public Performance in Late Medieval England* (Chicago and London: University of Chicago Press, 2007).

Brown, Peter (ed.), *Medieval English Literature and Culture, c.1350–c.1500* (2006; Oxford: Blackwell, 2007).

——, *The Rise of Western Christendom: Triumph and Diversity, A.D. 200–1000* (1996; Oxford: Blackwell, 2003).

Burrow, John A., 'Fantasy and language in *The Cloud of Unknowing*', *Essays in Criticism*, 27 (1977), 283–98.

Butler, Cuthbert, *Western Mysticism: The Teaching of SS Augustine, Gregory and Bernard on Contemplation and the Contemplative Life* (1922; London: Arrow Books, 1960).

Camporesi, Piero, *Juice of Life: The Symbolic and Magic Significance of Blood*, trans. R. R. Barr (1995; New York: Continuum, 1998).

Cannon, Christopher, 'Enclosure', in Carolyn Dinshaw and David Wallace (eds), *The Cambridge Companion to Medieval Women's Writing* (Cambridge: Cambridge University Press, 2003), pp. 109–23.

Canatella, H. M., 'Long-distance love: the ideology of male–female spiritual friendship in Goscelin of Saint Bertin's *Liber confortatorius*', *Journal of the History of Sexuality*, 19, 1 (2010), 35–53.

Clark, Elizabeth A., 'Sane insanity: women and asceticism in late ancient Christianity', *Medieval Encounters: Jewish, Christian and Muslim Culture in Confluence and Dialogue*, 3 (1997), 211–30.

——, 'Perilous readings: Jerome, asceticism, and Heresy', *Proceedings of the PMR Conference*, 19–20 (1994–6), 15–33.

Clark, John P. H., 'Action and contemplation in Walter Hilton', *Downside Review*, 97 (1979), 258–74.

Clay, Rotha Mary, *The Hermits and Anchorites of England* (London: Methuen, 1914).

——, 'Further studies on medieval recluses', *Journal of the British Archaeological Association*, 16 (1953), 74–86.

Cohen, Esther, *The Modulated Scream: Pain in Late Medieval Culture* (Chicago and London: University of Chicago Press, 2010).

Constable, Giles, *Culture and Spirituality in Medieval Europe* (Aldershot: Variorum, 1996).

——, *Three Studies in Medieval Religious and Social Thought* (Cambridge: Cambridge University Press, 1995).

——, 'Moderation and restraint in ascetic practices in the Middle Ages', in Haijo J. Westra (ed.), *From Athens to Chartres: Neoplatonism and Medieval Thought. Studies in Honour of Edouard Jeauneau* (Leiden: E. J. Brill, 1992), pp. 315–27.

——, *Attitudes towards Self-inflicted Suffering in the Middle Ages* (Brookline, Mass.: Hellenic College Press, 1982).

Cushing, Kathleen G., *Reform and Papacy in the Eleventh Century: Spirituality and Social Change* (Manchester: Manchester University Press, 2005).

Dahood, Roger, 'The current state of *Ancrene Wisse* group studies', *Medieval English Studies Newsletter*, 36 (1997), 6–14.

——, 'The use of coloured initials and other division markers in early versions of *Ancrene Riwle*', in Edward D. Kennedy, Ronald Waldron and Joseph S. Wittig (eds), *Medieval English Studies Presented to George Kane* (Cambridge: D. S. Brewer, 1988), pp. 79–97.

Daniell, Christopher, *From Norman Conquest to Magna Carta: England, 1066–1215* (London and New York: Routledge, 2005).

Darwin, Francis D. S., *The English Mediaeval Recluse* (London: SPCK, 1944).

D'Evelyn, Charlotte, 'Instructions for religious', in J. B. Severs, A. E. Hartung and J. E. Wells (eds), *A Manual of the Writings in Middle English, 1050–1500*, 10 vols (New Haven: Connecticut Academy of Arts and Sciences, 1967–98), vol. 2, p. 21.

Dobson, Eric J., *The Origins of 'Ancrene Wisse'* (Oxford: Clarendon Press, 1976).

Duffy, Eamon, *The Stripping of the Altars: Traditional Religion in England, c.1400–1580* (New Haven and London: Yale University Press, 1992).

Dutton, Elisabeth M., *Julian of Norwich: the Influence of Late-medieval Devotional Compilations* (Cambridge: D. S. Brewer, 2008).

Dutton, Marsha L., 'Christ our mother: Aelred's iconography for contemplative union', in E. Rozanne Elder (ed.), *Goad and Nail*, Studies in Medieval Cistercian History, 10 (Kalamazoo: Cistercian Studies Series, 1985), pp. 21–45.

Dyas, Dee, Valerie Edden and Roger Ellis (eds), *Approaching Medieval English Anchoritic and Mystical Texts* (Cambridge: D. S. Brewer, 2005).

Edsall, Mary Agnes, '"True anchoresses are called birds": asceticism as ascent and the purgative mysticism of the *Ancrene Wisse*', *Viator*, 34 (2003), 157–86.

Edwards, A. S. G. (ed.), *A Companion to Middle English Prose* (Cambridge: D. S. Brewer, 2004).

Elkins, Sharon K., *Holy Women of Twelfth-century England* (Chapel Hill: University of North Carolina Press, 1988).

Erler, Mary C., 'A London anchorite, Simon Appulby: his *Fruyte of Redempcyon* and its milieu', *Viator: Medieval and Renaissance Studies*, 29 (1998), 227–39.

Fanous, Samuel and Henrietta Leyser (eds), *Christina of Markyate: A Twelfth-century Holy Woman* (London and New York: Routledge, 2005).

Frassetto, Michael (ed.), *The Year 1000: Religious and Social Response to the Turning of the First Millennium* (Basingstoke and New York: Palgrave Macmillan, 2002).

Frost, Cheryl, 'The attitude to women and the adaptation to a feminine audience in the *Ancrene Wisse*', *AUMLA: The Journal of the Australasian Universities Language and Literature Association*, 50 (1978), 235–50.

Fulton, Rachel, *From Judgement to Passion: Devotion to Christ and the Virgin Mary, 800–1200* (New York and Chichester: Columbia University Press, 2002).

Georgianna, Linda, *The Solitary Self: Individuality in the 'Ancrene Wisse'* (Cambridge, Mass. and London: Harvard University Press, 1981).

Gilchrist, Roberta, *Contemplation and Action: The Other Monasticism* (London and New York: Leicester University Press, 1995).

Glasscoe, Marion, *English Medieval Mystics: Games of Faith* (London and New York: Longman, 1993).

—— (ed.), *The Medieval Mystical Tradition in England 1982: Symposium Proceedings* (Exeter: Exeter University Press, 1982).

Grayson, Janet, *Structure and Imagery in 'Ancrene Wisse'* (Hanover, NH: University Press of New England for the University of New Hampshire, 1974).

Griffiths, Fiona J., '"Men's duty to provide for women's needs": Abelard, Heloise, and their negotiation of the *cura monialium*', in Constance Hoffman Berman (ed.), *Medieval Religion: New Approaches* (New York and London: Routledge, 2005), pp. 209–315.

Gunn, Cate, *'Ancrene Wisse': From Pastoral Literature to Vernacular Spirituality* (Cardiff: University of Wales Press, 2008).

——, *'Ancrene Wisse*: a modern lay person's guide to a medieval religious text', *Magistra: A Journal of Women's Spirituality in History*, 8 (2002), 3–25.

——, '"Efter the measse-cos, hwen the preost sacreð": when is the moment of ecstasy in *Ancrene Wisse?*', *Notes and Queries*, 246 (2001), 105–8.

Hallier, Amédée, *The Monastic Theology of Aelred of Rievaulx: An Experiential Theology* (Shannon: Irish University Press, 1969).

Hamburger, Jeffrey F., *The Visual and the Visionary: Art and Female Spirituality in Late Medieval Germany* (New York: Zone, 1998).

Hamilton, Bernard, 'Ideals of holiness: crusaders, contemplatives, and mendicants', *International History Review*, 17 (1995), 693–712.

Haskins, Susan, *Mary Magdalen: Myth and Metaphor* (London: Riverhead, 1993).

Herbert McAvoy, Liz, *Medieval Anchoritisms: Gender, Space and the Solitary Life* (Cambridge: D. S. Brewer, 2011).

—— (ed.), *Rhetoric of the Anchorhold: Space, Place and Body within the Discourses of Enclosure* (Cardiff: University of Wales Press, 2008).

—— and Mari Hughes-Edwards (eds), *Anchorites, Wombs and Tombs: Intersections of Gender and Enclosure in the Middle Ages* (Cardiff: University of Wales Press, 2005).

——, *Authority and the Female Body in the Writings of Julian of Norwich and Margery Kempe* (Cambridge: D. S. Brewer, 2004).

——, '"Neb ... sumdeal ilich wommon ant neddre is behinden": reading the monstrous in the anchoritic text', in Edward A. Jones (ed.), *The Medieval Mystical Tradition in England: Papers Read at Charney Manor, July 2004 [Exeter Symposium VII]* (Cambridge: D. S. Brewer, 2004), pp. 51–69.

——, '"The Moder's service": motherhood as matrix in Julian of Norwich', *Mystics Quarterly*, 24 (1998), 181–97.

Hollis, Stephanie, 'Strategies of emplacement and displacement: St Edith and the Wilton community in Goscelin's Legend of Edith and *Liber confortatorius*', in C. A. Lees and G. R. Overing (eds), *A Place to Believe In: Locating Medieval Landscapes* (Pennsylvania: The Pennsylvania State University Press, 2006), pp. 150–69.

Hollywood, Amy, *Sensible Ecstasy: Mysticism, Sexual Difference, and the Demands of History* (Chicago and London: University of Chicago Press, 2002).

——, *The Soul as Virgin Wife: Mechthild of Magdeburg, Marguerite Porete, and Meister Eckhart* (Notre Dame, Ind.: University of Notre Dame Press, 1995).

Howie, Cary, *Claustrophilia: The Erotics of Enclosure in Medieval Literature* (Basingstoke and New York: Palgrave Macmillan, 2007).

Hubnik, Sandi J., '(Re)constructing the medieval recluse: performative acts of virginity and the writings of Julian of Norwich', *The Historian*, 67, 1 (2005), 43–61.

Hudson, Anne, *Lollards and their Books* (London: Hambledon, 1985).

Hudson, Vivian K., 'Clothing and adornment imagery in *The Scale of Perfection*: a reflection of contemplation', *Studies in Spirituality*, 4 (1994), 116–14.

Hughes, Jonathan, *Pastors and Visionaries: Religion and Secular Life in Late Medieval Yorkshire* (Woodbridge: Boydell and Brewer, 1988).

Hughes-Edwards, Mari, 'The role of the anchoritic guidance writer: Goscelin of St Bertin', in Catherine Innes-Parker and Naoë Kukita Yoshikawa (eds), *Anchoritism in the Middle Ages: Texts and Traditions* (Cardiff: University of Wales Press, forthcoming 2012).

——, 'Anchoritism: the English tradition', in Liz Herbert McAvoy (ed.), *Anchoritic Traditions of Medieval Europe* (Woodbridge: Boydell and Brewer, 2010), pp. 131–52.

——, '"How good it is to be alone"? Sociability, solitude and medieval English Anchoritism', *Mystics Quarterly*, 35 (2009), 31–61.

——, 'Hedgehog skins and hairshirts: the changing role of asceticism in the anchoritic ideal', *Mystics Quarterly*, 28 (2002), 6–25.

Hussey, Stanley S., 'From *Scale* I to *Scale* II', *Analecta Cartusiana*, 130 (1995), 46–67.

——, 'Walter Hilton: traditionalist?', in Marion Glasscoe (ed.), *The Medieval Mystical Tradition in England: Papers Read at the Exeter Symposium, July 1980* (Exeter: Exeter University Press, 1980), pp. 1–16.

Innes-Parker, Catherine, 'Fragmentation and reconstruction: images of the female body in *Ancrene Wisse* and the Katherine Group', *Comitatus: A Journal of Medieval and Renaissance Studies*, 26 (1995), 27–52.

——, 'Virgin, bride and lover: a study of the relationship between sexuality and spirituality in anchoritic literature' (unpublished diss., Memorial University of Newfoundland, 1992).

James, M. R. and C. Jenkins, *A Descriptive Catalogue of the Manuscripts in the Library of Lambeth Palace* (Cambridge: Cambridge University Press, 1930–2).

Jollife, Peter S., *A Check-list of Middle English Prose Writings of Spiritual Guidance* (Toronto: Pontifical Institute of Mediaeval Studies, 1974).

Jones, Edward A., 'Anchoritic aspects of Julian of Norwich', in Liz Herbert McAvoy (ed.), *A Companion to Julian of Norwich* (Cambridge: D. S. Brewer, 2008), pp. 75–87.

——, 'A new look into the *Speculum inclusorum*', in Marion Glasscoe (ed.), *The Medieval Mystical Tradition in England, Ireland and Wales: Papers Read at Charney Manor, July 1999 (Exeter Symposium VI)* (Cambridge: D. S. Brewer, 1999), pp. 123–45.

——, 'The hermits and anchorites of Oxfordshire', *Oxoniensia*, 63 (1998), 51–77.

——, 'Langland and hermits', *Yearbook of Langland Studies*, 11 (1997), 67–86.

——, 'Rotha Clay's *Hermits and Anchorites of England*', *Monastic Research Bulletin*, 3 (1997), 46–8.

Kaelber, Lutz, *Schools of Asceticism: Ideology and Organization in Medieval Religious Communities* (Pennsylvania: The Pennsylvania State University Press, 1998).

Keen, Maurice, 'Wyclif, the Bible, and transubstantiation', in Anthony Kenny (ed.), *Wyclif in his Times* (Oxford: Clarendon Press, 1986), pp. 1–16.

Kerby-Fulton, Kathryn, *Books Under Suspicion: Censorship and Tolerance of Revelatory Writing in Late Medieval England* (Notre Dame, Ind.: University of Notre Dame Press, 2006).

Kieckhefer, Richard, *Unquiet Souls: Fourteenth Century Saints and their Religious Milieu* (Chicago and London: University of Chicago Press, 1984).

Knowles, David, *The Monastic Order in England: A History of its Developments from the Times of St Dunstan to the Fourth Lateran Council, 940–1216* (Cambridge: Cambridge University Press, 1963).

——, *The English Mystical Tradition* (New York: Harper, 1961).

——, *The Religious Orders in England, Volume II: The End of the Middle Ages* (Cambridge: Cambridge University Press, 1955).

Kocher, Suzanne, *Allegories of Love in Marguerite Porete's 'Mirror of simple souls'*, Medieval Women: Texts and Contexts, 17 (Turnout: Brepols, 2008).

Kroll, Jerome and Bernard Bachrach, *The Mystic Mind: The Psychology of Medieval Mystics and Ascetics* (New York and London: Routledge, 2005).

Lambert, Malcolm, *Medieval Heresy: Popular Movements from the Gregorian Reform to the Reformation* (1977; Oxford: Blackwell, 2002).

Latzke, Therese, 'Robert von Arbrissel, Ermengard und Eva', *Mittellateinisches Jahrbuch*, 19 (1984), 116–54.

Lawless, George, *Augustine of Hippo and his Monastic Rule* (1987; Oxford: Clarendon Press, 1991).

Lawrence, Clifford H., *Medieval Monasticism: Forms of Religious Life in Western Europe in the Middle Ages* (London and New York: Longman, 1989).

Leff, Gordon, *Heresy in the Later Middle Ages: The Relation of Heterodoxy to Dissent, c.1250–1450*, 2 vols (Manchester: Manchester University Press, 1967).

——, *Bradwardine and the Pelagians: A Study of His 'Dei Causa Dei' and Its Opponents* (Cambridge: Cambridge University Press, 1957).

Lehmijoki Gardner, Maiju, *Dominican Penitent Women* (New York and Mahwah: Paulist Press, 2005).

Leyser, Conrad, *Authority and Asceticism from Augustine to Gregory the Great* (Oxford: Clarendon Press, 2000).

Leyser, Henrietta, *Hermits and the New Monasticism. A Study of Religious Communities in Western Europe 1000–1150* (Basingstoke and New York: Palgrave Macmillan, 1984).

Licence, Tom, *Hermits and Recluses in English Society: 950–1200* (Oxford: Oxford University Press, 2011).

——, 'Evidence of recluses in eleventh-century England', in Malcolm Godden and Simon Keynes (eds), *Anglo-Saxon England*, 36 (2007), 221–34.

Liddell, Henry G. and Robert Scott, *A Greek–English Lexicon*, 2 vols (Oxford: Clarendon Press, 1843).

Lochrie, Karma, 'The language of transgression: body, flesh and word in mystical discourse', in Allen J. Frantzen (ed.), *Speaking Two Languages: Traditional Disciplines and Contemporary Theory in Medieval Studies* (Albany: SUNY, 1991), pp. 115–41.

McDonnell, Ernest W., *The Beguines and Beghards in Medieval Culture with Special Emphasis Upon the Belgian Scene* (New Brunswick, NJ: Rutgers University Press, 1954).

McGinn, Bernard, 'Contemplation in Gregory the Great', in John C. Cavadini (ed.), *Gregory the Great: A Symposium* (Notre Dame, Ind.: University of Notre Dame Press, 1995), pp. 146–67.

McGowan, Joseph P., 'An introduction to the corpus of Anglo-Latin literature', in Phillip Pulsiano and Elaine M. Treharne (eds), *A Companion to Anglo-Saxon Literature* (Oxford: Blackwell, 2001), pp. 11–49.

McGuire, Brian Patrick, *Friendship and Community: The Monastic Experience, 350–1250* (Kalamazoo: Cistercian Publications, 1988).

McHardy, A. K., 'Bishop Buckingham and the Lollards of Lincoln diocese', in Derek Baker (ed.), *Schism, Heresy and Religious Protest*, Studies in Church History, 9 (Cambridge: Cambridge University Press, 1972), pp. 131–45.

McIlroy, Claire Elizabeth, *The English Prose Treatises of Richard Rolle* (Cambridge: D. S. Brewer, 2004).

McSheffrey, Shannon, *Gender and Heresy: Women and Men in Lollard Communities, 1420–1530* (Philadelphia: University of Pennsylvania Press, 1995).

Magill, Kevin J., *Julian of Norwich: Mystic or Visionary?* (London and New York: Routledge, 2006).

Maitland, Sarah, 'Passionate prayer: masochistic images in women's experience', in L. Hurcombe (ed.), *Sex and God: Some Varieties of Women's Religious Experience* (London and New York: Routledge and Kegan Paul, 1987), pp. 125–40.

Martin, Thomas F., *Our Restless Heart: The Augustinian Tradition* (London: Darton, Longman & Todd, 2003).

Mayr-Harting, Henry, 'Functions of a twelfth-century recluse', *History: The Journal of the Historical Association*, 60 (1975), 337–52.

Meale, Carol M. (ed.), *Women and Literature in Britain: 1150–1500* (Cambridge: Cambridge Studies in Literature, 1993).

Millett, Bella, '*Ancrene Wisse* and the life of perfection', *Leeds Studies in English*, 33 (2002), 53–76.

——, '*Ancrene Wisse* and the book of hours', in Denis Renevey and Christiania Whitehead (eds), *Writing Religious Women: Female Spiritual and Textual Practices in Late Medieval England* (Cardiff: University of Wales Press, 2000), pp. 21–40.

——, *Ancrene Wisse, The Katherine Group and the Wooing Group: Annotated Bibliographies of Old and Middle English Literature*, vol. 2 (Cambridge: Boydell and Brewer, 1996).

——, '*Mouvance* and the medieval author: re-editing *Ancrene Wisse*', in Alistair J. Minnis (ed.), *Late-medieval Religious Texts and Their Transmission: Essays in Honour of A. I. Doyle* (Cambridge: D. S. Brewer, 1994), pp. 9–20.

——, 'The origins of *Ancrene Wisse*: new answers, new questions', *Medium Aevum*, 60 (1991), 206–28.

Mills, Robert, *Suspended Animation: Pain, Pleasure and Punishment in Medieval Culture* (London: Reaktion Books, 2005).

——, 'Gender, sodomy, friendship, and the medieval anchorhold', *Journal of Medieval Religious Cultures*, 36, 1 (2010), 1–27.

Milosh, Joseph E., *'The Scale of Perfection' and the English Mystical Tradition* (Madison, Milwaukee and London: University of Wisconsin, 1966).

Minnis, Alistair J., 'Affection and imagination in *The Cloud of Unknowing* and Hilton's *Scale of Perfection*', *Traditio*, 39 (1983), 323–66.

Mulder-Bakker, Anneke B., *Lives of the Anchoresses: The Rise of the Urban Recluse in Medieval Europe* (Philadelphia: University of Pennsylvania Press, 2005).

——, 'Was Mary Magdalen a Magdalen?', in R. I. A. Nip et al. (eds), *Media Latinitas: A Collection of Essays to Mark the Occasion of the Retirement of L. J. Engels* (Turnhout: Brepols, 1996), pp. 269–74.

——, 'The reclusorium as an informal centre of learning', in J. W. Drijvers and A. A. MacDonald (eds), *Centres of Learning: Learning and Location in Pre-modern Europe and the Near East* (Leiden: E. J. Brill, 1995), pp. 245–55.

Newman, Barbara, 'Liminalities: literate women in the long twelfth century', in Thomas F. X. Noble and John van Engen (eds), *European Transformations: The Long Twelfth Century* (Notre Dame, Ind.: University of Notre Dame Press, 2012), pp. 145–98.

——, 'Flaws in the golden bowl: gender and spiritual formation in the twelfth century', *Traditio*, 45 (1989–90), 111–46.

Otter, Monika, 'Entrances and exits: performing the Psalms in Goscelin's *Liber confortatorius*', *Speculum*, 83, 2 (2008), 283–302.

——, 'Inclusae exclusus: desire, identification and gender in the *Liber confortatorius*', in Goscelin of St Bertin, *The Book of Encouragement and Consolation (Liber confortatorius). The Letter of Goscelin to the Recluse Eva*, trans. Monika Otter (Cambridge: D. S. Brewer, 2004), pp. 151–67.

Park, Tarjei, 'Reflecting Christ: the role of the flesh in Walter Hilton and Julian of Norwich', in Marion Glasscoe (ed.), *The Medieval Mystical Tradition in England V: Papers Read at Dartington Hall, July 1992* (Exeter: Exeter University Press, 1992), pp. 17–37.

Petroff, Elizabeth A. (ed.), *Medieval Women's Visionary Literature* (New York and Oxford: Oxford University Press, 1986).

Pollard, William F. and Richard Boenig (eds), *Mysticism and Spirituality in Medieval England* (Cambridge: D. S. Brewer, 1997).

Potts, Jennifer, Lorna Stevenson and Jocelyn Wogan-Browne (eds), *Concordance to 'Ancrene Wisse': MS Corpus Christi College, Cambridge 402* (Cambridge: D. S. Brewer, 1993).

Power, Eileen E., *Medieval English Nunneries: c.1275 to 1535* (Cambridge: Cambridge University Press, 1922).

Price, Jocelyn, '"Inner" and "outer": conceptualizing the body in *Ancrene Wisse* and Aelred's *De institutione inclusarum*', in Gregory Kratzmann and James Simpson (eds), *Medieval Religious and Ethical Literature. Essays in Honour of G. H. Russell* (Cambridge: D. S. Brewer, 1986), pp. 192–208.

Ranft, Patricia, *Women and the Religious Life in Premodern Europe* (1996; New York: St Martin's Press, 1998).

Renevey, Denis, 'Looking for a context: Rolle, anchoritic culture and the office of the dead', in G. D. Caie and D. Renevey (eds), *Medieval Texts in Context* (London and New York: Routledge, 2008), pp. 192–211.

——, *Language, Self and Love: Hermeneutics in the Writings of Richard Rolle and the Commentaries on the Song of Songs* (Cardiff: University of Wales Press, 2001).

Renna, Thomas, 'Virginity in the Life of Christina of Markyate and Aelred of Rievaulx's *Rule*', *American Benedictine Review*, 36 (1985), 79–92.

Rex, Richard, *The Lollards* (Basingstoke: Palgrave Macmillan, 2002).

Riches, Samantha J. E. and Sarah Salih (eds), *Gender and Holiness: Men, Women and Saints in Late Medieval Europe* (London and New York: Routledge, 2002).

Ridyard, Susan J., 'Functions of a twelfth-century recluse revisited: the case of Godric of Finchale', in Richard Gameson and Henrietta Leyser (eds), *Belief and Culture in the Middle Ages: Studies Presented to Henry Mayr-Harting* (Oxford: Oxford University Press, 2001), pp. 236–50.

Riehle, Wolfgang, *The Middle English Mystics* (London, Boston and Henley: Routledge and Kegan Paul, 1981).

Robertson, Elizabeth, 'Medieval medical views of women and female spirituality in the *Ancrene Wisse* and Julian of Norwich's *Showings*', in Linda Lomperis and Sarah Stanbury (eds), *Feminist Approaches to the Body in Medieval Literature* (Philadelphia: University of Pennsylvania Press, 1993), pp. 142–67.

——, *Early English Devotional Prose and the Female Audience* (Knoxville: University of Tennessee Press, 1990).

Rosof, Patricia J. F., 'The anchoress in the twelfth and thirteenth centuries', in John A. Nichols and Lillian Thomas Shank (eds), *Medieval Religious Women, Vol. Two: Peaceweavers* (Kalamazoo: Cistercian Studies Series, 1987), pp. 123–45.

Rubin, Miri, *Mother of God: A History of the Virgin Mary* (London, New York, Victoria, Ontario and Auckland: Penguin, 2009).

——, *Corpus Christi: The Eucharist in Late Medieval* Culture (Cambridge: Cambridge University Press, 1991).

Salih, Sarah, 'When is a bosom not a bosom? Problems with "erotic mysticism"', in Anke Bernau, Ruth Evans and Sarah Salih (eds), *Medieval Virginities* (Toronto and Cardiff: University of Wales Press and University of Toronto Press, 2003), pp. 14–32.

——, *Versions of Virginity in Late Medieval Europe* (Cambridge: D. S. Brewer, 2001).

Salomon, David A., '*Corpus Mysticum*: text as body/body as text', in Susannah Mary Chewning (ed.), *Intersections of Sexuality and the Divine in Medieval Culture: The Word Made Flesh* (Hampshire: Ashgate, 2005), pp. 140–55.

Sargent, Michael G. (ed.), *De Cella in Seculum: Religious and Secular Life and Devotion in Late Medieval England* (Cambridge: D. S. Brewer, 1989).

——, 'Walter Hilton's *Scale of Perfection*: the London manuscript group reconsidered', *Medium Aevum*, 52 (1983), 189–216.

——, 'Contemporary criticism of Richard Rolle', *Analecta Cartusiana*, 55 (1981), 160–205.

Sauer, Michelle, '"Prei for me mi leue suster": the paradox of the anchoritic "community" in late medieval England', *Prose Studies*, 26, 1–2 (2003), 153–75.

Sharpe, Richard, 'Anselm as author: publishing in the late eleventh century', *Journal of Medieval Latin*, 19 (2009), 1–87.

Sheils, W. J. (ed.), *Monks, Hermits and the Ascetic Tradition*, Studies in Church History, 22 (Oxford: Blackwell, 1985).

Simons, Walter, *Cities of Ladies: Beguine Communities in the Medieval Low Countries, 1200–1565* (Philadelphia: University of Pennsylvania Press, 2001).

Smith, Lesley and Jane H. M. Taylor (eds), *Women, the Book and the Godly: Selected Proceedings of the St Hilda's Conference 1993* (Cambridge: D. S. Brewer, 1995).

Somerset, Fiona, 'Eciam mulier: women in Lollardy and the problem of sources', in Linda Olson and Kathryn Kerby-Fulton (eds), *Voices in Dialogue: Reading Women in the Middle Ages* (Notre Dame, Ind.: University of Notre Dame Press, 2005), pp. 261–78.

Sommerfeldt, John R., 'The rape of the soul: the vocabulary of contemplation in Aelred of Rievaulx's *Mirror of Love*, Book II', in J. R. Sommerfeldt (ed.), *Erudition at God's Service. Studies in Medieval Cistercian History*, 11 (Kalamazoo: Cistercian Studies Series, 1987), pp. 169–74.

Southern, Richard W., *Saint Anselm: A Portrait in a Landscape* (Cambridge: Cambridge University Press, 1990).

——, *Medieval Humanism and Other Studies* (Oxford: Blackwell, 1970).

——, *The Middle Ages*, The Pelican History of the Church, 10 vols (London, New York, Victoria, Ontario and Auckland: Penguin, 1970), vol. 2.

——, *Western Society and the Church in the Middle Ages* (London, New York, Victoria, Ontario and Auckland: Penguin, 1970).

Spence, Sarah, *Texts and the Self in the Twelfth Century* (Cambridge: Cambridge University Press, 1996).

Squire, Aelred, *Aelred of Rievaulx: A Study* (London: SPCK, 1969).

Stroud, Daphne, 'Eve of Wilton and Goscelin of St Bertin at Old Sarum, *c.*1070–1078', *Wiltshire Archaeological and Natural History Magazine*, 99 (2006), 204–12.

Sutherland, Jenifer, 'Amplification of the virgin: play and empowerment in Walter of Wimborne's *Marie Carmina*', in Bonnie Maclachlan and Judith Fletcher (eds), *Virginity Revisited: Configurations of the Unpossessed Body* (Toronto, Buffalo and London: University of Toronto Press, 2007), pp. 128–48.

Swanson, Robert N., *Religion and Devotion in Europe, c.1215–c.1515* (Cambridge: Cambridge University Press, 1995).

Tanner, Norman P., *The Church in Late-medieval Norwich, 1370–1532* (Toronto: Pontifical Institute of Medieval Studies, 1984).

Turner, H. Thackeray, 'Notes on Compton Church, Surrey', *The Proceedings of the Society of Antiquaries*, 12 March 1908, 4–7.

Turner, Victor, *The Ritual Process: Structure and Anti-structure* (1969; New York: Aldine de Gruyter, 1995).

Underhill, Evelyn, *Mysticism: A Study in the Nature and Development of Spiritual Consciousness*, 2 vols (London: Methuen, 1912).

van Rossum, Irene, '*Adest meliori parte*: a portrait of monastic friendship in exile in Goscelin's *Liber confortatorius*' (unpublished D.Phil. thesis, University of York, 1999).

Vauchez, André, *Sainthood in the Later Middle Ages*, trans. J. Birrell (Cambridge: Cambridge University Press, 1997).

Voaden, Rosalyn, *God's Words, Women's Voices: The Discernment of Spirits in the Writing of Late Medieval Women Visionaries* (Woodbridge: York Medieval Press, 1999).

Wada, Yoko (ed.), *A Companion to 'Ancrene Wisse'* (Cambridge: D. S. Brewer, 2003).

——, 'Dominican authorship of *Ancrene Wisse*: the evidence of the introduction', in (ed.), *A Book of Ancrene Wisse* (Suita, Osaka: Kansai University Press, 2002), pp. 95–110.

Wakelin, M. F., 'Richard Rolle and the language of mystical experience in the fourteenth century', *The Downside Review*, 5 (1979), 192–203.

Walker Bynum, Caroline, *Fragmentation and Redemption: Essays on Gender and the Human Body in Medieval Religion* (New York: Zone, 1992).

——, *Holy Feast and Holy Fast: The Religious Significance of Food to Medieval Women*, The New Historicism: Studies in Cultural Poetics (Berkeley, Los Angeles and London: University of California Press, 1987).

——, *Jesus as Mother: Studies in the Spirituality of the High Middle Ages* (Berkeley, Los Angeles and London: University of California Press, 1982).

Ward, Jennifer, *Women of the English Nobility and Gentry, 1066–1500* (Manchester: Manchester University Press, 1995).

Warren, Ann K., *Anchorites and their Patrons in Medieval England* (Berkeley, Los Angeles and London: University of California Press, 1985).

——, 'The nun as anchoress: England 1100–1500', in John A. Nichols and Lillian Thomas Shank (eds), *Medieval Religious Women, Vol. One: Distant Echoes* (Kalamazoo: Cistercian Studies Series, 1984), pp. 197–212.

Watson, Nicholas, '"With the heat of the hungry heart": empowerment and *Ancrene Wisse*', in Mary C. Erler and Maryanne Kowaleski (eds), *Gendering the Master Narrative: Women and Power in the Middle Ages* (Ithaca and London: Cornell University Press, 2003), pp. 52–70.

——, 'The Middle English mystics', in David Wallace (ed.), *The Cambridge History of Medieval English Literature* (Cambridge: Cambridge University Press, 1999), pp. 539–65.

——, 'Melting into God the English way: deification in the Middle English version of Marguerite Porete's *Mirouer des simples âmes anienties*', in Rosalyn Voaden (ed.), *Prophets Abroad: The Reception of Continental Holy Women in Late Medieval England* (Cambridge: D. S. Brewer, 1996), pp. 19–51.

——, 'Censorship and cultural change in late medieval England: vernacular theology, the Oxford translation debate, and Arundel's Constitutions of 1409', *Speculum*, 70 (1995), 822–64.

——, *Richard Rolle and the Invention of Authority* (Cambridge: Cambridge University Press, 1991).

——, 'The methods and objectives of thirteenth-century anchoritic devotion', in Marion Glasscoe (ed.), *The Medieval Mystical Tradition in England IV. The Exeter Symposium IV: Papers Read at Dartington Hall, July 1987* (Cambridge: D. S. Brewer, 1987), pp. 132–53.

Watt, Diane (ed.), *Medieval Women in their Communities* (Cardiff: University of Wales Press, 1997).

——, 'Reconstructing the word: the political prophecies of Elizabeth Barton (1506–1534)', *Renaissance Quarterly*, 50 (1997), 136–63.

——, *Secretaries of God: Women Prophets in Late Medieval and Early Modern England* (Cambridge: D. S. Brewer, 1997).

Weber, Max, *Essays in Sociology*, ed. and trans. H. H. Gerth and C. Wright Mills (New York: Oxford University Press, 1946).

Wenham, L. P. and C. J. Hatcher, 'The anchoress of Richmond, north Yorkshire', in *A Richmond Miscellany*, North Yorkshire County Record Office Publications, 25 (1980), 46–55.

Wheatley, Abigail, *The Idea of the Castle in Medieval England* (Woodbridge: York Medieval Press, 2004).

Wiethaus, Ulrike (ed.), *Maps of Flesh and Light: The Religious Experience of Medieval Women Mystics* (Syracuse, New York: Syracuse University Press, 1993).

Wilmart, André, 'Eve et Goscelin (I)', *Révue Bénédictine*, 46 (1934), 414–38.

——, 'Eve et Goscelin (II)', *Révue Bénédictine*, 50 (1938), 42–83.

Woolgar, Christopher M., *The Senses in Late Medieval England* (New Haven and London: Yale University Press, 2006).

Yohe, K. M., 'Sexual attraction and the motivations for love and friendship in Aelred of Rievaulx', *Benedictine Review*, 46 (1995), 283–307.

Zumthor, Paul, *Essai de poétique médiévale* (Paris: Seuil, 1972).

Online secondary sources

Academia.edu, *http://northwestern.academia.edu* (accessed 7 September 2011).

Gale, Colin, 'Treasure in earthen vessels: treasures from Lambeth Palace library', *Fulcrum: Renewing the Evangelical Centre*, *http://www.fulcrum-anglican.org.uk/page.cfm?ID=542* (accessed 7 September 2011).

Hermits and Anchorites of England, *http://hermits.ex.ac.uk* (accessed 7 September 2011).

The Middle English Dictionary, *http://quod.lib.umich.edu/m/med* (accessed 7 September 2011).

The Oxford English Dictionary, *http://www.oed.com* (accessed 7 September 2011).

Index

Abbey of the Holy Ghost 79, 93, 97
Achler, Elisabeth 106
Ad Jovinium (Jerome) 61–2
Ademar of Chabannes 85, 99
Aelred *see De institutione inclusarum*
    (Aelred)
Alexander, St 50, 53
Allen, Hope Emily 25
almsgiving 42, 47–8, 69
Ambrose, St 17, 53, 86, 94
anchorholds 1, 3–7. 15, 20–1, 33–4, 36–40,
    44–6, 50–1, 55–6, 62, 74, 80, 96–7,
    100–2, 108–9, 110
    Compton, Surrey 7
    gardens 7
    Leatherhead, Surrey 7
    rural locations 7, 51
    servants 45–6, 47
    urban locations 7, 51
anchoritic patrons 6, 22, 47
Ancren Riwle (Morton) 22, 46, 54, 63
Ancrene Wisse
    on asceticism 59–60, 63–4, 68, 69, 71, 72,
        73–4, 76
    on chastity 53, 54
    on contemplative experience 81, 83, 86,
        87, 90, 91–2, 93, 94
    on enclosure 32, 33, 34, 35, 36, 37, 38, 39
    on orthodoxy 100–101, 103
    overview 8, 9, 10, 11, 21–5, 30
    on social interaction 45–7, 48, 50–51
    on solitude 41, 42
Angela of Foligno 89, 91
Anselm, St
    Cur Deus Homo 75
    letters *see* letters of St Anselm
Antony, St 60
Appulby, Simon 97
Arundel's Constitutions 102
ascent metaphors 92–3
asceticism

aggressive 60, 62, 63–6, 72, 77
and chastity 63
and contemplation 69, 81
and discretion 61, 67–9, 71, 72
as distinct from penance 22, 59–60
early medieval period 62–9
history of 59–62
later medieval period 69–75
and meditation 75–80
passive 60, 66
as safeguarding enclosure 39
Augustine of Hippo, St 61, 94
    Confessiones 61, 99
    De Civitate Dei 99
    De Doctrina Christiana 61
Augustinian Rule 68–9, 72
Ayto, John 29

Bachrach, Bernard 60
Bacon, Robert 24
Baker, Denise 78, 82, 93
Baldwin (ascetic) 73
Baldwin of Ford 106
Barratt, Alexandra 20, 21, 29, 41, 53
Bartholomew of Farne 65–6
Bartlett, Ann Clark 48
Barton, Elizabeth 88
Beatrice of Nazareth 91
Beauchamp, Richard 5, 88
beguines 95, 106
Bell, Rudolph M. 64
Bendict, St 3, 61, 86
Benedictine Rule 3, 61, 62, 63, 64, 66, 67
Bernard of Clairvaux 67, 106
Bernau, Anke 54
Bestul, Thomas H. 101
Bhattacharji, Santha 78
bible
    2 Corinthians 89–90
    Ecclesiastes 90
    Luke 94

Proverbs 90
Psalms 60
Song of Songs 90, 92
vernacular translation of 102, 103
Bildhauer, Bettina 76
Biller, Peter 72
Bilney, Thomas 102
Blandina, St 65
blood imagery 76, 77–8
Boenig, Robert 82
Boethius 99
Book of Margery Kempe 96
Book to a Mother 89
Boswell, John 55
Bradley Warren, Nancy 42
Bradwardine, Thomas 103
Brantley, Jessica 69
Brian of Lingen 24
Bridget of Sweden 71, 101
Bridgettines 96
Brithric (recluse, death of) 32, 65
British Library, Harley MS 1740 79
Brown, Peter 86
Browne, William 31
Bruno of Colgne 69
Brut, Walter 48
Buckingham, Bishop 5
Burrow, John 35
Butler, Cuthbert 82

Caesarius of Heisterbach 73
Cagnoli, Gerard 72, 93
Camaldolese 66
Camporesi, Pietro 71
Canatella, H.M. 18, 19
Cannon, Christopher 35
Carrow Priory, Norwich 7
Carthusians 69, 96
Cassian, John 61, 69, 72
Catherine of Genoa 96
Catherine of Siena 71, 91, 93–4, 101
cells *see* anchorholds
ceremonies of enclosure 4–5
Chadwick, Henry 59
Charterhouse of Sheen 7, 31
chastity 21, 22, 29, 52–6, 63
Chester-le-Street 7
Christ 19, 26, 35, 41, 54, 71, 75–80, 87, 90–91, 105
Christina of Markyate 17, 20
Christina the Astonishing 65, 74
Christine (of St James's Church, Shere) 5
Chrystosom, John 54
Cistercians 50, 66–7
Clark, John P.H. 28

Clay, Rotha Mary 4, 5, 7, 8, 44, 63, 88, 102
Cloud of Unknowing 35, 83, 97
Cluniacs 66–7
communion *see* Eucharist
community, support for anchoritism 5, 6
community, virtual anchoritic 46–7
confession 22, 24, 28, 59–60
Confessiones (Augustine) 61, 99
confessors 45, 47, 101
Consolation of Philosophy (Boethius) 99
Constable, Giles 61, 62, 71, 94, 98
Consuetudines Cartusiae (Guigo) 69
contemplative experience
    active and contemplative lives 26, 40, 94–8
    and asceticism 69, 81
    contemplative fusion 89–94
    contemplative ravishment 92–3
    and orthodoxy 98–107
    and personal experience 26–7, 29
    and rationality 28–9
    as safeguarding enclosure 39, 40
    and the senses 22, 28–9
    and solitude 43, 94–5
    three stages of 26, 84–94
    terminology 82–4
Cottle, Basil 8
Cur Deus Homo (Anselm) 75
Cushing, Kathleen G. 98

Dahood, Roger 23
Damian, Peter 17, 66, 81
Daniell, Christopher 6, 66, 98
Darwin, Francis D.S. 44
Day, Mabel 22
de Gorran, Geoffrey 17
de Heton, Isolda 5
De causa Dei (Bradwardine) 103
De Civitate Dei (Augustine) 99
De Doctrina Christiana (Augustine) 61
De institutione inclusarum (Aelred)
    on asceticism 59, 63, 64, 67–8, 73–4, 76
    on chastity 53–5
    on contemplative experience 81, 83, 84–5, 87, 89, 94, 98
    on enclosure 32, 36, 37, 39
    on orthodoxy 100, 103
    overview 9, 20–21,
    on social interaction 41–2, 44, 45–6, 47, 48, 50–51
    on solitude 41–2
De institutione inclusarum (vernacular redaction extant in Oxford, Bodleian Library, MS Bodley 423)
    on asceticism 74

on chastity 54–5
on contemplative experience 84
on enclosure 32–3, 34, 37–8, 39
on orthodoxy 103
overview 9, 10, 11, 29
on social interaction 47–9, 51
De Ormesta Mundi (Orosius) 99
De Virginibus (St Ambrose) 53
death metaphors 4–5, 6, 35–8, 42
desert solitaries 3, 60, 61, 70
D'Evelyn, Charlotte 10
Dialogue on Miracles (Caesarius) 73
Dobson, Eric J. 23, 24, 47
Doctrine of the Heart, The 29
documentary records 4–6
Dominicans 24, 45, 69, 102
Duffy, Eamon 107

Edith of Wilton 16, 86
Edsall, Mary 81
Elijah 41
Elisabeth of Schönau 76, 87
Elliott, Dyan 16, 17–18
Ellis, Roger 30
Elzéar of Sabran 86
enclosure
    ceremonies of 4–5
    and fixity of place 32–3
    flights from 5
    length of 7
    licences for 4
    as living death 35–8
    purpose of 33–5
    safeguarding 39–40
    see also anchorholds
Eucharist 39–40, 48, 64, 75, 90–91,
    105–7
Eusebius of Caesarea 65
Evans, Ruth 96
Eve (addressee of *Liber confortatorius*) 15–
    18, 27, 34, 36, 38, 46, 52, 62, 65, 99

family members, of recluses 16, 46–7, 48
fear 8–9, 103
Finke, Laurie A. 82, 89
fire metaphors 29, 76, 93
Fishlake, Thomas 28
flights from enclosure 5
Flora of Beaulieu 71, 93
Fonte Avellana community 66
Fontevrault community 66
Form of Living, The (Rolle)
    on asceticism 70, 71, 72, 73–4
    on chastity 55–6
    on contemplative experience 81, 83–4, 85,

89, 92, 93, 95, 97
    on enclosure 34–5, 38, 40
    on orthodoxy 103–4, 105
    overview 9–10, 22, 25–7, 28–9
    on social interaction 47–8, 49, 51
    on solitude 42–3
Francis, St 76
Franciscans 69, 103
Frassetto, Michael 18, 85
Fruit of Redempcyon (Appulby) 97
Fulton, Rachel 91

Gale, Colin 19
Gambacorta, Clare 71–2
Genoveva (ascetic) 65
Georgianna, Linda 10, 35, 36, 44, 92
Germaine of Auxerre 65
Gerson, Jean 87, 101
Gertrude of Helfta, St 86, 87, 91
Gilbert of Sempringham 24
Gilchrist, Roberta 7
Glasscoe, Marion 82
Godric of Finchale 65
Godwine (hermit) 24
Goscelin of St Bertin's *see Liber
    confortatorius* (Goscelin)
Grandmontines 66
Grayson, Janet 35
Gregory, St 94
Griffiths, Fiona J. 99
Gualberto, John 66
Guigo 69
Gunn, Cate 24–5, 53, 82, 100

Hadewijch of Brabant 86–7, 91–2
Hamburger, Jeffrey F. 78–9, 90
Hanna, Ralph 25
Hasenfratz, Robert 6, 24
Hayward, Rebecca 17, 18, 41, 99
Henry V 5, 31, 88
Henry VI 5, 88
Henry VIII 88
Henry of Coquet 66
heresy 72, 96, 99–100, 102–6
Herman, Bishop of Ramsbury and Sherborne
    15, 16
hermits 3–4
Hervé of Vendôme 16
Hilary of Orléans 16
Hildegard of Bingen 87, 89
Hilton, Walter
    On Mixed Life 95–6
    Scale of Perfection see *Scale of Perfection*
    (Hilton)
Historia ecclesiastica (Eusebius) 65

Hollis, Stephanie 15–16, 17, 19, 52, 99
Hollywood, Amy 65, 87
Holy Name 105
homosexuality 53, 55
Howie, Cary 35, 44
Hubnik, Sandi J. 64
Hudson, Anne 102
Hudson, Vivian Kay 28
Hugh, hermit of Caen 19–20, 21, 27
Hughes, Jonathan 78, 95
Hussey, Stanley 27

Inge, Dean 82
Innes-Parker, Catherine 100
Innocent III, Pope 72

James of Vitry 65, 76
Jenkins, Jacqueline 96
Jerome, St 61–2, 94
Jestice, Phyllis G. 54, 75, 105
John the Baptist, St 41
John of Bridlington, St 88
Jones, Edward A. 3–4, 5, 8, 30, 31
Julian of Norwich 5, 78, 88–9, 91, 93, 96–7

Kempe, Margery 83, 89, 96, 98, 107
Kerby-Fulton, Kathryn 89
Kieckhefer, Richard 72
Kirkby, Margaret 25, 26
Knowles, David 26
Kroll, Jerome 60
Kügelin, Konrad 106

La Sainte Abbaye 84
Lampett, Julian 7
Lawrence, Clifford H. 66, 69
Leff, Gordon 102, 104
Lehmijoki Gardner, Maiju 71
letters of St Anselm
    on chastity 53
    on contemplative experience 81, 83, 84,
        86
    on orthodoxy 100, 101
    overview 9, 19–20, 21, 27
    on social interaction 45, 47, 49
    on solitude 41, 43
Leyser, Conrad 59, 60
Leyser, Henrietta 4
Liber confortatorius (Goscelin)
    on asceticism 60, 62–3, 64–5, 67,
        75–6
    on chastity 52–3, 54
    on contemplative experience 81, 83, 84,
        85–6, 90–91, 93
    on enclosure 32, 33–4, 36–7, 38, 39–40

    on orthodoxy 98–100, 106
    overview 9, 15–19, 22, 27
    on social interaction 45, 46, 50–51
    on solitude 41, 42
Licence, Tom 4, 6–7, 10, 19, 43–4
Lochrie, Karma 54, 83
Lollardy 102, 103, 106
Loricatus, Dominic 66
love 17–18, 20, 22, 26, 27, 40, 43, 49, 72,
    74, 75–6, 81, 92
Love, Nicholas 79, 97
Lutgard of Aywières 65
Lydgate, John 92–3
Lyndwood, William 7

McAvoy, Liz Herbert 6, 45, 97, 100
McDonnell, Ernest 106
McIlroy, Claire 27
MacPherson, Mary Paul 21, 53–4
Magdalene, Mary 54, 89, 97
Maitland, Sarah 100
Mann, Katherine 102
Martin, St 86
Marx, C.W. 79
Mary, sister of Lazarus 41, 94, 96, 97
Mary, the Virgin 41, 85, 87, 88, 91
Mary of Egypt 41, 64
Mary of Oignies 65, 71, 76, 81, 91, 106
masturbation 50, 53, 55
Matilda (of St Peter's, Leicester) 102
Mayr-Harting, Henry 6
Mechthild of Hackeborn 87, 91
Mechthild of Magdeburg 87, 91
meditation 21, 28, 30, 75–80, 83, 84–5
Meditationes vitae Christi 79, 97
Millett, Bella 9, 21–2, 23, 24, 25, 45, 46, 63
Mills, Robert 53
Mirror of St Edmund 89
Mirror of Simple Souls 88
Mirrour of the Blessed Lyf of Jesu Christi
    (Love) 79, 97
Modesta (visionary) 86
Morton, James 22, 63
Moses 41, 65
Mueller, Janel 28
Mulder-Bakker, Anneke B. 44–5, 86
Myrour of Recluses, The
    on chastity 55
    on contemplative experience 85, 88
    on enclosure 32, 33, 38, 39
    on orthodoxy 104, 105–6
    overview 10, 11, 30–31
    on social interaction 47, 48, 51
mysticism 82–3

Newman, Barbara 36
Nicholas, St 86
Norbert, St 69

Ogilvie-Thompson, Sarah 26
Oliger, P. Livario 30
On Mixed Life (Hilton) 95–6
Orosius, Paulus 99
orthodoxy 26, 98–107
Otter, Monika 10, 15, 16, 17, 18, 35, 40, 52, 60, 62, 63, 81, 83, 84

paganism 98–9
Pageants of Richard Beauchamp 88
Palmer, Anna 5, 102
Park, Tarjei 70–71
Parkes, Malcolm 21–2
Passion, the 15, 62, 75–80
patrons 6, 22, 47
Paul, St 41, 86, 89–90
Pearsall, Derek 25
penance 22, 30, 59–60
Perpetua, St 64–5
Peter of Luxembourg 71
pilgrimages, of recluses 6
place, anchoritic fixity of 22, 32–3
Pollard, William F. 28, 82
pollution metaphors 52
Poor, Herbert 24
Poor, Richard 24
Porete, Margaret 88
poverty 47–8, 69
Powell Harley, Marta 30, 39, 55
prayer 28, 30, 42, 48, 83, 85
Premonstratensians 24, 68, 69
Price, Jocelyn 45
purification 26, 60, 70, 74, 75, 77, 85, 105
Putter, Ad 93

Ranft, Patricia 8
ravishment 92–3
Rawghton, Emma 5, 88
reading 30, 39, 46, 69, 83, 99
relatives; *see* family members of recluses
Renevey, Denis 6, 26–7, 29
Richard II 5
Robert of Arbrissel 16, 17, 66
Robert of Molesme 67
Robertson, Elizabeth 17, 39, 44, 98
Roger of Markyate 65
Rolle, Richard *see The Form of Living* (Rolle)
Romuald of Ravenna 66
Rosof, Patricia J.F. 42

Ross, Ellen M. 78
Roy, Gopa 100
Rubin, Miri 37
Russell-Smith, Joy 28

St Augustine's, Canterbury 16
Saint-Eutrope 16
St James's Church, Shere 5
St Julian's Church, Conisford 7
St Peter's Church, Leicester 5, 102
St Peter's Church, Northampton 102
Saint-Sauveur-le-Vicomte, Angers 15–16
Salih, Sarah 53
Saloman, David A. 87
Salu, Mary 36
Sancii, Gonsalvo 72
Sargent, Michael 27
Sauer, Michelle 22, 46
Savage, Anne 24
Scale of Perfection (Hilton)
    on asceticism 69–71, 72–5, 77, 78
    on chastity 55
    on contemplative experience 84, 88, 89, 92, 93, 94–5, 97–8
    on enclosure 32, 34, 35, 38, 39, 40
    on orthodoxy 101, 103, 104–5
    overview 10, 11, 22, 25, 27–9
    on social interaction 48, 51–2
    on solitude 43
Scherman, Emma 6, 7
Schulenburg, Jane 86, 99
Scott, Elizabeth 7
Secreta Secretorum (Lydgate) 92–3
self-flagellation 64, 66, 71
self-knowledge 70
self-starvation 64
senses, the 22, 28, 39, 50–52, 54, 86
sexuality 5, 9, 50, 52–6, 63, 90–91
shared solitude 16
Sharpe, Richard 19
Shepherd, Geoffrey 22–3, 81
sickness 63, 69–70
sight 28, 39, 50–51, 86
silence 41–2, 43, 69, 95
Silvanus, Bishop of Toulouse 65
Simon of Ghent 24
Simons, Walter 106
sin 15, 28, 30, 34, 49, 54–5, 60, 64, 69–71, 74, 100
Sitwell, Gerard 81
social interaction, of recluses
    acceptable levels of 39, 43–9
    and chastity 52–6
    demonizing of 49–52

sodomy 55
solitude
   and contemplation 43, 94–5
   idealisation of 41–3
   qualification of 43–9
   safeguarding 49–52
   shared 16
Somerset, Fiona 48
Southern, Richard W. 19, 75, 99
Speculum inclusorum
   on asceticism 70, 71, 73, 77–8
   on chastity 55
   on contemplative experience 84, 85, 88,
      92, 97–8
   on enclosure 32, 33, 38
   on orthodoxy 104, 105–6
   overview 9, 10, 11, 29–31
   on social interaction 47–8, 51
   on solitude 43
spousal metaphors 91, 92
Squire, Aelred 20
Staley, Lynn 96
stigmatization 76, 106
Stratford, John, Bishop of Winchester 5
Stroud, Daphne 16, 18
suffering 59–60, 75–9; *see also* asceticism
Suso, Henry 72, 73, 93
Sutherland, Jenifer 91
syneisaktism 53, 55

Tanner, Norman 7
teaching 48
tears 85
Thomas of Cantimpré 65
Tolkien, J.R.R. 24

Trus, Sir John 31
Turner, Victor 37

Underhill, Evelyn 82
Urban V, Pope 71

Vallombrosa community 66
Victorines 24, 68
virginity 53, 54, 55; *see also* chastity
visions 78–9, 84, 85–9, 98, 101
Vitas Patrum 24, 60, 61
Voaden, Rosalynn 82

Waldensians 72
Walker Bynum, Caroline 64, 87, 96
Warner, Christopher 88
Warren, Ann K. 3, 4, 5, 6, 7–8, 10, 26, 44,
   47, 63, 81, 82, 83, 90
Watson, Nicholas 24, 25, 27, 35, 44, 81, 82,
   83, 92, 95, 96, 100
Watt, Diane 98
Watton community 54
Whalley Abbey 5
White, Hugh 36
Wigmore Abbey 24
William, Duke of Aquitaine 66
William of Ockham 103
Wilton community 15–16
womb metaphors 37
Woolgar, Christopher M. 51
worldly imagery 35–6
Wulfric of Haselbury 6, 65
Wyclif, John 102, 103, 106

Zumthor, Paul 25